Emergent Practices of Learning Analytics in K-12 Classrooms

Nurdan Kavaklı Ulutaş
Izmir Demokrasi University, Turkey

Devrim Höl
Pamukkale University, Turkey

A volume in the Advances in Early Childhood and K-12 Education (AECKE) Book Series

IGI Global
PUBLISHER of TIMELY KNOWLEDGE

Published in the United States of America by
IGI Global
Information Science Reference (an imprint of IGI Global)
701 E. Chocolate Avenue
Hershey PA, USA 17033
Tel: 717-533-8845
Fax: 717-533-8661
E-mail: cust@igi-global.com
Web site: http://www.igi-global.com

Library of Congress Cataloging-in-Publication Data

Names: Ulutaş, Nurdan Kavaklı, 1988- editor. | Höl, Devrim, 1979- editor.

Title: Emergent practices of learning analytics in K-12 classrooms / Edited by Nurdan Kavaklı Ulutaş, Devrim Höl.
Description: Hershey, PA : Information Science Reference, [2024] | Includes bibliographical references and index. | Summary: "This book compiles conceptual, empirical, and theoretical research that contributes to the understanding of learning analytics to make more informed choices for student success"-- Provided by publisher.
Identifiers: LCCN 2023049172 (print) | LCCN 2023049173 (ebook) | ISBN 9798369300664 (hardcover) | ISBN 9798369300671 (paperback) | ISBN 9798369300688 (ebook)
Subjects: LCSH: Education--Research--Data processing. | Educational statistics. | Academic achievement.
Classification: LCC LB1028.43 .E4475 2024 (print) | LCC LB1028.43 (ebook) | DDC 370.285--dc23/eng/20231101
LC record available at https://lccn.loc.gov/2023049172
LC ebook record available at https://lccn.loc.gov/2023049173

This book is published in the IGI Global book series Advances in Early Childhood and K-12 Education (AECKE) (ISSN: 2329-5929; eISSN: 2329-5937)

British Cataloguing in Publication Data
A Cataloguing in Publication record for this book is available from the British Library.

All work contributed to this book is new, previously-unpublished material.
The views expressed in this book are those of the authors, but not necessarily of the publisher.

For electronic access to this publication, please contact: eresources@igi-global.com.

Advances in Early Childhood and K-12 Education (AECKE) Book Series

Jared Keengwe
University of North Dakota, USA

ISSN:2329-5929
EISSN:2329-5937

MISSION

Early childhood and K-12 education is always evolving as new methods and tools are developed through which to shape the minds of today's youth. Globally, educational approaches vary allowing for new discussions on the best methods to not only educate, but also measure and analyze the learning process as well as an individual's intellectual development. New research in these fields is necessary to improve the current state of education and ensure that future generations are presented with quality learning opportunities.

The **Advances in Early Childhood and K-12 Education (AECKE)** series aims to present the latest research on trends, pedagogies, tools, and methodologies regarding all facets of early childhood and K-12 education.

COVERAGE

- Early Childhood Education
- Diverse Learners
- Standardized Testing
- Reading and Writing
- Literacy Development
- STEM Education
- Individualized Education
- Head Start and Pre-K Programs
- Pedagogy
- K-12 Education

IGI Global is currently accepting manuscripts for publication within this series. To submit a proposal for a volume in this series, please contact our Acquisition Editors at Acquisitions@igi-global.com or visit: http://www.igi-global.com/publish/.

The Advances in Early Childhood and K-12 Education (AECKE) Book Series (ISSN 2329-5929) is published by IGI Global, 701 E. Chocolate Avenue, Hershey, PA 17033-1240, USA, www.igi-global.com. This series is composed of titles available for purchase individually; each title is edited to be contextually exclusive from any other title within the series. For pricing and ordering information please visit http://www.igi-global.com/book-series/advances-early-childhood-education/76699. Postmaster: Send all address changes to above address.

Titles in this Series

For a list of additional titles in this series, please visit: http://www.igi-global.com/book-series/

PK-12 Professionals' Narratives of Working as Advocates Impacting Today's Schools
Patrick S. De Walt (California State University, Fresno, USA) and Dara N. Nix-Stevenson (Sincecombahee Educational Consulting, USA)
Information Science Reference • © 2024 • 220pp • H/C (ISBN: 9781668492369) • US $225.00

Perspectives on Empowering Intergenerational Relations in Educational Organizations
Soner Polat (Kocaeli University, Turkey) and Çağlar Çelik (Ministry of National Education, Turkey)
Information Science Reference • © 2023 • 388pp • H/C (ISBN: 9781668488881) • US $230.00

Mindful Listening Instruction in the Elementary Classroom Authentic Strategies Using Picturebooks
Donna Jessie Fortune (Virginia Tech, USA) and Mary Alice Barksdale (Independent Researcher, USA)
Information Science Reference • © 2023 • 287pp • H/C (ISBN: 9781668450772) • US $215.00

Meaningful and Active Family Engagement IEP, Transition and Technology Integration in Special Education
Millicent M. Musyoka (Lamar University, USA) and Guofeng Shen (University of Northern Colorado, USA)
Information Science Reference • © 2023 • 394pp • H/C (ISBN: 9798369313848) • US $230.00

Developing and Sustaining STEM Programs Across the K-12 Education Landscape
Jessica L. Spott (Texas Tech University, USA) Lane J. Sobehrad (Lubbock Independent School District, USA) and Rebecca L. Hite (Texas Tech University, USA)
Information Science Reference • © 2023 • 286pp • H/C (ISBN: 9781668477717) • US $215.00

IGI Global
PUBLISHER of TIMELY KNOWLEDGE

701 East Chocolate Avenue, Hershey, PA 17033, USA
Tel: 717-533-8845 x100 • Fax: 717-533-8661
E-Mail: cust@igi-global.com • www.igi-global.com

Table of Contents

Detailed Table of Contents

was administered on eight dyslexic children at the middle school on the west coast of the country. The present study was carried out utilizing a dyslexia checklist involving vocabulary and grammar items. Small group instruction with the learners was conducted and a dyslexia checklist was used on a weekly basis to measure the learners' improvement in vocabulary and grammar skills. Findings revealed that learners exhibited high performance in grammar and vocabulary.

Organizations of every size and industry are embracing data analytics to extract insightful information from the data with the goal of enhancing decision-making, boosting productivity, streamlining workflows, and reducing costs. The adoption of data, more especially learning analytics, which is the act of obtaining, measuring, and analyzing data on learners in order to better understand their requirements and learning preferences, is an excellent possibility for the education industry. Predictive learner analytics can be used to gain a variety of insights that can help institutions improve learner retention, engagement, and performance measurement, particularly in asynchronous online learning where students feel helpless and distracted. In light of this, the chapter suggests a methodology and model for integrating asynchronous learning and predictive analytics.

This chapter explores the dynamic synergy between artificial intelligence (AI) and learning analytics (LA) as catalysts for self-regulated learning (SRL). By examining the intersection of AI, LA, and SRL, this chapter sheds light on the evolving landscape of education and the opportunities it offers for tailored, data-driven learning experiences. It delves into the transformative potential of AI-powered LA, providing personalized insights, prediction, recommendation, and interactive scaffolding; thus promoting SRL development among learners. It also addresses ethical considerations, challenges, and the need for interdisciplinary collaboration among educators, data scientists, and policymakers. Ultimately, this chapter underscores the importance of responsible implementation and continuous research to harness the full benefits of AI-powered LA in supporting SRL and improving educational outcomes.

This chapter explores the design of social learning analytics for collaborative learning, incorporating virtual reality, life skills, and a STEM approach. Researchers employ social learning analytics, an emerging field that combines social network analysis and learning analytics, to gain insights into collaborative learning environments. The chapter emphasizes integrating virtual reality, life skills, and STEM in social learning analytics, covering data collection methods, data analysis techniques, and pedagogical applications. It also explores key considerations for designing social learning analytics in collaborative learning, encompassing the development of tools and assessment strategies. Finally, the chapter looks ahead to future directions and prospects for social learning analytics in collaborative learning.

As a result of the advancements in technology and the changes in the student profiles, which can be categorized as the digital natives, it is an indispensable practice for today's English as a Foreign Language (EFL) teachers to effectively apply digital tools to develop their students' language skills and increase their motivation and enthusiasm for communication in the target language. Based on this necessity, the current chapter of the book tries to give insights to EFL teachers to use digital tools for technology-enhanced practices with the aim of enhancing their students' willingness to communicate (WTC). It also suggests some ways for the teachers to collect data about their student's progress and the learning process, which is called learner analytics, while performing these technology-enhanced practices.

Since human beings are not only physical entities, albeit constituted by complex social and emotional features, their well-being also depends on learning how to communicate their needs to the others in an effective way, and to manage their emotions in a healthy way. From the learning perspective, emotional health also contributes to enhanced academic success, leading to improvement in learning. It is, thus, of critical importance to develop an understanding for learning engagement through the utilization of a novel concept of emotional learning analytics (ELA) to transform education systems with the purpose of molding a future that strengthens improved academic success as well as nestling peace and well-being. Accordingly, this review aims to provide a double dividend to the learners in K-12 classrooms

Foreword

Throughout history, scholars have been trying to understand the potentials and complexities of learning and have attempted to identify best practices to impact students' learning. With this purpose in mind, the present book, *Emergent Practices of Learning Analytics in K-12 Classrooms* has a series of research on learning analytics (LA) to be able to suggest some solutions to the challenges in K-12 education. Therefore, a group of scholars presented practical perspectives on classroom applications of LA in terms of their expertise. Hence, the chapters of the book cover a wide range of topics such as predictive analytics and social learning analytics, self-regulated learning perspectives, language learning, evaluation frameworks, and technology-enhanced learning, which also nurtures 21st-century skills. Using qualitative and quantitative methodologies for data collection, the book also discusses the benefits and challenges of the application of LA in K-12 education and suggests future directions for LA research.

In addition, *Emergent Practices of Learning Analytics in K-12 Classrooms* is an indispensable resource for scholars, educators, and administrators because it not only helps teachers make data-driven decisions by making use of various resources but also creates engaging learning experiences that lead to improved student outcomes. Concisely, this book addresses various topics such as practical classroom applications, suggestions for alternative tasks and assessment procedures, integrating artificial intelligence (AI) into classes to make use of the dynamic synergy between AI and LA, dealing with social learning analytics for collaborative learning, incorporating virtual reality, life skills, and STEM, using digital tools for technology-enhanced practices, and embracing the significance of social-emotional learning.

Essentially, the book is composed of 10 chapters, each dealing with specific issues in K-12 education. Chapter 1 deals with reflections from classroom practices to forecast the future of LA. Chapter 2 covers the language learning challenges of dyslexics, and Chapter 3 suggests a methodology and model for integrating asynchronous learning and predictive analytics. In addition, Chapter 4 attempts to explore the dynamic synergy between AI and LA as catalysts for self-regulated learning (SRL). While Chapter 5 investigates collocations and lexico-grammatical patterns in English coursebooks of K12, Chapter 6 deals with developing a framework for online LA in schools. Next, Chapter 7 integrates virtual reality, life skills, and STEM in social learning analytics (SLA), and Chapter 8 provides insights to EFL teachers to use digital tools for technology-enhanced practices. Finally, Chapter 9 provides an understanding of learning engagement through the utilization of emotional learning analytics (ELA) and Chapter 10 discusses the value of LA analytics in educational settings by presenting future directions.

Turan Paker
Pamukkale University, Turkey

Preface

In the constantly changing world of education, technology has become an indispensable tool, revolutionizing teaching, and learning practices worldwide. However, the widespread adoption of technology, especially in response to the global spread of Covid-19, has led to the gathering of vast amounts of data from students' digital footprints. While this data has the potential to provide valuable insights through learning analytics (LA), the challenge lies in effectively harnessing and interpreting this information to optimize teaching, learning, and assessment practices in K-12 classrooms. Academic scholars are faced with the task of understanding the potentials and complexities of learning analytics, navigating ethical considerations, and identifying best practices to ensure data-driven decision-making that positively impacts student outcomes.

Accordingly, the present co-edited book proposes a series of research on LA to provide a foundation as a solution to the challenges presented by different perspectives in K-12 education to improve student learning. Therefore, this book brings together a diverse group of academic scholars, leveraging their expertise to explore and present practical perspectives on classroom applications of LA. By offering a balance between qualitative and quantitative methodologies, this book equips scholars with the necessary tools to harness the full potential of LA in K-12 classrooms. More specifically, this it takes an informed look at researching perspectives on LA through reflections on classroom applications by giving recommendations to strengthen quality student learning by drawing on a variety of research methodologies. Covering a wide range of topics, from predictive analytics and social learning analytics to self-regulated learning perspectives, language learning, evaluation frameworks, and technology-enhanced learning. It not only highlights the benefits of applying LA in K-12 education but also addresses the barriers and concerns surrounding data privacy, transparency, and trust. Moreover, this book identifies future directions for LA, allowing academic scholars to stay ahead of the curve and proactively shape the future of K-12 education.

The target audience of this coedited book is composed of professionals, educators, high-stake holders, researchers working in the field of LA together with those who would like to improve student learning in general. Basically, as academics seek to enhance the quality of teaching, learning, and assessment practices, *Emergent Practices of Learning Analytics in K-12 Classrooms* serves as an indispensable resource. By drawing on innovative research and real-world applications, this book empowers educators to make data-driven decisions, optimize resources, and create engaging learning experiences that lead to improved student outcomes. By embracing the insights and recommendations presented in this book, academic scholars, educators, and administrators can confidently navigate the realm of LA and pave the way for a brighter future in K-12 education.

ORGANIZATION OF THE BOOK

Chapter 1

Prof. Kavaklı Ulutaş and Prof. Höl provide a recent contribution of learning analytics (LA) to K-12 education by means of an introduction to support learners and teachers together with researchers in the field as a promising area of research as summarized below:

Hailing the value of learning analytics, this chapter embarks on reflections from classroom practices to forecast the future of learning analytics to support learners and teachers as well as scrutinizing how data can transform learning environments to enhance learner engagement and performance together with the utilization of LA for educational purposes to provide pedagogical applications of LA as a promising area of research.

Chapter 2

Mr. Akpınar and Prof. Çubukçu explore the language learning challenges of dyslexics since their ability to learn the language is impaired by a specific learning disability, dyslexia. Since these individuals have difficulties in some aspects of language (e.g., reading, writing, vocabulary, grammar, and spelling), their performance improvement is highlighted via LA perspective with specific focus on grammar and vocabulary as summarized below:

This chapter is an attempt to find out the challenges that the learners with dyslexia encounter in vocabulary and grammar skills in learning a foreign language. Elaborating a qualitative research paradigm, this chapter embarks on an instrumental case study utilizing a dyslexia checklist involving vocabulary and grammar item laced with a small group instruction on a weekly basis to measure learners' improvement in both vocabulary and grammar skills.

Chapter 3

Prof. Dhamija and Prof. Dhamija introduce the predictive learning analytics to provide fruitful insights into the improvement of learner retention and engagement for performance measurement specifically in asynchronous online learning environments as summarized below:

This chapter suggests a methodology and model for integrating asynchronous learning and predictive analytics since predictive learner analytics can be used to gain a variety of insights that can help institutions improve learner retention, engagement, and performance measurement, particularly in asynchronous online learning where students feel helpless and distracted.

Chapter 4

Prof. Yildirim-Erbasli, Ms. Gorgun, and Prof. Bulut introduce the transformative potential of AI-powered LA, providing personalized insights, prediction, recommendation, and interactive scaffolding, and thus promoting SRL development among learners also addressing the ethical considerations and challenges as summarized below:

This chapter explores the dynamic synergy between artificial intelligence (AI) and learning analytics (LA) as catalysts for self-regulated learning (SRL). By examining the intersection of AI, LA, and SRL, this chapter sheds light on the evolving landscape of education and the opportunities it offers for tailored, data-driven learning experiences.

Chapter 5

Prof. Özbay and Ms. Çıtlak present how learning analytics and corpus linguistics can be merged to achieve the five steps of learning analytics by answering the information-based questions to detect whether a corpus-based data-driven learning approach can be suggested as a contributor to learning analytics as summarized below:

This chapter investigates collocations and lexico-grammatical patterns in English coursebooks of K12 published by the Ministry of Language Education in Türkiye and by native English speakers to provide a basis for the representations of the word clusters and collocations that are mostly used in the reference native corpora of English coursebooks.

Chapter 6

Mrs. Klinck-Van der Merwe and Prof. Goosen introduce a framework for online learning analytics against the background of emergent practices related to learning analytics in kindergarten/grade R through grade-12 classrooms as summarized below:

This chapter attempts to develop a framework for online Learning Analytics (LA) in schools as a precursor for personalized learning to present researchers' perspectives on learning analytics in open and distance learning environments, as well as barriers to, and discuss future research directions for K-12 classrooms.

Chapter 7

Mr. Singha, Prof. Singha, Ms. Haokip, Ms. Thomas, Ms. Sabeena, and Prof. Natal emphasize integrating virtual reality, life skills, and STEM in social learning analytics, covering data collection methods, data analysis techniques, and pedagogical applications exploring key considerations for designing social learning analytics in collaborative learning, encompassing the development of tools and assessment strategies as summarized below:

This chapter probes into the design of social learning analytics for collaborative learning, incorporating virtual reality, life skills, and a STEM (Science, Technology, Engineering, and Mathematics) approach looking ahead to future directions and prospects for social learning analytics in collaborative learning.

Chapter 8

Prof. Kanat-Mutluoglu and Prof. Kahraman-Ozkurt introduce how English as a Foreign Language (EFL) teachers can effectively apply digital tools to develop their students' language skills and increase their motivation and enthusiasm for communication in the target language using a learning analytics approach as summarized below:

This chapter tries to give insights to EFL teachers to use digital tools for technology-enhanced practices with the aim of enhancing their students' willingness to communicate (WTC) suggesting some ways for teachers to collect data about their student's progress and the learning process through learner analytics, while performing technology-enhanced practices.

Chapter 9

Prof. Kavaklı Ulutaş provides an understanding for learning engagement through the utilization of a novel concept of emotional learning analytics (ELA) to transform education systems with the purpose of molding a future that strengthens improved academic success as well as nestling peace and well-being as summarized below:

This chapters provides a double dividend to the learners in K-12 classrooms to embrace the significance of social-emotional learning (SEL) and mindfulness to rethink learning engagement by synthesizing the findings, challenges, and recommendations compiled from latest research through ELA to nurture emphatic learners for a sustainable society across the world.

Chapter 10

Prof. Höl and Prof. Kavaklı Ulutaş promote an understanding of learning analytics (LA) to revolutionize educational settings and learning systems as well as supporting researchers by means of future directions as summarized below:

This chapter highlights the value of learning analytics in educational settings to provoke researchers on future directions tailoring the improvement of students' learning results through innovative and revolutionary approaches, methods, and techniques for K-12 education.

Nurdan Kavaklı Ulutaş
Izmir Demokrasi University, Turkey

Devrim Höl
Pamukkale University, Turkey

Acknowledgment

This co-edited book would have not existed without the amazing efforts of authors, unified through learning analytics (LA), although geographically apart. We are extremely excited to have authors from Türkiye, Canada, South Africa, and India. Their studies, journeys, and commitment to the field of LA within the scope of socio-emotional learning and mindfulness, personalized learning, willingness to communicate, self-regulated learning, artificial intelligence-powered learning, asynchronous learning, collaborative learning, social learning, and language learning are remarkable. We hope that this co-edited book will engage us all in the future local and international collaborations with each other.

We are grateful to our Editorial Advisory Board for their diligent work and support throughout the process of this book; specifically for their valuable editing and feedback on the chapters submitted.

We would also like to thank all the Chapter Reviewers for without their attention to detail, expertise, and thoughtful care for topics, this project would have not been complete. Despite their hard work on their own chapters, these authors took the extra time to review the assigned chapters, with extreme care for quality. Many thanks to: Ankit Dhamija, Surjit Singha, Deepika Dhamija, Seyma N. Yildirim-Erbasli, Sibel Özkurt, Arzu Kanat-Mutluoglu, Okan Bulut, and Tuğba Çıtlak.

We extend special thanks to Prof. Dr. Turan Paker (Pamukkale University) for supporting our effort through writing of the Foreword to this co-edited book, and for the relentless advocacy in the understanding of learning analytics for K-12 education.

We are deeply touched by the IGI Global commitment to both local and international endeavors and inquiries. Special thanks to the supportive staff at IGI Global, in particular, to Nina Eddinger together with her colleagues from the Development and Marketing Teams.

We would also like to thank our families, partners and friends for their love, support and understanding throughout this project.

Nurdan Kavaklı Ulutaş
Izmir Demokrasi University, Türkiye

Devrim Höl
Pamukkale University, Türkiye

Chapter 1
Leveraging Learning Analytics to Support Learners and Teachers:
An Introduction

Nurdan Kavaklı Ulutaş
https://orcid.org/0000-0001-9572-9491
Izmir Demokrasi University, Turkey

Devrim Höl
https://orcid.org/0000-0001-5151-2581
Pamukkale University, Turkey

ABSTRACT

This chapter provides a brief introduction to learning analytics (LA) to support teaching and learning. In doing so, it attempts to enhance the perspectives to organize educational communities to showcase emergent practices specifically for K-12 education for a better learning design for both learners and teachers. Thus, how data can transform learning environments to enhance learner engagement and performance together with the utilization of LA for educational purposes are scrutinized by means of evidence-based research in related literature to provide pedagogical applications of LA as a promising area of research.

DOI: 10.4018/979-8-3693-0066-4.ch001

LEARNING ANALYTICS (LA): ABOVE AND BEYOND

"Data analytics and adaptive learning are two critical innovations gaining a foothold in higher education that we must continue to support, interrogate, and understand if we are to bend higher education's iron triangle and realize the sector's longstanding promise of catalyzing equitable success. The oppor- tunity and peril of these pioneering 21st century technologies (made availa- ble by recent advances in the learning sciences, high performance computing, cloud data storage and analytics, AI, and machine learning) requires our full engagement and study. Without the foundational and advanced insights compiled in this volume and continued careful measurement, transparency around assumptions and hypotheses testing, and open debate, we will fail to devise and implement both ethical and more equitable enhancements to the student experience – improvements that are both urgent and vital for real- izing higher education's promise on delivering greater opportunity and value to current and future generations of students." (Rahim S. Rajan, Deputy Director, Bill & Melinda Gates Foundation)

In today's time, it has increasingly become a commonplace chalk to support learning and teaching environment with technology. Yet, it does not only mean to utilize a specific type or form of technology to guarantee learner performance development, and/or success. Then, which types are more compatible to put forward success? How are we going to analyze the results? What is the best method for analysis? Does that information have something to tell teachers to positively impact their pedagogical practice(s)? Which type of technologies are more data rich?

At this point, learning analytics (LA) has emerged as a novel approach to provide responses to such questions by means of data collection, analysis, and application of the results to promote better learning by means of statistical techniques, interactive visuals, frameworks, and computer-aided modeling. Herein, the goal is to optimize learning for both learners and teachers to redefine better pedagogical strategies and speculate on potential pedagogies to provoke learner engagement in a fine-tuned alternate. As the data speculate on real-time analysis, learners can see their strengths and weaknesses on a subject-matter whereas teachers can observe their own educational efficacy. In each case, LA caters insights to all stakeholders irrespective of material being exploited, topic being covered, and activity leveraging in the classroom environment, even outside the classroom environment, just to improve learning and teaching (Elias, 2011).

Encompassing a myriad of models, algorithms, methods, and technologies to provide performance-based data, LA opens a window into the trajectories of learning and teaching to prioritize quality education. In doing so, the footprints of the learners can be extracted from the digital data to form educational databases to identify the achievement gap and provide remedial solutions to increase the level of achievement (Hwang et al., 2017). Herein, teachers do not only get a comprehensive view of learner progress but also monitor how learners are interacting with the course materials together with others (e.g., peers and teachers) in that clarification of the concepts through observation, questions, advice, and alternative views are of critical importance to maximize learning. LA can also be tool to support decision-making processes for course design and development. The results of the data analysis may require the improvement of course content and instructional resources on a regular basis. Besides, learners' interactions can be dissolved through timely feedback which is one of the key features of the learning process that is of utmost importance for both learners and teachers (Brookhart, 2017), which can improve the learning outcomes in turn (Merceron et al., 2015) apart from the six aspects that LA can support to enhance the learning and teaching process (Wong, 2017).

These aspects can be noted as (1) enhancing learner retention; (2) backing up informed decision-making; (3) pinpointing cost-effectiveness; (4) comprehending learners' behaviors; (5) establishing assistance to learners for self-paced learning; (6) giving feedback on a timely manner and providing intervention if needed. To note, these aspects are interactant to each other, albeit not segregated as entities.

In terms of student retention, it can be noted that educational settings are full of signs for learners which may either rise problems or provide suggestions at social and emotional scales. Learners having difficulties can be provided with interventions to overcome these issues and/or problems; and thus, their sense(s) of belonging to a learner community together with their level(s) of motivation get higher (Sclater et al., 2016). Regarding informed decision-making, LA can support certain pedagogical patterns suggesting activity plans and types for specific learning designs. Yet, it is still questionable to discover whether specific learning design are more meaningful for getting better learning outcomes although LA is proved to be successful (Toetenel & Rienties, 2016). Considering cost-effectiveness, in lieu of LA, it is easier to track and record learner progress as a key indicator of sustainable education. In this context, learning management systems (LMS) can be given as examples since results can be generated automatically, and learners can be informed thanks to its cost-effective nature where, in the meantime, learner behaviors can be better understood as the key components in the teaching and learning process.

Beyond question, LA can also assist learners through self-paced learning thanks to the advantages of educational data mining (EDM) and algorithms. After carefully analyzing the results of the LA, teacher(s) can identify learners who are in need personalized assistance, counselling, and/or intervention (Karkhanis & Dumbre, 2015). In doing so, LA can also provide feedback assisting teachers since feedback has the central role in educational settings. In turn, this may increase the level of learner motivation. Besides, with differing possibilities to predict learner success in advance, advanced LA can detect learner performance via generative, iterative, and discriminative classification models to provide a universal design for learning (UDL).

Considering the future of LA in education, LA is highly distributed across disciplines. As a promising indicator with a growing interest to build a theoretical foundation, it encourages critical reflection; however, may raise concerns about ethical and privacy issues (Lawson et al., 2016). In that, LA provides data collection and analysis for all, even at-risk learners. Thus, the ethical dilemma surrounds the practitioners since transparency is needed to avoid missteps. Hence, the crossroad is "none of the current leaders in the learning analytics field were trained as learning analysts." (Kizilcec & Davis, p. 150).

Simply put, LA is positioned as a unique field of study to guide professionals ranging from learners to educational administrators. However, since the primary inputs are derived from classroom environment, putting changes into action is of critical importance for learners and teachers. Thus, this co-edited book attempts to provide ranging studies with high-impact results with the aim of helping researchers showcasing the latest results to illuminate what remains unexplored. Pushing the field yet further forward, the purpose of this book is to navigate the extant literature of LA consolidated by the chapters putting forth common problems in learning and teaching with specific concern to K-12 education. It is also the hope of the editors to offer insights to the readers rather than simply summarizing the current literature in LA; henceforth, the chapters powerfully demonstrate its promise and take stock of varying stakeholders who would like to benefit from LA.

REFERENCES

Brookhart, S. M. (2017). *How to give effective feedback to your students*. ASCD.

Elias, T. (2011). *Learning analytics: The definitions, the processes, and the potential*. Learning Analytics. http://learninganalytics.net/LearningAnalyticsDefinitionsProcesses Potential.pdf

Hwang, G. J., Chu, H. C., & Yin, C. (2017). Objectives, methodologies, and research issues of learning analytics. *Interactive Learning Environments*, *25*(2), 143–146. doi:10.1080/10494820.2017.1287338

Karkhanis, S. P., & Dumbre, S. S. (2015). A study of application of data mining and analytics in education domain. *International Journal of Computer Applications*, *120*(22). doi:10.5120/21393-4436

Kizilcec, R. F., & Davis, D. (2023). Learning analytics education: A case study, review of current programs, and recommendations for instructors. In O. Viberg & A. Grönlund (Eds.), *Practicable Learning Analytics* (pp. 133–176). Springer. doi:10.1007/978-3-031-27646-0_8

Lawson, C., Beer, C., Rossi, D., Moore, T., & Fleming, J. (2016). Identification of 'at risk' students using learning analytics: The ethical dilemmas of intervention strategies in a higher education institution. *Educational Technology Research and Development*, *64*(5), 957–968. doi:10.100711423-016-9459-0

Merceron, A., Blikstein, P., & Siemens, G. (2015). Learning analytics: From big data to meaningful data. *Journal of Learning Analytics*, *2*(3), 4–8. doi:10.18608/jla.2015.23.2

Sclater, N. (2016). Developing a code of practice for learning analytics. *Journal of Learning Analytics*, *3*(1), 16–42. doi:10.18608/jla.2016.31.3

Toetenel, L., & Rienties, B. (2016). Analysing 157 learning designs using learning analytic approaches as a means to evaluate the impact of pedagogical decision making. *British Journal of Educational Technology*, *47*(5), 981–992. doi:10.1111/bjet.12423

Wong, B. T. M. (2017). Learning analytics in higher education: An analysis of case studies. *Asian Association of Open Universities Journal*, *12*(1), 21–40. doi:10.1108/AAOUJ-01-2017-0009

ADDITIONAL READING

Fischer, C., Pardos, Z. A., Baker, R. S., Williams, J. J., Yu, P., Sm, R., Slater, S., & Baker, S. (2020). Mining big data in education: Affordances and challenges. *Review of Research in Education*, *44*(1), 130–160. doi:10.3102/0091732X20903304

Gašević, D., Dawson, S., & Siemens, G. (2015). Let's not forget: Learning analytics are about learning. *TechTrends*, *59*(1), 64–71. doi:10.100711528-014-0822-x

Hernández-Leo, D., Martinez-Maldonado, R., Pardo, A., Munoz-Cristobal, J., & Rodríguez-Triana, M. J. (2019). Analytics for learning design: A layered framework and tools. *British Journal of Educational Technology*, *50*(1), 139–152. doi:10.1111/bjet.12645

Kizilcec, R. F., Pérez-Sanagustín, M., & Maldonado, J. J. (2017). Self-regulated learning strate- gies predict learner behavior and goal attainment in massive open online courses. *Computers & Education*, *104*, 18–33. doi:10.1016/j.compedu.2016.10.001

Uttamchandani, S., & Quick, J. (2022). An introduction to fairness, absence of bias, and equity in learning analytics. Handbook of Learning Analytics (pp. 205–212). Society for Learning Analytics Research (SOLAR).

Viberg, O., & Grönlund, A. (2023) (Eds.) Practicable learning analytics. Springer.

Wasson, B., & Kirschner, P. A. (2020). Learning design: European approaches. *TechTrends*, *64*(6), 815–827. doi:10.100711528-020-00498-0

KEY TERMS AND DEFINITIONS

Educational Data Mining (EDM): It delves into learning outcomes through mining and analyzing data as taught.

K-12 Education: It is the 12 years of compulsory education from kindergarten to Grade 12.

Learner Engagement: It reflects both quality and quantity of a student's participation into an educational program through efficiency echoed by interaction and cooperation with other students and teachers in the learning environment.

Learning Analytics (LA): It is a kind of an analysis of learning, processing data to improve students' learning using computational methods and techniques.

Learning Management System (LMS): It is a web-based technology or a software application that is executed to design, utilize, and evaluate the learning process.

Universal Design for Learning (UDL): It is an approach that gives equal opportunities to learners to accomplish through needs analysis, accommodation of learners' abilities, and elimination of uncanny hurdles of the learning process.

Chapter 2
Exploring the Language Learning Challenges of Dyslexics

Ömer Akpınar
https://orcid.org/0009-0002-6083-2944
Ministry of National Education, Turkey

Feryal Çubukçu
Dokuz Eylul University, Turkey

ABSTRACT

Dyslexia is a specific learning disability which influences the ability to learn the language. Dyslexic individuals have difficulties in some aspects of the language such as reading, writing, vocabulary, grammar, and spelling. Hence, this chapter is an attempt to find out the challenges that learners with dyslexia encounter in vocabulary and grammar skills in learning a foreign language. In this study, the qualitative research paradigm was undertaken where an instrumental case study was administered on eight dyslexic children at the middle school on the west coast of the country. The present study was carried out utilizing a dyslexia checklist involving vocabulary and grammar items. Small group instruction with the learners was conducted and a dyslexia checklist was used on a weekly basis to measure the learners' improvement in vocabulary and grammar skills. Findings revealed that learners exhibited high performance in grammar and vocabulary.

DOI: 10.4018/979-8-3693-0066-4.ch002

INTRODUCTION

In this chapter, the author aims to find out language learning challenges of dyslexics in vocabulary and grammar skills while learning a foreign language. Dyslexia is a language based disorder which makes language learning challenging for the learners and it is not so that easy to define dyslexia as it is comprised of many symptoms and features. Dyslexic individuals have their own symptoms, which differentiate among each other (Knudsen, 2012). However, the disorder includes some common traits observed in most of the dyslexics. To start with, dyslexia is regarded as genetic and the males having the disorder outnumber the females (Ott, 1997). It is considered to be a language processing disability, which leads the dyslexic individual to be unable to control some aspects of the language involving phonology, semantic system, grammar and pragmatics (Snowling, 2006).

It should not be viewed that dyslexic individuals experience difficulties in all sides of the language, but there are some skills, which are affected most. The influence of dyslexia over reading, writing and spelling skills cannot be overlooked (Knudsen, 2012).The dyslexic learners attend the same school setting with the peers growing up typically and do not have any intelligence problem. The learning opportunities they receive do not differ from the other learners developing regularly. However, what is challenging for dyslexic individuals is to read, write and spell properly (British Psychological Society, 1999). This study has the intention to explore the language learning challenges of dyslexics in vocabulary and grammar skills and eight learners with special educational needs and disability studying in the middle school are the participants of the study.

BACKGROUND

DYSLEXIA

A language learning problem called dyslexia affects up to one in five people worldwide (Knudsen, 2012). Dyslexia can include a variety of deficiencies, making it challenging to find a definition that fully captures the range of challenges that a dyslexic person may encounter (Morente, 2020). British Dyslexia Association (2007) sees dyslexia as a specific learning difficulty that essentially influences the development of literacy and the skills that are connected with language. It is believed to exist at birth and to have long-lasting consequences. Another definition is done by the Department for Education and Skills (2004) which views dyslexia as a special challenge associated with an outstanding balance of abilities. Reading, writing, utilizing symbols, and performing computations are all influenced.

Dyslexia is frequently considered to be a reading handicap since dyslexic individuals often struggle in school due to its association with reading difficulties. They become worried because they believe that they will make blunders and people will laugh at them. Dyslexics may struggle to concentrate and recall words in a stressful situation because their retrieval time lengthens and deteriorates. But, in relaxed circumstances, they will find it simpler to retract the words. What is more, as a result of being unable to distinguish between different sounds, dyslexics tend to pronounce words that sound alike. (Dimililer & Istek, 2018). However, a lot of dyslexic learners can succeed in decoding words, comprehending the text, and ultimately learning to read with the aid of specialist instruction (Sykes, 2008).

What Is Not Dyslexia

Even though there are many scientific researches and studies about the dyslexia, some myths and misconceptions still exist (Lyon et al., 2003; Snowling, 2013). The first one is the letter reversal which is considered to be the indicator of dyslexia, but the truth is that dyslexia is directly related to the language (Thorwarth, 2014). Secondly, dyslexia is generally seen to be connected with low intelligence. However, dyslexic individuals are not less intelligent than their age-peers. Thirdly, despite the common misconception of the dyslexia to be curable, it is incurable (Gray, 2008).

Moreover, it is thought that the percentage of the male having dyslexia is more than that of the female with dyslexia. The fact is that males and females have almost equal rates in terms of having the disorder (Shaywitz, 2003). Furthermore, dyslexia is considered to show up in primary school, but the signs of dyslexia can be seen during the preschool, too (Neuropedia Children's Neuroscience Center [CNC], 2021). Another misconception is that English is the only language in which dyslexia emerges, but all languages may include the learners having the disorder, dyslexia (Hudson et al., 2007). Lastly, insufficient reading at home is thought to be responsible for the existence of dyslexia, but the truth is that the disorder is not related to the reading span of the learners (CNC, 2021).

History of Dyslexia

The term *dyslexia* first appeared after extensive research that dates back a long period, possibly when the first people tried to read but were unable to do it (Akhtar, 2009). Reading difficulties were initially attributed to brain injury by a physician, Berlin (1872), and the word *dyslexia* was first used to describe them. It was suggested that dyslexia results from brain injury that impairs one's ability to read and write (Castles et al., 2006; Hooper & Hynd, 1985). Currently, *acquired dyslexia* could be described using this definition. Hence, studies at the time (Castles et al., 2006;

Hooper & Hynd, 1985) primarily focused on acquired dyslexia, where reading difficulties appeared as a result of sudden brain damage. However, *developmental dyslexia*, which manifested during a child's development, was recognized as another significant form of reading difficulty, and those who had it were the attention of educators and medical professionals (Akhtar, 2009).

Orton, an American neurologist and psychiatrist, made significant contributions to the study of dyslexia in the 1930s, and his insights are still relevant today. He stated that the issue of abnormality was inherited and that the unusual brain condition preventing the normal processing of visual perception of letters was the primary cause of why the disorder occurred (Masutto et al., 1994; Orton, 1930, 1937 cited in Regehr, 1987). Afterwards, modern hypotheses of dyslexia drew on research in cognitive psychology and neuroscience. The phonological deficit hypothesis, which was developed in the 1970s by paying attention to the Orton's approach component, initially defined dyslexia as a deficit in memorizing visual images of letters but later added that people found it harder to focus on an auditory form of a word than a written form (Bradley & Bryant, 1983; Brady, 1986; Bryant & Bradley, 1985; Frith, 1981).

Types of Dyslexia

Carlson (cited in Castles et al., 2006) and Brousseau (2006) state that dyslexia is divided into two main types: developmental form and acquired form. The former one has connection with poor reading skill and shows up in early childhood. It is hereditary and considered to be the most common type of dyslexia having impacts on children (Shaywitz, 1998). On the other hand, acquired dyslexia is proved to emerge as a result of brain illnesses or injury which leads to the reading disorder (Akhtar, 2009). Other than developmental dyslexia and acquired dyslexia, dysnemkinesia, dysphonesia and dyseidesia are mentioned to be the main types of dyslexia by Sandra Stark (2015) in *The Dyslexia Debate*. Meanwhile, Brousseau (2006) adds that dyslexia involves such subtypes as phonological dyslexia, surface dyslexia and deep dyslexia.

Dyslexia in L1 Learning

Since dyslexia develops continuously and leads the indicators to change over time, there are no reliable indicators that can be used to identify dyslexic learners at the start of their academic careers. Learners with dyslexia are initially difficult to diagnose, but as they progress in their education, it becomes evident. (Gray, 2008). Despite its significance, top experts believe it is challenging to identify them before the third grade. (Muter, 2003; Shaywitz, 2003). The most notable causes for this are that, up until the second grade, these learners have read novels with repetitive words and dealt with reading passages that have been supported by drawings and memory. They have nothing to do with decoding. Consequently, it becomes challenging to recognize the dyslexic students as a result of repetitive reading and predictable text (Gray, 2008).

It becomes simpler to identify dyslexic individuals from the third grade. Their ability to comprehend or remember the components of the words is initially aided by illustrations. However, as they go along, it's unavoidable that they will run into too many unfamiliar and infrequent words, which makes them anxious because they realize that memorization and illustrations are no longer adequate. In this case, instructors will observe that there is no correlation between the cues that the learners use and the appropriate word. By guessing and relying on the first consonant, they will attempt to read the unidentified words. Furthermore, their reliance on visual clues will increase as a result of their poor phonological abilities. Teachers need to be aware of these strategies because dyslexic individuals cover their tracks by hearing, comprehending, and responding in class. Teaching should be done with more efficient ways to assist them (Aaron, 1994; Davis & Braun, 1997).

Dyslexia in L2 Learning

It is widely believed that dyslexic individuals who have low L1 proficiency are likely to experience comparable challenges in their L2, and that is directly connected with the transition from one language to the other (Chung & Ho, 2010). It is stated that if the learners encounter challenges in native language learning process, they may have the possibility to face similar difficulties while learning a foreign language (da Fontoura & Siegel, 1995). The goal of the current study is to find out the language learning challenges of dyslexics in vocabulary and grammar skills hence, it is beneficial to investigate these skills to understand the relationship between dyslexia and L2 learning.

Vocabulary. Łockiewicz and Jaskulska (2015) aimed to explore the relationship between thememental lexicon and the knowledge of the English vocabulary. A comparison between 26 Polish students with dyslexia and 24 non-dyslexic students was made. It was found out that the dyslexic individuals experienced difficulties in reaching the information from the mental lexicon. Lack of vocabulary knowledge resulted in challenges while learning a foreign language. Another study conducted by Everatt (1999) suggested that control group in the study performed better than adult dyslexics in reading non-words. In a similar vein, it was stated that in terms of vocabulary, auditory short-term memory, and speed in processing the vocabulary, dyslexic adults were not as successful as non-dyslexic adults (Zabell, 2003).

Grammar. Having difficulties in grammar means that learners encounter challenges in syntactic coding which affects acquiring the grammatical rules, the form of grammatical sentences and mechanical rules. A study administered by Pavlidou and Williams (2010) showed that the learners growing up typically performed better in identifying grammatical and interrelatedly weak objects than the learners having developmental dyslexia. The result of the study conducted by Cantiani et al. (2015) was in line with the result of the study above. Despite the fact that individuals with developmental dyslexia identified morphosyntactic errors in phrases, they tried hard to notice the differences among the sentences in terms of grammatical correctness. Moreover, it was discovered that learners with dyslexia whose grades varied from one to three had a tendency to show some challenges in grammar use which was usual for their ages. However, as they moved onto their education from the fourth to the eighth grades, the difficulty in comprehending the texts emerged as a result of impaired grammar (Apriani & Supardan, 2018).

Inclusive Education

Inclusive education has been practiced in many nations since the 1960s which implies that students who are developing normally and those who are having difficulty in learning are educated together in the same classroom (Yazıcıoğlu, 2018). Salend (1998) states that the goal of inclusion is to create educational and social institutions that suit the requirements of all students while also empowering them to recognize and respect one another's individual characteristics. Inclusive education was first put into practice in the US in the 1970s, and it was quickly embraced by many other nations as the foundation for their education policy. In Türkiye, inclusive education began to be practiced in 1983 with the passage of the "Children with Special Needs Act," which was designated as Law Number 2916. "The Special Education Services Regulation" was enacted into law in 2000 after the "Decree Law on Special Education Law," also known as 573, was placed into effect in 1997 (Yazıcıoğlu, 2018).

Inclusive education is carried out using three different approaches known as full-time inclusion, half-time inclusion, and reverse inclusion. In the full-time inclusion model, students with learning disability continue their academic work alongside regularly progressing peers; in the half-time inclusion model, students with learning disability continue their academic work alongside peers who are not academically deficient in some lessons in the same setting or extracurricular activities. In addition, when it comes to the reverse inclusion model, special education schools and foundations set up a separate classroom if students who are progressing normally intend to enroll in classes with students who continue receiving special education. The administration of inclusive education is not enough to meet the needs of the learners having the disorder, dyslexia in Türkiye, as the number of the learners whose priority is to receive special education has been increasing day by day (Yazıcoğlu,

2018). The learners with special educational needs and disability share the same school environment with the peers in the education system of Türkiye.

METHOD

The present study attempted to find out the answers to these questions:

1. What are the challenges that the learners with dyslexia encounter in vocabulary?
2. What are the challenges that the learners with dyslexia encounter in English grammar?

Setting

The study was conducted at one of the state middle schools on the west coast of the country. The research took seven weeks and was applied in the first term of 2022-2023 education year. To implement the study, the ethics committee approval of the Dokuz Eylül University Institutional Board of the School was acquired on 21 June 2022. Since the study would be administered in one of the state middle schools, the researcher consulted the ethics committee of the Ministry of National Education. The committee approved of the research on 15 September 2022 and permitted the researcher to carry out the study.

Participants

Eight learners with special educational needs and disability (SEND) were recruited to the implementation. The informed consent forms had to be obtained from the parents as the participants of the study were below 18 years old. Therefore, the parents were informed about the aim of the study and agreed to sign the informed consent form. Table 1 below can show the features of the participants.

Data Collection Instrument and Procedure

The data in this paper came from a dyslexia checklist including vocabulary and grammar items. There were nine items in vocabulary part and the items were prepared by Coskun and Mitrani (2020). The permission for using the data collection instrument was obtained through e-mail. The grammar items were taken from the website (ghotit, n.d) which was designed to search for the mistakes that were made most commonly by the dyslexic learners. 14 items were found in grammar part and the total number of the items in the dyslexia checklist was 23. The researcher himself taught English to the participants and observed them on their English course, hence he had the opportunity to realize how the learners struggled or succeeded in while improving their foreign language. *Yes* or *No* options found on the dyslexia checklist were ticked when the observation and teaching sessions were over. The performance of the participants was measured on a weekly basis through the dyslexia checklist.

Table 1. Features of the participants

Pseudonyms of the participants	Grade	Age	Gender
Student 1	eighth	13	male
Student 2	eighth	13	male
Student 3	eighth	13	male
Student 4	seventh	12	female
Student 5	seventh	12	male
Student 6	sixth	11	female
Student 7	sixth	11	female
Student 8	fifth	10	male

Data Analysis Procedure

The researcher prepared the lesson plans in advance and benefitted from them during the seven-week administration. The data was gathered via the dyslexia checklist including vocabulary and grammar items and the frequency table involving the challenges that learners with special educational needs and disability had in vocabulary and grammar skills was formed to analyze the data. The frequencies of each potential value of a categorical variable were summarized using the frequency table of the qualitative data. The frequency table was the technique that was most frequently used to analyze the qualitative data. The researcher observed the participants for seven weeks in their own classrooms and filled in the checklists during the observation. To ensure the trustworthiness of the study, Guba (1981) suggests using four criteria which he thinks qualitative researchers should take into account while conducting a reliable research:

1. credibility
2. transferability
3. dependability
4. confirmability

Credibility is one of the key criteria which deals with the concept to ensure that the study really measures what is essentially determined (Shenton, 2004). To ensure the credibility, the researcher in this study held frequent meetings with his thesis supervisor to discuss the flow of the study. Peer scrutiny was also welcomed in this study. Moreover, the researcher adopted well established research methods employed in earlier comparable studies which contributed to the credibility of the qualitative study.

The second criteria, transferability is related to how the qualitative researcher shows that the results of the study are applicable to other circumstances (Merriam, 1998) and it assesses how well the study's findings can be applied in different situations, conditions, and places. The researcher conducted the study at one of the public secondary schools with eight students with special educational needs and disability and to achieve the transferability, the author attempted to assure the readers that the findings of the study could be applicable to the other contexts and situations related to the language learning challenges of the participants having the same disorder.

The third factor, dependability refers to the extent to which the study could be reproduced by other researchers in the same contexts, with the same informants and results (Shenton, 2004). The researcher in this study tracked precise methods for collecting, analyzing and interpreting data. Case study as a research design and observation and teaching as data collection tools contributed to the dependability of the study, because the researcher provided the future researchers with an in-depth methodological description of these sections to enable them to improve their comprehension of the efficiency of the methods.

Finally, the concept of confirmability is concerned with the degree of the objectivity and the important point in confirmability is to ensure as much as possible that the findings of the study are reached through the experiences and the ideas of the participants (Shenton, 2004). The researcher in this study ensured the issue of confirmability through describing the methodology in a detailed way. This approach contributed to the integrity of the findings to be analyzed thoroughly.

RESULT

The frequency table below revealed the data which was gathered from the dyslexic learners in vocabulary and grammar learning process and the items showed the performance of the learners during the seven-week implementation.

Table 2. Data analysis

		first week		seventh week	
	Items	**n**	**%**	**n**	**%**
		yes/no		**yes/no**	
The items which show increase	**Vocabulary**				
	2) Matches the words with the pictures	3/5	37.5/62.5	8/0	100/0
	3)Matches the words with the definitions	4/4	50/50	8/0	100/0
	4) Chooses the correct word to complete a sentence	2/6	25/75	8/0	100/0
	5) Matches the word with the synonym / antonym	1/7	12.5/87.5	8/0	100/0
	6) Identifies the missing parts of speech in the sentence	1/7	12.5/87.5	5/3	62.5/37.5
	7) Identifies the noun/verb/ adjective/ adverb form of the word	0/8	0/100	5/3	62.5/37.5
	8) Writes the different forms of the word	0/8	0/100	8/0	100/0
	9) Chooses the correct form of the word	1/7	12.5/87.5	8/0	100/0
	Grammar				
	10) Uses the form of 'to be' correctly	2/6	25/75	3/5	37.5/62.5
	11) is careful about the use of articles 'a, an, the'	1/7	12.5/87.5	6/2	75/25
	12) Uses the 'prepositions' properly	0/8	0/100	3/5	37.5/62.5
	13) Pays attention to the use of 'to' in 'verbs' or in 'to infinitive'	1/7	12.5/87.5	2/6	25/75
	16) Agrees on the plurality of 'subject' or 'verb'	0/8	0/100	7/1	87.5/12.5
	17) is careful about the sequence of tenses in English sentence	0/8	0/100	2/6	25/75
	19) Does not add possessive 's' when necessary in English sentence	7/1	87.5/12.5	4/4	50/50
	21) is careful about noun plurality agreement – plural to singular and singular to plural	1/7	12.5/87.5	4/4	50/50
	23) States the subject/verb/object of the sentence	0/8	0/100	5/3	62.5/37.5
The items which show no change	**Vocabulary**				
	1) Defines vocabulary words	0/8	0/100	0/8	0/100
	Grammar				
	14) Fails in the agreement of 'continuous' or 'to infinitive'	8/0	100/0	8/0	100/0
	15) Uses the 'continuous form '(ing)' correctly	0/8	0/100	0/8	0/100
	18) Notices the difference between verb forms of past and past participle in English sentence	0/8	0/100	0/8	0/100
	20) Fails in comparing things	8/0	100/0	8/0	100/0
	22) Fails in 'tense correction' according to the context	8/0	100/0	8/0	100/0

It can be seen in Table 2 that a tremendous increase occurred in choosing the correct word to complete a sentence, matching the word with the synonym/antonym, choosing the correct form of the word and writing the different forms of the word. In terms of matching the words with the definitions and pictures, identifying the missing parts of speech in the sentence and identifying the noun/verb/ adjective/ adverb form of the word, a notable rise was observed in vocabulary. When it comes to grammar, it could be mentioned that there was a minor increase in using ''to be'', the tenses sequentially and ''to'' in verbs or infinitives. Besides, a significant increase was seen in using the prepositions, plural and singular words and possessive ''s''. Moreover, there was a considerable rise in using the articles, plural forms of ''subject'' or ''verb'' and stating the elements of the sentences. Meanwhile, there was no change in comparing things, defining vocabulary, using the continuous form (-ing), noticing the difference between verb forms of past and past participle and using the tenses correctly.

The findings of the study implied that learners improved their grammar skills. Being able to do the exercises in the coursebook during the implementation led the learners to take part in classroom activities. However, they were not able to do some exercises, which were challenging for them. In terms of vocabulary, the learners exhibited the best performance. This study contributed to the learners' capacity to increase vocabulary.

DISCUSSION

This qualitative research sought to explore the challenges that the learners with special educational needs and disability encountered in vocabulary and grammar skills while learning a foreign language. Eight learners took part in the study and the dyslexia checklist involving vocabulary and grammar items was used to collect the data. To measure the learners' improvement, the frequency table was formed. The results of the study indicated that the dyslexic individuals improved their vocabulary skills and made progress in grammar studies during the seven-week implementation.

In terms of vocabulary, the dyslexia checklist had nine items and eight out of nine showed increase. The picture that emerged in the finding indicated that learners with dyslexia performed well in the activities related to the vocabulary. There was only one item in which no change was observed. With regard to vocabulary, many studies are found to pay attention to the roles of vocabulary and memory in reading comprehension (Carroll, 1993; Krasowicz-Kupis, 1999; Mather & Wendling, 2012; Ouellette, 2006). The studies suggested that more complex texts could only be comprehended when the learners had sufficient proficiency in vocabulary and it was crucial for the dyslexic learners, too. Another study carried out by Dimililer and Istek (2018) showed that learners with dyslexia had difficulties in naming the objects, retrieving the words and remembering them easily. Likewise, it was found out that the performance of the dyslexic individuals was worse than their age-peers growing up typically on silent reading vocabulary and understanding the reading passages (Ferraro & Doyle, 1981).

Regarding the grammar, the dyslexia checklist included 14 items related to the grammar skills and the data gathered revealed that dyslexic individuals did well in nine items. No change occurred in five items. The study of Helland and Kaasa (2005) agreed with the items showing positive results as the researchers presented *'L2 Comprehension test assessed receptive language' and 'model sentences assessed expressive language'* to the participants to evaluate the grammatical abilities. 15 sentences were utilized and it was found out that creating accurate syntax with the model sentences was easier than creating accurate semantics and morphology. In a similar vein, Snowling and Hulme (1989) carried out a study which involved a participant having challenges in short-term memory and naming the objects. Despite the difficulties, the learner could improve his ability in grammar. On the other hand, another study administered by Reid et al. (2008) revealed that learners with dyslexia had many difficulties while learning a foreign language and the challenges existing in the grammar of the target language could be said to be responsible for not being able to develop a rewarding interlanguage.

CONCLUSION AND RECOMMENDATIONS

The study had the purpose to explore the language learning challenges of dyslexics in vocabulary and grammar skills while learning a foreign language. Eight learners with special educational needs and disability took part in the study. The learners' grades varied from the fifth to the eighth grades in the state middle school. The dyslexia checklist including vocabulary and grammar items was utilized to collect the data and the frequency table was constructed to analyze the data. The researcher prepared lesson plans for each teaching sessions and taught English for seven weeks. Along with the teaching, the learners were observed.

Small group and one-to-one special instructions with the learners with special educational needs and disability had positive impacts on the learners' vocabulary and grammar skills. The increase on the performance of the learners' in vocabulary studies emerged as a result of conducting small group and one-to-one special instructions with the learners. The instructions gave more opportunity to the researcher to pay attention to the learners individually. Moreover, the current study revealed the fact that children with dyslexia improved their grammar skills with the help of the individualised and small group instructions. The instructions enabled the learners to acquire the grammar subjects as much as they could and to practice more activities in an effective way.

Meanwhile, some recommendations can be made for further research. Firstly, teachers should be aware of the existence of dyslexia as they have much more interaction with the dyslexic learners than other people. Secondly, the fact of dyslexia is so common that it is ordinary to come across a dyslexic learner in every classroom. Classroom environment and teaching methods can be designed to make the dyslexic learners feel relaxed and secured in education setting. The next thing is that the parents of the peers normally developing should know what dyslexia is and inform their own children about how to behave towards their dyslexic friends. To achieve this, the parents of the peers normally developing can attend the seminars to learn about the dyslexia. Moreover, it is beneficial to adapt inclusive education more in schools to prevent the isolation of the learners with special educational needs and disability in the classrooms. The learners should be given the opportunity to maintain their education in the same school setting with their peers developing regularly.

ACKNOWLEDGMENT

This article has been adapted from the first researcher's dissertation supervised by the second author. The authors of this publication declare there are no competing interests. This research received no specific grant from any funding agency in the public, commercial, or not-for-profit sectors. Funding for this research was covered by the authors of this article.

REFERENCES

Aaron, P. G. (1994). *Dyslexia and hyperlexia: Diagnosis and management of developmental reading disabilities.* Springer Dordrecht., doi:10.1007/978-94-009-1065-2

Akhtar, S. (2009). *The nature of developmental dyslexia.* [Unpublished MA thesis, Long Island University, Brooklyn].

Apriani, E., & Supardan, D. (2018). Language learning disabilities: How can I help my students with dyslexia. *English Franca, 2*(2), 187–200. doi:10.29240/ef.v2i2.598

Bradley, L., & Bryant, P. E. (1983). Categorizing sounds and learning to read: A casual connection. *Nature, 301*(3), 419–421. doi:10.1038/301419a0

Brady, S. (1986). Short-term memory, phonological processing, and reading ability. *Annals of Dyslexia, 36*(1), 138–153. doi:10.1007/BF02648026 PMID:24243456

British Dyslexia Association. (2007). *What is Dyslexia?* BDA. https://www.bdadyslexia.org.uk/dyslexia/about-dyslexia/what-is-dyslexia

British Psychological Society. (1999). *Dyslexia, literacy, and psychological assessment*. British Psychological Society.

Brousseau, R. G. (2006). *An Investigation into the progression of early acquired dyslexia* [Unpublished Doctoral dissertation, University of Windsor]. https://scholar.uwindsor.ca/cgi/viewcontent.cgi?article=8216&context=etd

Bryant, P., & Bradley, L. (1985). *Children's reading problems*. Blackwell.

Cantiani, C., Lorusso, M. L., Perego, P., Molteni, M., & Guasti, M. T. (2015). Developmental dyslexia with and without language impairment: ERPs reveal qualitative differences in morphosyntactic processing. *Developmental Neuropsychology, 40*(5), 291–312. doi:10.1080/87565641.2015.1072536 PMID:26285096

Carroll, J. B. (1993). *Human cognitive abilities: A survey of factor-analytic studies*. Cambridge University Press. doi:10.1017/CBO9780511571312

Castles, A., Bates, T. C., & Coltheart, M. (2006). John Marshall and the developmental dyslexia. *Aphasiology, 20*(9-11), 871–892. doi:10.1080/02687030600738952

Chung, K. K. H., & Ho, C. S. (2010). Second language learning difficulties in Chinese children with dyslexia: What are the reading-related cognitive skills that contribute to English and Chinese word reading? *Journal of Learning Disabilities, 43*(3), 195–211. doi:10.1177/0022219409345018 PMID:19897734

Coskun, N., & Mitrani, C. (2020). An instructional design for vocabulary acquisition with a hidden disability of dyslexia. *New Trends and Issues Proceedings on Humanities and Social Sciences, 7*(1), 220–241. doi:10.18844/prosoc.v7i1.4901

Da Fontoura, H. A., & Siegel, L. S. (1995). Reading, syntactic, and working memory skills of bilingual Portuguese-English Canadian children. *Reading and Writing, 7*(1), 139–153. doi:10.1007/BF01026951

Davis, R. D., & Braun, E. M. (1997). *The gist of dyslexia*. Perigee Books.

Department for Education and Skills. (2004). *A framework for understanding Dyslexia*. https://www.achieveability.org.uk/files/1270740075/dfes-framework-for-understanding-dyslexia.pdf

Dimililer, C., & Istek, E. (2018). Experiences of a dyslexic child in an English as a foreign language class. *Springer Science+Business Media B.V., part of Springer Nature, 20*(52), 1391-1398.

Everatt, J., Steffert, B., & Smythe, I. (1999). An eye for the unusual: Creative thinking in dyslexics. *Dyslexia (Chichester, England), 5*(1), 28–46. doi:10.1002/(SICI)1099-0909(199903)5:1<28::AID-DYS126>3.0.CO;2-K

Ferraro, M. P., & Doyle, B. A. (1981, April 12-17). *Syntactic and reading abilities in normal and learning disabled high school students.* [Paper Presentation]. Annual International Convention of the Council for Exceptional Children 59th Council for Exceptional Children, New York. https://journals.sagepub.com/doi/abs/10.1177/001440298104700514

Frith, U. (1981). Experimental approaches to developmental dyslexia: An introduction. *Psychological Research, 43*(2), 97–109. doi:10.1007/BF00309824 PMID:7302094

Ghotit Dyslexia Writing and Reading Assistant. (n.d.). *Grammar corrections* [Data set]. https://www.ghotit.com/dyslexia-grammar-corrections

Gray, E. S. (2008). Understanding dyslexia and its instructional implications: A case to support intense intervention. *Literacy Research and Instruction, 47*(2), 116–123. doi:10.1080/19388070701878790

Guba, E. G. (1981). Criteria for assessing the trustworthiness of naturalistic inquiries. *Educational Communication and Technology, 29*(2), 75–91. doi:10.1007/BF02766777

Heigham, J., & Croker, R. A. (2009). *Qualitative research in applied linguistics: A practical introduction*. Palgrave Macmillan. doi:10.1057/9780230239517

Helland, T., & Kaasa, R. (2005). Dyslexia in English as a second language. *Dyslexia (Chichester, England), 11*(1), 41–60. doi:10.1002/dys.286 PMID:15747806

Hooper, S. R., & Hynd, G. W. (1985). Differential diagnosis of subtypes of developmental dyslexia with the Kaufman Assessment Battery for children (K- ABC). *Journal of Clinical Child Psychology, 14*(2), 145–152. doi:10.120715374424jccp1402_8

Hudson, R. F., High, L., & Otaiba, S. A. (2007). Dyslexia and the brain: What does current research tell us? *The Reading Teacher, 60*(6), 506–515. doi:10.1598/RT.60.6.1

Knudsen, I. (2012). *Dyslexia and foreign language learning*. [Unpublished MA thesis, Malmö University, Malmö]. https://www.diva-portal.org/smash/get/diva2:1498521/FULLTEXT01.pdf

Krasowicz-Kupis, G. (1999). *Rozwój metajęzykowy a osiągnięcia w czytaniu u dzieci 6-9 letnich.* Wydawnictwo UMCS.

Łockiewicz, M., & Jaskulska, M. (2015). Mental lexicon, working memory and L2 (English) vocabulary in Polish students with and without dyslexia. *Center for Educational Policy Studies Journal*, *5*(1), 71–89. doi:10.26529/cepsj.155

Lyon, G. R., Shaywitz, S. E., & Shaywitz, B. A. (2003). A definition of dyslexia. *Annals of Dyslexia*, *53*(1), 1–14. doi:10.100711881-003-0001-9 PMID:24234186

Masutto, C., Bravar, L., & Fabbro, F. (1994). Neurolinguistic differentiation of children with subtypes of dyslexia. *Journal of Learning Disabilities*, *27*(8), 520–526. doi:10.1177/002221949402700807 PMID:7989856

Mather, N., & Wendling, B. J. (2012). *Essentials of dyslexia assessment and intervention.* John Wiley & Sons, Inc.

Merriam, S. B. (1998). *Qualitative research and case study applications in education.* Jossey-Bass Publishers.

Morente, B. Y. (2020). *Learning an L2 with dyslexia: Phonological working memory effects, accuracy, and lexical richness.* [Unpublished MA thesis, University of Wyoming, Laremie].

Muter, V. (2003). *Early reading development and dyslexia.* Whurr Publishers.

Neuropedia Children's Neuroscience Center. (2021). 7 common myths about dyslexia. *Neuropedia.ae.* https://neuropedia.ae/Blog/7-common-myths-about-dyslexia

Ott, P. (1997). *How to detect and manage dyslexia – A reference and resource manual.* Heinemann Educational Books.

Ouellette, G. P. (2006). What's meaning got to do with it: The role of vocabulary in word reading and reading comprehension. *Journal of Educational Psychology*, *98*(3), 554–566. doi:10.1037/0022-0663.98.3.554

Pavlidou, E. V., & Williams, J. M. (2010). Developmental dyslexia and implicit learning: Evidence from an AGL transfer study. *Procedia: Social and Behavioral Sciences*, *2*(2), 3289–3296. doi:10.1016/j.sbspro.2010.03.503

Regehr, S. M. (1987). The genetic aspects of developmental dyslexia. *Canadian Journal of Behavioral Science/Revue Canadienne. Science et Comportement*, *19*(3), 239–253.

Reid, G., Fawcett, A., Manis, F., & Siegel, L. (2008). *Handbook of dyslexia.* SAGE Publications. doi:10.4135/9780857020987

Salend, S. J. (1998). *Effective mainstreaming creating inclusive classrooms*. Prentice Hall.

Shaywitz, S. E. (1998). Current Concepts: Dyslexia. *The New England Journal of Medicine, 338*(5), 307–312. doi:10.1056/NEJM199801293380507 PMID:9445412

Shaywitz, S. E. (2003). *Overcoming dyslexia*. Alfred A. Knopf.

Shenton, A. K. (2004). Strategies for ensuring trustworthiness in qualitative research projects. *Education for Information, 22*(2), 63–75. doi:10.3233/EFI-2004-22201

Snowling, M., & Hulme, C. (1989). A longitudinal case study of developmental phonological dyslexia. *Cognitive Neuropsychology, 6*(4), 379–401. doi:10.1080/02643298908253289

Snowling, M. J. (2006). *Dyslexia speech and language: The practitioner's handbook*. Wiley.

Snowling, M. J. (2013). Early identification and interventions for dyslexia: A contemporary view. *Journal of Research in Special Educational Needs, 13*(1), 7–14. doi:10.1111/j.1471-3802.2012.01262.x PMID:26290655

Stark, S. (2015, February 19-21). *The dyslexia debate* [Conference session]. International Association for Cognitive Education, Southern Africa. http://www.iacesa.co.za/wp-content/uploads/2015/07/Stark-Sandra.-The-ReadingBrain1.pdf

Sykes, J. (2008). *Dyslexia, design and reading: Making print work for college students with dyslexia a qualitative interaction design study*. [Unpublished Doctoral dissertation, Carnegie Merlon University, Pennsylvania].

Thorwarth, C. (2014). Debunking the myths of dyslexia. *Leadership and Research in Education, 1*, 51–66.

Yazıcıoğlu, T. (2018). Kaynaştırma uygulamalarının tarihsel süreci ve Türkiye'de uygulanan kaynaştırma modelleri. *Nevşehir Hacı Bektaş Veli Üniversitesi SBE Dergisi, 8*(1), 92–110. doi:10.30783/nevsosbilen.420028

Zabell, C. (2003). *Individual differences in dyslexia*. [Unpublished Doctoral dissertation, University of Surrey, Guildford]. https://openresearch.surrey.ac.uk/esploro/outputs/doctoral/Individual-Differences-in-Dyslexia/99516562702346#file-0

ADDITIONAL READING

Arnbak, E., & Elbro, C. (2000). The effects of morphological awareness training on the reading and spelling skills of young dyslexics. *Scandinavian Journal of Educational Research, 44*(3), 229–251. doi:10.1080/00313830050154485

Beauvois, M. F., & Derouesne, J. (1979). Phonological alexia: Three dissociations. *Journal of Neurology, Neurosurgery, and Psychiatry, 42*(12), 1115–1124. doi:10.1136/jnnp.42.12.1115 PMID:533850

Catts, H., & Kamhi, A. (1999). *Language and reading disabilities*. Allyn and Bacon.

Department for Education and Skills. (2004). *A framework for understanding Dyslexia*. Department for Education and Skills. https://www.achieveability.org.uk/files/1270740075/dfes-framework-for-understanding-dyslexia.pdf

Dyslexia Scotland. (2009). *Defining dyslexia*. Dyslexia Scottland. https://dyslexiascotland.org.uk/wp-content/uploads/2022/06/WhatIsDyslexia.pdf

Felton, R. H., Naylor, C. E., & Wood, F. B. (1990). Neuropsychological profile of adult dyslexics. *Brain and Language, 39*(4), 485–497. doi:10.1016/0093-934X(90)90157-C PMID:2076492

Ganschow, L., & Sparks, R. L. (2000). Reflections on foreign language study for students with language learning problems: Research, issues, and challenges. *Dyslexia (Chichester, England), 6*(2), 87–100. doi:10.1002/(SICI)1099-0909(200004/06)6:2<87::AID-DYS153>3.0.CO;2-H PMID:10840509

Liberman, I. Y., Mann, V. A., Shankweiler, D., & Werfelman, M. (1982). Children's memory for recurring linguistic and nonlinguistic material in relation to reading ability. *Cortex, 18*(3), 367–375. doi:10.1016/S0010-9452(82)80035-X PMID:7151446

McGuinness, C., McGuinness, D., & McGuinness, G. (1996). Phono-Graphix: A new method for remediation reading difficulties. *Annals of Dyslexia, 46*(1), 73–96. doi:10.1007/BF02648172 PMID:24234268

Saldana, J., & Omasta, M. (2018). *Qualitative research: Analyzing life*. Sage Publications.

KEY TERMS AND DEFINITIONS

A Child with Special Educational Needs and Disability: A learner having a learner disability or difficulty.

Dyslexia: Specific learning disability which affects the person most in a neurobiological way.

Dyslexia Checklist: A checklist used for measuring the difficulties that the learners with dyslexia experience in the specific context.

Foreign Language: A language which is not the mother tongue of the speaker. It is a target language that is learned after the native language.

Inclusive Education: Part-time or full-time education conducted most on the students with special educational needs and disabilities in normal classes which provides the least restrictive educational environments for them with the help of the necessary support services.

Observation: A way of collecting and recording data which is used mostly in scientific research.

Small Group Instruction: A kind of instruction which enables the teachers to teach the learners in small groups varying from 2-6 learners.

Chapter 3
Integrated Model for Asynchronous Learning and Predictive Analytics for Enhanced Learner Experience

Ankit Dhamija
https://orcid.org/0000-0003-4456-9680
Amity University, Gwalior, India

Deepika Dhamija
Amity University, Gwalior, India

ABSTRACT

Organizations of every size and industry are embracing data analytics to extract insightful information from the data with the goal of enhancing decision-making, boosting productivity, streamlining workflows, and reducing costs. The adoption of data, more especially learning analytics, which is the act of obtaining, measuring, and analyzing data on learners in order to better understand their requirements and learning preferences, is an excellent possibility for the education industry. Predictive learner analytics can be used to gain a variety of insights that can help institutions improve learner retention, engagement, and performance measurement, particularly in asynchronous online learning where students feel helpless and distracted. In light of this, the chapter suggests a methodology and model for integrating asynchronous learning and predictive analytics.

DOI: 10.4018/979-8-3693-0066-4.ch003

INTRODUCTION

With the advancements in information technology, Online learning or e-learning is becoming more accessible and it is being embraced and accepted as an education method. The COVID-19 pandemic's effects have led to a significant increase in the usage of e-learning due to its great temporal and geographic flexibility, low knowledge acquisition threshold, and wealth of learning resources. A major technological advancement in online learning is the adoption of Artificial Intelligence (AI) (Anderson et al., 1985; Baker, 2016; Roll et al., 2018; Seo et al., 2020b; VanLehn, 2011), where AI capabilities are being utilized to provide personalized learning experiences to learners. It is also assisting in automating the Assessments where the manual processes on instructors' part are being taken care of by AI systems. All these benefits that AI can deliver were not possible if the associated data was unavailable. As it is well known that online learning is delivered through a Learning Management System (LMS) which captures all the learner data including their grades, activities, and performance. This data from LMS becomes the most important input for AI systems since all the insights about learner performance levels and behavioral aspects will be based on LMS data.

Despite the availability of several features and a variety of additional functionality on the LMS, instructors find it difficult to gauge their students' learning progress, raising concerns about the efficacy of e-learning. Hence, it becomes important that the educational institutions empower their LMS with AI capabilities to gain deep insights about the learner's performance. Getting access to such deep insights is an upcoming area which is popularly known as learning analytics (LA). LA ensures that the learner data is collected, measured, analyzed, and used for reporting purposes. The objective of using learning analytics is to understand and optimize the learning environment. The field itself has grown to the next level in the recent past where so many new areas have now become part of learning analytics. Learning Analytics now comprises assessment, LMS, educational research and technology from the academic side, AI, data science, data visualization and statistics from the technical and analytics side.

The most relevant sort of learning analytics is predictive analytics, which aims to predict future events based on prior and present data (Gandomi & Haider 2015). As the name implies, predictive analytics seeks to forecast future occurrences, patterns, and trends under varied settings (Joseph & Johnson 2013). It uses several techniques, such as regression analysis, forecasting, pattern matching, predictive modeling, and multivariate statistics (Gandomi & Haider 2015; Waller & Fawcett 2013). The goal of prediction is to forecast students' and teachers' activities to generate data that can assist teachers in making decisions (Chatti et al., 2013).

To answer the question, "What will happen next?" predictive analytics is applied. What interventions and preventive measures, for example, might a teacher apply to lower the failure rate? Herodotou et al. (2019) provided evidence on how teachers can use predictive analytics to support active learning. Predictive analytics, according to a large body of research, can help teachers improve their teaching practice (Barmaki & Hughes, 2015; Prieto et al., 2016; Prieto et al., 2018; Suehiro et al., 2017) as well as identify groups of students who may require additional support to achieve desired learning outcomes (Goggins et al., 2016; Thomas, 2018).

The need of learning analytics is mostly felt in asynchronous learning where the learner is engaged in his learning tasks on their own. There is minimum or zero live interaction with the peers and instructor and the learner is expected to independently carry on with the learning tasks and complete the assignments and assessments as per the course schedule. This type of learning is more demanding for learners and studies reveal that learners may feel isolated, dejected, and lost. They may also feel the need for real time assistance from the instructor. Despite the efforts from the instructors and use of several innovative instructional strategies like gamification (Dhamija & Dhamija, 2022), storytelling, role-play to mention a few, the learner feels helpless (Dhamija & Dhamija, 2020). Hence, it would not be incorrect to say that the chances of a learner failing a course or quitting the course are most likely. Hence, for education institution and members of academic fraternity, measures must be taken to avoid such a situation and efforts must be made to ensure student retention and their meaningful engagement. Predictive learning analytics have the potential to address this aspect. It can assist the educational institutions in identifying students who are in danger of failing a course or quitting their studies, predicting their academic achievements in the future, providing them with personalized and timely feedback (*K*, 2022; Kidecha, 2022; McGavisk, 2023), helping them in identifying their strength areas and honing their skill sets and supporting the growth of crucial abilities like teamwork, critical thinking, communication, and creativity (Full Fabric, n.d.; Judge, n.d.)

Hence, the purpose of this chapter is to bring to fore, important features of asynchronous learning and highlighting the necessary elements linked to student learning with an objective to enhance students' learning experience and their active engagement. Since the chapter discussed the importance of learning analytics, a discussion of several types of learning analytics methodologies will follow. Since the chapter is inclined towards using predictive analytics in asynchronous learning, the processes to execute and apply predictive analytics tools and techniques on the student data to get insightful knowledge about student learning will then be demonstrated using a model. Thereafter, the authors propose best practices to be implemented in the asynchronous learning environment by the educational institution.

The chapter also aims to discuss and evaluate the top learning analytics solutions from the perspective of the capabilities they provide.

The chapter will assist instructors, learners as well as academic administrators & educators in understanding the concepts of learning analytics, predictive analytics in an asynchronous learning environment. This chapter will provide instructors and academic administrators with relevant knowledge, techniques, and approaches about asynchronous online learning and predictive analytics, and inform them how the latter can be effectively used to enhance the learning experiences of learners. For students, the chapter will bring in a new perspective in the way they learn and how their educational institution can bring a change in the way they learn and gain knowledge. For academic administrators and educators, the chapter is going to bring a realization that the asynchronous teaching-learning environment requires modern methods and innovative pedagogies to remain relevant. Also, the chapter can provide deep insights about to LMS designers and managers in the way modern LMS is designed and the type of features and technologies that can be integrated in the LMS for smooth navigation of the platform. In this way, the chapter is quite relevant to all the stakeholders.

This chapter begins with a detailed background and analysis of recent advancements in asynchronous learning environments. Findings from the studies that focus on usage of learning analytics in online learning are discussed and efforts have been made to explain the need of learning analytics techniques in modern day teaching-learning. Further, the chapter proposes a model about how to effectively apply predictive analytics in an asynchronous learning environment. Finally, the chapter ends with the challenges associated with implementation of predictive learning analytics, followed by a conclusion.

BACKGROUND AND LITERATURE REVIEW

The improvements in asynchronous online learning and the use of predictive analytics in online learning are discussed in this section, along with their interrelationships. An extensive literature review of current studies highlights the developments in asynchronous online learning up to this point. Similarly, the focus of the next subsection is on studies pertaining to predictive analytics.

Table 1 provides an overview of the key findings from papers on Asynchronous Learning, AI, and Learning Analytics.

Table 1. Summary of recent work in asynchronous learning, AI, and predictive analytics

Author	Year	Focus Areas	Key Findings
Moorhouse & Wong	2022	Asynchronous Online Learning	● Examined the methods for delivering information in Synchronous and asynchronous online settings. ● Employed a qualitative-dominant sequential mixed method.
Fabriz, Mendzheritskaya & Stehle	2021	Asynchronous Online Learning	● The impact of synchronous and asynchronous online teaching in higher education was explored. ● Students in synchronous settings reported more peer-centered activities and higher satisfaction levels. ● Teachers noticed fewer distinctions between the two formats, especially concerning feedback activities.
Varkey et al.	2022	Asynchronous Online Learning	● Explored the application of instructional and learning science in asynchronous learning environments. ● Covered topics like spacing, interleaving, meta-cognition, multimedia principles, and clear feedback for various student groups, highlighting their importance in creating effective online classrooms.
		Asynchronous Online Learning	● Synchronous learning was perceived as sometimes unpleasant and increased student responsibility due to prolonged screen time. ● Asynchronous learning provided students with the opportunity for independent investigation and research but was considered burdensome due to a high volume of written tasks with tight deadlines.
Ghiley	2022	Asynchronous Online Learning	● The key benefits of asynchronous learning included the ability to study anywhere and anytime, at a personalized pace, with the flexibility to review lessons indefinitely, leading to time savings.
Rahman et al.	2018	AI and Predictive Analytics	● Online education can utilize AI techniques to create virtual assistants for direct communication with students, leveraging big data processing to analyze patterns and categorize outcomes. ● Expert systems, chatbots, and virtual assistants are examples of AI solutions in online education model.
Villegas-Ch et al.	2019	AI and Predictive Analytics	● The integration of AI techniques in online education, such as data mining, aims to identify student weaknesses and provide valuable insights to enhance learning quality. ● By leveraging educational databases and BI architectures, educators can implement targeted remedial procedures and optimize the learning experience for individual students.
Villegas-Ch et al.	2017	AI and Predictive Analytics	● Employing Business Intelligence (BI) with multiple data sources allows for a detailed analysis of factors influencing academic desertion in virtual or online educational models.

continues on following page

Table 1. Continued

Author	Year	Focus Areas	Key Findings
Villegas-Ch et al.	2020	AI and Predictive Analytics	● Proposed an enhanced online education model by integrating AI, data analysis, and LMS. ● Virtual assistants driven by AI, such as machine learning, communicate with students, analyze their interactions, and use data analysis to identify patterns for personalized learning experiences. ● Integrated model prioritizes student learning by providing personalized support, such as notifying students about academic schedules, monitoring performance, and aiding improve learning outcomes.
Rets et al.	2023	AI and Predictive Analytics	● Limited understanding of how proposed ethical norms are implemented in routine Learning Analytics (LA) decisions. ● To ensure ethical application of LA in higher education, he suggested six actionable recommendations, including involving end users, considering diverse student needs, acting on gathered data, providing student support, involving various stakeholders, and regularly reviewing and updating ethical standards in LA policies.
Herodotou et al.	2019	AI and Predictive Analytics	● Employs machine-learning techniques for the early detection of students at risk of not submitting (or failing) their next assignment.
Wolff et al.	2014	AI and Predictive Analytics	● Proposed solution can identify students at risk early on and empower teachers to effectively and pro-actively monitor and support their students before they fail.
Herodotou et al.	2017	AI and Predictive Analytics	● The use of PLA data and visualizations with teacher.
Leeuwen et al.	2014	AI and Predictive Analytics	● Observed that teachers who got learning analytics visualizations of collaboration activities were better able to recognize participation issues. ● Teachers who did not receive learning analytics visualizations, they intervened. more frequently in "Problematic" groups.
McKenney & Mor	2015	AI and Predictive Analytics	• The use of analytics software helped instructors' professional growth.
Herodotou et al.	2017	AI and Predictive Analytics	• ·The use of Predictive Learning Analytics (PLA) showed mixed effects on student performance.
Herodotou et al.		AI and Predictive Analytics	• Highlights the importance of teachers' active involvement with predictive data in positively impacting student outcomes.
Dazo et al.	2017	AI and Predictive Analytics	• Predictive Learning Analytics (PLA) can vary based on different situations, emphasizing the need for more extensive, longitudinal studies across diverse settings and disciplines.
Bailie	2020	AI and Predictive Analytics	• Studied the relationship between a specific online learner behavior, documented in an LMS, and academic performance indicated by final grades.
Badal & Sungkur	2022	AI and Predictive Analytics	• Developed a predictive model which utilized machine learning techniques and quantitative data analysis to predict a student's final grade and engagement level.

Studies Focusing on Asynchronous Online Learning

The most crucial component of any educational setting is the learner, and in an online situation this is even truer. Since there are many different delivery methods for online learning, the most important is the asynchronous online learning model, in which interactions between students and instructors take place solely through written communication, such as but not limited to LMS, messages, discussion forums, and emails. Students in this approach do not have live interaction sessions with the instructors, thus they are expected to study alone from the e-learning resources offered to them on the LMS. The importance of this model is increased due to the nature and limitations of the model. With no live student teacher interaction, students are expected to do self-study most of the time where they may feel helpless and demotivated. Due to these limitations, the significance of ensuring student engagement in asynchronous online learning is increased. This paradigm has advantages and disadvantages of its own. On the one hand, this model makes sure that students start their educational journey freely and with the least amount of help, which encourages self-paced learning. This model does, however, have several drawbacks, such as a lack of personal touch and attention.

Moorhouse and Wong (2022) examined the methods for delivering information in synchronous and asynchronous online settings with the aim of promoting and evaluating student learning and facilitating effective interaction between students and parents. Their research employed a qualitative-dominant sequential mixed-method study with follow-up interviews, and the results revealed that the optimum asynchronous and synchronous learning models for online learning are a combination of the two.

The impact of synchronous and asynchronous settings of online teaching and learning in higher education on students' learning experiences was examined in another study by Fabriz, Mendzheritskaya, and Stehle (2021). The findings showed that, in comparison to students who studied largely in asynchronous settings, students who studied mostly in synchronous settings reported more peer-centered activities, such as feedback. Teachers noticed fewer distinctions between synchronous and asynchronous learning environments, particularly when it came to feedback activities. Additionally, compared to students in predominantly asynchronous settings, students in mostly synchronous settings felt that their basic psychological requirements for relatedness and competence support were met to a higher extent, and they were also more satisfied overall with the online term.

Asynchronous learning was examined by Varkey et al. (2022) from the standpoint of how instructional science and learning science might be applied to produce the best classroom for both students and instructors. The study's topics included the use of the principles of spacing and interleaving and several specific examples of how that could be used, the principle of meta-cognition and one actual example of how it can be used, the twelve multimedia principles and the significance of the virtualization in the creation of resources, and the twelve multimedia principles. The use of these in various classrooms, including those for elementary school children, college students, medical and graduate school students, and finally adult working professionals, with some specific examples for working physicians, was further discussed. Finally, it was made obvious how important it is for instructors to provide students clear and concise feedback to facilitate learning and change in behavior.

During the COVID-19 Pandemic, research by Dhamija and Dhamija (2020) set out to examine how students perceived synchronous and asynchronous learning. According to their research, synchronous learning can be unpleasant at times and increases student responsibility primarily due to greater screen time. Asynchronous learning also gives the pupils the chance to independently investigate and research the subjects that have been given to them. Another reason why asynchronous activities were perceived as burdensome by students was the large number of written tasks that had to be turned in quickly.

The effects of synchronous and asynchronous distance learning in quantitative courses were examined in another study by Ghilay (2022). The results demonstrate that pupils much prefer asynchronous learning to synchronous learning. The capacity to learn anywhere, anytime, at the right pace, and the flexibility to repeat lessons forever are the key benefits of this. Other benefits include time savings.

Studies Focusing on AI and Predictive Analytics

AI is the process by which machines simulate human intelligence. In general, it is the branch of science that seeks to develop machines with human-like learning and thinking abilities. These systems can compare information, do logical tasks, learn from experience, and solve issues in specific situations. An AI system can often analyze large amounts of data, spot patterns and trends, and create predictions that are automatic, quick, and accurate. Predictive analytics and other AI techniques are incorporated into frequently used applications to make everyday encounters smarter (Chen et al., 2020)

An online education model can make use of a variety of AI techniques to give systems unique properties that enable the development of virtual assistants that communicate with students directly. The goal of the AI is to examine patterns in the data that has already undergone big data processing. This allows the system to automatically categorize the outcomes and suggest several courses of action to the modality's students and tutors (Rahman et al., 2018). Expert systems, chatbots, and virtual assistants are a few examples of AI solutions that can do this kind of task.

The use of AI or tools for analyzing educational data in LMS has been highlighted in several related publications that have been reviewed (Villegas-Ch & Luján-Mora, 2017; Roos, 2018; Thomas, 2020; Murphy, 2019). However, the primary goal of boosting learning is not presented in these works, making this integration helpful to individuals involved. The use of data mining techniques for knowledge discovery in educational databases has been proposed in certain research (Villegas-Ch et al., 2019). This feature seeks to show which students in a certain course have weaknesses. The areas or individuals in charge of the learning quality are given this knowledge, and they are the ones who implement the appropriate remedial procedures.

Other works include business intelligence (BI) which includes data collecting, analysis, and visualization methods and approaches to enhance executive decision-making (Bharadiya, 2023). It is suggested to employ BI to incorporate multiple data sources to offer the study more nuance (Villegas-Chet et al., 2017). The level of detail in the data enables us to pinpoint the factors that influence academic desertion, one of the issues that has the biggest bearing on virtual or online educational models.

The integration of artificial intelligence (AI), data analysis, and LMS is proposed by Villegas-Ch et al. (2020) to enhance an online education model and subsequently enhance student learning. They promoted the use of virtual assistants to support students while they learn. This paradigm incorporates an AI system, such as machine learning, that oversees communicating with students and controlling their performance. The model is aware of every piece of information about the learner, both from interactions with them and from information gleaned from their analyses. Finding student patterns that enable classification of students and their learning style is the goal of data analysis, which also enables the development of an adaptable model that is tailored to the needs of each individual student. Learning is prioritized by combining these technologies with the LMS; as a result, the student will encounter a virtual assistant when entering the LMS who is familiar with their academic schedule and all the details of their performance. The assistant is aware of what must be done through the academic agenda and sends notifications to ensure compliance. Another characteristic that the assistant can regulate is grades; as a result, it continuously analyzes student performance and can communicate with them to help them learn.

There is little knowledge of how proposed ethical norms are applied in routine learning analytics (LA) decisions, according to Rets et al. (2023). The application of ethics in LA should be guided by practical ethics and multidisciplinary research. As a result, Rets et al. (2023) offered six doable suggestions for the moral application of LA in higher education institutions. The suggestions covered topics like involving end users in the creation and use of LA tools, considering a variety of student needs, acting on gathered LA data by higher education institutions (HEI), providing students with support through LA data, enlisting the help of various stakeholders to test LA data by HEI, and reviewing and updating the LA policy's ethical standards on a regular basis.

The usage of OUAnalyse (OUA), cutting-edge predictive analytics learning algorithm that employs machine-learning techniques for the early detection of students at risk of not submitting (or failing) their next assignment, was suggested by Herodotou et al. (2019).

Results from studies by Wolff et al. (2014) showed that predictive learning analytics (PLA), in addition to current practices, can identify students at risk early on and empower teachers to effectively and pro-actively monitor and support their students before they fail.

Studies evaluating the use of PLA data and visualizations (Herodotou et al., 2017; Leeuwen et al., 2014; Leeuwen et al., 2015) with teachers have yielded contradictory results. Leeuwen et al. (2014) found, for instance, that teachers who got learning analytics visualizations of collaboration activities were better able to recognize participation issues. The study involved 28 teachers. Additionally, compared to a control group of teachers who did not receive learning analytics visualizations, it was discovered that they intervened more frequently in "problematic" groups.

McKenney and Mor (2015) report that using analytics software helped instructors' professional growth, which is another example of positive effects. When 240 teachers in 10 modules were given access to PLA, Herodotou et al. (2017) found mixed effects on student performance. However, usage analysis revealed that teachers used PLA only sparingly in their practice, which could account for these mixed effects. It was also discovered that teachers had favorable opinions about using PLA in the classroom because they recognized their value in enhancing instruction and being "on top of things." (Herodotou, 2017, p.5)

Additionally, Herodotou et al. (n.d.), in a multi-methods study, found that teachers' overall engagement with predictive data is the second most important factor explaining student performance, after previous best performance. The frequency of learning analytics visits also reduced between semesters, according to Dazo et al. (2017) analysis of utilization data from 14 teachers. A second focus group with six teachers revealed that there were difficulties in comprehending learning analytics data, which caused some of them to switch to alternative ways of keeping track of their students' development, such as reading their blog postings. Overall, there is growing evidence that PLA can be successful in some situations but not in others, highlighting the need for more thorough, longitudinal study that is not restricted to a single setting or discipline.

The association between a certain online learner behavior as documented in a learning management system and academic performance as determined by final grades was examined by Bailie (2020). Findings showed that perfect-scoring students had read more than 95% of their classmates' discussion entries. The surprising element of the results was that students could have watched the same post more than once, as those with the lowest grades (10%tile) did not necessarily have the lowest viewing.

To estimate student performance (grade/engagement) and analyze the impact of online learning platform features, Badal and Sungkur (2022) offer a predictive model. Their model predicted a student's final grade and engagement level using machine learning techniques and a quantitative approach to the gathering and processing of student data. The findings showed that the grade and engagement predictions had recorded accuracy of 85% and 83% respectively.

LITERATURE REVIEW SUMMARY

A close examination of the above table reveals that most studies in asynchronous and synchronous online learning tried to find out the factors that impact student learning. It is also observed that the area of learning analytics has grown in popularity and is being adopted as the preferred technological tool by higher education institutions to gain deep insights about learners, their learning patterns. It is also being embraced by instructors to know the learners better and guide them towards their strength areas. Also, the usage of artificial intelligence techniques and algorithms based on predictive analytics are being employed by the educational institutions to study and analyze the learner data.

MODEL PREREQUISITES

To create a model for applying predictive analytics in an asynchronous learning setting, the following steps are followed:

1. Identify the System Components

It is important to identify the various aspects of the proposed system that need to serve as input, what data processing operations to be carried out on the data and the output in the form of a student performance database with only the required data. Since every system that exists in this world has three major components: Input, processing, and output. Same holds true in this scenario as well. Table 2 describes these three components:

a. **Input Data:** Deciding on the input data is a challenging task as there are so many types of data that would be needed. To start with, aspects like the learner's basic information, different types of assignments and activities that a learner participates in and the type of assessments or quizzes that they are required to attempt. The most convenient way to fetch this type of information will require access to the Learning Management System (LMS) through which the learners access the course contents. Figure 1 describes the various types of data sources that may be needed from the LMS.

Table 2. Model components

Input	Processing	Output
Learner Data Source: LMS	Data preprocessing, Activities: extraction, transformation, loading	Learner Performance Database

Figure 1. Detailed system overview

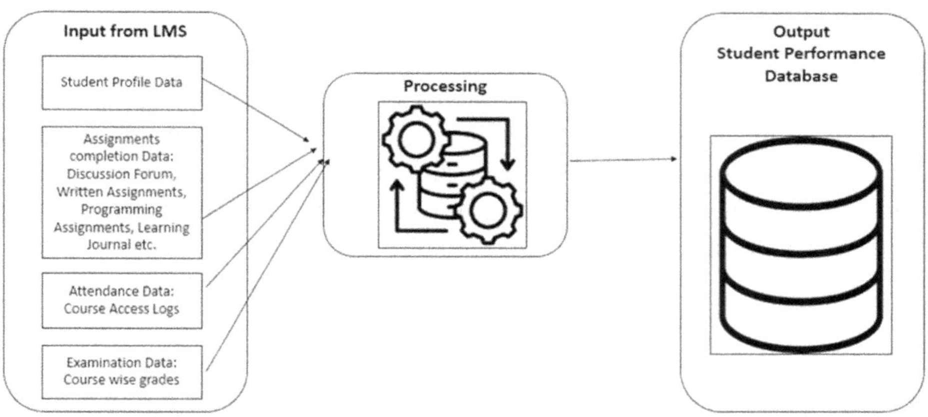

b. **Processing:** Processing of the input data holds great significance in any system. For any conclusions and inferences that are to be drawn from the input data, it is necessary to process and preprocess that input data, extract it from diverse data sources, then filter it to remove the unwanted and unnecessary information and finally load it into a common repository which we are referring to as Student Performance Database. This task requires considerable brainstorming and decision making in each of the sub steps of the processing stage.

c. **Output:** The output stage is somewhat a convenient stage to be since it now consists of a data set which is cleaned, filtered, and consists of data from all possible data sources. At this stage, this database will become the input for applying the predictive analytics algorithms. The last part in Figure 1 describes the output component.

2. Predictive Analytics Algorithms Selection

The next step is to select the best possible predictive analytics algorithm which is a challenging task due to the availability of a variety of machine learning algorithms. The purpose of predictive analytics, a broad set of methodologies, is to forecast future behavior. Given that predictive models are the foundation of predictive analytics, selecting the appropriate prediction modeling approach is possibly the most crucial stage in the entire process.

Hence, to perform this step, the following sub-steps are performed:

a. Identification of predictive analytics algorithms

The characteristics of the dataset and the effectiveness of the algorithms determine how effective a predictive analytics solution is. It is difficult to choose a learning algorithm that is appropriate for a given application in a certain domain. The reason for this is that predictive analytics algorithms serve a different purpose. Depending on the peculiarities of the data, even the results of several learning algorithms in the same category can change (Sarker et al., 2019). The research community has used many machine learning algorithms. The following are some of the most significant and well-known approaches that appear in predictive analytics literature: Decision Trees, Linear Regression, Logistic Regression, Time Series, K-Means, and Factor Analysis.

Decision Tree

A decision tree is a form of probability tree that allows you to decide on a given process. For example, you might want to decide whether to manufacture item A or item B, or whether to invest in option 1, option 2, or option 3 (Patel & Prajapati, 2018). Trees are a good tool for dealing with these types of complex decisions, which typically involve a variety of considerations and always entail some degree of ambiguity. Although they can be drawn by hand, software is frequently utilized since the trees can quickly grow complex. A decision tree starts with a node called the root node. Users divide each node recursively from this node using an if-then decision tree learning technique (Yadav & Pal, 2012). As a result, a decision tree is formed, with each branch representing a decision scenario and its conclusion (Sungkur & Maharaj, 2022). Figure 2 describes a sample decision tree.

Figure 2. A sample decision tree

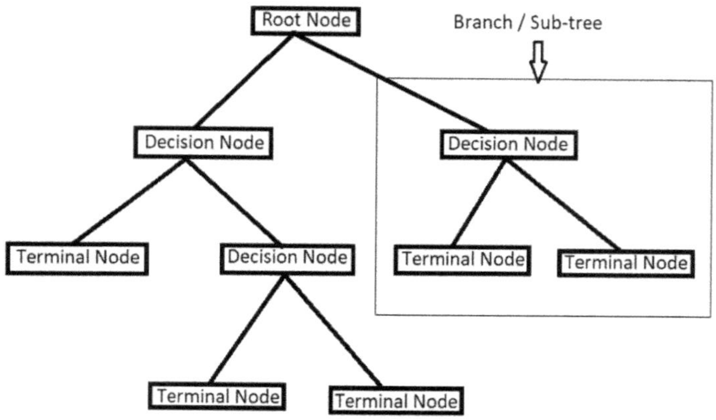

The use of Decision Tree algorithm in predictive learning analytics is demonstrated by Gotardo (2019) who used data mining techniques, notably the J48 algorithm, to construct the Decision Tree Model in forecasting student performance in data structures and algorithms. The produced Decision Tree Model results revealed that Finals had the highest instance and in predicting student achievement in the Data Structures and Algorithms course. It also demonstrates that Finals has the highest likelihood of receiving one of the following remarks: Pass, Failed, or Conditional. The model also identified the attributes Pass with 85.31% accuracy, Conditional with 79.41% accuracy, and failed with 91.67% accuracy. Figure 3 presents the model created using Decision Trees in their study.

Figure 3. Student performance decision rule

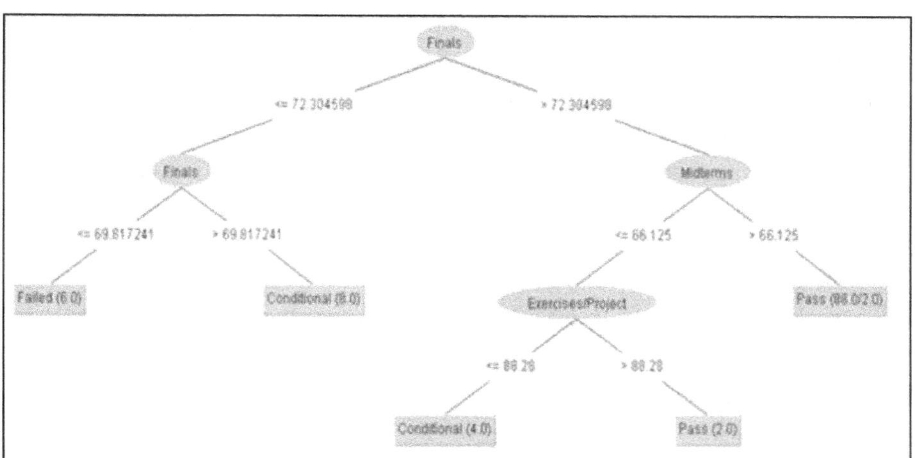

Raut & Nichat (2017) proposed a classification model that classifies a students' performance based on the Decision tree algorithm where they predicted student performance in a specific subject based on their performance of test result components during the performance by applying the C4.5 decision tree.

Pallathadka et al. (2023) used a decision tree classification methodology on learners' assessment data to identify learners at risk of low performance to improve the quality management of the teaching learning process. The research gap is that this methodology does not reveal specific limitations in learners.

In each of the research papers discussed above, it has been observed that though decision trees are an integral part of the work carried out, it is supported by other techniques like Data mining algorithms and statistics. Hence, Decision tree Algorithms alone are insufficient to create a model for predictive analytics as they are dependent on other algorithms. There are many more constraints with a decision tree. A slight change in the data might induce a big change in the structure of the decision tree, resulting in instability. When compared to other algorithms, a Decision tree's calculation can be significantly more complex at times. The training period for a decision tree is frequently longer.

Correlation and Regression Analysis

Regression and correlation are, in essence, the same statistical method. The distinction is simply in the goal - what one is attempting to discover. Correlation is concerned with the strength of a link between two variables, P and Q, whereas regression is concerned with how well Q can be predicted from P.

In education research, examples of regression include defining and detecting underachievement or specific learning issues, such as determining whether a student's reading attainment (Q) is at the level suggested by an IQ test (P). Another example would be screening tests to identify children who are at risk of dropping out of school so that they can receive additional assistance or engage in 'early intervention' activities. Essentially, linear regression is used to find the links between two or more variables that influence each other and to generate predictions by analyzing the changes. In the presence of outliers, linear regression is prone to producing erroneous decision limits. Logistic regression was created to help with categorization challenges. The goal of logistic regression is to translate a function from the dataset's attributes to the targets to assess the likelihood that a new entry corresponds to one of the target classes (Bisong, 2019).

In regression (Figure 4), P is the explanatory (or predictor/independent) variable and Q is the outcome (or dependent) variable. We're interested in understanding how well P predicts Q.

It is critical to understand which variable is the outcome (Q) and which variable is the explanatory variable (P). This may seem apparent, but it is not always clear in education studies - For example, there is no straightforward answer to the question if enhanced enthusiasm in reading indicate higher reading skills. Such uncertainties do exist in educational studies, hence, while performing a regression analysis, it is important to understand the hypothesis regarding the relationship because it is critical to the interpretation.

Figure 4. Visualization of prediction using regression

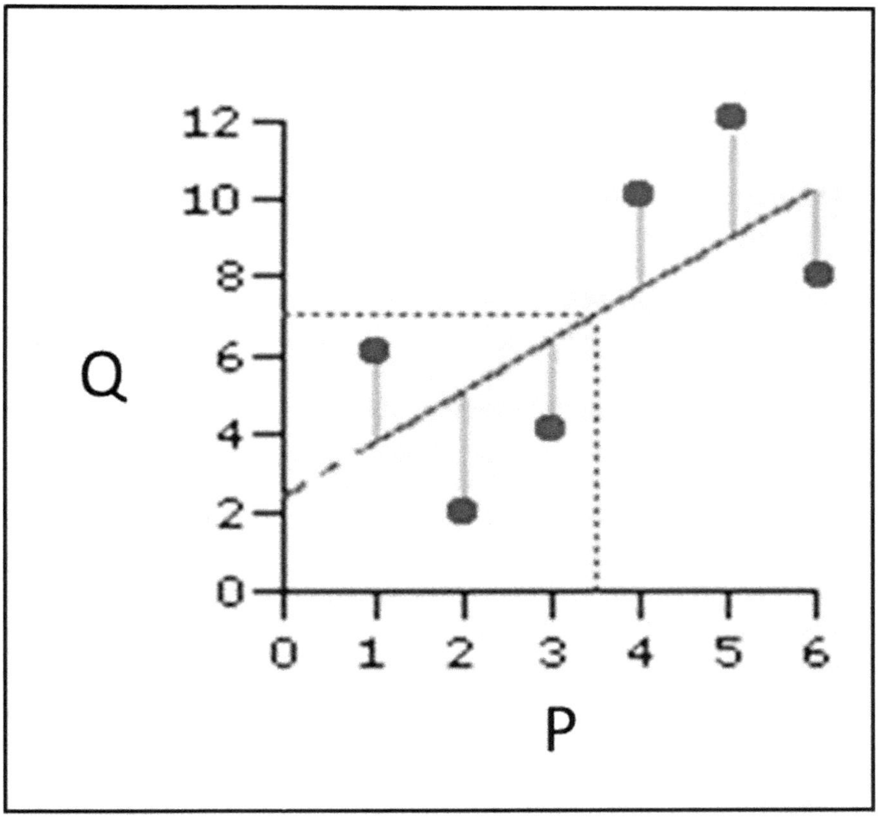

In a nutshell, regression analysis produces simply understood data that can be used to predict events, such as a learner's performance in a specific course.

Time Series

Time series forecasting is a machine learning technique that forecasts target values based on a known history of target values. The input to time series analysis is a sequence of goal values. The time series model calculates goal values for each step in a time range that can include up to 30 steps beyond the historical data. Time series models, like other regression models, compute a few statistics to measure their fit to historical data.

A widely used approach based on Time Series forecasting is Exponential smoothing which is a moving average method in which past observations are assigned exponentially diminishing weights. For nearly a half-century, exponential smoothing approaches have been frequently utilized in forecasting. It has applications at the strategic, tactical, and operational levels. Forecasting is used at the strategic level, for example, to project return on investment, growth, and the impact of innovations. Forecasting is used tactically to project expenses, inventory needs, and consumer satisfaction. Forecasting is used in operations to define goals and predict quality and compliance with standards (Chen & Cui, 2020).

In the higher education field, it can be used at various levels. At a strategic level, it can be used to project the growth of the institution and forecast the number of admissions that can be achieved based on the investments and campaigns. At tactical level, it can be used to project student satisfaction levels and at operational level, this method can be applied to ensure academic quality in content delivery is being followed.

Academic research on the use of time series in higher education has been done, with Haiyang et al. (2018) proposing a time-series classification approach for constructing data from students' behavior and activities on a range of online distance learning courses. Based on the TSF classification technique, the authors proposed a dropout prediction model. The proposed predictive model is independent of learning objectives and subject domains and is based on interaction data. The model predicts dropout rates without the need for instructional expertise. The results show that as the amount of data used in the model increases, so does the prediction accuracy on two selected datasets.

Similarly, Chen and Cui (2020) investigated student online temporal behaviors using LMS data for early course success prediction using a deep learning approach. The findings reveal that, when combined with a deep learning approach, time series data on click frequencies successfully provided early detection of at-risk children with reasonable prediction accuracy. In another study, Brooks, Thompson, and Teasley (2015) describe a unique method for turning educational log data into attributes that can be used to develop prediction models of student progress. These models, unlike cognitive modeling or content analysis approaches, are developed from interactions between learners and resources, requiring no input from instructional or domain specialists and being applicable across courses or learning contexts.

Hence, it is evident that Time series can be a useful method for higher education institutions to apply and gain access to learner analytics which can be helpful for the institution to retain students, assess their satisfaction levels and achieve academic quality.

K-Means

Another helpful method for analyzing comprehensive evaluation data on students is the K-means clustering analysis technology. Its objectives include accurately diagnosing learning issues, determining the regularity of data implications, and laying the groundwork for the creation of successful student management strategies (Liu, 2022). Academic research has been conducted on the usage of time series in higher education. For instance, Ifenthaler, Schumacher, and Kuzilek (2023) conducted a case study using learning analytics techniques to examine students' participation in self-assessments and how this relates to performance on final exams and self-reported self-testing techniques. To find students with comparable self-assessment interaction patterns, the k-means algorithm was employed to cluster students' participation with self-assessments. The findings offer a range of perspectives on how self-assessments are used and how they relate to academic success. They further suggested that prior to summative exams, students generally use self-tests. Engagement with self-assessments was divided into two distinct clusters, and engagement was positively correlated with performance on the final exam. These findings support the application of assessment analytics, along with frameworks that go along with it, to learning analytics, as well as the delivery of adaptive feedback to students.

Veluri et al. (2022) discussed the factors that influence college students' decision on a major and advocate the use of predictive tools and procedures to forecast student's behavior, attitudes, and performance with an objective of raising the achievement levels. They proposed a framework for student performance classification and prediction.

Factor Analysis

Mateus (2023) underlined the significance of the student experience (SX), which is based on interaction with multiple institution stakeholders. The SX is influenced by a variety of factors, including the design of institutional regulations, best practices in teaching, learning, and evaluation, as well as the accessibility of resources. They reported on how six factors—student-centered service, diversity and global citizenship, co-production of experience and learning, teacher dependence, accountability, and whole-person development—measured educational experiences affect their satisfaction with the university they chose.

The author conducted an exploratory factor analysis (EFA) on the collected data, and then they used Statistical Package for the Social Sciences (SPSS) AMOS to do a confirmatory factor analysis (CFA). They concluded that HEIs need instruments like the SX scale to accurately track the contribution they can provide to their students.

Wainwright et al. (2019) developed a descriptive tool to assess students' ideal and anticipated expectations of learning analytics services. A two-factor structure supported by the results of an exploratory factor analysis, an exploratory structural equation model, and confirmatory factor analysis best accounted for the data relating to ideal and predicted expectations. Ethical and privacy expectations are covered by component one, whereas service feature expectations are covered by factor two.

Using descriptive statistics for items and confirmatory factor analysis, Kostagiolas (2019) presents learning analytics data for assessing the effect of study pleasure on students' academic self-efficacy and performance. The investigation shows a link between students' contentment, self-efficacy, and academic achievement and assesses how academic information resources help students meet their information demands.

b. Evaluation of their suitability for the task to be performed

The next step in the process is suitability evaluation where suitability and compatibility of each of the predictive analytics can be assessed. This task is of great relevance and importance since a lot depends on the appropriate approach selection. Hence, to perform this task diligently, efforts must be made towards having a clarity of what exactly must be achieved. Questions like "do we want a solution to resolve and assess learner retention? Do we need to monitor their attendance in live classes, how to ensure maximum participation from learners in various assignments and activities, What are the chances of a learner failing or passing a particular course, how to shortlist the bright or poor candidates with good or bad performance so that they can be focused upon, what are the strengths or skills of a particular student and which skill they need to work upon" and so on, need to be thought about by the higher education institutions and then they should move to the next step.

c. Selection of single or multiple algorithms

In this step, a single or a combination of various predictive analytics approaches can be adopted, depending on the requirements of the institution. As discussed in point a, each of the approaches is suitable for a particular purpose and can answer a particular type of queries. Hence, it becomes important for higher education institutions to take this call with caution. It would be helpful if they take assistance from experts of Machine Learning and Data Analytics fields.

PROPOSED MODEL

Figure 5 presents the complete flow of sequence of events as the Proposed model where initially, the LMS serves as the input for the model. Since the requirements of the university or institution can be diverse, diverse learner data may be needed to perform predictive analytics. The author means by "diverse learner data" that information like a basic learner profile including their location, contact information, and pertinent personal characteristics is obtained. Similar information about how students attempt various types of projects, such as involvement in discussion forums, writing or programming assignments, and learning journals, also falls under the category of diversified information. Also included in the various data are the assessments that students attempt, such as practice quizzes, graded quizzes, end-of-semester exams, etc. The statistics regarding their access to the LMS as well as the e-learning content (eBooks, power point presentations, open-source links) also become crucial sources of diverse input data.

Figure 5. Proposed model

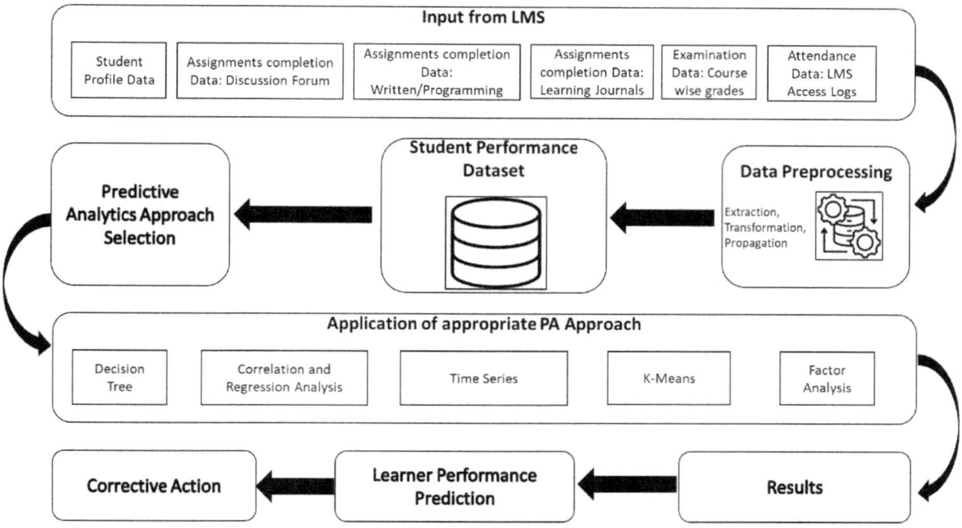

All this variety of input data is cleaned, transformed, and consolidated and loaded into a common repository called Student Performance Dataset. From this dataset, now the institution can apply the appropriate Predictive analytics approach, depending on their requirements. For example, algorithms based on Decision Trees can be helpful in forecasting student performance however they are accompanied with other techniques and algorithms like mining algorithms. Similarly, factor analysis can assist the institution to get such insights that help them in taking decisions that are of strategic nature like how to enhance learner satisfaction and experience. K-means can be used to measure the student engagement and interaction with the course and so on. Hence, predictive analytics have an algorithm or way for achieving every possible outcome related to learning analytics.

Now, after the desired algorithm is applied on the student performance data set and results are made available by the algorithms, the results can be verified and validated, and the learner performance can be predicted. If the results show a decline in learner performance or institutional performance or give a negative signal related to a learner failing a course or lack of participation is observed, appropriate corrective or preventive actions can be undertaken to ensure learner retention, enhance their performance and satisfaction levels. Finally, the model is flexible enough to include more algorithms and techniques to provide more customized solutions.

CHALLENGES OF PREDICTIVE LEARNING ANALYTICS

There is no doubt that predictive learning analytics is a boon for the institutions, and it allows them to find solutions to most pressing issues in higher education. However, there are several limitations and downsides to predictive analytics that stakeholders and educators should be aware of a variety of problems related to areas such as tracking, gathering, analyzing, and evaluating data; unsuitable learning environments; improving learning environments; and ethical and privacy concerns (Avella et al., 2016). Also, Gandhi (2022) emphasized the importance of recognizing the issue and the clear purpose of using predictive learning analytics must be clear to the higher education institutions. Below are the points concerning the challenges of predictive learning analytics.

a. Ethical and legal issues

Since the analytics works on a variety of learner data, it must be ensured that this data collection and analysis is done in an ethical manner and legally. There is a threat that sensitive learner information like academic performance, behavior, health, or demographics, could be misused or breached. Appropriate consent should be taken and the learner and their parents should be briefed about the purpose for which the information is being sought to establish trust.

b. Availability of Quality Data

Predictive analytics require a huge amount of data which is diverse in nature. Hence ensuring its availability and quality is quite challenging. If predictive analytics techniques are applied on incomplete or inconsistent data, the real picture of student performance cannot be predicted and the efforts would be wasted. Also, consolidating data from several sources is a challenging task and it requires coordination among all those data sources providers.

c. Requirement of technically sound personnel

Performing predictive analytics requires that the personnel are technically sound and possess knowledge of AI, machine learning, data science and visualization, advanced mathematics, and statistics. Further, the knowledge of the latest tools in these fields is mandatory and the personnel should also have experience in an academic environment. The personnel should also be capable of providing training and support to all other stakeholders including the institution management, learners, parents, and teachers.

d. Results Interpretation

Another difficulty in applying predictive analytics in education is ensuring that the results are validly and meaningfully applied. Predictive analytics, for instance, may yield results or suggestions that are ambiguous, incorrect, or irrelevant, such as false positives, false negatives, or overgeneralizations, which may result in poor decisions or actions. Therefore, utilizing techniques like cross-validation, testing, or feedback, educators and stakeholders should assess and confirm the quality and dependability of the predictive analytics outputs. Using techniques like storytelling, visualization, or dialogue, they should also effectively convey the findings and their implications.

e. Continuously evolving academic environment

Another challenge while applying predictive analytics is that the academic environment at institutions continues to evolve with new courses, assessment parameters and rubrics and curriculum modifications. Hence, performing predictive analytics in this changing environment is quite challenging as there can be issues with data capturing. Hence, the timeline when predictive analytics is to be performed must be chosen wisely.

CONCLUSION

The chapter focused on the importance of applying predictive analytics in an asynchronous learning environment. As analytics is being applied in several industries, its usage in the higher education industry has been quite limited as of now. Hence, if predictive learning analytics is embraced and applied by the universities and higher education institutions, a lot of challenges like student retention, student achievement tracking, student performance tracking and several other related issues can be dealt with appropriately. The chapter provided a detailed background study and an analysis of related work in the field of predictive analytics. Also, an integrated model for applying predictive analytics in an asynchronous learning environment is discussed in detail where several techniques are discussed and the situation where those can be applied is also discussed.

FUTURE RESEARCH DIRECTIONS

As part of future work, the model can be extended to include specific algorithms related with each of the techniques discussed in this chapter and, the model can include a combination of these approaches that can provide customized solutions to the institution's requirements. For all this to happen, the challenges mentioned in the chapter need to be tackled and data from all sources need to be fetched, cleaned, and consolidated so that the main data repository always remains updated.

REFERENCES

Anderson, J. R., Boyle, C. F., & Reiser, B. J. (1985). Intelligent tutoring systems. *Science*, *228*(4698), 456–462. doi:10.1126cience.228.4698.456 PMID:17746875

Apolinar-Gotardo, M. (2019). Using decision tree algorithm to predict student performance. *Indian Journal of Science and Technology*, *12*, 5.

Avella, J. T., Kebritchi, M., Nunn, S. G., & Kanai, T. (2016). Learning analytics methods, benefits, and challenges in higher education: A systematic literature review. *Online Learning : the Official Journal of the Online Learning Consortium*, *20*(2), 13–29.

Badal, Y. T., & Sungkur, R. K. (2023). Predictive modelling and analytics of students' grades using machine learning algorithms. *Education and Information Technologies, 28*(3), 3027–3057. doi:10.100710639-022-11299-8 PMID:36097545

Bailie, J. L. (2020). Online learner analytics of asynchronous discussions as a predictor of final grades. *Journal of Instructional Pedagogies, 24.*

Baker, R. S. (2016). Stupid tutoring systems, intelligent humans. *International Journal of Artificial Intelligence in Education, 26*(2), 600–614. doi:10.100740593-016-0105-0

Barmaki, R., & Hughes, C. E. (2015). Providing real-time feedback for student teachers in a virtual rehearsal environment. *The Proceedings of the 2015 ACM on International Conference on Multimodal Interaction* (pp. 531–537). ACM.

Bharadiya, J. P. (2023). A comparative study of business intelligence and artificial intelligence with big data analytics. *American Journal of Artificial Intelligence, 7*(1), 24.

Brooks, C., Thompson, C., & Teasley, S. (2015, March). A time series interaction analysis method for building predictive models of learners using log data. *The Proceedings of the fifth international conference on learning analytics and knowledge* (pp. 126-135).

Chatti, M. A., Dyckhoff, A. L., Schroeder, U., & Thüs, H. (2012). A reference model for learning analytics. *International Journal of Technology Enhanced Learning, 4*(5/6), 318–331. doi:10.1504/IJTEL.2012.051815

Chen, F., & Cui, Y. (2020). Utilizing student time series behavior in learning management systems for early prediction of course performance. *Journal of Learning Analytics, 7*(2), 1–17. doi:10.18608/jla.2020.72.1

Chen, L., Chen, P., & Lin, Z. (2020). Artificial intelligence in education: A review. *IEEE Access : Practical Innovations, Open Solutions, 8*, 75264–75278. doi:10.1109/ACCESS.2020.2988510

Cook, D. J., Augusto, J. C., & Jakkula, V. R. (2009). Ambient intelligence: Technologies, applications, and opportunities. *Pervasive and Mobile Computing, 5*(4), 277–298. doi:10.1016/j.pmcj.2009.04.001

Dazo, S. L., Stepanek, N. R., Chauhan, A., & Dorn, B. (2017). Examining instructor use of learning analytics. *Paper presented at the Proceedings of the 2017 CHI Conference Extended Abstracts on Human Factors in Computing Systems*. ACM. 10.1145/3027063.3053256

Dhamija, A., & Dhamija, D. (2020). Impact of innovative and interactive instructional strategies on student classroom participation. In M. Montebello (Ed.), Handbook of Research on Digital Learning (pp. 20-37). IGI Global. doi:10.4018/978-1-5225-9304-1.ch002

Fabriz, S., Mendzheritskaya, J., & Stehle, S. (2021). Impact of synchronous and asynchronous settings of online teaching and learning in higher education on students' learning experience during COVID-19. *Frontiers in Psychology*, *12*, 4544. doi:10.3389/fpsyg.2021.733554 PMID:34707542

Fernandez, C. J., Ramesh, R., & Manivannan, A. S. R. (2022). Synchronous learning and asynchronous learning during COVID-19 pandemic: A case study in India. *Asian Association of Open Universities Journal*, *17*(1), 1–14. doi:10.1108/AAOUJ-02-2021-0027

Gandhi, Y. (2022). *What is learning analytics? Challenges and types*. Analytics Steps – A leading source of Technical & Financial content. https://www.analyticssteps.com/blogs/what-learning-analytics-challenges-and-types

Gandomi, A., & Haider, M. (2015). Beyond the hype: Big data concepts, methods, and analytics. *International Journal of Information Management*, *35*(2), 137–144. doi:10.1016/j.ijinfomgt.2014.10.007

Ghilay, Y. (2022). Quantitative courses in higher education: A comparison between asynchronous and synchronous distance learning. *Journal of Education and Learning*, *11*(5), 93. doi:10.5539/jel.v11n5p93

Goggins, S. P., Galyen, K., Petakovic, E., & Laffey, J. M. (2016). Connecting performance to social structure and pedagogy as a pathway to scaling learning analytics in MOOCs: An exploratory study. *Journal of Computer Assisted Learning*, *32*(3), 244–266. doi:10.1111/jcal.12129

Haiyang, L., Wang, Z., Benachour, P., & Tubman, P. (2018, July). A time series classification method for behavior-based dropout prediction. *IEEE 18th international conference on advanced learning technologies (ICALT)* (pp. 191-195). IEEE.

Herodotou, C., Hlosta, M., Boroowa, A., Rienties, B., Zdrahal, Z., & Mangafa, C. (2019). Empowering online teachers through predictive learning analytics. *British Journal of Educational Technology*, *50*(6), 3064–3079. doi:10.1111/bjet.12853

Herodotou, C., Maguire, C., McDowell, N., Hlosta, M., & Boroowa, A. (2021). The engagement of university teachers with predictive learning analytics. *Computers & Education*, *173*, 104285. doi:10.1016/j.compedu.2021.104285

Herodotou, C., Maguire, C., McDowell, N., Hlosta, M., & Boroowa, A. (2021). The engagement of university teachers with predictive learning analytics. *Computers & Education*, *173*, 104285. doi:10.1016/j.compedu.2021.104285

Herodotou, C., Naydenova, G., Boroowa, A., Gilmour, A., & Rienties, B. (2020). How can predictive learning analytics and motivational interventions increase student retention and enhance administrative support in distance education? *Journal of Learning Analytics*, *7*(2), 72–83. doi:10.18608/jla.2020.72.4

Herodotou, C., Rienties, B., Boroowa, A., Zdrahal, Z., & Hlosta, M. (2019). A large-scale implementation of predictive learning analytics in higher education: The teachers' role and perspective. *Educational Technology Research and Development*, *67*(5), 1273–1306. doi:10.100711423-019-09685-0

Herodotou, C., Rienties, B., Hlosta, M., Boroowa, A., Mangafa, C., & Zdrahal, Z. (2020). The scalable implementation of predictive learning analytics at a distance learning university: Insights from a longitudinal case study. *The Internet and Higher Education*, *45*, 100725. doi:10.1016/j.iheduc.2020.100725

Full Fabric. (n.d.). How predictive analytics can boost student success rates. *Full Fabric*. https://www.fullfabric.com/

Ifenthaler, D., Schumacher, C., & Kuzilek, J. (2023). Investigating students' use of self-assessments in higher education using learning analytics. *Journal of Computer Assisted Learning*, *39*(1), 255–268. doi:10.1111/jcal.12744

Joseph, R. C., & Johnson, N. A. (2013). Big data and transformational government. *IT Professional*, *15*(6), 43–48. doi:10.1109/MITP.2013.61

Judge, L. (n.d.). *Predictive analytics in education: An introduction*. Tribal Group. https://www.tribalgroup.com/blog/predictive-analytics-in-education-an-introduction

K, S. (2022, October 18). *Role of predictive analytics in transforming education*. Bold BI. https://www.boldbi.com/blog/role-of-predictive-analytics-in-transforming-education

Kidecha, S. (2022, June 4). *Extensive guide on the role of predictive analytics in education*. Kody Technolab. https://kodytechnolab.com/blog/predictive-analytics-in-education/

Kostagiolas, P., Lavranos, C., & Korfiatis, N. (2019). Learning analytics: Survey data for measuring the impact of study satisfaction on students' academic self-efficacy and performance. *Data in Brief*, *25*, 104051. doi:10.1016/j.dib.2019.104051 PMID:31211203

Liu, R. (2022). Data analysis of educational evaluation using K-means clustering method. *Computational Intelligence and Neuroscience*, *31*, 3762431. doi:10.1155/2022/3762431 PMID:35958764

McGavisk, T. (2023, May 2). *Using predictive analytics to improve student education*. Time and Data security. https://www.timedatasecurity.com/blogs/using-predictive-analytics-to-improve-student-education

McKenney, S., & Mor, Y. (2015). Supporting teachers in data-informed educational design. *British Journal of Educational Technology*, *46*(2), 265–279. doi:10.1111/bjet.12262

Moorhouse, B. L., & Wong, K. M. (2022). Blending asynchronous and synchronous digital technologies and instructional approaches to facilitate remote learning. *Journal of Computers in Education*, *9*(1), 51–70. doi:10.100740692-021-00195-8

Murphy, R. F. (2019). Artificial intelligence applications to support K-12 teachers and teaching. Rand Corporation, 10.

Ndukwe, I. G., & Daniel, B. K. (2020). Teaching analytics, value, and tools for teacher data literacy: A systematic and tripartite approach. *International Journal of Educational Technology in Higher Education*, *17*(1), 1–31. doi:10.118641239-020-00201-6

Pallathadka, H., Wenda, A., Ramirez-Asís, E., Asís-López, M., Flores-Albornoz, J., & Phasinam, K. (2023). Classification and prediction of student performance data using various machine learning algorithms. *Materials Today: Proceedings*, *80*, 3782–3785. doi:10.1016/j.matpr.2021.07.382

Patel, H. H., & Prajapati, P. (2018). Study and analysis of decision tree-based classification algorithms. *International Journal on Computer Science and Engineering*, *6*(10).

Prieto, L. P., Sharma, K., Dillenbourg, P., & Jesús, M. (2016). Teaching analytics: towards automatic extraction of orchestration graphs using wearable sensors. *The Proceedings of the Sixth International Conference on Learning Analytics & Knowledge* (pp. 148–157). ACM.

Prieto, L. P., Sharma, K., Kidzinski, Ł., Rodríguez-Triana, M. J., & Dillenbourg, P. (2018). Multimodal teaching analytics: Automated extraction of orchestration graphs from wearable sensor data. *Journal of Computer Assisted Learning*, *34*(2), 193–203. doi:10.1111/jcal.12232 PMID:29686446

Rahman, A. M., Al Mamun, A., & Islam, A. (2017, December). Programming challenges of chatbot: Current and future prospective. *IEEE Region 10 Humanitarian Technology Conference (R10-HTC)* (pp. 75-78). IEEE.

Raut, A. B., & Nichat, M. A. A. (2017). Students performance prediction using decision tree. *International Journal of Computational Intelligence Research, 13*(7), 1735–1741.

Rets, I., Herodotou, C., & Gillespie, A. (2023). Six practical recommendations enabling ethical use of predictive learning analytics in distance education. *Journal of Learning Analytics*.

Roll, I., Russell, D. M., & Gašević, D. (2018). Learning at scale. *International Journal of Artificial Intelligence in Education, 28*(4), 471–477. doi:10.100740593-018-0170-7

Roos, S. (2018). *Chatbots in education: A passing trend or a valuable pedagogical tool?* Diva Portal. https://www.diva-portal.org/smash/get/diva2:1223692/FULLTEXT01.pdf

Sarker, I. H., Kayes, A. S. M., & Watters, P. (2019). Effectiveness analysis of machine learning classification models for predicting personalized context-aware smartphone usage. *Journal of Big Data, 6*(1), 1–28. doi:10.118640537-019-0219-y

Seo, K., Fels, S., Yoon, D., Roll, I., Dodson, S., & Fong, M. (2020b). Artificial intelligence for video-based learning at scale. *The Proceedings of the Seventh ACM Conference on Learning@ Scale* (pp. 215–217). ACM.

Sghir, N., Adadi, A., & Lahmer, M. (2022). Recent advances in predictive learning analytics: A decade systematic review (2012–2022). *Education and Information Technologies*, 1–35. PMID:36571084

Stefanakos, M., & Stefanakos, M. (2023). Predictive Analytics in Education: How can it help | AnalyticVue. https://analyticvue.com/predictive-analytics-in-education/

Suehiro, D., Taniguchi, Y., Shimada, A., & Ogata, H. (2017). Face-to-face teaching analytics: Extracting teaching activities from e-book logs via time-series analysis. *IEEE 17th International Conference On Advanced Learning Technologies (ICALT)*, 2017 (pp. 267–268). IEEE.

Sungkur, R. K., & Maharaj, M. (2022). A review of intelligent techniques for implementing SMART learning environments. In B. Sikdar, S. Prasad Maity, J. Samanta, & A. Roy (Eds.), *Proceedings of the 3rd International Conference on Communication, Devices and Computing: Lecture Notes in Electrical Engineering (*Vol. 851*)*. Springer. 10.1007/978-981-16-9154-6_69

Team, P. (2022, August 9). *Asynchronous learning explained: Examples, benefits, and more*. Panopto Video Platform. https://www.panopto.com/blog/asynchronous-learning-explained-examples-benefits-and-more/

Thomas, H. (2020). Critical literature review on chatbots in education. *IJTSRD*, *4*(6), 786–788.

van Leeuwen, A., Janssen, J., Erkens, G., & Brekelmans, M. (2014). Supporting teachers in guiding collaborating students: Effects of learning analytics in CSCL. *Computers & Education*, *79*, 28–39. doi:10.1016/j.compedu.2014.07.007

van Leeuwen, A., Janssen, J., Erkens, G., & Brekelmans, M. (2015). Teacher regulation of cognitive activities during student collaboration: Effects of learning analytics. *Computers & Education*, *90*, 80–94. doi:10.1016/j.compedu.2015.09.006

VanLehn, K. (2011). The relative effectiveness of human tutoring, intelligent tutoring systems, and other tutoring systems. *Educational Psychologist*, *46*(4), 197–221. do i:10.1080/00461520.2011.611369

Varkey, T. C., Varkey, J. A., Ding, J. B., Varkey, P. K., Zeitler, C., Nguyen, A. M., Merhavy, Z. I., & Thomas, C. R. (2022). Asynchronous learning: A general review of best practices for the 21st century. *Journal of Research in Innovative Teaching & Learning*, *16*(1), 4–16. doi:10.1108/JRIT-06-2022-0036

Veluri, R. K., Patra, I., Naved, M., Prasad, V. V., Arcinas, M. M., Beram, S. M., & Raghuvanshi, A. (2022). Learning analytics using deep learning techniques for efficiently managing educational institutes. *Materials Today: Proceedings*, *51*, 2317–2320. doi:10.1016/j.matpr.2021.11.416

Villegas-Ch, W., & Luján-Mora, S. (2017, March). Analysis of data mining techniques applied to LMS for personalized education. *IEEE 2017 World Engineering Education Conference (EDUNINE)* (pp. 85-89). IEEE.

Villegas-Ch, W., Luján-Mora, S., & Buenaño-Fernandez, D. (2017, December). Data mining toolkit for extraction of knowledge from LMS. *The Proceedings of the 9th International Conference on Education Technology and Computers* (pp. 31-35). ACM.

Villegas-Ch, W., Palacios-Pacheco, X., Ortiz-Garcés, I., & Luján-Mora, S. (2019). *Management of educative data in university students with the use of big data techniques*. Página personal - Sergio Luján Mora. https://sergiolujanmora.es/management-educative-data-university-students-use-big-data-techniques

Villegas-Ch, W., Román-Cañizares, M., & Palacios-Pacheco, X. (2020). Improvement of an online education model with the integration of machine learning and data analysis in an LMS. [MDPI AG.]. *Applied Sciences (Basel, Switzerland), 10*(15), 5371. doi:10.3390/app10155371

Waller, M. A., & Fawcett, S. E. (2013). Data science, predictive analytics, and big data: A revolution that will transform supply chain design and management. *Journal of Business Logistics*, *34*(2), 77–84. doi:10.1111/jbl.12010

Whitelock-Wainwright, A., Gašević, D., Tejeiro, R., Tsai, Y. S., & Bennett, K. (2019). The student expectations of learning analytics questionnaire. *Journal of Computer Assisted Learning*, *35*(5), 633–666. doi:10.1111/jcal.12366

Wolff, A., Zdrahal, Z., Herrmannova, D., Kuzilek, J., & Hlosta, M. (2014). Developing predictive models for early detection of at-risk students on distance learning modules. *Machine Learning and Learning Analytics Workshop at The 4th International Conference on Learning Analytics and Knowledge (LAK14)*, Indianapolis, Indiana, USA.

Yadav, S. K., & Pal, S. (2012). Data mining: A prediction for performance improvement of engineering students using classification. *arXiv preprint arXiv:1203.3832*.

ADDITIONAL READING

Al-Tameemi, G., Xue, J., Ajit, S., Kanakis, T., & Hadi, I. (2020, June). Predictive learning analytics in higher education: Factors, methods, and challenges. *2020 International Conference on Advances in Computing and Communication Engineering (ICACCE)* (pp. 1-9). IEEE. 10.1109/ICACCE49060.2020.9154946

Herodotou, C., Naydenova, G., Boroowa, A., Gilmour, A., & Rienties, B. (2020). How can predictive learning analytics and motivational interventions increase student retention and enhance administrative support in distance education? *Journal of Learning Analytics*, *7*(2), 72–83. doi:10.18608/jla.2020.72.4

Mubarak, A. A., Cao, H., & Ahmed, S. A. (2021). Predictive learning analytics using deep learning model in MOOCs' courses videos. *Education and Information Technologies*, *26*(1), 371–392. doi:10.100710639-020-10273-6

Ranjeeth, S., Latchoumi, T. P., & Paul, P. V. (2020). A survey on predictive models of learning analytics. *Procedia Computer Science*, *167*, 37–46. doi:10.1016/j.procs.2020.03.180

KEY TERMS AND DEFINITIONS

Artificial Intelligence: The simulation of human intelligence processes by machines, especially computer systems.

Assessment: Making inferences based on students' learning and development to design new learning opportunities for students.

Asynchronous Learning: A form of learning where the instructor and the students in the course all engage with the course content at different times.

Business Intelligence (BI): An organizational infrastructure that collects, stores, and analyzes the data produced by a company's activities.

Database: An organized collection of data.

Learning Analytics (LA): The measurement, collection, analysis and reporting of data about learners and their contexts, for purposes of understanding and optimising learning and the environments in which it occurs.

Learning Management System: (LMS): A software application or web-based technology used to plan, implement, and assess a specific learning process.

Machine Learning: A type of artificial intelligence (AI) focused on building computer systems that learn from data.

Predictive Analytics (PA): The use of statistics and modeling techniques to determine future performance based on current and historical data.

Chapter 4
Enhancing Self-Regulated Learning With Artificial Intelligence-Powered Learning Analytics

Seyma N. Yildirim-Erbasli
Concordia University of Edmonton, Canada

Guher Gorgun
https://orcid.org/0000-0002-0861-9225
University of Alberta, Canada

Okan Bulut
https://orcid.org/0000-0001-5853-1267
University of Alberta, Canada

ABSTRACT

This chapter explores the dynamic synergy between artificial intelligence (AI) and learning analytics (LA) as catalysts for self-regulated learning (SRL). By examining the intersection of AI, LA, and SRL, this chapter sheds light on the evolving landscape of education and the opportunities it offers for tailored, data-driven learning experiences. It delves into the transformative potential of AI-powered LA, providing personalized insights, prediction, recommendation, and interactive scaffolding; thus promoting SRL development among learners. It also addresses ethical considerations, challenges, and the need for interdisciplinary collaboration among educators, data scientists, and policymakers. Ultimately, this chapter underscores the importance of responsible implementation and continuous research to harness the full benefits of AI-powered LA in supporting SRL and improving educational outcomes.

DOI: 10.4018/979-8-3693-0066-4.ch004

INTRODUCTION

With recent advances in digital technologies, self-regulated learning (SRL) and learning analytics (LA) have become two essential areas of focus in education. SRL is the ability to regulate one's learning process metacognitively (involving planning, goal setting, organization, self-monitoring, and evaluation), motivationally (drawing upon intrinsic interest during learning), and behaviorally (utilizing adaptive adjustments) (Zimmerman, 1990). LA refers to the active use of past and real-time data to support and enhance learning outcomes (Siemens, 2012). SRL encompasses planning, monitoring, evaluating, and adapting learning strategies to achieve academic goals. LA complements SRL by providing insights into students' behaviors, interactions, and performance within educational contexts. LA provides a wealth of information about students' learning patterns, preferences, and progress that can be used to personalize instruction, support individual learning goals, and facilitate metacognitive development. LA leverages data analysis to create a feedback loop, helping students understand how they engage with the learning material and identify areas where improvements can be made. Through LA, educators and policymakers can better understand how students learn and identify ways to optimize teaching and learning practices to enhance student success. For example, LA can analyze how students engage with the online course materials and identify areas of difficulty. In response to this LA analysis, the instructor can provide personalized resources and support to help students overcome their challenges. As a result, students can gain a better understanding of the course material, aligning with their learning goals and improving their overall performance. This scenario illustrates how LA can personalize instruction and support individual learning goals by leveraging data analysis and creating a feedback loop.

In recent years, artificial intelligence (AI) has led to the emergence of AI-powered LA tools, which have the potential to support SRL. Integration of AI into LA enhances this symbiotic relationship between LA and SRL. AI can support LA by providing more sophisticated and accurate analyses of student data, as well as by automating certain aspects of the analytics process. AI can autonomously learn patterns and associations in data, and this feature can be leveraged to enhance the effectiveness of LA (Alam, 2021). AI can automatically capture and analyze a wealth of data related to students' SRL behaviors, including their study habits, progress, and even their emotional or metacognitive states. As a result, cutting-edge techniques, such as AI, in learning analytics have gained popularity in recent years (Alam, 2021). By combining AI's capabilities with LA's mechanisms, we can gain the power to offer personalized recommendations and support based on students' specific learning profiles. This integration streamlines the process of adapting instruction to meet individual needs, ultimately fostering more effective SRL and improving overall learning outcomes. For example, an AI-powered LA can adjust the difficulty level and content of learning materials based on students' performance to ensure that they are challenged but not overwhelmed. This can help the students develop better self-regulation skills and improve their learning outcomes.

In this chapter, we embark on an exploration of the dynamic synergy between AI and LA and their role as catalysts for SRL. The complete potential of SRL becomes a formidable challenge in the absence of the insights and support delivered by LA. The gap lies between the benefits of SRL and the challenges learners face in harnessing these benefits. It is a challenge to realize that, without an intelligent and data-driven framework, these benefits may remain underutilized or even inaccessible. This chapter aims to address this challenge by providing a comprehensive exploration of how AI-powered LA can bridge this gap and empower learners. The integration of AI-powered LA becomes not just advantageous but a necessity, particularly in an educational landscape increasingly reliant on data-driven decision-making and personalized learning experiences. This chapter provides an overview of the role of AI-powered LA in supporting SRL and explores the benefits and ethical considerations associated with the use of AI-powered LA for SRL support. The chapter includes the following sections: theoretical background, AI-powered LA for SRL support, and ethical considerations and challenges.

THEORETICAL BACKGROUND

With the advancement of technology-enhanced or online learning environments, there is a growing trend of autonomous education activities undertaken by students (Kim & Moon 2019). At the essence of essential human skills and competencies lies the ability to self-regulate, enabling individuals to take initiative, establish goals, and monitor themselves and others. The development of SRL skills is crucial for effective lifelong learning, empowering learners with a sense of agency and equipping them with the capacity to adapt and regulate their behavior in diverse challenging situations across various domains. Consequently, the need for SRL has become increasingly important. Specifically, in online learning environments, where students are more entrusted with making their own decisions throughout the learning process, the ability to self-regulate one's learning becomes crucial (Azevedo et al., 2022). Students are expected to possess the competency to independently manage and engage in learning activities, taking ownership of their educational journey. SRL is considered an essential learning skill that renders learners as autonomous agents in a learning environment. That is, students with higher levels of SRL skills tend to engage in metacognitive skills, monitor their learning, demonstrate better time management skills, and adapt study tactics to improve their learning. The theoretical background section of this chapter provides an overview of SRL, LA, and AI, defining and exploring the respective roles of LA and AI in the development of SRL. This section also highlights the importance of an evidence-based approach by outlining some key findings in this area. This provides a strong foundation for the discussion of AI-powered LA and its potential to support SRL.

Self-Regulated Learning

The self-regulation of learning refers to students' ability to manage their cognitive (i.e., acquisition of knowledge and skills), metacognitive (i.e., monitoring and controlling learning), and affective (i.e., regulating effort for engaging with the learning materials) processes by employing strategies to achieve their established goals (Panadero & Alonso-Tapia, 2014). SRL is a key element of effective learning, encompassing students' ability to plan, monitor, and evaluate their own learning (Zimmerman, 1990). It is framed as an intentional and goal-directed process, whereby learners actively make conscious decisions to steer themselves towards their desired learning objectives (Azevedo et al., 2022). Zimmerman's model of SRL (2000) is a comprehensive and cyclical framework that encompasses three phases: forethought, performance, and self-reflection. At the forethought phase of learning, students engage in metacognitive activities that involve analyzing the task for orientation, setting goals, and devising a plan. During the performance phase, they execute the task using cognitive strategies as well as monitor and control the processing of learning content and the strategies applied to the task. Finally, in the self-reflection phase, students evaluate and reflect on their learning progress by comparing it to previously established goals or standards. Therefore, SRL encompasses dynamic processes that actively regulate one's own learning through monitoring and controlling SRL activities in pursuit of personal goals.

Self-regulated learners exhibit a distinctive ability to establish and pursue their own learning objectives while meticulously overseeing their advancement and adjusting strategies as needed. This proficiency extends beyond the mere possession of a comprehensive array of learning tactics; it encompasses the motivational competence to apply effort in executing these cognitive processes. As a result, students who are adept at regulating their learning through deliberate and reflective means tend to exhibit heightened academic achievement (e.g., Sabourin et al., 2013). Although SRL holds theoretical importance and has demonstrated empirical benefits, typically, some students may not inherently or naturally self-regulate their learning without external guidance or support, and they can encounter challenges in effectively regulating their learning (Lim et al., 2023). However, providing scaffolding support to learners in their activities (e.g., feedback and intelligent tutors) can significantly enhance learning outcomes. Several studies have been conducted to develop and implement computer-generated scaffolds aimed at supporting SRL and have revealed varying degrees of positive effectiveness (Guo, 2022; Munshi et al., 2023). Recognizing this issue, researchers have undertaken a growing number of studies in LA to gain a deeper understanding of SRL processes (Saint et al., 2020). Their objective is to identify strategies and interventions that can effectively promote and enhance students' SRL.

By monitoring students' SRL skills, data about the learners' thought processes, motivation, metacognition, and management strategies can be obtained and then used to inform LA-based tools. For example, self-regulated learners may be more likely to complete assignments, participate in discussions, or seek additional learning resources. This data can be used to identify patterns and relationships in learner behavior and performance, which can inform the development of LA tools and strategies. On the other hand, LA is the process of using data analytics to gain insights into the learning process, providing information that can be used to improve teaching and learning outcomes. By collecting and analyzing data on learner behavior and performance, LA can provide learners with feedback on their progress and help them identify areas where they may need to adjust their learning strategies (Ifenthaler et al., 2018). Thus, self-regulated learners can generate data that can inform LA, while LA can provide feedback and support that can help learners become effective self-regulated learners. SRL and LA can work together in a mutually reinforcing cycle.

Research has shown that LA can be used to support SRL in several ways, including providing feedback (Bulut et al., 2022), personalizing learning (Blumenstein, 2020), and developing metacognitive skills (Chen et al., 2019). LA systems can track students' progress, identify areas of difficulty, and generate individualized feedback. This feedback can include specific recommendations for improvement and supplementary resources tailored to each student's needs. In addition, LA systems can monitor and analyze emotional responses, attitudes, and engagement levels and provide valuable insights into students' motivational states. They can help students better regulate their emotions and attitudes, ultimately fostering a more conducive environment for self-regulation. This use of LA can be a key driver in influencing and enhancing students' motivation, a pivotal aspect of SRL.

AI has also the potential to provide invaluable tools for students seeking to enhance their SRL (e.g., Xia et al., 2022). AI applications that analyze students' activities in real-time play a pivotal role in providing valuable feedback and support, which in turn assist students in enhancing their SRL. Students' varying levels of prior knowledge can play a crucial role in how they engage with AI-driven learning tools (Yang et al., 2018). Students with strong prior knowledge often leverage AI to refine their understanding and skills further. They are inclined to adopt more effective approaches in navigating these AI-driven resources during their SRL processes. With their solid foundation, they may utilize AI tools to clarify specific, nuanced queries, delve deeper into complex topics, or seek advanced-level insights, and guidance. On the other hand, students with less prior knowledge might rely on AI tools for foundational explanations, basic concepts, and step-by-step guidance to bridge gaps in their understanding. AI can provide them with accessible and scaffolded content, gradually building their competence in the subject matter.

Learning Analytics

LA aims to comprehend and enhance learning and refers to the process of collecting, analyzing, reporting, and interpreting data concerning learners and their environments (Siemens, 2013). LA stands as an interdisciplinary field that draws from various research domains, including educational data mining, data visualization, and recommender systems (Salas-Pilco et al., 2022). LA typically employs two distinct analytical methodologies: descriptive analytics (focuses on examining the data-driven behaviors and actions that learners generate in online platforms) and predictive analytics (involves the use of student behavioral data, historical records, and sociodemographic information to forecast educational outcomes (Rets et al., 2021). Its primary objective is to harness the vast amount of data generated by students within the learning environment and apply advanced analytical techniques to gain insights that can enhance and refine both learning and teaching practices (Krikun, 2017). This multifaceted approach positions LA at the forefront of educational innovation, where data-driven decision-making plays a pivotal role in improving educational outcomes and fostering more effective learning experiences.

In digital learning environments, learners or agents leave traces of their interactions (e.g., page visits, clicks, quiz attempts) (Clow, 2013) providing rich information about themselves such as their behavior, affect, and performance. Such information gathered through LA can be used for designing learning dashboards (e.g., Verbert et al., 2013), developing automated detectors (e.g., Gorgun et al., 2022), creating visualizations (e.g., Park & Jo, 2015), supporting writing activities (e.g., Allen et al., 2017), providing feedback (e.g., Lee et al., 2019), personalizing learner experience (e.g., Liu et al., 2017), or enhancing decision-making process of teachers and school administrations (e.g., Wandera et al., 2019).

The underlying assumption in LA is that by monitoring and tracking data pertaining to learners, learning environments, and teachers, we may understand, explain, and improve the learning experiences and processes of learners (Clow, 2013). That is, LA is envisioned to provide actionable insight to enhance learning, thus an LA circle is proposed by some researchers which is composed of gathering data from learners, generating some metrics about their learning and interaction, and providing feedback and interventions to enhance the learning process (Clow, 2012).

LA is not only a promising tool for providing feedback and interventions to various actors of education to enhance learning, but also it is a noteworthy methodology for complementing research on learning and teaching by providing rich data about learners (Siemens, 2013). In other words, researchers may corroborate the theoretical underpinnings of learning as well as improve the understanding of learner behavior in different educational settings through using learner data obtained via LA tools (e.g., dashboards, and learning management systems).

Gabriel et al. (2022) propose that LA resides at the intersection of multiple disciplines, specifically learning, analytics, and human-centered design. Human-centered design encompasses usability and participatory design, contributing to the holistic framework of LA. Learning encompasses domains such as learning and assessment sciences and educational technology, while analytics incorporates fields such as statistics, visualization, and notably AI (also see Kim & Moon, 2019).

Artificial Intelligence in Education

In the realm of LA, there are challenges to overcome in terms of real-time collection and processing of data. These challenges aim to measure and track ongoing learning processes while providing learners with personalized SRL scaffolds to support their learning journey. AI stands as a rich source of promising and innovative solutions with the potential to address these challenges. AI encompasses machine-based systems with the ability to employ human-defined objectives for the purpose of generating predictions, offering recommendations, and making decisions (Dignum et al., 2020). AI includes a diverse range of components, each with its own unique applications and methodologies (Salas-Pilco et al., 2022). Two notable components of AI within the realm of education include machine learning, which involves the utilization of algorithms that leverage educational data to discern patterns, and natural language processing, which relies on algorithms designed for language recognition, enabling the extraction and analysis of textual information from educational materials. These AI components collectively contribute to enhancing educational experiences by automating tasks, providing data-driven insights, and facilitating more personalized and effective learning environments.

The continuously growing demand for personalized education highlights the pivotal role of AI in transforming the learning landscape. The integration of AI in education empowers students, enabling them to learn at their own pace, receive targeted support, and unlock their full potential in an ever-changing world. With the recognition that each student has unique needs and learning modes, researchers and educators are actively leveraging AI technologies to support students' performance by tailoring educational experiences (Ciolacu et al., 2017).

AI can enable the creation of adaptive learning platforms that dynamically adjust to students' abilities, progress, and preferences. In addition, these platforms should prioritize the cultivation of SRL, rather than assuming the sole responsibility of regulating learners themselves (Järvelä et al., 2021). Hybrid systems, integrating both humans and AI, are characterized by the dynamic and flexible boundaries between AI and human decision-making. Tasks can be shifted from humans to AI and vice versa (Buxbaum-Conradi et al., 2016) and hold promise in fostering complex learner skills (e.g., SRL) within educational contexts. These systems are a novel approach within adaptive learning technologies that supports the development of SRL skills through a hybrid intelligence approach, combining humans and AI (Molenaar, 2022).

AI-POWERED LA FOR SRL

Research has underscored the importance of further developing and implementing personalized scaffolding techniques rather than generalized or standardized support to all students to enhance and promote SRL (Guo, 2022; Lim et al., 2023). Recent studies have aimed to shed light on the mechanisms through which learners self-regulate their learning and bridge three interconnected research domains: SRL, LA, and AI (e.g., Molenaar et al., 2023). Interdisciplinary endeavors in these fields integrate SRL as a guiding theory to fuel investigations and employ advanced measurement and support techniques of SRL, in conjunction with LA and AI. This includes endeavors such as enhancing learning technologies with real-time SRL support. AI-driven features are utilized in online courses to enhance the learning experience, such as hands-on activities facilitated by virtual or augmented reality, gamification, and intelligent conversation platforms like Chatbots (Ciolacu et al., 2017). These emerging technologies assist learners in developing SRL across multiple domains (e.g., Azevedo et al., 2022). Empirical evidence indicates that incorporating emerging technology into SRL practices leads to superior learning outcomes compared to conventional methods (Azevedo et al., 2022).

The integration of AI and LA techniques holds the promise of ultimately enhancing students' learning performances (Darvishi et al., 2022). By harnessing the power of AI and LA, we can gain a deeper understanding of individual student needs and learning patterns. This synergy enables the development of personalized learning pathways, early intervention strategies, and personalized content delivery, all of which contribute to more effective and tailored learning experiences. This integration also excels in handling intricate, nonlinear information, enabling the extraction and representation of multi-level and high-dimensional features of student learning, a capability that outshines traditional learning analytics (Ouyang et al., 2023). By tapping into AI's capacity such as pattern recognition and data processing, coupled with LA's ability to dissect and interpret educational data, this synergy allows for a more comprehensive understanding of SRL. In addition, this carries the potential to cultivate students' awareness and self-reflection throughout their learning journey (Ouyang et al., 2023). Students can gain valuable insights into their learning processes, progress, and areas for improvement. This heightened awareness is expected to empower students to take a more active and intentional role in their learning. The section on AI-powered LA for SRL provides an overview as well as examples of AI-powered LA tools and techniques that have been developed and used to support SRL, such as adaptive learning systems, dashboards, machine learning, and conversational agents.

Adaptive Learning Systems for Personalization

AI-enabled adaptive learning systems have the potential to enhance both teaching and learning by providing instructors, learners, and researchers with valuable insights. These systems can effectively identify and deploy appropriate learning interventions by utilizing evidence from SRL experts, researchers, instructors, and learners (Kabudi et al., 2021). Thus, the data collected during learning activities can go beyond mere predictive analytics and instead leverage data in diverse ways, tailored to the specific learner and session objectives. Adaptive learning systems can track students' progress, assess their knowledge, and adjust instruction to meet their individual needs. By providing personalized learning experiences, these systems can help students take charge of their learning process. Adaptive learning systems can suggest personalized learning activities to address learning challenges, thus providing students with the support they need (e.g., Saadati et al., 2021). By providing personalized learning experiences that are tailored to each student's needs, adaptive learning systems help students become more self-regulated learners.

As aforementioned, scaffolding strategies to support learners can be instrumental in enhancing learning outcomes because students do not always possess innate or automatic SRL and may require additional guidance and structure to effectively regulate their learning. Xia and colleagues (2022) have identified a crucial element in enhancing SRL when utilizing AI, emphasizing the importance of catering to their autonomy, competence, and other fundamental psychological needs. In their study, Lim et al. (2023) claimed that scaffolds should be designed to be continuously adaptive and personalized and then gradually reduced based on students' evolving learning progress to promote SRL in an optimal manner. With this claim, they used trace data and investigated the impact of analytics-based personalized scaffolds, supported by a rule-based AI system, on students' learning process and outcomes progress on the fly. In their experiment, the student groups were assigned to receive different types of scaffolds during their learning sessions: personalized scaffolds, generalized scaffolds (i.e., standardized for all students), or no scaffolds. The results revealed that personalized scaffolds led to increased engagement in SRL activities, although no significant effects were observed on learning outcomes. Lim et al. (2023) concluded that analytics-based personalized scaffolds, informed by real-time measurement and supported with AI, represent an initial advancement towards adaptive SRL interventions that incorporate AI.

LA Dashboards for Monitoring Learning

Within the LA literature, a distinction is frequently drawn between two types of analytics: extracted analytics, which utilizes learner dashboards to provide explanations to learners on how to regulate their own learning, and embedded analytics, which employ advanced algorithms to detect learners' progress and dynamically adapt the learning material accordingly (van Leeuwen et al., 2021). Utilizing dashboards equipped with predictive analytics, recommender services, and intelligent agents can represent a valuable approach to enhancing learning environments and advancing SRL (Molenaar et al., 2023). These technologies empower educators and learners alike by providing valuable insights and tailored support to optimize the learning experience.

Dashboards can serve as an interface to enable learner-AI interaction, showcasing learners how their performance aligns with their goals (monitoring) and providing guidance on necessary adjustments for progress (control) (Molenaar, 2022). Initially, the AI takes an active role in regulating learning while the dashboards raise learners' awareness. Eventually, learners become self-regulated, and the AI transitions into an observer and supporter, assisting learners in understanding their own behavior. Thus, over time, learners gain increasingly detailed information through the dashboards, enabling them to self-regulate their own learning while reducing the reliance on AI regulation.

Machine Learning for Prediction and Recommendation

Machine learning is another example of AI-powered LA that has been used to support SRL. Machine learning, for example, can be used to analyze data and identify patterns in students' learning behaviors, such as their study habits or time management skills (e.g., Cui et al., 2020). Machine learning techniques are used for the analysis of clickstream, keystroke, mouse movement, and eye-tracking data to identify various learning strategies and learning outcomes (e.g., Matcha et al., 2020) as well as detect cognitive and metacognitive processes (e.g., Molenaar et al., 2019). They can be employed to intervene in a timely manner and provide personalized feedback and support to help students improve their SRL skills and thus achieve their academic goals. Both supervised and unsupervised machine learning approaches hold the potential to advance our comprehension of extracting valuable insights from learner data regarding their strategic actions, thereby enhancing their SRL.

Feedback and intervention, informed by AI predictions and recommendations, exert substantial influence on learning processes and environments. Ouyang et al. (2023) integrated AI (to predict student performance) with LA (to visualize the results and provide in-time and continuous feedback) aiming to enhance student learning outcomes within a collaborative learning environment. The findings revealed substantial advantages, including heightened engagement levels, improved attitudes towards and perceptions of the feedback received, increased self-reflection on writing practices, enhanced writing product quality, reduced requests for additional feedback and assistance, and a diminished sense of inefficiency in collaborative writing endeavors.

Ciolacu et al. (2018) aimed to decrease the failure rate of students in a blended learning course over the long term by employing machine learning techniques. They utilized and enhanced LA by developing an early recognition system equipped with real-time data and integrated with machine learning which generates personalized emails to alert students at risk. The system monitored task strategies and utilized predictive algorithms to provide students with an estimation of their learning activities based on previous experiences. The predictions encouraged students to modify their learning behavior during the reflection phase and achieved a significant reduction of almost half in the failure rates and thus had a substantial impact on students' performance by offering them a clear and transparent understanding of their progress. Xing and Du (2019) devised a dropout prediction model tailored for at-risk students, optimizing it by delivering personalized interventions that considered the unique circumstances and preferences of each student. In another study, an early warning system was established using machine learning, allowing for timely feedback and intervention for students at risk (Baneres et al., 2019). These examples underscore the transformative potential of AI-driven LA strategies to support SRL.

Pedagogical Agents for Interactive Scaffolding

The convergence of LA, AI agents, and SRL creates a dynamic educational landscape where the synergy of these components holds significant potential. AI agents, encompassing chatbots and virtual assistants, play a pivotal role in harnessing LA insights to craft personalized learning experiences. The agents can be guided in real-time analyses of multimodal data. These AI-driven entities possess the capability to process vast datasets, identify trends, assess individual progress, and provide timely feedback—all of which align closely with the core tenets of SRL. By doing so, AI agents can empower students, granting them greater autonomy in their learning journey while offering tailored guidance and support rooted in LA-derived insights. Thus, the integration of AI agents and LA can enrich the SRL, equipping students with the necessary tools to become self-regulated.

Incorporating embedded AI agents into the learning process can promote affective and motivational processes (i.e., SRL) through natural language processing, within a genuine interaction between agents and students. They can also include explicit or implicit modeling of specific affective and motivational states. For example, an embedded AI agent in a learning environment could include explicit modeling of specific affective and motivational states by displaying visual cues or facial expressions that represent emotions such as happiness, frustration, or curiosity. The agent could also provide implicit modeling by adapting its responses and feedback based on the student's engagement level, performance, or expressed interests. This dynamic modeling of affective and motivational states enhances the agent's ability to personalize the learning experience and effectively support the student's emotional and motivational needs. In their respective studies, both Azevedo et al. (2022) and Munshi et al. (2023) explored the integration of adaptive scaffolding within intelligent learning environments. Azevedo et al. (2022) implemented adaptive scaffolding features within the MetaTutor system, aimed at promoting SRL in the field of science education. Pedagogical agents within the MetaTutor system prompted learners to employ various SRL strategies based on their task progress, as measured by trace data. Similarly, Munshi et al. (2023) developed an adaptive scaffolding framework for Betty's Brain, a learning system that continuously detected students' learning behaviors to trigger suitable scaffolds.

ETHICAL CONSIDERATIONS AND CHALLENGES

As AI-powered LA continues to gain popularity, it offers various benefits for enhancing student learning through SRL both inside and outside the classroom. Nevertheless, like all AI applications that rely on human data, AI-powered LA systems are also not immune to ethical challenges. Therefore, it is crucial to consider and address these challenges to ensure that the implementation of AI-powered LA is effective, ethical, and fair for all students. This section delves into potential challenges and ethical considerations related to the use of AI-powered LA. The issues discussed include data privacy, transparency, fairness, and accountability.

Data Privacy and Transparency

Data privacy is one of the primary ethical challenges associated with AI-powered LA. Ensuring the ethical use of student data is paramount, as LA relies on the collection and analysis of often sensitive information. Research suggests that privacy and data protection continue to be major stumbling blocks for a data-driven educational future, including AI-powered LA applications (Hoel & Chen, 2018). The collection, storage, and analysis of large amounts of learner data can raise significant concerns about data confidentiality and the potential misuse of data (Heiser et al., 2023). In AI-powered applications, a significant challenge revolves around determining the permissible usage of learner information, including considerations about granting access to potentially personal data and establishing ethical protocols (Ifenthaler & Schumacher, 2019). Especially students' personal information, such as their academic performance, behavior, and demographic information, must be treated with utmost confidentiality to protect their privacy rights. Therefore, it is vital to prioritize and uphold confidentiality, reliability, security, and privacy, while also ensuring compliance with security and privacy policies (Ifenthaler & Tracey, 2016). To ensure data privacy, the collection and use of learner data must be transparent and secure. When students are aware that their data is being collected and used responsibly, they are more likely to engage with LA systems and take ownership of their learning processes, fostering a stronger sense of autonomy and self-regulation.

Transparency also poses a significant obstacle in the application of AI-driven LA. The algorithms used in AI-powered LA must be transparent because an explainable decision-making process is also essential to prevent biased outcomes. Both the data that underlies LA systems and the AI algorithms that generate the recommendations and decisions must be transparent to both educators and learners. Research has shown that the absence of transparency and undefined data in LA can lead to poor decision-making regarding student progress and performance in online learning environments (Dringus, 2012). Open communication regarding the data collection methods, the goals of LA implementation, and the potential impact on learners fosters trust and empowers students to make informed decisions about their engagement with LA. When students understand how LA works and how it can support their learning, they are more likely to take an active role in self-regulation, using LA insights to monitor their progress and make data-informed decisions. Furthermore, the complexity of AI algorithms can make it challenging for educators and students to understand how these algorithms arrive at their predictions or recommendations (Corrin et al., 2019). If students and educators do not comprehend how AI algorithms make decisions, this can result in distrust and skepticism, which can undermine the effectiveness of AI-powered LA tools. Therefore, disclosing more information to students and educators about how AI and LA operate can instill confidence in their use.

Fairness

As AI-powered LA tools become a more prevalent tool in education, there are growing concerns about fairness and equity. Ethical concerns surrounding fairness are a pivotal component influencing the support of SRL within the context of LA. One issue is the lack of consideration for ethical issues and challenges surrounding the use of LA. With the increased number of AI-powered tools in education, the development of LA has outpaced the ethical considerations (Pardo & Siemens, 2014). This raises serious concerns about the potential for bias and discrimination in the algorithms used in LA systems. AI algorithms have the potential to generate biased outcomes based on how they are trained and the features they use. Biased algorithms may disadvantage learners due to their personal characteristics, including their race, gender, and socio-economic status. This may result in unintentional discrimination against disadvantaged groups, and further exacerbate existing inequalities in education (Grimm et al., 2023). Therefore, it is important to ensure that LA systems are designed and implemented in a way that is fair and equitable for all students and that they do not perpetuate or amplify existing social inequalities (Pardo & Siemens, 2014).

Ensuring fairness in LA extends to guaranteeing equitable access and opportunities for all students, irrespective of their backgrounds, thereby broadening the reach of SRL. Ethical considerations also encompass mitigating algorithmic biases within LA systems, promoting fair assessment and evaluation practices, maintaining transparency and accountability in decision-making processes, and upholding ethical data use. By addressing these ethical concerns related to fairness, educators can create a more inclusive and just learning environment, fostering SRL and empowering students from diverse backgrounds to take control of their educational journeys with confidence.

Another issue is the absence of the student voice in decision-making about learning analytics. Students may not have equal access to technology or resources, which can impact their participation in online learning platforms and the data collected about their performance. Especially, students from disadvantaged backgrounds may have less access to technology and resources, making it harder for them to benefit from AI-powered LA tools. If the development teams behind these tools lack diversity, there is a risk that they may not consider or understand the specific needs of underrepresented groups. Therefore, considering student attitudes toward LA is crucial in shaping the design and implementation of these systems (Roberts et al., 2016). It is important to ensure diverse learner representation in the development and decision-making processes of LA tools to consider a wide range of learner perspectives and needs.

Accountability

AI-powered LA is a cutting-edge technology that could transform the education industry. Nevertheless, ethical concerns must be considered when integrating this technology. One of these concerns is accountability. Since AI algorithms make decisions based on complex data analyses, it can be difficult to attribute responsibility for errors or harm caused by AI-powered LA. Hence, it is vital to establish clear accountability and responsibility lines to guarantee that AI-powered LA is employed ethically and responsibly.

To guarantee ethical use, the accountability of AI-powered LA systems must be established to ensure that they are utilized for their intended purpose without harming students. Accountability for AI-powered LA can be achieved in several ways. First, the LA process must be made transparent by clearly communicating its purpose, data sources, methods, and potential outcomes to all stakeholders, including students, educators, and administrators. Second, it is essential to develop robust data governance policies and procedures that outline who has access to data, how data is collected, stored, and used, and what safeguards are in place to protect sensitive information. Third, an ethical framework or code of conduct must be established to guide the collection, analysis, and use of learner data. This framework should prioritize the principles of fairness, privacy, and equity. Fourth, LA systems should incorporate mechanisms for students to question, challenge, or appeal decisions made based on the data, thereby establishing a framework of ethical accountability that empowers learners and fosters trust in the LA process. When ethical accountability is prioritized, LA can serve as a tool for enhancing SRL by promoting responsible and transparent data practices that enable students to take charge of their learning journey confidently and securely.

Compliance with laws and regulations is also highly important in establishing accountability. Stakeholders involved in the design and implementation of AI-powered LA tools must remain informed about relevant data protection laws and regulations, such as the Family Educational Rights and Privacy Act (FERPA) in the United States or the General Data Protection Regulation (GDPR) in the European Union and ensure compliance. All personnel involved in LA systems should receive training to increase their awareness about ethical considerations, data privacy, and compliance with regulations. Additionally, it is essential to build a redress mechanism that would allow learners to seek redress or request corrections related to their data.

Potential Strategies to Deal With Ethical Considerations

Ensuring data privacy, transparency, fairness, and accountability is of utmost importance when utilizing AI algorithms in education. A proactive approach is necessary, which involves regular evaluation and monitoring of AI algorithms for bias and ensuring that the underlying data represents the diverse student population. Both educators and students, as end-users of AI-powered LA tools, must be aware of the limitations of these algorithms and should not solely rely on their recommendations (e.g., Jordan & Bake, 2022). Encouraging critical thinking and providing explanations for AI-generated recommendations can also mitigate the challenges associated with AI-powered LA. Additionally, conducting fairness audits of AI algorithms is crucial. These audits can detect any biases or unfairness in the AI algorithms used in LA applications, thereby ensuring that LA systems are fair and equitable for all students (Fernsel & Simbeck, 2022).

In summary, ethical considerations are paramount when it comes to AI-powered LA. It is worth noting that these systems must be designed and implemented in a way that safeguards students' privacy, promotes fairness and transparency, and establishes clear lines of accountability and responsibility.

CONCLUSION AND RECOMMENDATIONS

This chapter provides a thorough overview of various ways AI-powered LA can aid in supporting SRL as well as ethical concerns associated with its use. By exploring the theoretical underpinnings and importance of SRL, LA, and AI in education, the chapter highlights the potential of AI-powered LA in enhancing student learning experiences. The examples of AI-powered LA tools and techniques presented demonstrate their potential to provide timely feedback, personalize instruction, predict student performance, and provide interactive support. Like any technology, AI-powered LA also raises ethical considerations and challenges. This chapter also discusses these concerns and proposes strategies to address them.

AI leverages extensive data processing and analytics to emulate human-like cognitive processes and functionalities (e.g., Ouyang et al., 2023). This convergence of technology and cognitive science has emerged as a vibrant field of scientific inquiry. Through AI's ability to process vast amounts of data and adapt in real-time, it has the potential to transform educational experiences, offering personalized and interactive support and tailored content to learners, ultimately advancing the effectiveness and accessibility of learning environments. In addition, the integration of AI and LA provides educators with powerful tools to support SRL, helping students take charge of their learning process and become more self-regulated. Using AI-powered LA tools, educators can support students in their learning process and help them achieve their full potential.

The importance of interdisciplinary collaboration between the fields of LA, AI, and SRL cannot be overstated. This synergy is pivotal as AI continues to make significant strides that have the potential to propel the domain of SRL into new frontiers. As AI evolves, it becomes increasingly clear that its integration with LA is not just beneficial but essential for advancing the field and optimizing educational outcomes for learners of all backgrounds. AI capabilities for data analysis, predictive modeling, and personalization hold the key to unlocking deeper insights into how individuals regulate their learning processes. By forging connections between these disciplines, we can create a fertile ground for innovation and the development of AI-powered LA tools and techniques that can revolutionize our understanding of SRL. In essence, AI and LA offer a pathway toward more self-directed learning, ultimately benefiting students to gain SRL skills.

Implications for Educators and Policymakers

Implications for educators and policymakers are substantial in the context of the integration of AI-powered LA tools. AI-powered LA tools offer exciting possibilities for education but require thoughtful planning, training, and policy considerations for their effective implementation. Educators must consider weaving these advanced technologies, recognizing the potential for the enhancement of SRL. For example, educators should explore the integration of dashboards to monitor student progress and performance, enabling timely interventions and personalized support. In addition, they should undergo training to effectively employ adaptive learning systems. On the other hand, policymakers should allocate resources for teacher development programs and incentivize schools to adopt dashboards and adaptive learning technologies. It is imperative that educators receive training to effectively leverage AI-powered LA tools in the classroom.

Machine learning's predictive and recommendation capabilities necessitate educators' collaboration with data analysts to harness these insights for optimizing teaching and learning. Policymakers should encourage partnerships between schools and data experts while ensuring data privacy regulations are robust and ethically sound. Educators should explore ways to incorporate pedagogical agents into the learning process, guiding students and providing interactive support. Policymakers can aid this effort by promoting the development and ethical use of such tools in educational settings. Additionally, they should ensure equitable access to these technologies, bridging the digital divide and promoting inclusivity in education. Policymakers must establish and enforce robust data privacy and security regulations to safeguard students' sensitive data collected by AI-powered LA systems. Collaborative efforts between educators and policymakers are needed to develop ethical guidelines, emphasizing responsible data handling and algorithmic transparency in educational settings.

Final Thoughts and Recommendations for AI-Powered LA for SRL

This chapter makes a significant contribution to the field of education by exploring the potential of AI-powered LA to support SRL while highlighting the importance of ethical considerations and challenges associated with its use. This advances our understanding of the integration of AI and LA and its responsible use, which can inform better decisions to support SRL. Thus, this chapter serves as a valuable resource not only for its current context but also as a blueprint for forthcoming research endeavors. Its significance extends beyond the immediate subject matter, offering a comprehensive foundation for exploring the role of LA in enhancing SRL. By leveraging the insights presented in this chapter, researchers can embark on studies aimed at furthering our understanding of how AI can be harnessed with LA to improve the SRL process. It is important to conduct further research to better understand how AI and LA can be integrated and used to support SRL, as well as to establish clear guidelines to ensure its ethical use.

Researchers should continually explore AI techniques and algorithms that can enhance the accuracy and usability of LA tools to support SRL. Investigating emerging AI technologies like large language models and deep learning in the context of SRL can be particularly valuable. Future research should investigate how AI-powered LA impacts SRL in diverse cultural and educational contexts. This research can reveal potential cultural differences in the effectiveness and acceptance of these technologies. In addition, investigating how AI-powered LA impacts diverse groups of learners, including those with different learning abilities and needs, can provide insights into inclusive educational practices. Researchers should conduct longitudinal studies to assess the long-term impact of AI-powered LA on SRL to understand how these technologies influence students' learning trajectories over time. Researchers should also explore students' experiences, perceptions, and behaviors to get a richer understanding of the complexities involved in AI-powered LA and SRL.

As we look ahead to the future of AI-powered LA in the context of SRL, further research should encompass a wide range of methodologies, ethical considerations, and collaborative efforts. By addressing these areas, researchers can continue to advance our understanding of how AI-powered LA can effectively support SRL and contribute to the enhancement of education for all students.

REFERENCES

Alam, A. (2021, December). Should robots replace teachers? Mobilisation of AI and learning analytics in education. *The Proceedings of the International Conference on Advances in Computing, Communication, and Control* (ICAC3) (pp. 1-12). ACM.

Allen, L. K., Perret, C., Likens, A., & McNamara, D. S. (2017). What'd you say again? *The Proceedings of the Seventh International Learning Analytics & Knowledge Conference*. Association for Computing Machinery. 10.1145/3027385.3027445

Azevedo, R., Bouchet, F., Duffy, M., Harley, J., Taub, M., Trevors, G., Cloude, E., Dever, D., Wiedbusch, M., Wortha, F., & Cerezo, R. (2022). Lessons learned and future directions of MetaTutor: Leveraging multichannel data to scaffold self-regulated learning with an intelligent tutoring system. *Frontiers in Psychology*, *13*, 813632. doi:10.3389/fpsyg.2022.813632 PMID:35774935

Baneres, D., Rodríguez-Gonzalez, M. E., & Serra, M. (2019). An early feedback prediction system for learners at-risk within a first-year higher education course. *IEEE Transactions on Learning Technologies*, *12*(2), 249–263. doi:10.1109/TLT.2019.2912167

Blumenstein, M. (2020). Synergies of learning analytics and learning design: A systematic review of student outcomes. *Journal of Learning Analytics*, *7*(3), 13–32. doi:10.18608/jla.2020.73.3

Bulut, O., Gorgun, G., Yildirim-Erbasli, S. N., Wongvorachan, T., Daniels, L. M., Gao, Y., Lai, K. W., & Shin, J. (2022). Standing on the shoulders of giants: Online formative assessments as the foundation for predictive learning analytics models. *British Journal of Educational Technology*, *54*(1), 19–39. doi:10.1111/bjet.13276

Buxbaum-Conradi, S., Redlich, T., & Branding, J. H. (2016, January). Conceptualizing hybrid human-machine systems and interaction. *The 49th Hawaii International Conference on System Sciences (HICSS)* (pp. 551-559). IEEE. 10.1109/HICSS.2016.75

Chen, L., Lu, M., Goda, Y., & Yamada, M. (2019, November). Design of learning analytics dashboard supporting metacognition. *The Proceedings of the 16th International Conference on Cognition and Exploratory Learning in the Digital Age (CELDA)* (pp. 175-182). IADIS. 10.33965/celda2019_201911L022

Ciolacu, M., Tehrani, A. F., Beer, R., & Popp, H. (2017, October). Education 4.0—Fostering student's performance with machine learning methods. *IEEE 23rd International Symposium for Design and Technology in Electronic Packaging (SIITME)* (pp. 438-443). IEEE. https://doi.org/10.1109/SIITME.2017.8259941

Ciolacu, M., Tehrani, A. F., Binder, L., & Svasta, P. M. (2018, October). Education 4.0-Artificial Intelligence assisted higher education: Early recognition system with machine learning to support students' success. *IEEE 24th International Symposium for Design and Technology in Electronic Packaging (SIITME)* (pp. 23-30). IEEE. 10.1109/SIITME.2018.8599203

Clow, D. (2012). The learning analytics cycle: Closing the loop effectively. *The Proceedings of the 2nd International Conference on Learning Analytics and Knowledge* (LAK12), (pp. 134-138). IEEE.

Clow, D. (2013). An overview of learning analytics. *Teaching in Higher Education, 18*(6), 683–695. doi:10.1080/13562517.2013.827653

Corrin, L., Kennedy, G., French, S., Buckingham Shum, S., Kitto, K., Pardo, A., West, D., Mirriahi, N., & Colvin, C. (2019). *The ethics of learning analytics in Australian higher education: A discussion paper.*

Cui, Y., Chen, F., & Shiri, A. (2020). Scale up predictive models for early detection of at-risk students: A feasibility study. *Information and Learning Science, 121*(3/4), 97–116. doi:10.1108/ILS-05-2019-0041

Darvishi, A., Khosravi, H., Sadiq, S., & Gašević, D. (2022). Incorporating AI and learning analytics to build trustworthy peer assessment systems. *British Journal of Educational Technology, 53*(4), 844–875. doi:10.1111/bjet.13233

Dignum, V., Penagos, M., Pigmans, K., & Vosloo, S. (2020). *Policy guidance on AI for children.* UNICEF Office of Global Insight and Policy.

Dringus, L. P. (2012). Learning analytics considered harmful. *Journal of Asynchronous Learning Networks, 16*(3), 87–100.

Fernsel, L., & Simbeck, K. (2022). Data synthesis for fairness audits of learning analytics algorithms. Monographien (AKWI-Tagungsband zur 35), 316-320. https://doi.org/ doi:10.30844/AKWI_2022_21

Gabriel, F., Cloude, E. B., & Azevedo, R. (2022). Using learning analytics to measure motivational and affective processes during self-regulated learning with advanced learning technologies. In *Social and Emotional Learning and Complex Skills Assessment: An Inclusive Learning Analytics Perspective* (pp. 93–108). Springer. doi:10.1007/978-3-031-06333-6_6

Gorgun, G., Yildirim-Erbasli, S. N., & Demmans Epp, C. (2022). Predicting cognitive engagement in online course discussion forums. In A. Mitrovic, & N. Bosch (Eds.), *Proceedings of the 15th International Conference on Educational Data Mining*, (pp. 276-289). Durham, UK: International Educational Data Mining Society. 10.5281/zenodo.6853149

Grimm, A., Steegh, A., Kubsch, M., & Neumann, K. (2023). Learning analytics in physics education. *Journal of Learning Analytics*, *10*(1), 71–84. doi:10.18608/jla.2023.7793

Guo, L. (2022). Using metacognitive prompts to enhance self-regulated learning and learning outcomes: A meta-analysis of experimental studies in computer-based learning environments. *Journal of Computer Assisted Learning*, *38*(3), 811–832. doi:10.1111/jcal.12650

Heiser, R., Stritto, M., Brown, A., & Croft, B. (2023). Amplifying student and administrator perspectives on equity and bias in learning analytics. *Journal of Learning Analytics*, *10*(1), 8–23. doi:10.18608/jla.2023.7775

Hoel, T., & Chen, W. (2018). Privacy and data protection in learning analytics should be motivated by an educational maxim—Towards a proposal. *Research and Practice in Technology Enhanced Learning*, *13*(1), 1–14. doi:10.118641039-018-0086-8 PMID:30595748

Holstein, K., & Doroudi, S. (2019, March). Fairness and equity in learning analytics systems (FairLAK). *The Proceedings of the 9th International Conference on Learning Analytics & Knowledge* (LAK 2019) (pp. 1-2).

Ifenthaler, D., Gibson, D., & Dobozy, E. (2018). Informing learning design through analytics: Applying network graph analysis. *Australasian Journal of Educational Technology*, *34*(2), 117–132. doi:10.14742/ajet.3767

Ifenthaler, D., & Schumacher, C. (2019). Releasing Personal Information Within Learning Analytics Systems. In D. Sampson, J. M. Spector, D. Ifenthaler, P. Isaías, & S. Sergis (Eds.), *Learning Technologies for Transforming Large-Scale Teaching, Learning, and Assessment* (pp. 3–18). Springer. doi:10.1007/978-3-030-15130-0_1

Ifenthaler, D., & Tracey, M. W. (2016). Exploring the relationship of ethics and privacy in learning analytics and design: Implications for the field of educational technology. *Educational Technology Research and Development*, *64*(5), 877–880. doi:10.100711423-016-9480-3

Järvelä, S., Malmberg, J., Haataja, E., Sobocinski, M., & Kirschner, P. A. (2021). What multimodal data can tell us about the students' regulation of their learning process? *Learning and Instruction*, *72*, 101203. doi:10.1016/j.learninstruc.2019.04.004

Jordan, R., & Bake, R. (2022). Implementing flipped classroom that used an intelligent tutoring system into learning process: Formative assessment in the design of instructional systems. *AI and Ethics*, 1–10. doi:10.1002374543681-022-0001274-z

Kabudi, T., Pappas, I., & Olsen, D. H. (2021). AI-enabled adaptive learning systems: A systematic mapping of the literature. *Computers and Education: Artificial Intelligence*, *2*, 100017. doi:10.1016/j.caeai.2021.100017

Kim, K., & Moon, N. (2019). Activity index model for self-regulated learning with learning analysis in a TEL environment. *The Journal of Supercomputing*, *75*(4), 1971–1989. doi:10.100711227-018-2446-y

Krikun, I. (2017, November). Applying learning analytics methods to enhance learning quality and effectiveness in virtual learning environments. *5th IEEE workshop on Advances in Information, Electronic and Electrical Engineering (AIEEE)* (pp. 1-6). IEEE. https://doi.org/10.1109/AIEEE.2017.8270532

Lee, H. S., Pallant, A., Pryputniewicz, S., Lord, T., Mulholland, M., & Liu, O. L. (2019). Automated text scoring and real-time adjustable feedback: Supporting revision of scientific arguments involving uncertainty. *Science Education*, *103*(3), 590–622. doi:10.1002ce.21504

Lim, L., Bannert, M., van der Graaf, J., Singh, S., Fan, Y., Surendrannair, S., Rakovic, M., Molenaar, I., Moore, J., & Gašević, D. (2023). Effects of real-time analytics-based personalized scaffolds on students' self-regulated learning. *Computers in Human Behavior*, *139*, 107547. doi:10.1016/j.chb.2022.107547

Liu, D. Y. T., Bartimote-Aufflick, K., Pardo, A., & Bridgeman, A. J. (2017). Data-driven personalization of student learning support in higher education. In A. Peña-Ayala (Ed.), *Learning analytics: Fundaments, applications, and trends: A view of the current state of the art to enhance e-learning* (pp. 143–169). Springer., doi:10.1007/978-3-319-52977-6_5

Lyell, D., & Coiera, E. (2017). Automation bias and verification complexity: A systematic review. *Journal of the American Medical Informatics Association : JAMIA*, *24*(2), 423–431. doi:10.1093/jamia/ocw105 PMID:27516495

Matcha, W., Gasevic, D., Uzir, N. A. A., Jovanovic, J., Pardo, A., Lim, L., & Tsai, Y. S. (2020). Analytics of learning strategies: Role of course design and delivery modality. *Journal of Learning Analytics*, *7*(2), 45–71. doi:10.18608/jla.2020.72.3

Molenaar, I. (2022). The concept of hybrid human-AI regulation: Exemplifying how to support young learners' self-regulated learning. *Computers and Education: Artificial Intelligence*, *3*, 100070. doi:10.1016/j.caeai.2022.100070

Molenaar, I., de Mooij, S., Azevedo, R., Bannertd, M., Järveläe, S., & Gaševićf, D. (2023). Measuring self-regulated learning and the role of AI: Five years of research using multimodal multichannel data. *Computers in Human Behavior*, *107540*, 107540. doi:10.1016/j.chb.2022.107540

Molenaar, I., Horvers, A., & Dijkstra, R. (2019). Young learners' regulation of practice behavior in adaptive learning technologies. *Frontiers in Psychology*, *10*, 2792. doi:10.3389/fpsyg.2019.02792 PMID:31920837

Munshi, A., Biswas, G., Baker, R., Ocumpaugh, J., Hutt, S., & Paquette, L. (2023). Analysing adaptive scaffolds that help students develop self-regulated learning behaviours. *Journal of Computer Assisted Learning*, *39*(2), 351–368. doi:10.1111/jcal.12761

Ouyang, F., Wu, M., Zheng, L., Zhang, L., & Jiao, P. (2023). Integration of artificial intelligence performance prediction and learning analytics to improve student learning in online engineering course. *International Journal of Educational Technology in Higher Education*, *20*(1), 1–23. doi:10.118641239-022-00372-4 PMID:36683653

Panadero, E., & Alonso-Tapia, J. (2014). How do students self-regulate? Review of Zimmerman's cyclical model of self-regulated learning. *Anales de Psicología*, *30*(2), 450–462. doi:10.6018/analesps.30.2.167221

Pardo, A., & Siemens, G. (2014). Ethical and privacy principles for learning analytics. *British Journal of Educational Technology*, *45*(3), 438–450. doi:10.1111/bjet.12152

Park, Y., & Jo, I. H. (2015). Development of the learning analytics dashboard to support students' learning performance. *Journal of Universal Computer Science*, *21*(1), 110.

Rets, I., Herodotou, C., Bayer, V., Hlosta, M., & Rienties, B. (2021). Exploring critical factors of the perceived usefulness of a learning analytics dashboard for distance university students. *International Journal of Educational Technology in Higher Education*, *18*(1), 1–23. doi:10.118641239-021-00284-9 PMID:34778534

Roberts, L., Howell, J., Seaman, K., & Gibson, D. (2016). Student attitudes toward learning analytics in higher education: "The Fitbit version of the learning world". *Frontiers in Psychology*, *7*. doi:10.3389/fpsyg.2016.01959 PMID:28066285

Saadati, Z., Zeki, C. P., & Vatankhah Barenji, R. (2021). On the development of blockchain-based learning management system as a metacognitive tool to support self-regulation learning in online higher education. *Interactive Learning Environments*, *31*(5), 1–24. doi:10.1080/10494820.2021.1920429

Sabourin, J. L., Shores, L. R., Mott, B. W., & Lester, J. C. (2013). Understanding and predicting student self-regulated learning strategies in game-based learning environments. *International Journal of Artificial Intelligence in Education*, *23*(1-4), 94–114. doi:10.100740593-013-0004-6

Saint, J., Whitelock-Wainwright, A., Gašević, D., & Pardo, A. (2020). Trace-SRL: A framework for analysis of microlevel processes of self-regulated learning from trace data. *IEEE Transactions on Learning Technologies*, *13*(4), 861–877. doi:10.1109/TLT.2020.3027496

Salas-Pilco, S. Z., Xiao, K., & Hu, X. (2022). Artificial intelligence and learning analytics in teacher education: A systematic review. *Education Sciences*, *12*(8), 569. doi:10.3390/educsci12080569

Siemens, G. (2012, April). Learning analytics: Envisioning a research discipline and a domain of practice. *The Proceedings of the 2nd International Conference on Learning Analytics and Knowledge* (pp. 4-8).

Siemens, G. (2013). Learning analytics: The emergence of a discipline. *The American Behavioral Scientist*, *57*(10), 1380–1400. doi:10.1177/0002764213498851

van Leeuwen, A., Knoop-van Campen, C. A., Molenaar, I., & Rummel, N. (2021). How teacher characteristics relate to how teachers use dashboards: Results from two case studies in K-12. *Journal of Learning Analytics*, *8*(2), 6–21. doi:10.18608/jla.2021.7325

Verbert, K., Duval, E., Klerkx, J., Govaerts, S., & Santos, J. L. (2013). Learning analytics dashboard applications. *The American Behavioral Scientist*, *57*(10), 1500–1509. doi:10.1177/0002764213479363

Wandera, H., Marivate, V., & Sengeh, M. D. (2019). Predicting national school performance for policy making in South Africa. *6th International Conference on Soft Computing Machine Intelligence (ISCMI)* (pp. 23–28). Springer. 10.1109/ISCMI47871.2019.9004323

Xia, Q., Chiu, T. K., & Chai, C. S. (2022). The moderating effects of gender and need satisfaction on self-regulated learning through Artificial Intelligence (AI). *Education and Information Technologies*, *28*(7), 8691–8713. doi:10.100710639-022-11547-x

Xing, W., & Du, D. (2019). Dropout prediction in MOOCs: Using deep learning for personalized intervention. *Journal of Educational Computing Research, 57*(3), 547–570. doi:10.1177/0735633118757015

Yang, T. C., Chen, M. C., & Chen, S. Y. (2018). The influences of self-regulated learning support and prior knowledge on improving learning performance. *Computers & Education, 126*, 37-52. https://doi.org/. compedu.2018.06.025 doi:10.1016/j

Zimmerman, B. J. (1990). Self-regulated learning and academic achievement: An overview. *Educational Psychologist, 25*(1), 3–17. doi:10.120715326985ep2501_2

Zimmerman, B. J. (2000). Attaining self-regulation: A social cognitive perspective. In M. Boekaerts, P. R. Pintrich, & M. Zeidner (Eds.), *Handbook of self-regulation* (pp. 13–39). Academic Press. doi:10.1016/B978-012109890-2/50031-7

ADDITIONAL READING

Aguiar, E., Lakkaraju, H., Bhanpuri, N., Miller, D., Yuhas, B., & Addison, K. L. (2015). Who, when, and why? *The Proceedings of the Fifth International Conference on Learning Analytics and Knowledge* (pp. 93-102). ACM. 10.1145/2723576.2723619

Azevedo, R., & Gašević, D. (2019). Analyzing multimodal multichannel data about self-regulated learning with advanced learning technologies: Issues and challenges. *Computers in Human Behavior, 96*, 207–210. doi:10.1016/j.chb.2019.03.025

Chango, W., Cerezo, R., Sanchez-Santillan, M., Azevedo, R., & Romero, C. (2021). Improving prediction of students' performance in intelligent tutoring systems using attribute selection and ensembles of different multimodal data sources. *Journal of Computing in Higher Education, 33*(3), 614–634. doi:10.100712528-021-09298-8

D'Mello, S. K., & Kory, J. (2015). A review and meta-analysis of multimodal affect detection systems. *ACM Computing Surveys, 47*(3), 1–36. doi:10.1145/2682899

Daumiller, M., & Dresel, M. (2019). Supporting self-regulated learning with digital media using motivational regulation and metacognitive prompts. *Journal of Experimental Education, 87*(1), 161–176. doi:10.1080/00220973.2018.1448744

de Sousa, E. B., Alexandre, B., Ferreira Mello, R., Pontual Falcão, T., Vesin, B., & Gašević, D. (2021). Applications of learning analytics in high schools: A systematic literature review. *Frontiers in Artificial Intelligence, 4*, 737891. doi:10.3389/frai.2021.737891 PMID:34647016

France, L., Heraud, J.-M., Marty, J.-C., Carron, T., & Heili, J. (2006). Monitoring virtual classroom: Visualization techniques to observe student activities in an e-learning system. *The Proceedings of the Sixth International Conference on Advanced Learning Technologies* (pp. 716-720). IEEE.

Govaerts, S., Verbert, K., Duval, E., & Pardo, A. (2012). The student activity meter for awareness and self-reflection. *The Proceedings of the 2012 ACM Annual Conference on Human Factors in Computing Systems extended abstracts* (pp. 869-884). ACM.

Long, P., & Siemens, G. (2014). Penetrating the fog: Analytics in learning and education. *Italian Journal of Educational Technology, 22*(3), 132–137.

Ramos-Soto, A., Lama, M., Vázquez-Barreiros, B., Bugarín, A., Mucientes, M., & Barro, S. (2015, July). Towards textual reporting in learning analytics dashboards. *IEEE 15th International Conference on Advanced Learning Technologies* (pp. 260-264). IEEE.

Schumacher, C., & Ifenthaler, D. (2021). Investigating prompts for supporting students' self-regulation–A remaining challenge for learning analytics approaches? *The Internet and Higher Education, 49*, 100791. doi:10.1016/j.iheduc.2020.100791

KEY TERMS AND DEFINITIONS

Adaptive Learning System: It refers to an educational technology or platform that uses data analytics to personalize the learning experience for individual learners.

Artificial Intelligence: It involves creating computer systems capable of performing tasks that typically simulate human-like cognitive functions and require human intelligence.

Dashboard: It refers to a visual interface displaying key metrics, trends, and information related to students' learning behaviors, performance, and progress derived from learning analytics.

Learning Analytics: It is the process of collecting, analyzing, and interpreting data from learning environments.

Machine Learning: It refers to employing computer algorithms to discover and learn patterns and trends within a given dataset without explicit instruction.

Pedagogical Agent: It refers to speech-based or text-based agents designed to support and enhance the learning experience.

Self-regulated Learning: It refers to the ability of individuals to actively monitor, control, and regulate their own learning processes.

Chapter 5
The Integration of Corpus Tools in the Design and Implementation of a Novel Analytical Model for the Learning of K12 Classrooms

Ali Şükrü Özbay
https://orcid.org/0000-0002-3421-0650
Karadeniz Technical University, Turkey

Tuğba Çıtlak
https://orcid.org/0000-0002-5152-3069
Karadeniz Technical University, Turkey

ABSTRACT

Learning analytics provides language teaching professionals both with the support to observe the learners' learning process and with tracking language teaching professionals' performances in the teaching process, enabling feedback and a trigger to be up to date. In this study, the authors proposed a framework for novel learning analytics models, which attempts to present how learning analytics and corpus linguistics can be merged to achieve the five steps of learning analytics by answering the information-based questions. To that end, they investigated collocations and lexico-grammatical patterns in English coursebooks of K12 published by the Ministry of Language Education in Türkiye and by native English speakers. It was found that the English coursebooks of K12 in Türkiye underrepresented word clusters and collocations that are mostly used in the reference native corpora of English coursebooks. Hereby, a corpus-based data-driven learning approach was suggested as a contributor to learning analytics.

DOI: 10.4018/979-8-3693-0066-4.ch005

INTRODUCTION

The use of online technologies has been situated in conjunction with every area including teaching. One of the online technologies that can be utilized for tracking the learners' online traces is learning analytics. Learning analytics has been one of the recent fields of scientific inquiry that specifically deals with the processes of learning from various perspectives and dimensions. It is also a term popularly used to analyze the big data of learners as a piece of evidence in the process of learning. The digital traces that emerged in online environments resulted in the emergence of big data, and the idea of using this emerging data in the processing stages of many learners at various levels and the subsequent efforts to delve into learning analytics through multi-dimensional perspectives brought new projections as well as challenges. One of the main provisions is that language teaching professionals and stakeholders are provided with the data gathered from the learners to help them create an environment in which the learning takes place better (Bozkurt, 2016). In this regard, it can be defined as "developing tools and techniques for capturing, storing, and finding patterns in large amounts of electronic data; representing them in generative and useful ways; and integrating them into intelligent tools that personalize and optimize learning environments" (Martin & Sherin, 2013, p. 511). Learning analytics can enrich the learning process by providing real-time feedback. Moreover, it provides language teaching professionals both with the support to observe the learners' learning process and with tracking language teaching professionals' performances in the teaching process, which enables the language teaching professionals to give the learners feedback more efficiently and to give the necessary trigger to be up to date. Learning analytics in which many approaches, methods, and tools are used together can also delve into the teaching materials given by the educational institutions and run by the states to find out to what extent these teaching materials are effective in terms of various dimensions (Bozkurt, 2016; Tutsun, 2020).

An especially significant approach is the integration of the corpus linguistics approach as a means of tracking the learners' developments and processes of learning as part of perspectives on learning analytics. Using concordances may help to detect native and non-native language patterns by analyzing naturally occurring language samples (Hunston, 2022). This type of pattern analysis may have positive indicators for K12 learners who are good at technology and discovery-based learning approaches, searching for patterns as language detectives (Martin & Sherin, 2013).

Being an inductive instructional approach, the corpus-based data-driven learning approach holds promise for diverse groups of K12 learners at various levels and it supports the constructivist approach in that it transforms learners into linguistic researchers actively taking responsibility for their learning and language teaching professionals into research leaders guiding learners (Sinclair, 1991; Marlowe &

Page, 2005; Roblyer & Doering, 2013). Since learning analytics is constituted into five steps: capture, report, predict, act, and refine (Campbell et al., 2007), DDL and corpus tools offer opportunities to achieve these five steps in a predictable order. First, it captures the data produced by the learners and reports the use of language patterns according to the frequency of usage. Then, according to the report, analysis can be done to predict what will happen next. This prediction will trigger the stakeholders to act to make the language learning environment better as well as more refined for the prospective users. The process of realizing language learning analytics should be a viable model to tap the benefits of the approach for K12 learners. Thus, the information level of learning analytics involves questions related to the past, present, and future and attempts to answer the questions of "what happened", "what is happening now", and "what will happen" (Davenport et al., 2010, p. 81). These questions are related to the reporting, alerts, and extrapolation processes in learning analytics.

BACKGROUND

There are previous studies focusing on how to design, implement, and evaluate learning analytics in the context of K12 classrooms. The varying designs and implementations of learning analytics in K12 classrooms have been proposed multiple times because the implementation of learning analytics in K12 classrooms can be a more complex procedure than it seems. One reason may be that the attitudes of schools toward technology can be mixed, and they can be politically charged (Aguerrebere et al., 2022). Thus, the previous studies have shown examples of how to design, implement, and evaluate learning analytics in K12 classrooms according to different contexts.

One of the studies that implemented learning analytics in K12 classrooms was conducted by Monroy et al. (2014). They (2014) used an online education environment with a 5E learning approach to implement learning analytics in K12 classrooms. Learning analytics showed the traces of the language teaching professionals' use of the curriculum in detail along with the most visited step of the 5E approach. The results revealed that the use of the model changed according to the person and the purpose. It was found useful in observing the patterns of use and questioning the curriculum and its effectiveness in the K12 context.

Another study conducted by Tan et al. (2017) was the first study to design the implementation of learning analytics in computer-assisted collaborative critical reading in the K12 context of Singapore. It was found that it fostered the students' self-awareness, reflective skills, self-regulation, motivations, and engagement in the activities. Although peer-referenced visualizations of the learning analytics dashboard were intended to trigger competition and learning with games, it was observed that it can also demoralize the students.

Another study conducted by Macarini et al. (2020) implemented education data mining and learning analytics in the national education system of K12 in Uruguay. As a result, it provided support for the improvement of decision-makers. However, several challenges were identified during the study, such as the understanding of nuances of different traces in the educational system and the ethical and legal restrictions.

Moreover, Ruipérez-Valiente and Kim (2020) investigated the effects of individual and collaborative gameplay with K12 students by implementing learning analytics to trace the patterns of the students. Learning analytics implemented to find out the students' patterns while playing solo and in collaboration with the other students showed that the students who played games solo completed the tasks most efficiently while the students who played collaboratively interacted more for further exploration in the game. In this regard, it was suggested that solo or collaborative gameplay can be chosen according to the purpose. Furthermore, the students' feedback was positive; however, the question of whether the lower level of activities can cause disengagement in students or not was given as a limitation.

All in all, previous studies attempted to find new ways to implement learning analytics in the K12 context. However, there is still room for improvement regarding the different school systems in different contexts. A meta-analysis study conducted by Du et al. (2021) shows that there is a lack of data in the K12 context which might be due to the lack of training in learning analytics and data resources of the schools. In this regard, they (2021) state that it is more available in online systems of K12 education. In addition, Selwyn (2019) suggests potential areas of learning analytics to change as a reply to the possible challenges that learning analytics can face. These areas include the economical aspect of learning analytics and designing of learning analytics involving an understanding of "different social contexts in which they are likely to be used, as well as the diverse needs and rights of users" (Selwyn, 2019, p. 16). Therefore, more studies can be conducted to investigate the implementation of learning analytics in K12 classrooms in different contexts to show more examples to the language teaching professionals and decision-makers on how to design, implement, and evaluate learning analytics in the K12 context.

Corpus Tools and Applications in K12 Classrooms

Previous studies using corpus tools and applications in K12 classrooms investigated the implementation of data-driven learning and teaching vocabulary and lexico-grammatical patterns. They investigated the coursebooks used in K12 classrooms concerning the lexemes and lexico-grammatical patterns used in these coursebooks. One of the studies that examined the use of vocabulary and lexico-grammatical patterns was conducted by Kara (2020) who extended the study of Özbay (2015) by applying corpus-based analysis in the context of K12. It was found that English K12 coursebooks published by the Ministry of Education in Türkiye were found to have a limited range of word clusters and collocation.

Similarly, a study conducted by Yu (2020) investigated whether the English textbooks used in Turkish K12 public schools align with the high-stakes high school and university entrance exams for the past decade. It was revealed that the most frequently used words, lexical bundles, and lexical diversity were found to have little overlap in the two corpora. The lexical diversity of the textbooks of K12 in Türkiye was lower than that of high-stake exams in Türkiye.

Another study conducted by Alhudithi (2017) investigated the use of vocabulary in K12 textbooks in Saudi Arabia through a corpus-based analysis. Different from Kara's (2020) study, it was found that a wide range of collocations were given with the most frequent words and repetitions. However, newly introduced words were found to have lower repetitions in the textbooks.

Moreover, for implementing the most frequent words and collocations in K12 classrooms, one of the studies that was conducted by Ehsanzadehsorati (2018) created a dictionary with the most frequently used words for K12 learners. Ehsanzadehsorati (2018) created a mobile application for K12 learners to reach low, medium, and high-frequency words along with the two groups of words: academic and stem words.

Differently, the other studies examined the implementation of corpus tools and applications through a corpus-based data-driven learning approach. Thus, Smith et al. (2007) proposed that corpus-based descriptive grammar can be utilized in the context of K12 for combining pedagogical knowledge and practice in K12 language classrooms along with social interaction. In addition, in the context of K12 classrooms, corpus linguistics can be one of the efficient ways to provide insights into the academic aspect and specific features of language for K12 students (Ranney, 2012). Similarly, Yaylali et al. (2021) suggested that using learner corpora through data-driven learning activities can enhance the awareness of K12 learners on a wide range of example phrases for writing tasks. On the other hand, most of the previous studies focused on the corpus-based analysis of vocabulary and collocations used in K12 classrooms instead of the implementation of corpus tools and a corpus-based data-driven learning approach in K12 classrooms. Therefore, there is still room for the implementation of corpus tools and applications in the context of K12.

Data-Driven Learning

Consisting of the active employment of the tools and techniques of corpus linguistics, Data-Driven Learning (DDL) proposes a larger framework of authentic classroom activities aiming for filling the gap between pedagogy and implementation. Having an autonomous nature, DDL brings a larger number of linguistic instances for practice, which is described as "condense exposure" by Gabrielatos (2005, p. 10), who also stated that such awareness-raising classroom activities based on the premises of DDL may have potential for increasing vocabulary learning with a focus on meaningful content. Moreover, the linguistic instances obtained through corpus tools may have a corrective function in the learners' English. This will be possible when they compare their language productions with those of native speakers. This kind of comparison between non-native and native data is likely to bring some other benefits such as heightened awareness of patterned structure, error correction opportunities, observing the overrepresentation, underrepresentation patterns, and other interlanguage features.

Another feature of the DDL approach is its' potential to open the gates of discovery-based language learning, turning learning into an autonomous practice. The learners in this regard are generally referred to as "travelers" (Bernardini 2001, p. 22), "researchers" (Johns 1997, p. 101), or "detectives" with John's (1997, p. 101) slogan "Every student a Sherlock Holmes".

Discovery-Based Language Learning

Being essentially an instructional approach, discovery-based language learning gives the learners various opportunities for exploration and knowledge construction, turning the process into an engaging and effective learning experience. Rooted in the constructivist theory of learning, discovery-based learning occurs with the combination of problem solutions, experience sharing in an environment, and prior knowledge activation with the data available to them. When applied to language classrooms, discovery-based language learning may help language learners develop their understanding of language through observation, inference, prediction, and hypothesis formulation. This circular experience is also referred to as experiential learning and the language teaching professionals are responsible for guiding and encouraging the learners to predict, observe and notice the gap for further learning. Through several classroom activities that are done inductively, language learners are given ample opportunities to observe the data, draw hypotheses and formulate new rules and check their validity from other sources. This active involvement in the learning process has a role in transforming the learners into more autonomous people who are empowered and self-confident (Mair, 2002). The use of DDL in the classroom brings crucial learning skills for language learners such as "predicting, observing and noticing the gap, thinking, reasoning, reflecting on the data and exploring, and drawing inferences from these data" (O'Sullivan, 2007, p. 277).

The use of DDL applications through DIY (do-it-yourself) corpora may help young EFL learners in K12 classrooms perceive the frequency of combinations as well as notice their gaps. The innovative capacity of corpus-based and teacher-led DDL activities with data visuals and natural language examples support learning in K12 classrooms together with increased motivation for discovering something new. Although DDL for young learners is a relatively unexplored area in the literature, learners in K12 classrooms may have the potential to discover new patterns and rules in the concordance data using contextual clues and content and observing new patterns. In other words, the active involvement of K12 learners in the discovery process may result in the identification of various recurring patterns in context and formulating of new rules or revising the old ones controlling these lexical patterns through "inductive type of reasoning" (Rhalmi, 2021, p. 3). This inductive type of reasoning and active involvement takes place in basically four steps that are contextualizing the target structure, consciousness-raising, appropriation, and production.

One good example by Liontou (2019) from the literature is the experimental approach to investigate young EFL learners' (K12 learners) ability to process idiomatic expressions when exposed to authentic examples by studying corpus data in the form of concordance lines and extended sentences. The analysis showed that there was a significant increase in the ability of learners to guess the right meaning from the contextual clues and content and to learn to use idiomatic expressions in writing.

K12 Language Learning in Türkiye

The expectations for English language education in Türkiye have increased gradually and the changing needs of the Turkish education system have been met in English language teaching (Demirpolat, 2015). Regarding this, before the 2012-2013 academic year, the students could start learning a foreign language only in the 4th grade. Furthermore, in 2006, a new curriculum that was put into practice enabled English language teaching to adopt both a holistic and communicative approach (Haznedar, 2003). This new curriculum aimed to raise the awareness, interest, and motivation of the students, support positive attitudes, provide joyful and meaningful activities to the students, and help the students to develop their communicative competence (Kirkgöz, 2007). However, the hours that the students were exposed to English language learning in the classroom were less than those of other countries. Therefore, in the 2012-2013 academic year, with the advent of the 4 + 4 + 4 education system, the age of starting primary school was reduced to 5 and the grade of starting English education was reduced to the second grade (Bayyurt, 2012).

In this regard, Bayyurt (2012) mentions the points of further focus with the advent of the 4 + 4 + 4 education system. It involves curriculum development and application applicable to the age groups of students, training language teaching professionals who can give foreign language lessons to students at an early age, and developing and evaluating course materials for the needs of students who will start learning a foreign language from the 2nd grade, and lastly development processes of assessment and evaluation tools for those students. This education system adapts communicative language teaching and an action-oriented approach within the Common European Framework of Reference for Languages (CEFR) (Kara, 2020). Moreover, this new education system suggests that a child starts to learn English at the age of 6. Thus, at the end of K12 education, the student will have taken 1850 hours of English language lessons in total, which shows the time and energy spent on English education in K12 in Türkiye.

The motivation for this study dates to earlier studies by Kara's (2020) and Özbay (2015). Özbay (2015), who compiled a corpus from the argumentative essays of freshmen and sophomores (KTUCLE), concluded that the students employed a limited category of common word clusters in terms of word usage, diversity, types, and frequencies. The main reasons for these results were suggested as the learners' limited previous language learning experiences and the English course materials used by the learners in high school. Kara (2020) investigated the use of word clusters and collocations by comparing English coursebooks for high schools published by the Ministry of Education in Türkiye with a reference corpus compiled from the corpus-based English coursebooks written by native speakers of English. The results suggested that English coursebooks for high schools published by the Ministry of Education in Türkiye were found to have a limited range of word clusters and collocation. Secondly, foreign language education was decided to begin in the 2nd grade of primary school, and the 5th grades of primary school were transformed into foreign language preparatory classes. Despite these developments in English teaching in Türkiye, most of the students have not yet reached the desired levels of proficiency in the English language (Demirpolat, 2015). One of the reasons for the low proficiency levels can be the limited exposure to the word clusters and collocations having low saliency and frequency in English teaching materials currently used in Turkish schools.

Thus, this study attempted to shed light on the use of word clusters and collocations in English coursebooks of high schools published by the Ministry of Education in Türkiye. Based on the evidence, in the next part of this study, the research questions were answered and the use of corpus-based DDL approach and DDL-based teaching and learning have been proposed along with the publications of corpus-based coursebooks as future implementation.

As part of the efforts to apply learning analytics in K12 education, it was aimed to propose some viable ways to promote the learning of specific language patterns used in K12 English coursebooks, published by the Ministry of Language Education in Türkiye. To that end, this study investigated collocations and lexico-grammatical patterns that were used in both English coursebooks of K12 and corpus-based English coursebooks by native English speakers.

Based on the questions directed by Davenport et al. (2010) for the learning analytics, the use of language patterns was investigated by using a corpus software program, Sketch Engine, to answer the research questions regarding the lexical content of materials of English language teaching in high schools in Türkiye. To answer the question of what must be done in the future, an interview was made and a reference corpus involving corpus-based English coursebooks by native writers was examined to detect the common and frequent collocations and lexico-grammatical patterns that can also be used in English language teaching coursebooks. Based on the findings, pedagogical implications were made regarding the learners, language teaching professionals, material writers, and other stakeholders.

In the study, we used the five steps of learning analytics by capturing the data from the coursebooks, reporting the patterns and collocations, using, and predicting the possible contents that can be contained in the Turkish coursebooks in the future. For the act and refine steps, we have made suggestions for the DDL approach and aimed to trigger the necessary actions to be taken for improving the learning environment and keeping this process regularly reviewed for ensuring sustainability.

With this original study on learning analytics, we aimed to highlight the missing points in learning analytics applications in Türkiye and expand the use of simple corpus tools during learning as well as create new areas of use, and an analysis model for evaluating and revising the words and multi-word combinations and related grammatical structures that exist in English coursebooks currently used in public schools.

To strengthen the learning environment and process, we examined words and multi-word combinations, and grammatical content on a corpus database based on the frequency and contextual data, aiming to create an analysis model for evaluating and revising the lexical content and the related grammatical structures existing in English coursebooks currently used in K12 schools as well as to create a framework of novel learning analytics models. Therefore, this study attempted to give insights into how these two areas can be merged to achieve the five steps of learning analytics.

This study attempted to answer these questions through a corpus-based analysis of English coursebooks of high schools published by the Ministry of Education. In the insight level of learning analytics (Davenport et al., 2010), recommendations were made by suggesting the implementation of DDL and the use of corpus linguistics in creating the coursebook for the most effective action that can be taken in the future.

This study is an original one since it is the first study to combine learning analytics and corpus linguistics to be used together for tracking the learning processes involving pedagogical materials. One element that strengthens the originality of this study is that it emphasizes the combinational characteristics of English words for K12 learners. When the learner corpus named KTUCLE, which has strict design criteria and consists of 5 million words, compiled by Özbay (2015) over a period of eight years (2011-2018), is examined, it is seen that K12 learners use word combinations seldom although the multiple word groups or patterns are "very strong" in English (Sinclair, 1991). Therefore, as stated earlier, we examined words and multi-word combinations, and grammatical content on a corpus database based on the frequency and contextual data to strengthen the learning environment and the process. The present study answered the following questions:

1. What are the top twenty-word clusters in TurkCorp and the reference corpora?
2. What are the top twenty nouns in TurkCorp and the reference corpora?
3. What are the top twenty verbs in TurkCorp and the reference corpora?
4. What are the most common verb+noun patterns in all the corpora?
5. What are the perceptions of the language teaching professionals regarding the use of word clusters and lexemes in the K12 English coursebooks used in Türkiye?
6. What can be done regarding the use of word clusters and collocations in the K12 English coursebooks and classes in the future?

Method

This study is a mixed-method study involving both quantitative and qualitative analysis. A corpus-based analysis was conducted as an indicator of the situation in terms of the use of lexemes and collocations in the English coursebooks of the Ministry of Education. In the quantitative part of the analysis, the frequencies of the verbs, nouns, and collocations that were used in TurkCorp, FaceCorp, and NewpassCorp and their log-likelihood results were compared to see if there were any statistically significant differences among the three corpora regarding the top five verbs and nouns. The reference corpora involving FaceCorp and NewpassCorp were investigated to answer the question of future implementations by detecting the possible collocations and lexico-grammatical patterns to be used in English coursebooks in Türkiye. Regarding the five steps of learning analytics, the researchers first captured the data from the three corpora. Then, the most frequently used words and collocations were found and reported. With the corpus-based analysis of the reference corpora, the possible contents for the future English coursebooks in Türkiye were observed. Lastly, the DDL approach was suggested for the act and refine steps of learning analytics.

When it comes to the qualitative analysis of the study, a focus group interview was conducted with the English language teaching professionals (n=9). After the focus group interview, a content analysis was conducted to see the common patterns of the English language teaching professionals concerning their perceptions of the use of lexemes, word clusters, and collocations in the English coursebooks in Türkiye. The qualitative part of the study enabled the researchers to find out the present situation of English coursebooks from the eyes of English language teaching professionals.

All in all, this study attempted to propose a novel model for the evaluation of English coursebooks used in K12 schools within the framework of learning analytics. Thus, the present study may give insightful suggestions on how corpus linguistics and learning analytics can be merged via the inclusion of corpus-based analysis into the five steps of learning analytics and the information-based questions of learning analytics involving the present and the future.

Corpus Analysis

A corpus analysis was conducted to find out the most frequently used lexemes, word clusters, collocations, and n-grams in the native and non-native English coursebooks. It enabled the researchers to compare the uses of lexemes and collocations used in the coursebook published by the Ministry of Education in Türkiye with those of native speakers of English. The comparison revealed how English coursebooks published in Türkiye used the lexemes and collocations which are most frequently employed in reference corpora. Regarding this, the differences, and similarities between these coursebooks were investigated through a corpus methodology.

Sketch Engine. As for the corpus concordance tool for the quantitative analysis of the corpora, Sketch Engine was used. Sketch Engine is "a corpus tool which takes as input a corpus of any language and a corresponding grammar pattern and which generates word sketches for the words of that language" (Kilgarriff et al. 2008, p. 297). We used "word list, word sketch, and concordance" functions for the study. The concordance function enables the researcher to see the larger context of the keyword with the frequency. The word list function provides the frequency lists. Lastly, we used the word sketch function to observe the collocations and word combinations. The frequency lists of the most used verbs and nouns were investigated through the word list function. Then, the most frequent collocations with the top verbs and nouns were found via the word sketch function. Lastly, the concordance function was used to see the normalized frequencies. In this regard, raw frequencies were normalized per 100,000 "to adjust raw frequency counts from texts of different lengths so that they can be compared accurately" (Biber et al., 1998, p. 263).

Corpora. We used three corpora consisting of English coursebooks: TurkCorp, FaceCorp, and NewpassCorp. The corpus called TurkCorp consists of English coursebooks for high schools published by the Ministry of Education in Türkiye. As for the reference corpora, FaceCorp and NewpassCorp were compiled. FaceCorp was compiled from the English coursebooks named as Face2Face whereas NewpassCorp was compiled from the English coursebook called New Password.

Table 1 shows that the English coursebooks in Türkiye consist of the coursebooks preparatory classes, 9, 10, 11, and 12. classes with 342,540 corpus size. As for the reference corpora, the Face2Face corpus involves elementary, pre-intermediate, intermediate, and upper-intermediate levels with 23,046 corpus size while the New Password corpus includes 1,2,3, and 4 levels with 41,281 corpus size. Since the sizes of corpora were not equal, normalized frequencies were used.

Table 1. Corpora used in this study

Name of the Coursebooks	Levels of the Coursebooks	Corpus Size
High school	Preparatory Classes, 9, 10, 11, 12. Classes	342,540
Face2Face	Elementary, pre-intermediate, intermediate, and upper-intermediate	23,046
New Password	1, 2, 3, and 4	41,281

Participants, Settings, and Focus Group Interview

The qualitative part of the study involved focus group interviews with 10 English language teaching professionals. For the selection of the participants, a convenience sampling method was used to reach the most suitable English language teaching professionals to access in Türkiye for this study. Focus group interviews enabled the researchers to conduct a qualitative analysis and in-depth content analysis by shedding light on the perceptions of the English language teaching professionals in Türkiye regarding the inclusion of words and collocations, which are used in the target language, in the English coursebooks of the high school published by the Ministry of Education in Türkiye. Therefore, two questions in the focus group interview were asked:

Q1. What are your perceptions regarding the use of word clusters and lexemes in the K12 English coursebooks for high and secondary schools in Türkiye?

Q2. What can be done regarding the use of word clusters and collocations in the K12 coursebooks and K12 classes for high and secondary schools in Türkiye in the future?

The researchers aimed to find out the perceptions of English language teaching professionals on the currently used English coursebooks. Since quantitative analysis investigated frequencies and collocations, qualitative analysis via a focus group interview is expected to help reveal how English language teaching professionals perceive word usage patterns in the English coursebooks in Türkiye. Therefore, a content analysis was conducted to categorize the common themes emerged from the interview data.

Results and Discussions

Corpus-based Quantitative Results

In Table 2, the results of the top twenty nouns used in TurkCorp, FaceCorp, and NewpassCorp show that the noun *people* was used with the highest frequency in the three corpora. The second most frequent noun in TurkCorp and NewpassCorp was *time* while it was *day* in FaceCorp. Moreover, the nouns *people, day, time*, and *year* were used with high frequencies in NewpassCorp and FaceCorp whereas TurkCorp underrepresented these nouns. Another interesting finding was that FaceCorp and NewpassCorp mostly used nouns that can be applicable to real-life situations such as *day, job, money, food, holiday*, and *number* while TurkCorp had mostly the nouns related to the activities, such as *question, theme, text, sentence,* and *dialogue*. The overall findings indicated that TurkCorp underrepresented the nouns for the themes of real life, which may be due to the lack of meaningful input and pragmatic competence.

Table 3 presents the results of the top twenty verbs used in the three corpora. The verb *be* was used with the highest frequencies in the three corpora. It was followed by *do* and *have* in TurkCorp and NewpassCorp while they were *have* and *do* used in FaceCorp in a sequence. Furthermore, the verbs *be, do, have, make, go, get,* and the other verbs were underrepresented in the TurkCorp. It was also found that FaceCorp and NewpassCorp used the verb *say* more than the verbs *write, read, and listen* and more than the TurkCorp did; on the other hand, TurkCorp used the verbs *write, read*, and *listen* more than the verb *say* and more than the other two corpora did. This indicates that TurkCorp underrepresented the verb *say* even though it was used as one of the verbs to initiate an activity based on production. Instead of the verb *say*, TurkCorp overrepresented the verb *write* for the command of a production-based activity. In addition, the verbs *read* and *listen* were overrepresented in TurkCorp to initiate an activity based on the reception. It is seen that even though the activities in the TurkCorp were initiated with the verbs used for the receptive skills, these activities were followed by one of the productive skills, which is writing rather than speaking. On the other hand, in FaceCorp and NewpassCorp, speaking was emphasized with a higher frequency with the verb *say*.

Table 2. Top twenty nouns used in three corpora

TurkCorp		FaceCorp		NewpassCorp	
Nouns	***nf***	**Nouns**	***nf***	**Nouns**	***nf***
People	22,5	People	39	People	77,2
Time	18,4	Day	34,2	Time	28,8
Friend	14,8	Time	29,9	Food	27,8
Question	14,4	Year	21,6	Year	25,9
Theme	14,1	Thing	19,5	Thing	23,9
School	13,3	Week	17,7	Day	22,2
Word	12,9	TV	17,3	Way	16,7
Text	11,8	World	16,9	Part	15,9
Life	11,2	Man	16,4	Example	15,5
Sentence	11	Course	13,4	Student	14,5
Day	10,3	Life	12,5	Brain	13,8
Student	10,3	Friend	12,1	School	13,5
Work	9,6	Home	11,7	Job	13,3
Dialogue	9	Number	11,7	Life	13
World	8,8	Holiday	11,2	Country	12,8
Picture	8,4	Night	10,8	Word	12,8
Year	7,9	Child	10,4	Eye	11,6
Story	7,7	Restaurant	10,4	Money	11,1
Country	7,1	House	9,9	United	10,9
Read	7	Family	9,5	Something	10,9

As it was shown in Table 4, analyzing word clusters used in the three corpora, we see that the word cluster *work in pairs* was mostly used in the TurkCorp whereas *I don't* was mostly in the FaceCorp, and the word cluster *the United States* was mostly used in the NewpassCorp. Also, the word clusters *a lot of* and *one of the* were highly used in FaceCorp and NewpassCorp whereas they were underrepresented in the TurkCorp. Moreover, the word clusters that were mostly used in the TurkCorp were the imperatives concerning the activities in the coursebooks, such as *look at the, the following questions, listen to the,* and *answer the following*. However, the word clusters used in the FaceCorp and the NewpassCorp were not based on the imperatives for the activities; instead, they were from the contextualized texts related to real-life situations, such as *I don't, a lot of, the end of, all the time, part of the, the people who*, and *make a living*.

Table 3. Top twenty verbs used in three corpora

TurkCorp		FaceCorp		NewpassCorp	
Verbs	***nf***	**Verbs**	***nf***	**Verbs**	***nf***
Be	258,3	Be	408,3	Be	339,6
Do	71,3	Have	114,9	Do	96,8
Have	64,6	Do	86,3	Have	88,9
Use	23,9	Go	59,4	Make	42,1
Go	22,2	Get	45,1	Say	40,2
Write	21,1	Know	26,9	Get	34,8
Make	18,4	Want	23,8	Go	28,3
Get	15,9	Say	22,9	Use	23,2
Give	13,8	Think	22,9	Work	23
Read	13,5	Live	21,2	Know	21,3
Listen	13,4	See	19,5	Think	21
Take	12,5	Like	18,6	Take	21
Think	12,2	Work	16,4	Eat	19,8
See	12	Love	16	Want	19,3
Like	9,6	Leave	13,4	Need	16,7
Follow	9,6	Need	13	Come	16,7
Know	9,3	Stay	13	Find	15,2
Find	8,7	Look	12,5	Look	14,7
Want	8,1	Make	12,5	Learn	14,7
Talk	8,1	Watch	12,5	Like	14,2

The top twenty-word clusters of the noun *people* were found in the three corpora in subject and object positions as in Table 5. For the verbs with the noun *people* as subjects, the most frequent verb was *be* in TurkCorp, *think* in FaceCorp, and *do* in NewpassCorp. TurkCorp used the verbs *have, use*, and *do* in a sequence other than the verb *be*. As for FaceCorp, the verb *be, have,* and *live* was used sequentially other than the verb *think*. Lastly, NewpassCorp used *have, be,* and *think* in a sequence other than the verb *do*. All in all, the verbs that were used with the noun *people* as subjects were underrepresented in TurkCorp when compared to FaceCorp and NewpassCorp.

Table 4. Top twenty 3-4-grams used in three corpora

TurkCorp		FaceCorp		NewpassCorp	
Word-Clusters	***nf***	**Word-Clusters**	***nf***	**Word-Clusters**	***nf***
Work in pairs	5,5	I don't	9,5	the United States	10,6
Look at the	5,4	A lot of	8,6	In the United States	6,7
The following questions	4,7	The end of	4,7	A lot of	6,2
Listen to the	3,9	All the time	4,3	Part of the	3,3
Answer the following	3,2	One of the	3,9	The people who	2,6
In the blanks	3,2	All over the	3,4	One of the	2,1
One of the	3,2	N't want to	3	Make a living	2,1
A lot of	3,2	Over the world	3	Have to be	1,9
Check this out	3,2	Don't want	3	Percent of the	1,9
I don't	3,1	You want to	3	People in the	1,9
Read the text	3,1	In the world	3	Around the world	1,9
Do you think	2,8	All over the world	3	To go to	1,6
What do you	2,6	Don't know	3	Of the world	1,6
Answer the questions	2,3	To live with	2,6	Of the body	1,6
With your friends	2,1	Do n't want to	2,6	It is the	1,6
Fill in the blanks	1,8	I don't know	2,6	A lot of time	1,6
In the world	1,6	In the UK	2,6	All the time	1,6
In the example	1,6	The Full Moon	2,6	Not want to	1,6
As in the example	1,5	I didn't	2,6	During the day	1,6
Do you think	1,5	I want to	2,6	Such as the	1,6

For the verbs that were used with the noun *people* as object, the verb *do* was used in TurkCorp the most whereas the verb *be* was used the most in the FaceCorp, and the verb *help* was used the most in the NewpassCorp. TurkCorp used the verbs *help* and *think* after the verb *be*. FaceCorp used the verbs *meet* and *kill* after the verb *want*. Lastly, NewpassCorp used *be* and *do* after the verb *help*. Moreover, the word clusters used with the noun *people* as object and the verbs were used in NewpassCorp and FaceCorp more than in TurkCorp.

When it comes to the top five verb + noun patterns for the verb *be*, the noun *student* was used with the verb *be* the most as a pattern in TurkCorp as in Table 6. It was followed by the nouns *child, place, year*, and *friend*. For FaceCorp, the noun *thing* was used the most, and it was followed by the nouns *love, person, people*, and *work*. In the NewpassCorp, the noun *part* was the one used with the verb *be* the most. It was followed by the nouns *thing, type, student*, and *way*. TurkCorp underrepresented the verb + noun patterns used in the other two corpora. In addition, TurkCorp underrepresented other verb + noun patterns for the verb *be*, which revealed that the verb *be* was hardly used with the nouns as patterns when compared to the reference corpora.

Table 5. Twenty word-clusters used with the noun "people" in three corpora

Verbs as Subject						Verbs as Object					
TurkCorp		FaceCorp		NewpassCorp		TurkCorp		FaceCorp		NewpassCorp	
Verbs	***nf***	**Verbs**	***nf***	**Verbs**	***nf***	**Verbs**	***nf***	**Verbs**	***nf***	**Verbs**	***nf***
Be	1,3	Think	2,6	Do	5,57	Do	1,02	Be	2,16	Help	2,42
Have	0,55	Be	2,6	Have	2,18	Be	0,64	Meet	1,3	Be	1,69
Use	0,52	Have	2,16	Be	2,18	Help	0,49	Kill	0,86	Do	1,45
Do	0,49	Live	1,3	Think	1,93	Think	0,23	Want	0,86	Meet	1,21
Travel	0,26	Watch	1,3	Speak	1,45	Make	0,23	Know	0,86	Ask	0,72
Live	0,26	Do	1,3	Work	1,45	Use	0,2	Injure	0,43	Need	0,72
Prefer	0,23	Like	0,86	Believe	1,21	Meet	0,17	Interview	0,43	Have	0,72
Feel	0,23	Say	0,86	Like	1,21	Ask	0,14	Think	0,43	Want	0,48
Wear	0,23	Get	0,86	Make	1,21	Know	0,11	Call	0,43	See	0,48
Talk	0,23	Kiss	0,43	Say	1,21	Warn	0,08	Make	0,43	Make	0,48

Table 6. Top five be + noun patterns used in three corpora

TurkCorp		FaceCorp		NewpassCorp	
Patterns	***nf***	**Patterns**	***nf***	**Patterns**	***nf***
Be + Student	1,25	Be + Thing	3,47	Be + Part	4,36
Be + Child	0,87	Be + Love	2,6	Be + Thing	2,42
Be + Place	0,87	Be + Person	2,6	Be + Type	2,18
Be + Year	0,84	Be + People	2,16	Be + Student	2,18
Be + Friend	0,84	Be + Work	1,73	Be + Way	2,18

Table 7 shows that the verb + noun patterns for the verb *do* was found in the three corpora. TurkCorp used the noun *something* the most, and it was followed by the nouns *people, homework, sport,* and *exercise*. FaceCorp used the noun *anything* the most while it was followed by the nouns such as *thing, shopping, exercise*, and *something*. For NewpassCorp, the noun *job* was used with the verb *do* the most, and it was followed by the nouns *people, research, something*, and *thing*. The noun *something* was found in the top five of the three corpora. Furthermore, NewpassCorp and FaceCorp used the top five verbs *do* and noun patterns more than TurkCorp did.

Table 7. Top five do + noun patterns used in three corpora

TurkCorp		FaceCorp		NewpassCorp	
Patterns	*nf*	**Patterns**	*nf*	**Patterns**	*nf*
Do + Something	1,05	Do + Anything	1,73	Do + Job	2,18
Do + People	1,02	Do + Thing	1,73	Do + People	1,45
Do + Homework	0,52	Do + Shopping	1,3	Do + Research	1,21
Do + Sport	0,49	Do + Exercise	0,86	Do + Something	1,21
Do + Exercise	0,46	Do + Something	0,86	Do + Thing	1,21

As for the top five *have* and noun patterns used in three corpora, TurkCorp used the noun *time* the most, and it was followed by the nouns *chance, right, money,* and *problem* as in Table 8. FaceCorp used the noun *dinner* the most while it was followed by the nouns *problem, time, holiday*, and *lunch*. Lastly, NewpassCorp used the noun *time* with the verb *have* the most, and it was followed by the nouns *problem, rule, fun,* and *job*. The nouns *time* and *problem* were used in the top five of the three corpora. Furthermore, NewpassCorp and FaceCorp used the top five patterns for the verb *have* and noun more than TurkCorp did.

Table 8. Top five have + noun patterns used in three corpora

TurkCorp		FaceCorp		NewpassCorp	
Patterns	*nf*	**Patterns**	*nf*	**Patterns**	*nf*
Have + Time	1,25	Have + Dinner	1,73	Have + Time	1,69
Have + Chance	0,55	Have + Problem	1,73	Have + Problem	1,45
Have + Right	0,55	Have + Time	1,73	Have + Rule	0,96
Have + Money	0,46	Have + Holiday	1,3	Have + Fun	0,96
Have + Problem	0,46	Have + Lunch	0,86	Have + Job	0,96

When it comes to the top five verb *use* and noun pattern in the three corpora, TurkCorp used the noun *expression* the most, and it was followed by the nouns *medium, word, tense*, and *phone* as in Table 9. FaceCorp used the noun recipe with the verb *use* the most and the nouns *calculator, colour, medicine,* and *box* in sequence. Moreover, NewpassCorp used the noun *kit* the most with the verb *use*, and the nouns *internet, computer, calculator*, and *resource* sequentially. NewpassCorp used the top five verb *use* and noun patterns more than FaceCorp and TurkCorp.

Table 9. Top five use + noun patterns used in three corpora

TurkCorp		FaceCorp		NewpassCorp	
Patterns	*nf*	**Patterns**	*nf*	**Patterns**	*nf*
Use + Expression	0,49	Use + Recipe	0,86	Use + Kit	0,96
Use + Medium	0,46	Use + Calculator	0,43	Use + Internet	0,72
Use + Word	0,46	Use + Colour	0,43	Use + Computer	0,72
Use + Tense	0,4	Use + Medicine	0,43	Use + Calculator	0,48
Use + Phone	0,37	Use + Box	0,43	Use + Resource	0,48

Lastly, Table 10 illustrates the top five verbs *make* and noun patterns in the three corpora. TurkCorp used the noun sentence with the verb *make* the most, it was followed by the nouns *plan, list, difference*, and *dialogue*. FaceCorp used the noun *difference* the most and used the nouns *programme, face, grade*, and *noise* in sequence. On the other hand, NewpassCorp used the noun *decision* the most, and it was followed by the nouns *living, life, movie*, and *money*. Moreover, NewpassCorp was the one that used the verb *make* and noun patterns more than FaceCorp and TurkCorp. However, TurkCorp underrepresented the patterns for the verb *make* and nouns.

Table 10. Top five make + noun patterns used in three corpora

TurkCorp		FaceCorp		NewpassCorp	
Patterns	*nf*	**Patterns**	*nf*	**Patterns**	*nf*
Make + Sentence	0,61	Make + Difference	0,86	Make + Decision	2,9
Make + Plan	0,58	Make + Programme	0,86	Make + Living	2,18
Make + List	0,46	Make + Face	0,43	Make + Life	1,45
Make + Difference	0,35	Make + Grade	0,43	Make + Movie	1,21
Make + Dialogue	0,35	Make + Noise	0,43	Make + Money	1,21

The log-likelihood tests for the top five nouns in TurkCorp and FaceCorp showed that there is a statistically significant difference between TurkCorp and FaceCorp regarding the use of nouns *people, question,* and *day* as in Table 11. While FaceCorp used the nouns *people* and *day* more than TurkCorp, TurkCorp used the noun *question* more than FaceCorp. Even though the difference between these two corpora concerning the nouns *time* and *friend* was not found statistically significant, FaceCorp used the noun *time* more than TurkCorp, and TurkCop used the noun *friend* more than FaceCorp. It was found that TurkCorp underrepresented the nouns *people* and *day*, and it overrepresented the noun question when compared to the reference corpus.

Table 11. Log-Likelihood tests for the top five nouns in TurkCorp and FaceCorp

Nouns	TurkCorp	FaceCorp	LL		p-value
People	22,5	39	4.48	-	0.02
Time	18,4	29,9	2.76	-	0.10
Day	10,3	34,2	13.54	-	0.00
Friend	14,8	12,1	0.27	+	0.69
Question	14,4	4,3	5.76	+	0.01

As for the log-likelihood tests for the top five nouns used in TurkCorp and NewpassCorp, Table 12 shows that there is a statistically significant difference between TurkCorp and NewpassCorp regarding the use of nouns *day, year,* and *people.* NewpassCorp used these nouns more than TurkCorp did; TurkCorp underrepresented the nouns *day, year,* and *people.* Although there is not any statistically significant difference regarding the nouns *time* and *friend*, TurkCorp underrepresented the noun *time* and overrepresented the noun *friend.*

Table 12. Log-Likelihood tests for the top five nouns in TurkCorp and NewpassCorp

Nouns	TurkCorp	NewpassCorp	LL		p-value
People	22,5	77,2	31.73	-	0.00
Time	18,4	28,8	2.31	-	0.13
Day	10,3	22,2	4.46	-	0.03
Friend	14,8	8,23	1.9	+	0.19
Year	7,9	25,9	10.10	-	0.00

When it comes to the log-likelihood tests for the top five verbs in TurkCorp and FaceCorp, it was found that there is a statistically significant difference between these two corpora in terms of the verbs *use, be*, and *have* as in Table 13. TurkCorp underrepresented the verbs *be* and *have* and overrepresented the verb *use*. There was no difference regarding the verbs *do* and *make*; however, TurkCorp underrepresented the verb *do* and overrepresented the verb *make*.

Table 13. Log-Likelihood tests for the top five verbs in TurkCorp and FaceCorp

Verbs	TurkCorp	FaceCorp	LL		p-value
Be	258,3	408,3	11.09	-	0.00
Do	71,3	86,3	1.43	-	0.23
Have	64,6	114,9	14.29	-	0.00
Use	23,9	11,7	4.27	+	0.03
Make	18,4	12,5	1.13	+	0.27

Lastly, Table 14 shows the results of log-likelihood tests for the top five verbs used in TurkCorp and NewpassCorp. According to the results, there is a statistically significant difference between the two corpora regarding the use of verbs *do, have, make*, and *be*. TurkCorp underrepresented these verbs; FaceCorp used them more than TurkCop did. On the other hand, there was no difference between them concerning the verb *use*.

Table 14. Log-Likelihood tests for the top five verbs in TurkCorp and NewpassCorp

Verbs	TurkCorp	NewpassCorp	LL		p-value
Be	258,3	339,6	11.09	-	0.00
Do	71,3	96,8	3.88	-	0.05
Have	64,6	88,9	3.86	-	0.05
Use	23,9	23,2	0.01	+	1
Make	18,4	42,1	9.54	-	0.00

Qualitative Results: Focus Group Interview

For the first interview question, the qualitative analysis indicated that most participants think that word clusters are not common in the K12 English coursebooks as in Table

15. Instead, the lexemes are usually presented in isolation, which may not provide authentic use of language (n=7). The other participants revealed that although word clusters and lexemes are frequently used in the K12 English coursebooks, they are not authentic language samples (n=2).

Table 15. Codes/Themes emerged in the focus group interview for the question one

Question 1	Codes/Themes	Participants
What are your perceptions regarding the use of word clusters and lexemes in the K12 English coursebooks for high and secondary schools in Türkiye?	Word clusters are not common.	1, 2, 4, 5, 7, 8, 9
	Word clusters are common, but not authentic.	3, 6

Regarding this, the following excerpt gives the perceptions of English language teaching professionals on the use of word clusters and lexemes in the K12 English coursebooks:

According to my perception, K-12 English coursebooks are so transmitted through a very narrow window and is out of date. Unfortunately, the fact that the book is equipped with visuals does not save the situation. The number of sentence patterns used in the book is very few, directing students to learn only simple vocabulary. The coursebooks do not contain sentence structures and phrases used by native speakers. [Participant 1]

Participant 1 indicates that the use of word clusters and patterns in the K12 English coursebooks is not common. He thinks that the students learn only the lexemes rather than the word clusters of lexemes. In addition, he suggests that the phrases in the K12 English coursebooks are not related to the real-life usage of native speakers.

On the other hand, participant 3 thinks that there are various word clusters and lexemes in the K12 English coursebooks (n=2). Whereas he indicates that these word clusters and lexemes are presented in a meaningful way, the other participant maintained that they are not in correlation with real-life situations:

There are various word clusters and lexemes in English coursebooks for high and secondary school. Yet, as far as I observed, there is little correlation between the word clusters or lexemes and real-life situations because most of them are uncommon for authentic language. [Participant 3]

Based on the responses, although the word clusters and lexemes are presented in the English coursebooks of K12, they do not present the authentic language use regarding the real-life situations of the target language.

As Table 16 shows, regarding what can be done with the use of word clusters and collocations in the K12 coursebooks in Türkiye in the future, most participants indicated that there should be more exercises, activities, and examples of word clusters and collocations (n=8).

Table 16. Codes/Themes emerged in the focus group interview for the question two

<table>
<tr><th>Question 2</th><th colspan="2">Codes/Themes</th><th>Participants</th></tr>
<tr><td rowspan="3">In your opinion, what can be done regarding the use of word clusters and collocations in the K12 coursebooks for high and secondary schools in Türkiye in the future?</td><td rowspan="2">The implementation through</td><td>activities</td><td>4, 6, 8</td></tr>
<tr><td>materials</td><td>1, 2, 3, 5, 9</td></tr>
<tr><td colspan="2">Create difficulty</td><td>7</td></tr>
</table>

Only one participant maintained that having more collocations can be difficult to understand for the students:

In terms of middle school coursebooks, it is possible to come across collocations often. Sometimes they might be confusing for the students since they try to translate every word to Turkish. [Participant 7]

In this regard, the participant suggested that the students might try to translate the collocations word for word. Thus, having more collocations in the middle school English coursebooks can create difficulty in understanding the meaning of these collocations. On the other hand, most participants stated that coursebooks should be redesigned regarding the implementation of word clusters and collocations in the activities, texts, exercises, and examples in the coursebooks by considering authentic language use:

It is essential for the coursebook writers to investigate the authentic use of language and implement the word clusters and collocations into the coursebook. [Participant 3]

Therefore, the participants seem to agree that the use of word clusters and collocations in the coursebooks is essential. Moreover, they think that coursebook writers should redesign the English coursebooks and include more word clusters and collocations in the lexical content.

As in Table 17, in the final interview question, most participants signified the role of English language teaching professionals in the use of word clusters and collocations in the classroom regarding the awareness of the language teaching professionals on the use of these patterns (n=6).

Table 17. Codes/Themes emerged in the focus group interview for the question three

Question 3	Codes/Themes	Participants
In your opinion, what can be done regarding the use of word clusters and collocations in the K12 classes for high and secondary schools in the future?	The awareness of the teachers	2, 3, 4, 5, 8, 9
	The use of word clusters and collocations via the materials	1, 4, 7, 8
	The use of word clusters and collocations via the activities	5, 6

Also, they suggested the use of word clusters and collocations through the materials (n=4) and activities (n=2). In this regard, one of the participants stated that English language teaching professionals should be aware of the use of collocations and word clusters:

Prospective and in-service teachers' awareness regarding the importance of collocational knowledge in language learning/teaching should be raised. Their vocabulary teaching in class should be more focused on word clusters and collocations rather than individual words. [Participant 9]

The participant signified the role of the English language teaching professionals and the importance of being aware of the word clusters and collocations in terms of the English language teaching professionals. Moreover, the participant suggested that English language teaching professionals, who are aware of these patterns, should teach the word clusters and collocations instead of individual words that have no context.

Other participants maintained that materials should be designed by implementing word clusters and collocations that are in connection with authentic language use:

If the texts used are more authentic, I think the problem will be minimized since it will include such structures and phrases. [Participant 1]

This participant stated that the texts that are used in the K12 classrooms should be more authentic in terms of lexical content.

In this study, we used both qualitative and corpus-based quantitative research methods and the quantitative data obtained through corpus-based comparisons indicated the lexical content of the corpora under investigation. Therefore, qualitative data through focus group interviews complemented the findings of the quantitative data.

The first research question asked the top twenty nouns in all the corpora. The analysis showed almost similar nouns with the highest frequencies. The nouns found in the TurkCorp were mostly representing verbal events rather than real-life situations as represented in the reference corpora.

The second research question asked the top twenty-word clusters in all the corpora. The analysis showed that the word clusters in Turkish corpora were different from the reference corpora in terms of function. Word clusters in TurkCorp mainly consisted of instructions unlike those in the reference corpora.

The third research question asked the top twenty verbs in all the corpora. Although there were similar common verbs in all the corpora, this was largely because those verb patterns have already greater saliency in English. We observed an underrepresentation of other common verb patterns in the Turkish corpus, and this indicates the need to re-design coursebook contents according to the expected saliency.

The fourth research question asked the most common verb+noun patterns in all the corpora. The patterns with be, do, have, use, and make were investigated and the results showed that Turkish corpus over- and underrepresented these common words when compared to reference corpora.

For space considerations, we have not given a detailed account of the possible causes and the reasons for such over and underrepresented patterns in this study. Rather, we have attempted to indicate the existence of possible divergences between the Turkish corpus and the reference corpora in the form of over and underrepresented patterns.

The remaining questions (5-6-7) asked the perceptions of language teaching professionals regarding the word cluster, lexeme, and collocational content of English coursebooks in K12 classrooms and these questions were investigated through focus group interviews. The interview results emphasized the need to greater focus on lexical content with meaningful contexts to ensure effective learning and that language teaching professionals are responsible for bringing more lexically focused content into their teaching.

CONCLUSION AND RECOMMENDATIONS

In this study, we focused on the possibility of integrating corpus-based data-driven learning methodology with rich lexical content from collocations to word clusters to propose a novel way of developing learning analytics. The inclusion of lexical content in English coursebooks for K12 learners is likely to increase awareness as well as the amount of learning, creating a viable classroom setting where learning is maximized through consciousness-raising activities, autonomous learners, and supportive language teaching professionals. We also compared corpora of coursebooks in terms of lexical content. A log-likelihood significance test was applied and significant overuses and underuses in the Turkish and English coursebook corpora were reported. The interview data also indicated the need to revise the content of K12 English coursebooks and bring more authentic content with a focus on consciousness-raising activities. Finally, new data obtained through the corpus provides a solid and reliable source for making decisions about learning analytics in terms of past, present, and future applications.

Within this scope, this chapter has presented a brief introduction to learning analytics from a corpus perspective. Then, several related concepts were discussed considering the existing literature. Finally, pedagogical implications highlighting the need to bring a new perspective into language learning were presented.

The findings provide significant pedagogical implications for K12 learning analytics. K12 learners should learn the lexical aspects of the English language with a focus on common collocations and word clusters. We believe that more corpus data should be included in the design and implementation of a new analytical model for K12 classrooms. The use of corpus data coupled with a focus on the multi-word combinations in all types and senses will most probably be effective in creating a sense of novelty in language teaching and learning. Corpus-informed coursebook content and the inclusion of a new collocational syllabus would be helpful for quick learning.

Secondly, the learners and their learning contexts need to be optimized through inductive learning, discovery-based language practices, and data-driven learning methodology. Language learners as detectives, continuously looking for discoveries based on the corpus data they are given by language teaching professionals will be likely to maximize their learning. Coupled with corpus evidence and the integration of phraseological content into the English coursebooks in K12 schools, learners are likely to improve learning in an autonomous style.

Finally, as stated earlier, when the steps of learning analytics are fostered through DDL and corpus-based language practices in a predictable order, the gains will be greater on the part of the learners.

ACKNOWLEDGMENT

This research received no specific grant from any funding agency in the public, commercial, or not-for-profit sectors.

REFERENCES

Aguerrebere, C., He, H., Kwet, M., Laakso, M. J., Lang, C., Price-Dennis, C. M. D., & Zhang, H. (2022). Global perspectives on learning analytics in K12 education. In C. Lang, A. F. Wise, A. Merceron, D. Gaševic, & G. Siemens (Eds.), *The handbook of learning analytics* (pp. 223–231). SOLAR. doi:10.18608/hla22.022

Alhudithi, E. (2017). *A corpus-based analysis of English vocabulary input provided in K-12 textbooks used in Saudi Arabia* [Unpublished Doctoral dissertation, Colorado State University]. ProQuest Dissertations and Theses Global.

Bayyurt, Y. (2012). Proposing a model for English language education in the Turkish sociocultural context. In Y. Bayyurt & Y. Bektaş-Çetinkaya (Eds.), *Research perspectives on teaching and learning English in Turkey: Policies and practices* (pp. 301–312). Peter Lang.

Bernardini, S. (2001). Spoilt for choice: A learner explores general language corpora. In G. Aston (Ed.), *Learning with corpora* (pp. 220–249). Athelstan.

Biber, D., Conrad, S., & Reppen, R. (1998). *Corpus linguistics: Investigating language structure and use*. Cambridge University Press. doi:10.1017/CBO9780511804489

Bozkurt, A. (2016). Öğrenme analitiği: E-öğrenme, büyük veri ve bireyselleştirilmiş öğrenme. *Açıköğretim Uygulamaları ve Araştırmaları Dergisi*, *2*(4), 55–81.

Campbell, J. P., DeBlois, P. B., & Oblinger, D. G. (2007). Academic analytics: A new tool for a new era. *EDUCAUSE Review*, *42*(4), 40.

Davenport, T. H., Harris, J. G., & Morison, R. (2010). *Analytics at work: Smarter decisions, better results*. Harvard Business Press.

Demirpolat, B. C. (2015). *Türkiye'nin yabancı dil öğretimiyle imtihanı: Sorunlar ve çözüm önerileri*. SETA. http://file.setav.org/Files/Pdf/20150707131308_131_yabancidil_web.pdf

Du, X., Yang, J., Shelton, B. E., Hung, J. L., & Zhang, M. (2021). A systematic meta-review and analysis of learning analytics research. *Behaviour & Information Technology*, *40*(1), 49–62. doi:10.1080/0144929X.2019.1669712

Ehsanzadehsorati, S. (2018). *A corpus-driven approach toward teaching vocabulary and reading to English language learners in US-based K-12 context through a mobile app*. [*Dissertation, FIU*]. https://digitalcommons.fiu.edu/etd/3860

Gabrielatos, C. (2005). Corpora and language teaching: Just a fling or wedding bells? *Tesl-Ej*, *8*(4), 1–35.

Haznedar, B. (2003). *Neden erken yaşta yabancı dil eğitimi. İ. Erdoğan (Haz.), Türk eğitim sisteminde yabancı dil eğitimi ve kalite arayışları*. Özel Okullar Derneği Yayınları.

Hunston, S. (2022). *Corpora in applied linguistics* (2nd ed.). Cambridge University Press. doi:10.1017/9781108616218

Johns, T. (1991). Should you be persuaded - Two examples of data-driven learning materials. In T. Johns & P. King (Eds.), *Classroom concordancing: English language research journal* (pp. 1–16). Birmingham University.

Kara, S. (2020). *EFL teachers' views and corpus analysis of English coursebooks used in Turkish state schools in terms of authentic grammatical and lexical contents with a specific focus to the use of "must"*. [Unpublished MA thesis, Karadeniz Technical University, Trabzon].

Kilgarriff, A., Pavel, R., Pavel, S., & David, T. (2008). The sketch engine. In T. Fontenelle (Ed.), *Practical lexicography: A reader* (pp. 297–306). Oxford University Press. doi:10.1093/oso/9780199292332.003.0020

Kirkgöz, Y. (2007). Language planning and implementation in Turkish primary schools. *Current Issues in Language Planning*, *8*(2), 174–191. doi:10.2167/cilp114.0

Liontou, T. (2019). The effect of data-driven learning activities on young EFL learners' processing of English idioms. In P. Crosthwaite (Ed.), *Data-driven learning for the next generation: Corpora and DDL for pre-tertiary learners* (pp. 208–227). Routledge., doi:10.4324/9780429425899-12

Macarini, L. A., Lemos dos Santos, H., Cechinel, C., Ochoa, X., Rodés, V., Pérez Casas, A., Lucas, P. P., Maya, R., Alonso, G. E., & Díaz, P. (2020). Towards the implementation of a countrywide K-12 learning analytics initiative in Uruguay. *Interactive Learning Environments*, *28*(2), 166–190. doi:10.1080/10494820.2019.1636082

Mair, C. (2002). Empowering non-native speakers: The hidden surplus value of corpora in continental English departments. In B. Kettemann & G. Marko (Eds.), *Teaching and learning by doing corpus analysis* (pp. 119–130). Rodopi. doi:10.1163/9789004334236_011

Marlowe, B. A., & Page, M. L. (2005). *Creating and sustaining the constructivist classroom* (2nd ed.). Corwin Press.

Martin, T., & Sherin, B. (2013). Learning analytics and computational techniques for detecting and evaluating patterns in learning: An introduction to the special issue. *Journal of the Learning Sciences*, *22*(4), 511–520. doi:10.1080/10508406.2013.840466

Monroy, C., Rangel, V. S., & Whitaker, R. (2014). A strategy for incorporating learning analytics into the design and evaluation of a K-12 science curriculum. *Journal of Learning Analytics*, *1*(2), 94–125. doi:10.18608/jla.2014.12.6

O'Sullivan, Í. (2007). Enhancing a process-oriented approach to literacy and language learning: The role of corpus consultation literacy. *ReCALL*, *19*(3), 269–286. doi:10.1017/S095834400700033X

Özbay, A. Ş. (2015). *Corpus analysis of the support verb construction development and use by EFL learners*. [Unpublished Doctoral dissertation, Karadeniz Technical University, Trabzon].

Ranney, S. (2012). Defining and teaching academic language: Developments in K-12 ESL. *Language and Linguistics Compass*, *6*(9), 560–574. doi:10.1002/lnc3.354

Rhalmi, M. (2021, February 25). Discovery learning: Guiding language discovery. *My English Pages*. https://www.myenglishpages.com/blog/discovery-learning-guiding-languagediscovery/

Roblyer, M. D., & Doering, A. H. (2013). *Integrating educational technology into teaching* (6th ed.). Pearson.

Ruipérez-Valiente, J. A., & Kim, Y. J. (2020). Effects of solo vs. collaborative play in a digital learning game on geometry: Results from a K12 experiment. *Computers & Education*, *159*, 104008. doi:10.1016/j.compedu.2020.104008

Selwyn, N. (2019). What's the problem with learning analytics? *Journal of Learning Analytics*, *6*(3), 11–19. doi:10.18608/jla.2019.63.3

Sinclair, J. (1991). *Corpus, concordance, collocation*. Oxford University Press.

Smith, C., Butler, N. L., Griffith, K. G., & Allan, W. (2007). The role of communication context, corpus-based grammar, and scaffolded interaction in ESL/EFL instruction. *Online Submission, 4*.

Tan, J. P. L., Koh, E., Jonathan, C., & Yang, S. (2017). Learner dashboards a double-edged sword? Students' sense-making of a collaborative critical reading and learning analytics environment for fostering 21st-century literacies. *Journal of Learning Analytics*, *4*(1), 117–140. doi:10.18608/jla.2017.41.7

Tutsun, E. (2020). Öğrenme analitikleri ve yükseköğretimdeki uygulama alanları. *Bilişim Teknolojileri Dergisi, 13*(3), 243–254. doi:10.17671/gazibtd.688052

Yaylali, A., Banat, H., & Novikov, A. (2021). Use of corpus-based materials in K-12 language classrooms. *TESOL SLWIS Newsletter*. http://newsmanager.commpartners.com/tesolslwis/issues/2021-02-26/3.html

Yu, X. (2020). *Examining and comparing English textbooks and high-stakes exams in Turkey: A Corpus-based study*. Corpora and Discourse International Conference, Brighton, England. https://hdl.handle.net/11511/92609

ADDITIONAL READING

Boulton, A., & Cobb, T. (2017). Corpus use in language learning: A meta-analysis. *Language Learning, 67*(2), 348–393. doi:10.1111/lang.12224

Boulton, A., & Vyatkina, N. (2021). Thirty years of data-driven learning: Taking stock and charting new directions over time. *Language Learning & Technology, 25*(3), 66–89. http://hdl.handle.net/10125/73450

Cheng, W. (2010). What can a corpus tell us about language teaching? In A. O'Keeffe & M. McCarthy (Eds.), *Routledge handbook of corpus linguistics* (pp. 319–332). Routledge. doi:10.4324/9780203856949-23

Crosthwaite, P., & Steeples, B. (2022). Data-driven learning with younger learners: Exploring corpus-assisted development of the passive voice for science writing with female secondary school students. *Computer Assisted Language Learning*, 1–32. doi:10.1080/09588221.2022.2068615

Ferdig, R. E., Hartshorne, R., Baumgartner, E., Kaplan-Rakowski, R., & Mouza, C. (Eds.). (2023). What preK-12 teachers should know about educational technology in 2023: A research-to-practice anthology. Association for the Advancement of Computing in Education (AACE).

Flowerdew, L. (2015). Data-driven learning and language learning theories: Whither the Twain shall meet. In A. Leńko-Szymańska & A. Boulton (Eds.), *Multiple affordances of language corpora for data-driven learning* (pp. 15–36). John Benjamins. doi:10.1075cl.69.02flo

Gilquin, G., & Granger, S. (2010). How can data-driven learning be used in language teaching? In A. O'Keeffe & M. McCarthy (Eds.), *Routledge handbook of corpus linguistics* (pp. 359–370). Routledge. doi:10.4324/9780203856949-26

Godwin-Jones, R. (2021). Big data and language learning: Opportunities and challenges. *Language Learning & Technology*, *25*(1), 4–19. http://hdl.handle.net/10125/44747

KEY TERMS AND DEFINITIONS

Corpus: Any collection of more than one text, referring to a large collection of natural texts compiled and considered to be representative of a variety or a genre of a language in machine-readable form.

Data-driven Learning: An approach to foreign language learning in which most language learning is guided by teachers and textbooks and is treated as data through which students as researchers are undertaking guided discovery tasks.

N-Grams: They are continuous sequences of words or symbols, or tokens in a document.

Sketch Engine: A tool to explore how language works and analyzes authentic texts of billions of words to identify typicality in language.

Word Clusters: They are words found repeatedly together in each other's company, in sequence, representing a tighter relationship than collocates.

Word Pattern: They are the sequences or patterns within words.

Chapter 6
A Framework for Online Learning Analytics in K-12 Classrooms as a Precursor for Personalized Learning:
Emergent Practices in Schools

Ronelle Klinck Van der Merwe
University of South Africa, South Africa

Leila Goosen
https://orcid.org/0000-0003-4948-2699
University of South Africa, South Africa

ABSTRACT

The purpose of the research study reported on in this chapter is to develop a framework for online learning analytics (LA) in schools as a precursor for personalized learning. Against the background of emergent practices related to learning analytics in Kindergarten/grade R through grade-12 classrooms, the chapter will present the authors' perspectives on learning analytics in open and distance learning environments, as well as barriers, and discuss future research directions for K-12 classrooms.

DOI: 10.4018/979-8-3693-0066-4.ch006

INTRODUCTION

Learning Analytics (LA) involve "the measurement, collection, analysis, and reporting of data about learners and their contexts, … and the environments in which it occurs" (Siemens, 2013, p. 1382), "in order to understand and" optimize learning (Ferguson, Clow, Griffiths, & Brasher, 2019, p. 43). As a rapidly growing field, LA is identified as a 'midterm horizon' for education (New Media Consortium, 2015), since many educational institutions have been using LA, albeit scarcely, and mostly through small-scale projects (Siemens, Dawson, & Lynch, 2013). Beyond question, LA research as a field embarks and draws on data gathered, analyzed and reported about and "from learners' interactions with educational technologies" and learning environments "to provide information and insights into" their learning (Lim, Dawson, Joksimovic, & Gašević, 2019, p. 250) in order to benefit from the potential of digital footprints (Siemens & Gašević, 2012).

In doing so, data science methods are utilized "with the goal to harness vast amounts of data about learning collected by the extensive use of" technologies (Gašević, Kovanović, & Joksimović, 2017, p. 63) to evaluate such data and present the findings in a myriad of textual and visual formats. Given the growing interest in this research field and practice, LA had matured into a rich praxis for many disciplines (Li & Wong, 2019) with promising results in order to shape pedagogical shifts, feasible allocation of institutional resources, and retention strategies that students can employ (Gašević, Dawson, & Siemens, 2015; Lim, et al., 2019). The journal article by Gašević, et al. (2015, p. 64) first introduced "the field of learning analytics and" outlined some of the lessons learned. Thus, like that of the edited book that it proposes to form part of, the target audience of this chapter will be composed of professionals, educators and researchers working in the field of education, together with "graduate *students* in education who used to be (or are planning to become) educators, teachers, school administrators", etc., who might "have little to no technical background" (Schneider, Reilly, & Radu, 2020, p. 91). The research findings of Avella, Kebritchi, Nunn, and Kanai (2016) implored educational *stakeholders*, who work with data, to have the relevant training in learning analytics and be able to understand how to apply the data effectively to achieve meaningful results.

Benefits of Applying Learning Analytics in K-12 Education

Using learning "analytics is receiving increased attention, in part because it offers to assist educational institutions in increasing student retention," as well as to predict (and improve) student success (Dietz-Uhler & Hurn, 2013, p. 17). A faculty perspective was provided by the latter authors in a journal article on interactive online learning, since "it is envisaged that education systems that do make the transition towards data-informed planning, decision making, and teaching and learning will hold significant competitive and quality advantages over those that do not" (Siemens et al., 2013, p. 2). Conversely, despite the promise of learning analytics that these "will use educational data to improve the quality and value of the learning experience within" schools and universities (Ferguson & Clow, 2017, p. 2), towards avoiding the failures that learning analytics have had, the *Educause review online* journal article by the latter authors indicated that researchers are questioning whether it potentially contributes to student success originating mainly from the type of educational delivery: residential, traditional, or distributed. More to note, the field may lack maturity since the possible outcomes of LA have not yet been translated into teaching and learning accurately (Siemens et al., 2013), and if not managed cautiously, LA may pose some risks (e.g., accountability, marginalization of professional practice, utility of LA, faculty engagement, decision-making, ethical and privacy principles for learning analytics, etc.) for students, teachers, and administrative staff (Pardo & Siemens, 2014). From the start, LA is concerned with the ways for enhancing education by detecting constructs that may impede learning. However, it is yet limited by the direct impact that LA may impose on K-12 education.

Therefore, as part of this edited book, the chapter proposes to compile conceptual, empirical, and theoretical research that contributes to the understanding of LA to make more informed choices for student success. The aim of the research study reported on in this chapter is to enhance the personal learning experience of school learners by applying a rigorous online learning analytics framework, while the objectives of the study include:

1. Identifying the strategies and behaviors that lead to a successful learning experience;
2. Finding empirical evidence that measures how personalized learning improves learning outcomes;
3. Evaluating and comparing the benefits of various learning analytical tools;
4. Digitizing a section of the curriculum for specific grades and subjects;
5. Designing a professional development program for educators to use and be able to effectively interpret the results from learning analytic tools;
6. Analyzing and interpreting the data derived from the digital learning experience;
7. Quantifying the critical elements for an effective learning analytics framework.

BACKGROUND

This section of the chapter will provide broad definitions and discussions of the topic on a framework for online learning analytics in schools as a precursor for personalization and incorporate the views of others (in the form of a literature review) into the discussion to support, refute, or demonstrate the authors' position on the topic.

Perspectives on Learning Analytics in Distance Learning Environments

Educational technologies can be implemented in distance learning environments and Goosen and Van Heerden (2017) described how to take this beyond the horizon when learning programming in the proceedings of the South Africa International Conference on Educational Technologies (SAICET).

Perspectives on Learning Analytics in Multimodal Learning Environments

Language teachers' investment in Digital Multimodal Composing (DMC) as a manifold application of computer-mediated communication was the focus of the chapter by Kavaklı Ulutaş and Abuşka (2023, p. 17) in a book on the multidisciplinary applications of computer-mediated communication. "As an instructional potential for language learning purposes to integrate digital technologies," DMC had "mushroomed as a textual practice".

Likewise, standardized testing in Türkiye was discussed in the international journal article on curriculum and instruction by Höl (2023, p. 984). The study evaluated English Foreign *Language* (EFL) teachers' perceptions and experiences of the Cambridge Young Learner Examinations (YLE). "In this context, the purpose of the research" was "to determine the perceptions of Turkish EFL" teachers.

Similarly, a *qualitative* study, which focused on the "pedagogical implications and evaluation of listening skills in an English as a Foreign Language context" and Turkish classes was presented by Kasimi and Höl (2023, p. 91) in their journal article featuring *Research on Youth and Language.*

"Second language writers can adapt their creative skills to acquire and reflect new knowledge with fewer sophisticated words through more contextual and *inclusive* language". The chapter by Hancı-Azizoglu and Kavaklı Ulutaş (2021, p. 250) provided a multilingual perspective on creative digital writing as part of a book on digital pedagogies and the transformation of *language* education.

Correspondingly, sustainable, and *inclusive* quality education can be achieved through research-informed practice on information and communication technologies, as described by Goosen (2018) in the proceedings of the 26th conference of the Southern African Association for Research on Mathematics, Science and Technology Education (SAARMSTE).

Moreover, Ölmez and Kavaklı Ulutaş (2023, p. 359), in their Indonesian journal article on English *language* teaching and applied linguistics, indicated that while pervading "almost all areas of society, technology has its roots in education in two alternates", the first of which is related to education systems integrating digital competencies. A diachronic view into an understanding of technology acceptance led the latter authors to ask where to go through the Technology Acceptance Model (TAM) for teacher education from global to local.

Strategies for engagement in online courses about engaging with the content, instructor, and other students were also provided in the chapter by Dietz-Uhler and Hurn (2015, p. 41), as well as quick hits for adjunct faculty and lecturers. The former author taught "in the Department of Psychology", where the "basic teaching philosophy is that students learn better and enjoy learning more when they think and do rather than listen".

Furthermore, according to Kılıçkaya (2022, p. 109), against the background the new normal of online *language* education, many studies had "shown that it is more efficient and effective to teach new words in a specific context" across "various activities which provide necessary comprehensible input".

Also in an English *language* teaching context, Höl and Küçük (2023, p. 228) showed that pre-service teacher and student shyness "appears as an important factor affecting teachers', pre-service teachers' and students' performance and how teachers handle classroom management situations".

Additionally, the purpose of the study reported on by Ayşenur and Höl (2023, p. 446) was to determine "the impact of DigiFlyers, a digital storytelling program," to improve "the listening comprehension and performance of young learners."

In addition, in the *Handbook of Research on Perspectives in Foreign Language Assessment*, the chapter reported on by Höl and Akman (2023, p. 329) aimed to examine "e-assessment in second/foreign language teaching-themed international publications from" Web of Science (WoS) using a bibliometric analysis method.

Benefits of Applying Learning Analytics in K-12 Education

There is significant research regarding online learning analytics and its benefits for Higher Education (HE). Most studies refer to how online learning analytics aid higher education institutions to make decisions about course offerings, identifying at risk students and categorizing which students will benefit from specific resources (Avella, et al., 2016). There is, however, a lack of research covering the benefits of learning analytics for primary or secondary schools, i.e., Basic Education as it is referred to in South Africa.

Furthermore, there is also a significant gap in research studies, linking online learning analytics and personalized learning. Questions, such as how can online learning analytics create or support opportunities for personalized learning, and if so, to what extent does this improve learning outcomes? What are the elements that create a successful learning experience to support personalized learning interventions? Furthermore, what are the benefits of introducing Information Communications Technology (ICT) tools such as learning analytics in education?

A scoping review by Bond, Viberg and Bergdahl (2023, p. 240) considered the current state of using learning analytics to measure and support K-12 student engagement. "Given the emergence and increasing application of learning analytics" within K-12 education, the paper published by the latter authors "focused on LA and student engagement in K-12 contexts and indexed in five international databases."

A systematic narrative review of learning analytics research in K-12 and schools was presented by Hirsto, Saqr, López-Pernas and Valtonen (2022, p. 1), including research where learning analytics was "the target of the study" (e.g., "dashboards) and papers in which learning analytics" on school-level featured, "as well as papers that deliver a real impact".

Towards demonstrating the value of learning analytics for K-12 education, the chapter by Baker and Koedinger (2018, p. 49) in a book on learning analytics in education indicated that in "recent years, educational data mining (EDM) and learning analytics ... methods have matured into approaches that can be used to analyze and enhance learning at" the K–12 level.

Perspectives on Learning Analytics in Mobile Learning Environments

Consequently, ICT provides significant benefits for the teaching and learning environment. Studies conducted by Delgardo et al. (2022) indicated that introducing the Web to learners improved their critical thinking and helped them to master learning, as well as allowing learners to work at their own pace. In other research findings related to ICTs in education, a case study conducted on mobile learning in schools, highlighted the following benefits, i.e., active engagement from learners, increased collaboration and communication between educator and learner, improved information literacy and digital citizenship (Chou, Block, & Jesness, 2012, p. 11). These are only some of the benefits of introducing ICTs into education and learning analytics could be a new and progressive way to evolve education in schools.

However, the journal article on educational technology development and exchange by the latter authors presented a case study of a mobile learning pilot project in K-12 schools, also warned that the "challenge for student learning is mainly distraction by the multitude of irrelevant" applications or 'apps' and student learning should be technology-supported "through innovative approaches to transform one-to-one learning".

Perspectives on Learning Analytics in Open Learning Environments

In a comparative study of students, academics, and industries, the paper on learning analytics of core competencies presented at the 23rd International Conference on Computers in Education (ICCE) by Chou, Tseng, Chen, et al. (2015) proposed "an approach for developing curriculum-level open student models. This approach" entailed evaluating student core competencies.

Following the theme of ICT in education, according to Brown (2012), the process of systematically collecting and analyzing large data sets from online sources for the purpose of improving learning processes is called learning analytics. Sources, such as Brown (2012) and Stewart (2017), will be interrogated to better understand the challenges and benefits of learning analytics. The research of leading thinkers in learning analytics will be examined to predict the future of learning (Niemi, Pea, Saxberg, & Clark, 2018). In addition, studies that focus on the different types of learning analytics tools such as learning dashboards (Jivet, Scheffel, Specht, & Drachsler, 2018) and Contextualized Attention Metadata (CAM) (Wolpers, Najjar, Verbert, & Duval, 2007), which combines different ICT tools will be compared.

Over the past decade, Kitto, et al (2020, p. v) had "witnessed a proliferation of new technologies involving an increasingly sophisticated use of data. In education, the field of" learning analytics is being taken beyond the Learning Management System (LMS) towards enabling connected learning via open-source analytics in 'the wild'. Popular ICT or LMS tools, such as Blackboard, Modular Object-Oriented Dynamic Learning Environment (MOODLE), Microsoft Teams Education Edition, Courseara, Udacity and edX will also form part of the comparative analysis as they have elements of built-in features or extensions for learning analytics (Clow, 2013). Research studies related to the relationship between learning analytics and personalized or adaptive learning will also form part of this study, as it relates to improving learning outcomes and strategies (Papamitsiou & Economides, 2014). A key success factor in implementing learning analytics in schools, is the digital savviness of educators and their ability to apply the findings to improve learning outcomes and personalized learning (Stewart, 2017). This key factor will also be evaluated to construct a rigorous professional development program for educators to apply and interpret the results of learning analytics.

In addition, an integral part of this study will also interrogate the validity and benefits of personalized learning pedagogy. Traditionally, personalized learning was not focused on evolving the learning process or providing sufficient collaboration to justify it as learner centric (McLoughlin, 2013). In addition, this study will focus on personalized learning and its relation to learning theories by Dewey (1938), Piaget (1983), Skinner (1974) and Vygotsky (1994). To ascertain the validity and relevance it is important that more modern learning styles such as personalized learning be scrutinized against the backdrop of traditional and well formulated learning theories. Furthermore, traditional theories will also be referenced and aligned to learning analytics models developed by other researchers in the field.

"Having set out learning analytics and its context in broad terms," the journal article on teaching in higher education by Clow (2013, p. 686) presented "a set of more concrete examples of learning analytics practice to provide a more grounded" overview of learning analytics.

MAIN FOCUS OF THE CHAPTER

Issues, Gaps, Problems

This section of the chapter will present the authors' perspectives on the issues, barriers, problems, etc., as these relate to the main theme of Emergent Practices of Learning Analytics in K-12 Classrooms and arguments supporting the authors' position on a framework for online learning analytics in schools as a precursor for personalization. It will also compare with what has been, or is currently being, done as it relates to the specific topic of the chapter.

Siemens and Gašević (2012) introduced a special issue on learning and knowledge analytics in the context of *educational technologies and society.*

In a similar context, the journal article on *educational technologies and society* by Wolpers, et al. (2007, p. 106) indicated that the "information overload in learning and teaching scenarios is a main hindering factor for efficient and effective learning. New methods are needed to help teachers and students in" tracking their actual usage, which could be achieved by implementing the attention metadata approach.

Likewise, a systematic literature review by Mian, Khalid, Qun and Ismail (2022, p. 2914) described the "application of Learning Analytics in educational" contexts, as well as exploring the advantages and "issues related to the use of Learning Analytics for" creative education.

According to the study reported on by Höl and Kasimi (2022, p. 421), English speaking anxiety-in-EFL classrooms is a growing dilemma. A review of research by the latter authors aimed "to discuss the current situation of research on speaking anxiety of" EFL learners through various variables.

"In addition to shifting the culture of the organization to be able to focus more on" learning analytics, the journal article on empowering teaching excellence by Stewart (2017, p. 101) benefited "from the knowledge gained through analytics", although "there is still a gap" when shifting from theory to practice.

As indicated by Jivet, et al. (2018, p. 31) in the proceedings of the 8th international conference on learning analytics and knowledge, learning "analytics can bridge the gap between learning sciences and data analytics, *leveraging* the expertise of both fields in exploring the vast amount of data generated" by preparing learning analytics dashboards for educational practice.

Although Pardo, Dawson, Gašević and Siemens (2019, p. 285) had "seen significant progress in the wealth of data captured in learning environments and the tools and techniques to deploy learning analytics methods, the true" supporting feedback processes at scale with an on-task hands-on tutorial were only revealed in the paper by the latter authors presented at the international learning analytics and knowledge conference.

In the era of 'big data', there are 'big opportunities' "for the higher education sector. However, there are also significant challenges to overcome before the potential of analytics can be" implemented towards improving the quality and productivity of the higher education sector (Siemens, et al., 2013, p. 1).

The study reported on by Chou, et al. (2018, p. 2169) pointed to the effect of learning analytics on graduates' academic records to reflect on a competency-based curriculum. As "classroom teaching in universities gathers limited data for analytics", the latter authors "applied learning analytics to the design of a competency-based curriculum and" reported their results in their journal article on *computer applications in engineering education.*

Ethical Considerations in K-12 Learning Analytics

Uunona and Goosen (2023) were *leveraging* ethical standards in artificial intelligence technologies towards a guideline for responsible teaching and learning applications.

In a review of the field of ethical issues in learning analytics, the journal article on *educational technology research and development* by Tzimas and Demetriadis (2021, p. 1101) described LA ethics as "an interdisciplinary field of study that addresses moral, legal, and social issues", with many "of the ethical issues raised" applying "equally to educational data sets of any size."

To begin with, Jones and Hinchliffe (2023, p. 2) outlined existing ethical issues in the context of learning analytics and asked whether academic library practitioners were prepared for learning analytics. Next, the latter authors described their "research questions and survey methodology" in their journal article on academic librarianship.

In a systematic literature review (2011–2021) of emerging trends and issues in Massive Open Online Course (MOOC) learning analytics empirical research, the journal article on *education and information technologies* by Zhu, Sari and Lee (2022, p. 10136) found that such "research and practice can help researchers and educators understand and address" applicable issues, including those that Zhu, et al. (2022, p. 10137) pointed out related to "the Society for Learning Analytics Research (SoLAR)".

Jones et al. (2020, p. 570) presented a comprehensive primer on library learning analytics practices, initiatives, and privacy issues, which indicated that the "adoption of these techniques leads to many professional ethics issues and practical concerns related to privacy." It also discussed "learning analytics, library adoption of these practices, and" identified "ethical and practical privacy issues".

Privacy, Transparency, and Trust in K-12 Learning Analytics

The ethical and privacy issues of learning analytics in higher education were discussed by Šlibar, Zlatić and Ređep (2021) in the 14th annual International Conference of Education, Research, and Innovation (ICERI) proceedings. Although these need to be weighed against "the opportunity to improve learning and teaching processes through the application of learning analytics", as well as an improved "understanding of learning habits and teaching designs".

Unresolved privacy and ethics issues related to learning analytics in higher education and academic librarianship were presented by Currier (2021, p. 117) regarding emerging library trends and information perspectives. "Learning analytics involve big data collection" and analysis, which could lead to "privacy concerns about learning analytics" that can be mitigated by attention to ethics of the procedures used for data "gathered for the purpose of learning analytics."

A complete validated learning analytics framework for designing issues from data use perspective were provided by Tlili, Essalmi, Jemni, Kinshuk and Chen (2019, p. 59) in an international journal on ICT education. Areas of the research interests of the latter authors included "learning analytics; learning technologies; mobile, ubiquitous and location aware learning systems; cognitive profiling; and interactive technologies."

Barriers to K-12 Learning Analytics

Klein, Lester, Rangwala and Johri (2019, p. 608), in their journal article on computing in higher education, reported on organizational incentives and technological "barriers related to technologies that inform both perception and adoption of learning analytics tools" in higher education, based on insights from users. "These incentives and barriers include personal and institutional commitment to technologies".

To meet the overarching aim of the paper by Jones (2019, p. 150) in the proceedings of the 36th International Conference on Innovation, Practice and Research in the Use of Educational Technologies in Tertiary Education (ASCILITE), the latter author considered "the enablers and barriers to academics" and showed how knowledge can be gained "of the barriers, enablers, and complex motivational issues" related to staff adoption of learning analytics, towards insights for professional learning opportunities from an Australian university.

Towards overcoming the barriers to health information, Veena and Gowrishankar (2021, p. 484), in their paper from *Image Processing and Capsule Networks (ICIPCN 2020)*, were using various "algorithms and techniques in machine learning … compared and classified based on the applications of Healthcare Analytics."

"Game learning analytics (GLA) is" one of the emerging trends regarding technologies "that facilitates teachers' evidence-based pedagogical design and assessments. Despite its affordances and potential in K–12 classrooms," several barriers remain to in-service teachers' integration of game learning analytics in K–12 classrooms (Liu, Ng, Hu, Ma, & Lai, 2023, p. 1).

Perspectives on Learning Analytics in Multimodal Learning Environments

The journal article on Science, Technology, Engineering and Mathematics (STEM) education research by Schneider, et al. (2020, p. 91) described "a class on Multimodal Learning Analytics" aimed at lowering barriers to *accessing* sensor data in education based on lessons learned from teaching multimodal learning analytics to educators.

Exploration of student cognitive and affective states during problem solving through multimodal data can benefit from lessons learned from a *programming* activity (Mangaroska, Sharma, Gašević, & Giannakos, 2022, p. 40). In their journal article on computer-assisted learning, the latter authors indicated that problem-solving "is a multidimensional and dynamic process that requires and interlinks cognitive, metacognitive, and affective dimensions of learning. However, current approaches practiced in computing education research (CER) are not sufficient to capture information beyond the basic programming process data".

Statement of the Problem

Perspectives on Learning Analytics in Blended Learning Environments

Technology in education is a powerful tool. Since the rise of online or *blended learning environments*, learning analytics had supported the development of new learning and assessment methodologies and identified **gaps** in learning management systems and tools. In an **issue** brief on enhancing teaching and learning through the use of concepts such as educational data mining, data visualization, machine learning and artificial intelligence, which had become synonymous with learning analytics, Bienkowski, Feng and Means (2012, p. 1) from the Office of Educational

Technology in the United States of America indicated that as more "commerce, entertainment, communication, and learning are occurring over the Web, the amount of" online data activities generated is skyrocketing. The **problem** is that despite the increase in learning analytics research, there is still insufficient data related to primary and secondary education in schools and to support how or if it influences learning outcomes. For example, there is a lack of research focusing on assessing how learning interventions change learner behavior or improve education through stakeholders' ability to interpret learning data or educator's competency to apply analytical tools. In addition, a deeper look into online learning analytics is necessary to evaluate the relationship to personalized learning and adaptive learning design.

A systematic literature review of analytics-driven design to enhance learning presented in the journal article on learning technologies by Mangaroska and Giannakos (2018, p. 516) indicated that as "the fields of learning analytics and learning design mature, the convergence and synergies between the two are becoming an important area for research." As much as this study answers a request from the latter authors for the development of a framework that aligns with learning analytics and learning theory, this study takes it one step further by examining to what extent learning outcomes can thus be improved.

Significance of the Study

The purpose of the chapter on the Industry Revolution 4.0 and its impact on education by Minasi (2023) in the *Encyclopedia of Data Science and Machine Learning* was "to discuss what will happen to the education system in the area of" the "Industrial Revolution 4.0. Information management is the most challenging problem faced".

The fourth industrial revolution has led to a significant paradigm shift in education. Disruptive technologies, such as the internet of things, artificial intelligence, machine learning and learning analytics, had led to new opportunities and **challenges** in education. According to a systematic literature review by Avella, et al. (2016, p. 13), higher "education for *the 21st century* continues to promote discoveries in the field through learning analytics". Learning analytics methods provide **benefits** for curriculum development, improving learning outcomes and behavior, personalized learning, and improved educator performance. Furthermore, learning analytics allow for real-time feedback for every learner and inform areas of improvement for educators. "The **problem** is that the rapid embrace of" LA diverts educators' focus from **challenges** in higher education.

Innovation in education is critical to learner success and improving the quality of teaching. Learners' success as it relates to the construction of personalized learning environments requires technological learning resources (Ramírez-Mera & Tur, 2023) that lead to better retention of information and processing at a deeper level.

Furthermore, personalized learning enabled by technologies and analytical tools can prepare learners for a global and competitive workforce.

Also, in the *Encyclopedia of Data Science and Machine Learning*, Marmo (2023) indicated that e-learning "is conducted via electronic media, typically the internet, in order to transfer knowledge to students." However, many "**problems** are involved in content creation" and assessment, and the personalized and adaptive learning tools and artificial intelligence required in e-learning systems highlight that the roadmap to success is different for each learner.

Research Questions

The research questions of this study include:

1. What are the characteristics for creating a successful learning environment?
2. How does personalized learning influence learning outcomes?
3. What are the functionalities of an effective learning analytics tool?
4. What are the most efficient methods that exist to digitize curriculum?
5. How can one create an effective professional development program to support educators with the application and interpretation of learning analytics tools?
6. What is the relationship between personalized learning and learning analytics?

To inform this study and the conceptualization of an effective framework for learning analytics implementation, reference to models employed by other researchers will be examined. Models such as the Learning Awareness Tools User eXperience (LATUX) workflow, propose a five-stage approach that includes **problem** identification, low-fidelity prototyping e.g., paper-based visualizations, high fidelity prototyping, e.g., simulated lessons, pilot studies and classroom use (Martinez-Maldonado, et al., 2015). The LATUX framework aligns to the **problem** statement of this study, as it relates to designing of an iterative workflow for validating and deploying of learning analytics.

A multi-level learning analytics framework and methods for learning analytics integrated learning design that will be referenced in this study promotes alignment to pedagogical intentions, technology tools that can be used by educators to design better learning experiences and a scaffolding process to support educators (Law & Liang, 2020, p. 98). The journal article on learning analytics by the latter authors described "the learning analytics and feedback in each case," as well as "the learning analytics to be" used. The LA framework is "integral to the learning design (LD) rather than constructed after the LD is completed" and is a necessary inclusion in this study, as it supports and guides educators with the implementation of learning analytical tools. In addition, Del Blanco, Serrano, Freire, Martínez-Ortiz and Fernández-Manjón

(2013) emphasized that the goals of learning analytics implementation are achievable when e-Learning standards such as Institute of Electrical and Electronics Engineers (IEEE) Standard for Learning Technology and Experience API are applied. The LATUX workflow, LA framework and e-Learning standards are examples of the models developed and referenced by other researchers which will help structure the framework for this study.

The study presented at the seventh conference on Learning@Scale by Shen, Liang, Law, Hemberg and O'Reilly (2020, p. 136) was "based on research in the areas of learning design and learning analytics that tries to achieve the goal of" understanding learner behavior through "learning design informed learning analytics."

Research Methodology

To investigate the **problem** statement for this study, i.e., how can learning analytics be applied to primary and secondary education and support the improvement of learning outcomes in schools, the research methodology listed below will be followed.

Research Approach

The research approach for this study will apply a mixed method, to ensure that each approach, i.e., qualitative, and quantitative will provide a more complete and comprehensive understanding of the research **problem** (Almalki, 2016). A qualitative approach is critical in this study to understand the strategies and behaviors required by research participants that lead to a successful learning experience. Furthermore, to grasp and better understand how personalized learning influences learning outcomes, a qualitative approach is required. On the other hand, a quantitative approach will allow quantifying behaviors of research participants to predict how learning analytics influences learning outcomes. A quantitative research approach will also be applied to analyze and interpret the data derived from the digital learning experience. The success of this study is also heavily reliant on testing by quantifying the benefits of various learning analytical tools. Lastly, this study will test the validity of various learning analytical models developed by other researchers to derive at a point of **conclusion** about the research **problem**.

Instrumentation and Data Collection Techniques

As part of the qualitative evaluation in this study and data collection, action research will be carried out. Action research allows for the researcher who is part of the same community i.e., education community to form a community of practice to solve the **problem** statement, how can learning analytics be applied to primary and secondary education and support the improvement of learning outcomes in schools. In conjunction to the qualitative data collection method, the main data collection method for the quantitative approach will be collected through surveys with closed ended questions that allow for quantifying the results according to percentages, tables, and graphs. Although surveys will be used, observations during the communities of practice will be used to support the survey findings.

Data Analysis

To conduct a thorough analysis of the research **problem**, the data analysis techniques are described below.

Firstly, a cyclical approach to analysis of the qualitative data collection method i.e., action research and observations will be conducted. This cyclical approach is known as the constant comparative method which comprises of joint coding and analysis during a continuous review of data to progressively form categories (Glaser & Strauss, 1967). This type of analysis includes four stages i.e., comparing incidents applicable to each category, integrating categories and their properties, delimiting the theory, and finally writing the theory (Glaser B. G., 1965). According to Westbrook (1994), the consistent comparative method leads to more accurate coding categories, its dimensions, identifying its limitations and the relationship between categories.

Juxtaposed to the constant comparative approach applied for the analysis of the qualitative data, the descriptive statistics technique will be applied to analyze the quantitative data collected. Fisher and Schneider (2016, p. 238) defined descriptive statistics as procedures "that allow researchers to describe, organize and summarize raw data". Using the raw data collected from the surveys can be described, organized, and presented as tables, various types of graphs, i.e., line graph, pie chart, scatter plots and histograms. This technique provides for a visual representation of the data.

SOLUTIONS AND RECOMMENDATIONS

This section of the chapter will discuss **solutions and recommendations** in dealing with the **issues, barriers** or **problems** presented in the preceding section.

Despite the apparent opportunities and benefits of learning analytics, there are significant **challenges** that impede progress. Tracking unsupervised learning had always been **problematic** and therefore learning analytics provides a **solution** to assess the progress per learner (DiCerbo, Shute, & Kim, 2017, p. 1). The chapter on learning, design, and technology in an international compendium of theory, research, practice, and policy by the latter authors indicated that several assessment experts had "advanced a vision of assessment in schools that relies on ongoing, performance-based, formative assessment. While there are many" **benefits** of learning analytics, since "the initial efforts to make sense of large learning-related datasets", LA had still not been implemented to support large-size classes (Joksimović, Kovanović, & Dawson, 2019, p. 37).

The journey of learning analytics this far had shown these to be powerful technological tools "for capturing various proxies of learning" that can support personalized, timely assessment, feedback, and learning, as indicated by researchers in the Higher Education Research and Development Society of Australasia (HERDSA) review of higher education.

The chapter by Griffiths (2020, p. 40), as part of a book offering radical **solutions**, open science, and an open approach to boost higher education, cited references on learning analytics, which "the Society for Learning Analytics Research" published. "It soon became clear that this work raised **ethical issues**, and" had "been an ongoing **concern** since the early days of" LA. Important **ethical issues** related to learning analytics in their historical context had "been identified, the possible courses of action analyzed in depth, and **recommendations**" were made (Griffiths, 2020, p. 41).

Barriers to K-12 Learning Analytics

Learning analytics technologies provide effective **solutions** to various **problems**. In the contexts of **emerging trends** and **barriers regarding learning analytics** in European higher education, as well as computers and education, Tsai, et al. (2020, p. 12) had "made some institutional decisions based on the results of learning analytics".

FUTURE RESEARCH DIRECTIONS

This section of the chapter will discuss **future** and **emerging trends** and provide insight about the **future** of the theme of **Emergent Practices of Learning Analytics in K-12 Classrooms**, from the perspective of the chapter focus on **a framework for online learning analytics in schools as a precursor for personalization**. The viability of a paradigm, model, implementation **issues** of proposed programs, etc., may also be included in this section. **Future research directions for K-12 learning analytics** will finally be suggested.

In terms of **emerging trends** (at the time) in the discipline of learning analytics, Siemens (2013, p. 1385), as an American behavioral scientist, did not attempt to "either modify or extend the range of features within established products. However, the growth in this field" had "also prompted the emergence of a new suite of commercial analytics tools". A bibliometric analysis in an international online journal article on education and teaching by Höl (2022, p. 2058) examined twenty-eight years on "the characteristics of the overall" **emerging** "research **trends**, patterns of productivity, and publications on" 'Assessing Pronunciation in English as a Second/Foreign Language Classes' (1993-2021).

In the IEEE Transactions on **Emerging trends** and Topics in Computing, Chou, Tseng, Chih et al. (2015) were using "**analytics** of student **learning** and" reflection, which were "applied to promote awareness, reflection, self-assessment, learning autonomy, planning, independent learning," etc. The latter authors visualized **learning analytics** as part of open student models of core competencies at the curriculum level. Ferguson, et al. (2019) offered expert views on moving forward with learning analytics in their journal article on learning analytics. **Emerging** technology **trends** presented by Gašević, et al. (2015, p. 65) included "learning analytics research to outline a few of the major topics that the learning analytics", as well as not forgetting that learning analytics are about learning.

Future Research Directions for K-12 Learning Analytics

In the *Handbook of Research on **Perspectives** in Foreign Language Assessment*, the chapter by Kavaklı Ulutaş (2023, p. 1) was revisiting the past to shape and "forecast the **future** of foreign language assessment". "Hailing the value of foreign language assessment," the latter author embarked "on reflections from classroom practices in order to" complete assessments of learners' foreign language abilities. According to DiCerbo, et al. (2017), the **future** of assessment in technology-rich environments should take on board psychometric **considerations**. As Niemi et al. (2018, p. xvii) were considering the **future** of learning analytics in education, one of the **emerging trends** seemed "clear: the accelerating rate of change as education continues to undergo fundamental transformations as traditional analog tools are replaced by digital systems and analytic tools."

CONCLUSION

This section of the chapter will provide a discussion of the overall coverage and concluding remarks. In **conclusion**, the data analysis techniques mentioned in this chapter, i.e., the constant comparative method and descriptive statistics, will lead to greater insights about learning analytics in relation to personalized learning.

REFERENCES

Almalki, S. (2016). Integrating quantitative and qualitative data in mixed methods research--challenges and benefits. *Journal of education and learning, 5*(3), 288-296.

Avella, J. T., Kebritchi, M., Nunn, S. G., & Kanai, T. (2016). Learning analytics methods, benefits, and challenges in higher education: A systematic literature review. *Online Learning : the Official Journal of the Online Learning Consortium, 20*(2), 13–29.

Ayşenur, A. V., & Höl, D. (2023). DigiFlyers:a digital storytelling program to improve the listening performance of young learners. *Mehmet Akif Ersoy Üniversitesi Eğitim Fakültesi Dergisi*, (66), 446–474.

Baker, R. S., & Koedinger, K. R. (2018). Towards demonstrating the value of learning analytics for K-12 education. In *Learning analytics in education* (pp. 49–62). Information Age Publishing.

Bienkowski, M., Feng, M., & Means, B. (2012). *Enhancing Teaching and Learning through Educational Data Mining and Learning Analytics: An Issue Brief.* Office of Educational Technology, US Department of Education. https://files.eric.ed.gov/fulltext/ED611199.pdf

Bond, M., Viberg, O., & Bergdahl, N. (2023, March). The current state of using learning analytics to measure and support K-12 student engagement: A scoping review. *13th International Learning Analytics and Knowledge (LAK) Conference* (pp. 240-249). Arlington: ACM.

Brown, M. (2012). Learning analytics: Moving from concept to practice. *EDUCAUSE Learning Initiative, 7*, 1–5.

Chou, C. C., Block, L., & Jesness, R. (2012). A case study of mobile learning pilot project in K-12 schools. [JETDE]. *Journal of Educational Technology Development and Exchange, 5*(2), 11–26. doi:10.18785/jetde.0502.02

Chou, C. Y., Tseng, S. F., Chen, Z. H., Chao, P. Y., Peng, K. C., & Lin, Y. L. (2015). *Learning analytics of core competencies: A comparative study of students, academics, and industries. 23rd International Conference on Computers in Education (ICCE).* Asia-Pacific Society for Computers in Education. https://scholar.lib.ntnu.edu.tw/en/publications/learning-analytics-of-core-competencies-a-comparative-study-of-st-2

Chou, C. Y., Tseng, S. F., Chih, W. C., Chen, Z. H., Chao, P. Y., Lai, K. R., Chan, C.-L., Yu, L.-C., & Lin, Y. L. (2015). Open student models of core competencies at the curriculum level: Using learning analytics for student reflection. *IEEE Transactions on Emerging Topics in Computing*, *5*(1), 32–44. https://ieeexplore.ieee.org/document/7335629. doi:10.1109/TETC.2015.2501805

Chou, C. Y., Tseng, S. F., Wang, C. J., Chao, P. Y., Chen, Z. H., Lai, K. R., Chan, C.-L., & Yu, L. C. (2018). Learning analytics on graduates' academic records to reflect on a competency-based curriculum. *Computer Applications in Engineering Education*, *26*(6), 2168–2182. doi:10.1002/cae.22019

Clow, D. (2013). An overview of learning analytics. *Teaching in Higher Education*, *18*(6), 683–695. doi:10.1080/13562517.2013.827653

Currier, C. (2021). Unresolved privacy and ethics issues related to learning analytics in higher education and academic librarianship. *Emerging Library & Information Perspectives*, *4*(1), 117–142. doi:10.5206/elip.v4i1.13463

Del Blanco, Á., Serrano, Á., Freire, M., Martínez-Ortiz, I., & Fernández-Manjón, B. (2013, March). E-Learning standards and learning analytics. Can data collection be improved by using standard data models? *Global Engineering Education Conference (EDUCON)* (pp. 1255-1261). IEEE. 10.1109/EduCon.2013.6530268

Delgardo, M., Higgins, D., McCormick, K. L., Reid, P., Canoll, P., & McCormick, P. C. (2022). Clinical characteristics, outcomes, and pathology analysis in patients with dorsal arachnoid web. *Neurosurgery*, *90*(5), 581–587. doi:10.1227/neu.0000000000001884 PMID:35290255

Dewey, J. (1938). *Experience and education*. Macmillan.

DiCerbo, K., Shute, V., & Kim, Y. J. (2017). The future of assessment in technology rich environments: Psychometric considerations. In *Learning, design, and technology: An international compendium of theory, research, practice, and policy* (pp. 1–21). Springer. doi:10.1007/978-3-319-17727-4_66-1

Dietz-Uhler, B., & Hurn, J. E. (2013). Using learning analytics to predict (and improve) student success: A faculty perspective. *Journal of Interactive Online Learning*, *12*(1), 17–26.

Dietz-Uhler, B., & Hurn, J. E. (2015). Strategies for engagement in online courses: Engaging with the content, instructor, and other students. In *Quick Hits for Adjunct Faculty and Lecturers* (pp. 41–44). Indiana University Press.

Ferguson, R., & Clow, D. (2017). Learning analytics: avoiding failure. *Educause Review Online, 31*. https://oro.open.ac.uk/50385/

Ferguson, R., Clow, D., Griffiths, D., & Brasher, A. (2019). Moving forward with learning analytics: Expert views. *Journal of Learning Analytics*, *6*(3), 43–59. doi:10.18608/jla.2019.63.8

Fisher, M., & Schneider, Z. (2016). Analysing data in quantitative research. In Z. Schneider, D. Whitehead, G. Lo-Biondo-Wood, & J. Haber (Eds.), *Nursing and midwifery research methods and appraisal for evidence-based practice* (pp. 213–235). Elsevier.

Gašević, D., Dawson, S., & Siemens, G. (2015). Let's not forget: Learning analytics are about learning. *TechTrends*, *59*(1), 64–71. doi:10.100711528-014-0822-x

Gašević, D., Kovanović, V., & Joksimović, S. (2017). Piecing the learning analytics puzzle: A consolidated model of a field of research and practice. *Learning: Research and Practice*, *3*(1), 63–78.

Glaser, B., & Strauss, A. (1967). *The discovery of grounded theory*. Aldine Publishing Company.

Glaser, B. G. (1965). The constant comparative method of qualitative analysis. *Social Problems*, *12*(4), 436–445. doi:10.2307/798843

Goosen, L. (2018). Sustainable and inclusive quality education through research informed practice on information and communication technologies in education. In L. Webb (Ed.), *Proceedings of the 26th Conference of the Southern African Association for Research in Mathematics, Science and Technology Education (SAARMSTE)* (pp. 215-228). Gabarone: University of Botswana.

Goosen, L., & Van Heerden, D. (2017). Beyond the horizon of learning programming with educational technologies. In U. I. Ogbonnaya, & S. Simelane-Mnisi (Ed.), *Proceedings of the South Africa International Conference on Educational Technologies* (pp. 78 - 90). Pretoria: African Academic Research Forum.

Griffiths, D. (2020). The ethical issues of learning analytics in their historical context. In *Radical solutions and open science: An open approach to boost higher education* (pp. 39–55). Springer. doi:10.1007/978-981-15-4276-3_3

Hancı-Azizoglu, E. B., & Kavaklı Ulutaş, N. (2021). Creative digital writing: A multilingual perspective. In *Digital pedagogies and the transformation of language education* (pp. 250–266). IGI Global. doi:10.4018/978-1-7998-6745-6.ch013

Hirsto, L., Saqr, M., López-Pernas, S., & Valtonen, T. (2022). A systematic narrative review of learning analytics research in K-12 and schools. *Proceedings of the Finnish Learning Analytics and Artificial Intelligence in Education Conference (FLAIEC)*. Joensuu, Finland. https://ceur-ws.org/Vol-3383/FLAIEC22_paper_9536.pdf

Höl, D. (2022). A bibliometric analysis of twenty-eight years on 'assessing pronunciation in English as a second/foreign language classes' (1993-2021). *International Online Journal of Education & Teaching*, *9*(4), 2057–2075.

Höl, D. (2023). Standardized testing in Turkey: EFL teachers' perceptions and experiences on Cambridge YLE exams. *International Journal of Curriculum and Instruction*, *15*(2), 984–1007.

Höl, D., & Akman, E. (2023). A bibliometric analysis on "e-assessment in teaching English as a foreign language" publications in web of science (WoS). In D. Köksal, N. Kavaklı Ulutaş, & S. Arslan (Eds.), *Handbook of Research on Perspectives in Foreign Language Assessment* (pp. 329–355). IGI Global. doi:10.4018/978-1-6684-5660-6.ch016

Höl, D., & Kasımi, Y. (2022). A growing dilemma: English speaking anxiety-in-EFL classrooms: A review of research. *RumeliDE Dil ve Edebiyat Araştırmaları Dergisi*, (28), 421–438. doi:10.29000/rumelide.1132581

Höl, D., & Küçük, O. (2023). Pre-service teacher and student shyness: English language teaching context. *Van Yüzüncü Yıl Üniversitesi Eğitim Fakültesi Dergisi*, *20*(1), 228–253. doi:10.33711/yyuefd.1118901

Jivet, I., Scheffel, M., Specht, M., & Drachsler, H. (2018, March). License to evaluate: Preparing learning analytics dashboards for educational practice. *Proceedings of the 8th international conference on learning analytics and knowledge* (pp. 31-40). Sydney, NSW, Australia: ACM. 10.1145/3170358.3170421

Joksimović, S., Kovanović, V., & Dawson, S. (2019). The journey of learning analytics. *HERDSA Review of Higher Education*, *6*, 27–63.

Jones, H. (2019, January). Barriers, enablers, and motivations for staff adoption of learning analytics: Insights for professional learning opportunities from an Australian university. *Proceedings of the 36th International Conference on Innovation, Practice and Research in the Use of Educational Technologies in Tertiary Education (ASCILITE)* (pp. 149-158). Singapore: University of Social Sciences.

Jones, K. M., Briney, K. A., Goben, A., Salo, D., Asher, A., & Perry, M. R. (2020). A comprehensive primer to library learning analytics practices, initiatives, and privacy issues. *College & Research Libraries*, *81*(3), 570–591. doi:10.5860/crl.81.3.570

Jones, K. M., & Hinchliffe, L. J. (2023). Ethical issues and learning analytics: Are academic library practitioners prepared? *Journal of Academic Librarianship*, *49*(1), 102621. doi:10.1016/j.acalib.2022.102621

Kasimi, Y., & Höl, D. (2023). A qualitative study on listening skills in Turkish EFL classes. [Research on Youth and Language]. *Novitas-ROYAL*, *17*(1), 91–107.

Kavaklı Ulutaş, N. (2023). Revisiting the past to shape the future: Assessment of foreign language abilities. In D. Köksal, N. Kavaklı Ulutaş, & S. Arslan (Eds.), *Handbook of Research on Perspectives in Foreign Language Assessment* (pp. 1–10). IGI Global. doi:10.4018/978-1-6684-5660-6.ch001

Kavaklı Ulutaş, N., & Abuşka, A. (2023). Language teachers' investment in digital multimodal composing (DMC) as a manifold application of computer-mediated communication. In Multidisciplinary Applications of Computer-Mediated Communication (pp. 17-30). IGI Global.

Kılıçkaya, F. (2022). Teaching vocabulary online using internet resources: A language teacher's experience. In E. Duruk (Ed.), *The New Normal of Online Language Education* (pp. 109–124).

Kitto, K., Lupton, M., Bruza, P., Mallett, D., Banks, J., Dawson, S., & Siemens, G. (2020). *Learning analytics beyond the LMS: Enabling connected learning via open source analytics in "the wild"*. Australian Government Department of Education, Skills and Employmen. https://opus.lib.uts.edu.au/bitstream/10453/152210/2/ID14-3821_Kitto_Report_2020.pdf

Klein, C., Lester, J., Rangwala, H., & Johri, A. (2019). Technological barriers and incentives to learning analytics adoption in higher education: Insights from users. *Journal of Computing in Higher Education*, *31*(3), 604–625. doi:10.100712528-019-09210-5

Law, N., & Liang, L. (2020). A multilevel framework and method for learning analytics integrated learning design. *Journal of Learning Analytics*, *7*(3), 98–117. doi:10.18608/jla.2020.73.8

Li, M., & Wong, K. K. (2019). Pedagogical shifts: Learning analytics of mobile learning using rain classroom in theater arts classes. *International Conference on Applied Education, Technology and Innovation.* https://repository.vtc.edu.hk/thei-aeti-2019/Day3-Session13/Session13/1/

Lim, L., Dawson, S., Joksimovic, S., & Gašević, D. (2019, March). Exploring students' sensemaking of learning analytics dashboards: Does frame of reference make a difference? *Proceedings of the 9th international conference on learning analytics & knowledge* (pp. 250-259). ACM. 10.1145/3303772.3303804

Liu, Y., Ng, J., Hu, X., Ma, Z., & Lai, X. (2023). Adopt or abandon: Facilitators and barriers of in-service teachers' integration of game learning analytics in K–12 classrooms? *Computers & Education*. doi:10.1016/j.compedu.2023.104951

Mangaroska, K., & Giannakos, M. (2018). Learning analytics for learning design: A systematic literature review of analytics-driven design to enhance learning. *IEEE Transactions on Learning Technologies*, *12*(4), 516–534. doi:10.1109/TLT.2018.2868673

Mangaroska, K., Sharma, K., Gašević, D., & Giannakos, M. (2022). Exploring students' cognitive and affective states during problem solving through multimodal data: Lessons learned from a programming activity. *Journal of Computer Assisted Learning*, *38*(1), 40–59. doi:10.1111/jcal.12590

Marmo, R. (2023). Artificial intelligence in e-learning systems. In *Encyclopedia of Data Science and Machine Learning* (pp. 1531–1545). IGI Global. https://www.igi-global.com/chapter/artificial-intelligence-in-e-learning-systems/317567

Martinez-Maldonado, R., Pardo, A., Mirriahi, N., Yacef, K., Kay, J., & Clayphan, A. (2015). LATUX: An iterative workflow for designing, validating, and deploying learning analytics visualizations. *Journal of Learning Analytics*, *2*(3), 9–39. doi:10.18608/jla.2015.23.3

McLoughlin, C. E. (2013, June). The pedagogy of personalised learning: exemplars, MOOCS and related learning theories. *EdMedia+ Innovate Learning* (pp. 266-270). Association for the Advancement of Computing in Education (AACE).

Mian, Y. S., Khalid, F., Qun, A. W., & Ismail, S. S. (2022). Learning analytics in Education, advantages and issues: A systematic literature review. *Creative Education*, *13*(9), 2913–2920. doi:10.4236/ce.2022.139183

Minasi, R. (2023). Industry revolution 4.0 and its impact on education. In J. Wang (Ed.), *Encyclopedia of Data Science and Machine Learning* (pp. 2211–2222). IGI Global. https://www.igi-global.com/chapter/industry-revolution-40-and-its-impact-on-education/317617

New Media Consortium (NMC). (2015). *NMC Horizon Report*. British Columbia Teachers' Federation.

Niemi, D., Pea, R. D., Saxberg, B., & Clark, R. E. (Eds.). (2018). *Learning analytics in education*. Information Age Publishing, Inc.

Ölmez, R., & Kavaklı Ulutaş, N. (2023). A diachronic view into an understanding of technology acceptance: Where to go through TAM for teacher education from global to local? [IJELTAL]. *Indonesian Journal of English Language Teaching and Applied Linguistics*, *7*(2), 359–377.

Papamitsiou, Z., & Economides, A. A. (2014). Learning analytics and educational data mining in practice: A systematic literature review of empirical evidence. *Journal of Educational Technology & Society*, *17*(4), 49–64.

Pardo, A., Dawson, S., Gašević, D., & Siemens, G. (2019). *Supporting feedback processes at scale with ontask a hands-on tutorial*. International Learning Analytics & Knowledge Conference.

Pardo, A., & Siemens, G. (2014). Ethical and privacy principles for learning analytics. *British Journal of Educational Technology*, *45*(3), 438–450. doi:10.1111/bjet.12152

Piaget, J. (1983). Piaget's Theory. In Handbook of Child Psychology. New York: Wiley.

Ramírez-Mera, U., & Tur, G. (2023). Metacognitive skills and emotions in the construction of Personal Learning Environments. [RED]. *Revista de Educación a Distancia*, *23*(71). Advance online publication. doi:10.6018/red.526831

Schneider, B., Reilly, J., & Radu, I. (2020). Lowering barriers for accessing sensor data in education: Lessons learned from teaching multimodal learning analytics to educators. *Journal for STEM Education Research*, *3*(1), 91–124. doi:10.100741979-020-00027-x

Shen, H., Liang, L., Law, N., Hemberg, E., & O'Reilly, U. M. (2020, August). Understanding learner behavior through learning design informed learning analytics. *Proceedings of the Seventh Conference on Learning@Scale* (pp. 135-145). ACM. 10.1145/3386527.3405919

Siemens, G. (2013). Learning analytics: The emergence of a discipline. *The American Behavioral Scientist*, *57*(10), 1380–1400. doi:10.1177/0002764213498851

Siemens, G., Dawson, S., & Lynch, G. (2013, December). *Improving the quality and productivity of the higher education sector. Policy and Strategy for Systems-Level Deployment of Learning Analytics.* Canberra: Society for Learning Analytics Research for the Australian Office for Learning and Teaching. https://ltr.edu.au/resources/SoLAR_Report_2014.pdf

Siemens, G., & Gašević, D. (2012). Special issue on learning and knowledge analytics. *Journal of Educational Technology & Society*, *15*(3), 1–163.

Skinner, B. F. (1974). *About behaviorism*. Knopf.

Šlibar, B., Zlatić, L., & Ređep, N. B. (2021). *Ethical and privacy issues of learning analytics in higher education. 14th annual International Conference of Education, Research and Innovation (ICERI) Proceedings*. IATED. https://library.iated.org/view/SLIBAR2021ETH

Stewart, C. (2017). Learning Analytics: Shifting from theory to practice. *Journal on Empowering Teaching Excellence*, *1*(1), 95–105.

Tlili, A., Essalmi, F., Jemni, M., Kinshuk, P., & Chen, N. S. (2019). A complete validated learning analytics framework: Designing issues from data use perspective. [IJICTE]. *International Journal of Information and Communication Technology Education*, *15*(3), 42–59. doi:10.4018/IJICTE.2019070104

Tsai, Y. S., Rates, D., Moreno-Marcos, P. M., Muñoz-Merino, P. J., Jivet, I., Scheffel, M., Drachsler, H., Delgado Kloos, C., & Gašević, D. (2020). Learning analytics in European higher education—Trends and barriers. *Computers & Education*, *155*, 103933. doi:10.1016/j.compedu.2020.103933

Tzimas, D., & Demetriadis, S. (2021). Ethical issues in learning analytics: A review of the field. *Educational Technology Research and Development*, *69*(2), 1101–1133. doi:10.100711423-021-09977-4

Uunona, G. N., & Goosen, L. (2023). Leveraging ethical standards in artificial intelligence technologies: A guideline for responsible teaching and learning applications. In M. Garcia, M. Lopez Cabrera, & R. de Almeida (Eds.), *Handbook of Research on Instructional Technologies in Health Education and Allied Disciplines* (pp. 310–330). IGI Global., doi:10.4018/978-1-6684-7164-7.ch014

Veena, A., & Gowrishankar, S. (2021). *Healthcare Analytics: Overcoming the barriers to health information using machine learning algorithms. Image Processing and Capsule Networks (ICIPCN 2020)*. Springer.

Vygotsky, L. (1994). Academic concepts in school aged children. In R. van der Veer, & J. Valsiner (Eds.), The Vygotsky reader (Original work published 1934 ed., pp. 111–126). Oxford: Blackwell.

Westbrook, L. (1994). Qualitative research methods: A review of major stages, data analysis techniques, and quality controls. *Library & Information Science Research*, *16*(3), 241–254. doi:10.1016/0740-8188(94)90026-4

Wolpers, M., Najjar, J., Verbert, K., & Duval, E. (2007). Tracking actual usage: The attention metadata approach. *Journal of Educational Technology & Society, 10*(3), 106–121.

Zhu, M., Sari, A. R., & Lee, M. M. (2022). Trends and issues in MOOC learning analytics empirical research: A systematic literature review (2011–2021). *Education and Information Technologies, 27*(7), 10135–10160. doi:10.100710639-022-11031-6

ADDITIONAL READING

Blikstein, P. (2013, April). Multimodal learning analytics. In *Proceedings of the third international conference on learning analytics and knowledge* (pp. 102-106). ACM. 10.1145/2460296.2460316

Chatti, M. A., Dyckhoff, A. L., Schroeder, U., & Thüs, H. (2012). A reference model for learning analytics. *International Journal of Technology Enhanced Learning, 4*(5-6), 318–331. doi:10.1504/IJTEL.2012.051815

Dawson, S., Joksimovic, S., Poquet, O., & Siemens, G. (2019, March). Increasing the impact of learning analytics. In *Proceedings of the 9th international conference on learning analytics & knowledge* (pp. 446-455). ACM. 10.1145/3303772.3303784

Ferguson, R. (2012). Learning analytics: Drivers, developments, and challenges. *International Journal of Technology Enhanced Learning, 4*(5-6), 304–317. doi:10.1504/IJTEL.2012.051816

Ferguson, R., & Buckingham Shum, S. (2012, April). Social learning analytics: five approaches. In *Proceedings of the 2nd international conference on learning analytics and knowledge* (pp. 23-33). ACM.

Lang, C., Siemens, G., Wise, A., & Gasevic, D. (Eds.). (2017). Handbook of learning analytics. New York: Society for Learning Analytics and Research (SOLAR). doi:10.18608/hla17

Leitner, P., Khalil, M., & Ebner, M. (2017). Learning analytics in higher education—a literature review. In A. Peña-Ayala (Ed.), *Learning analytics: Fundaments, applications, and trends: A view of the current state of the art to enhance E-learning* (Vol. 94, pp. 1–23). Springer. doi:10.1007/978-3-319-52977-6_1

Shum, S. B., & Ferguson, R. (2012). Social learning analytics. *Journal of Educational Technology & Society, 15*(3), 3–26.

KEY TERMS AND DEFINITIONS

Blended Learning: Blended learning consists of a blend between online and traditional face-to-face learning.

Distance Learning: Distance learning occurs when then the teacher and learner are not in the same location.

Higher Education: The Higher Education and Training sector represents the post-school environment.

K-12 Classrooms: Kindergarten (or grade R in the South African context of this chapter) to grade 12 represent the Basic Education or school sector.

Learning Analytics: Learning Analytics (LA) is about measuring, collecting, analyzing, and reporting on data regarding learners and their environments.

Mobile Learning: Mobile learning is enabled by mobile learning devices like mobile/cell phones.

Online Learning: Online learning takes place over the Internet.

Open Learning: Open learning typically represents an environment where anyone, irrespective of their educational background, may participate in learning.

Chapter 7
Designing Social Learning Analytics for Collaborative Learning Using Virtual Reality, Life Skill, and STEM Approach

Ranjit Singha
https://orcid.org/0000-0002-3541-8752
Christ University, India

Surjit Singha
https://orcid.org/0000-0002-5730-8677
Kristu Jayanti College, India

Alphonsa Diana Haokip
https://orcid.org/0000-0003-2578-0114
Rajiv Gandhi University, India

Jishamol Thomas
https://orcid.org/0000-0002-2912-9188
Christ University, India

G. Sabeena
Christ University, India

Melita Stephen Natal
https://orcid.org/0009-0004-1240-7817
Amity University, India

ABSTRACT

This chapter explores the design of social learning analytics for collaborative learning, incorporating virtual reality, life skills, and a STEM approach. Researchers employ social learning analytics, an emerging field that combines social network analysis and learning analytics, to gain insights into collaborative learning environments. The chapter emphasizes integrating virtual reality, life skills, and STEM in social learning analytics, covering data collection methods, data analysis techniques, and pedagogical applications. It also explores key considerations for designing social learning analytics in collaborative learning, encompassing the development of tools and assessment strategies. Finally, the chapter looks ahead to future directions and prospects for social learning analytics in collaborative learning.

DOI: 10.4018/979-8-3693-0066-4.ch007

INTRODUCTION

Social learning analytics uses data analytics techniques and methods to understand and improve social learning processes. It involves collecting, analyzing, and interpreting data from social interactions, discussions, and collaborations within learning environments, such as online communities, social media platforms, or collaborative learning spaces. Social Learning Analytics aims to gain insights into how learners engage with each other, share knowledge, collaborate, and collectively construct meaning to enhance the effectiveness of social learning experiences. By leveraging data from social interactions, social learning analytics aims to inform instructional design, facilitate personalized learning, and support the development of social learning interventions and strategies. Collaborative learning is a teaching and learning approach that emphasizes active participation, cooperation, and interaction among students. Students collaborate in groups or teams to solve problems, complete projects, discuss ideas and learn from each other's perspectives. Collaborative learning holds significance in education across various vital aspects. Cooperative learning promotes more profound understanding and knowledge retention. Through active engagement in discussions and interactions, students can clarify their understanding, explore different viewpoints, and consolidate their learning. According to Lee & Yang (2023), the main finding of their study indicates that students' perspectives on practical collaborative learning tasks align with classic motivational research, specifically in terms of efficacy and autonomy. The study reveals that students find collaboration enjoyable and beneficial when they perceive the tasks as meaningful and have a sense of control and independence in their learning process. It implies that collaborative tasks' perceived value and relevance and the opportunity for students to exercise autonomy are crucial factors in facilitating compelling collective learning experiences. The study underscores the practical importance of these findings by providing actionable recommendations for designing collaborative learning tasks that foster motivation and engagement.

It also suggests that combining research on educational design and classical motivational theory on collaborative learning could lead to a more robust theoretical base, improving suggestions for putting collaboration into practice in real classrooms. Cooperative learning fosters the development of critical thinking skills as students analyze, evaluate, and synthesize information. By working together to solve problems, students can develop their problem-solving abilities and learn to approach complex tasks from multiple perspectives. Collaborative learning allows students to improve their communication and interpersonal skills. They learn to effectively express their ideas, listen to others, negotiate and resolve conflicts, and work as a team. These skills are essential for success in both academic and professional settings. Collaborative learning creates a dynamic and interactive learning environment to increase students' motivation and engagement. By actively participating in discussions and group activities, students become more invested in their learning and take ownership of their educational journey. Collaborative learning equips students with the necessary skills to thrive professionally, where teamwork and collaboration are highly esteemed. It helps them develop the skills to collaborate effectively, contribute to group projects, and work in diverse teams. Collaborative learning provides opportunities for social interaction, fostering students' sense of belonging and community. It promotes empathy, respect for others' opinions, and the ability to work cooperatively, contributing to students' social and emotional development. Collaborative learning supports a student-centered and interactive learning environment, promoting active knowledge, critical thinking, communication skills, and teamwork. It prepares students for the complexities of the modern world, enhances their learning outcomes, and fosters their overall development.

This chapter explores the design and implementation of social learning analytics for collaborative learning, focusing on integrating virtual reality, life skills, and STEM approaches. It aims to discuss the importance of social learning analytics in understanding and enhancing collaborative learning environments. The chapter will cover various aspects, including theoretical frameworks, data collection methods, data analysis techniques, pedagogical applications, and design considerations for social learning analytics. Additionally, it will discuss future directions and prospects for social learning analytics in collaborative learning and the potential of virtual reality, life skills, and STEM approaches in this context. Virtual reality provides immersive and interactive learning experiences that can enhance collaborative learning. By creating virtual environments, VR enables learners to engage in realistic simulations, problem-solving activities, and role-playing scenarios. In the context of social learning analytics, VR can capture and analyze learners' interactions, behaviours, and communication patterns within these virtual environments. This data can provide valuable insights into how learners collaborate, communicate, and construct knowledge, allowing educators to identify strengths, challenges, and areas for improvement in collaborative learning experiences.

Life skills are essential competencies that enable individuals to navigate and succeed in various aspects of life effectively. These skills include communication, critical thinking, problem-solving, teamwork, adaptability, and interpersonal skills. Life skills are crucial for effective communication, collaboration, and mutual understanding among learners in collaborative learning. Social learning analytics can assess and analyze how learners apply these life skills during joint activities, providing valuable feedback to learners and educators on their skill development and areas that need improvement. The STEM approach emphasizes the integration of science, technology, engineering, and mathematics disciplines in education. Collaborative learning with a STEM focus promotes inquiry-based learning, problem-solving, and critical thinking skills. Social learning analytics can help analyze how learners engage in STEM activities, collaborate on complex problems, and apply STEM concepts in real-world contexts. It enables educators to identify patterns, strategies, and effective practices in STEM collaborative learning, facilitating the design of tailored interventions and instructional strategies. Integrating virtual reality, life skills, and STEM approaches in social learning analytics enhances the depth and breadth of insights obtained from collaborative learning experiences. It comprehensively explains learners' interactions, skill development, and knowledge construction. By leveraging these elements, educators can optimize instructional design, provide personalized feedback, and foster effective collaboration in various educational settings.

THEORETICAL FRAMEWORK

Social learning analytics in collaborative learning refers to applying analytical techniques and methods to study social interactions, behaviours, and patterns within collaborative learning environments. It combines social network analysis and learning analytics to gain insights into how learners engage, collaborate, and learn from one another in collaborative settings. Social Learning Analytics provides a deeper understanding of how learners interact, communicate, and collaborate. It enables the identification of critical social networks, influential individuals, and communication patterns within collaborative learning environments. By analyzing social interactions, social learning analytics can provide insights into the learning processes occurring within collaborative settings. Social Learning Analytics identifies how learners share, co-construct, and transfer knowledge, shedding light on the effectiveness of cooperative learning approaches. Social learning analytics allows for recognizing patterns and challenges in collaborative learning. It helps identify common difficulties, misconceptions, and areas where learners may require additional support or intervention. With social learning analytics, educators can provide personalized feedback and support to learners based on their social interactions and collaborative behaviours. This tailored feedback can facilitate individualized learning experiences and address specific learning needs.

Social learning analytics aligns with the principles of social constructivism, which emphasize the importance of social interactions, collaborative knowledge construction, and shared understanding. It supports the notion that learning is a social process and that meaningful learning occurs through active participation in communal activities. Analyzing social interactions within collaborative learning environments helps identify and understand these communities of practice, facilitating knowledge sharing and expertise development. Social Learning Analytics applies this theory to study the structure and dynamics of social networks within collaborative learning environments, exploring how these networks impact learning outcomes and knowledge diffusion. Activity theory analyzes human activities within specific social and cultural contexts. Social Learning Analytics employs activity theory to examine the collaborative activities and practices in which learners engage, aiming to understand how these activities contribute to learning outcomes and the overall learning process. Drawing on these theoretical perspectives, social learning analytics provides a solid foundation for understanding, analyzing, and improving collaborative learning experiences. It offers insights into social interactions, learning processes, and patterns, enabling educators to design effective interventions, foster meaningful collaborations, and support learners' knowledge construction and skill development.

Social learning analytics is crucial to understanding and enhancing collaborative learning environments. Social Learning Analytics provides valuable insights into collaborative learning environments' social interactions and dynamics. It allows educators to understand how learners engage, communicate, and collaborate, identifying patterns, influential individuals, and communication networks. This understanding helps foster effective collaboration and create a supportive learning community. Social learning analytics provides a window into the learning processes in collaborative learning environments by analyzing social interactions and collective behaviours. Social Learning Analytics helps educators identify how learners share, co-construct, and transfer knowledge. This assessment of learning processes allows educators to evaluate the effectiveness of collaborative learning strategies and make informed instructional decisions. Social learning analytics helps identify common challenges, misconceptions, and areas where learners struggle in cooperative learning settings. It enables educators to pinpoint learning difficulties and provide targeted support and interventions.

Moreover, it highlights opportunities for scaffolding and promoting deeper learning by recognizing successful collaboration patterns and strategies. Social learning analytics enable personalized feedback and support for individual learners. Educators can provide tailored feedback, guidance, and resources to address specific learning needs by analyzing their social interactions and collaborative behaviours. This personalized approach enhances learner engagement, motivation, and achievement in joint learning activities. Social Learning Analytics allows educators to monitor and evaluate the effectiveness of cooperative learning initiatives over time. By analyzing data on social interactions and learning outcomes, they can identify areas for improvement, refine instructional strategies, and optimize collaborative learning experiences. This iterative process promotes continuous improvement and enhances the overall effectiveness of collaborative learning environments.

Social learning analytics is essential in collaborative learning as it provides insights into social interactions, facilitates the assessment of learning processes, identifies challenges and opportunities, enables personalized feedback and support, and supports continuous improvement. By leveraging data and analytics, educators can optimize collaborative learning experiences and enhance learner outcomes. Social learning analytics draws upon several theoretical perspectives to inform its understanding and application in collaborative learning. Social Learning Analytics aligns with the principles of social constructivism, which emphasize that learning is a social process that occurs through active participation, collaboration, and the co-construction of knowledge. This perspective recognizes the importance of social interactions and context in shaping learning experiences and outcomes. Social learning analytics seeks to analyze and understand the social interactions and collaborative processes contributing to knowledge construction within collaborative learning environments. Imagine an online literature discussion group where high school students study and discuss classic novels. Students read assigned chapters independently and then engage in collaborative discussions on an online platform. In this example, social learning analytics aligns with the principles of social constructivism by analyzing the social interactions and collaborative processes within the online literature discussion group. Educators can facilitate meaningful learning experiences that promote critical thinking, interpretation, and engagement with literature by understanding how students actively participate, construct knowledge collectively, and engage in context-rich discussions.

The concept of practice centres on the social aspect of learning, emphasizing that learning occurs within communities where individuals participate in shared activities, develop a collective identity, and mutually support each other in their learning endeavours. Social learning analytics can help identify and analyze communities of practice within collaborative learning environments, uncovering the relationships, interactions, and knowledge-sharing dynamics within these communities. Imagine a network of teachers from various schools collaborating online to improve their teaching practices. They share resources, discuss effective teaching strategies, and seek advice from one another. In this example, social learning analytics aid in identifying and analyzing the community of practice among teachers within an online network. Educators can foster an environment that supports collaborative learning, effective teaching practices, and continuous professional growth within the teacher network by understanding shared activities, relationships, and knowledge-sharing dynamics. Social network theory scrutinizes the relationships and connections among individuals within a social system. In social learning analytics, this theory analyzes the structure and dynamics of social networks within collaborative learning environments. It aids in identifying influential individuals, communication patterns, and information flow within these networks, shedding light on how learners distribute, access, and share information and knowledge.

Consider a university course where students form study groups to collaborate on assignments and prepare for exams. Each study group consists of a few students who regularly meet to discuss course material, share resources, and support each other's learning. In this example, social network theory helps educators gain insights into the structure and dynamics of social networks within study groups. By understanding how information flows, who the influential nodes are, and how communication patterns form, educators can support and optimize collaborative learning experiences within these study groups, ultimately enhancing students' engagement and knowledge sharing. Activity theory analyzes human activities within specific social and cultural contexts. Activity Theory recognizes that learning is embedded within social practices and emphasizes the interplay between individual actions, social interactions, and the broader socio-cultural environment. Social learning analytics can apply activity theory to examine the collaborative activities, tasks, and practices in which learners engage, seeking to understand how these activities contribute to learning outcomes and the overall learning process. These theoretical perspectives provide a foundation for understanding the social and collaborative aspects of learning and guide the application of social learning analytics in analyzing and improving collaborative learning environments. By considering these perspectives, educators and researchers can gain deeper insights into the social processes, learning dynamics, and knowledge construction within collaborative learning settings.

In this history class, students actively engage in project-based learning. Task each group of students with researching and creating a presentation about a specific historical event. In this example, activity theory helps educators analyze collaborative activities within a project-based learning context. By understanding the elements of the activity system, interactions, and socio-cultural influences, educators can optimize collective learning experiences, address challenges, and enhance learning outcomes for students involved in the project. VR simulations and environments can capture learners' interactions, behaviours, and communication patterns in a highly realistic and controlled setting. Analyzing this data provides insights into collaboration strategies, problem-solving approaches, and the effectiveness of virtual collaborative learning experiences. VR can also create virtual social networks, enabling the analysis of learners' social interactions and network dynamics in virtual collaborative spaces. In a classroom environment, virtual reality (VR) technology to facilitate social learning analytics presents a distinct prospect for augmenting collective learning encounters and acquiring significant observations on student interactions. This article discusses the potential use of virtual reality (VR) technology in a classroom environment to enhance the utilization of social learning analytics.

Select a virtual reality (VR) platform or tool that aligns with the specific requirements and available resources of your educational setting. A wide array of virtual reality (VR) headgear, software applications, and platforms are already accessible, including fully immersive systems and mobile-based VR experiences. Develop virtual reality (VR) simulations that accurately replicate collaborative settings seen in real-world environments. One potential use is creating a virtual laboratory environment whereby students may engage in joint problem-solving activities related to scientific inquiries. Establishing a historical context can also involve students cooperating to critically analyze and interpret significant historical events. Virtual reality (VR) settings can collect meaningful interaction data, including many aspects such as students' physical motions, gestures, patterns of visual attention, and communication behaviours. The data above provides valuable insights into students' collaborative behaviours, content engagement, and navigation of virtual environments. Utilize social learning analytics to scrutinize students' collaborative techniques in a virtual reality (VR) setting. Determine whether their communication is adequate and how they distribute duties and responsibilities. The current study holds the potential to reveal discernible patterns that aid in identifying effective cooperation strategies.

Students actively participate in problem-solving endeavours using virtual reality (VR) simulations. Examine the methodologies used by individuals in addressing obstacles encountered in the virtual reality (VR) milieu. Are individuals engaging in the application of critical thinking skills? Are the researchers investigating several potential solutions? Monitor the extent of students' active involvement in the virtual reality collaboration exercises. Do all students participate actively, or do some individuals assume a passive role as just observers? Identifying differences in involvement may facilitate the identification and resolution of possible concerns. Evaluate the efficacy of virtual reality (VR) as a medium for facilitating collaborative learning. Collect student comments on their experiences, degree of comfort with the technology, and perceived educational results. The objective is to create virtual social networks in virtual reality (VR). These networks can depict student relationships established through their interactions and partnerships. Analyze the networks' structure to ascertain the presence of essential persons and discern information dissemination patterns. After the virtual reality (VR) collaboration experience, facilitate reflective sessions where students share their viewpoints, challenges, and ideas. Encourage individuals to express their thoughts on successful aspects and improvement areas. Maintaining ethical concerns and prioritizing data privacy while gathering and analyzing students' interaction data is essential. It is necessary to ensure that students know about the data-gathering process and get permission that aligns with ethical and legal standards.

Utilize the knowledge acquired through social learning analytics in virtual reality to enhance and optimize pedagogical strategies. Determine domains where students demonstrate exceptional performance and may need further assistance and adapt pedagogical approaches accordingly. Provide comprehensive training and service to educators and students alike to foster their confidence and expertise in using virtual reality (VR) technology for collaborative learning. Successful virtual reality (VR) technology integration for social learning analytics in educational settings requires meticulous planning, seamless integration, and continuous assessment. It is essential to ensure that virtual reality (VR) experiences follow the curriculum goals and to evaluate their compatibility with other teaching approaches carefully. Through virtual reality (VR), one may use its immersive and interactive qualities to generate novel and captivating collaborative learning prospects while acquiring significant observations on student behaviours and interactions. Life skills are essential competencies that enable individuals to navigate and succeed in various aspects of life. Integrating life skills into social learning analytics involves assessing and analyzing how learners employ these skills during collaborative learning activities. For example, investigating communication patterns can provide insights into learners' effective communication, active listening, and interpersonal skills. Understanding how learners apply critical thinking, problem-solving, and teamwork skills within collaborative tasks can also be valuable. Analyzing life skills in social learning analytics helps identify areas for improvement, design targeted interventions, and foster the development of well-rounded learners.

Incorporating life skills into social learning analytics in a classroom environment necessitates a deliberate methodology that amalgamates cooperative learning exercises with data examination to evaluate and augment students' proficiency in diverse fundamental abilities. Define the life skills pertinent to the curriculum and educational goals. Prominent life skills include effective communication, analytical reasoning, proficient problem-solving, innovative thinking, collaborative cooperation, efficient time management, adaptation to changing circumstances, and emotional intelligence. Design joint learning activities that organically integrate opportunities for students to engage in and exhibit these essential life skills. For example, a collaborative endeavour may need proficient communication, adept problem-solving skills, and cohesive cooperation. It is necessary to effectively convey the life skills intended for students to prioritize during each collaborative engagement. Elucidate how these talents correspond with their individual growth and prospective achievements. Employ several methodologies to gather data on students' application of life skills throughout joint endeavours. The methods used in this research endeavour include several techniques, such as documenting interpersonal exchanges, witnessing collective deliberations, scrutinizing written correspondence, and evaluating the results of project endeavours.

Examine the communication patterns and content to assess students' competency in effectively expressing ideas, actively listening, and participating in courteous and productive conversations. Analyze the strategies used by students when faced with difficulties in collaborative assignments. Do individuals possess the capacity to examine issues critically, consider other viewpoints, and generate novel resolutions? This study aims to analyze the cooperative dynamics among students in group settings. Are students effectively distributing the work? Are there visible examples of leadership within the group? Integrate peer and self-assessment elements into the instructional framework, whereby students assess their and their peers' proficiency in life skills shown during joint endeavours. It fosters the growth of self-awareness and encourages personal responsibility. The task at hand involves the formulation of unambiguous rubrics and evaluation standards that provide specific guidelines for assessing life skills. This practice facilitates students' comprehension of the anticipated requirements and provides a structure for constructive criticism. Provide constructive criticism to pupils based on the gathered data. Encourage individuals to examine their aptitudes and areas for growth regarding life skills. This reflective exercise fosters the development of metacognitive skills and promotes self-directed learning.

Develop precise interventions by utilizing the knowledge acquired through social learning analytics. To illustrate, if there is a perceived difficulty with communication skills, it would be beneficial to include concise instructional sessions or engaging exercises to enhance communication abilities. In light of examining life skills, developing personalized learning programs for pupils is proposed. These plans may have well-defined objectives and methodologies aimed at improving specific competencies. Assist students in comprehending the significance of these life skills in contexts extending beyond the confines of the classroom by elucidating their applicability to future professional endeavours, interpersonal connections, and holistic welfare. It is vital to consistently evaluate the efficacy of one's approach to integrating life skills within the context of collaborative learning. Modify methodologies following feedback and data analysis. Integrating collective learning experiences with evaluating life skills using social learning analytics enables the establishment of a comprehensive educational setting that fosters academic development and equips students with the necessary proficiencies to excel in diverse domains of their lives.

The STEM approach integrates science, technology, engineering, and mathematics concepts and practices in education. Integrating the STEM approach into social learning analytics involves analyzing collaborative learning activities around STEM subjects. For example, studying how learners collaborate, problem-solve, and apply STEM knowledge and skills during group projects or experiments can provide insights into effective STEM collaboration strategies. It enables educators to identify patterns, processes, and challenges in STEM collaborative learning and design interventions that promote more profound STEM learning experiences. Educators can better understand collaborative learning environments by integrating VR, life skills, and the STEM approach into social learning analytics. This integration enables the analysis of learners' interactions, behaviours, and skills in immersive virtual environments, the assessment of essential life skills within collaborative activities, and the analysis of collaboration dynamics specific to STEM subjects. Such integration facilitates personalized feedback, targeted interventions, and optimizing collective learning experiences, ultimately enhancing learners' engagement, skill development, and knowledge construction. The successful use of the STEM approach, virtual reality (VR), life skills, and social learning analytics in a classroom environment requires meticulous preparation and coordination. Ensure that the curriculum aligns with the principles and methodologies of STEM education. This inquiry aims to identify domains where integrating STEM knowledge and skills can enhance collaborative learning activities. Develop joint learning activities centred on STEM disciplines. Consider collaborative experiments, engineering tasks, programming assignments, or scientific inquiries. Leverage virtual reality technology to develop immersive and interactive environments replicating STEM-related settings. Gather empirical data about the interactions among students, their problem-solving approaches, and their utilization of STEM principles in virtual locations. It is essential to ensure that the collaborative activities have elements that allow students to use and enhance necessary life skills, like communication, critical thinking, and collaboration. Achieve this objective through collaborative discussions, constructive peer criticism, and reflective contemplation.

This study analyzes the data obtained from real-world collaborative activities and virtual reality (VR) simulations. Examine the trends in students' combined efforts, problem-solving approaches in STEM disciplines, and the practical application of their acquired knowledge. The primary objective of this study is to analyze the strategies students use while engaging with STEM issues. Are they using scientific methodologies in their approach? Are they using mathematical concepts? This study facilitates the identification of productive tactics and areas that need improvement. Furnish pupils with an evaluation of their collaborative and problem-solving endeavours in STEM. It is essential to foster a sense of introspection among individuals, prompting them to contemplate their experiences and discern potential avenues for personal development. Drawing upon the acquired knowledge, devise focused interventions to tackle distinct issues or deficiencies in the field of STEM. The interventions may include supplementary exercises, facilitated dialogues, or brief instructional sessions. Highlight the practical applicability of the STEM subjects in which students are actively involved. Assist individuals in comprehending the practical applications of these proficiencies throughout diverse STEM vocations and sectors. Customizing interventions and assistance according to each child's unique requirements is essential. Pupils may require additional support in particular STEM disciplines or specialized life skills. Utilize social learning analytics to comprehend the intricacies of collaborative processes within STEM disciplines. This analysis examines students' contributions to the problem-solving process, the distribution of responsibilities within the group, and the influence of good communication on the results. Emphasize the interrelationships among various STEM disciplines in joint endeavours. One such instance highlights the indispensability of mathematics in addressing engineering complexities and the applicability of scientific ideas to technological advancements. Consistently assessing the effectiveness of the integrated strategy holds crucial importance. Using the insights obtained, gathering student feedback and adapting instructional approaches is advisable.

It is essential to engage in continuous professional development for both oneself and coworkers to acquire the necessary skills and knowledge to proficiently incorporate virtual reality (VR), life skills, science, technology, engineering, and mathematics (STEM), as well as social learning analytics, into teaching methodologies. By integrating the STEM methodology, virtual reality (VR), life skills, and social learning analytics, it is possible to provide an immersive and dynamic educational setting that not only facilitates the acquisition of STEM information but also fosters the development of essential life skills and encourages successful cooperation. The use of this integrated strategy serves to augment students' levels of involvement, promote the cultivation of various abilities, and provide a comprehensive and well-rounded educational experience.

METHODS OF DATA COLLECTION IN SOCIAL LEARNING ANALYTICS

Researchers commonly employ surveys and questionnaires to collect self-reported data on learners' perceptions, attitudes, and experiences in collaborative learning environments. These instruments offer insights into learners' satisfaction, engagement, and perceived learning outcomes. Administering surveys is possible before, during, or after collaborative learning activities to collect data on diverse aspects, encompassing communication patterns, collaboration effectiveness, and self-assessment of skills. Observational methods involve systematically observing and documenting learners' behaviours, interactions, and activities within collaborative learning settings. This can be done through direct observations by researchers or video recordings that capture the nuances of social interactions. Observational data can provide detailed insights into learners' collaborative processes, communication patterns, problem-solving strategies, and engagement levels.

Social network analysis involves mapping learners' social relationships and interactions within collaborative learning environments. It examines the structure of social networks, identifies influential individuals, and analyzes information flow within the network. Collect data for social network analysis from various sources, such as online discussion forums, communication logs, or digital traces of learners' interactions. Learning analytics platforms integrated into collaborative learning environments can automatically collect and analyze the data generated during learning activities. These platforms can capture data such as learners' participation rates, contributions to group discussions, completion of tasks, and performance metrics. Learning analytics platforms offer real-time data for monitoring learners' progress, identifying areas for improvement, and providing personalized feedback. Surveys and questionnaires quickly and efficiently gather learners' perspectives and self-reported data. They can provide valuable insights into learners' subjective experiences, attitudes, and perceptions of collaboration. Surveys rely on learners' self-reporting, which may introduce biases or inaccuracies. They may also need more depth to capture complex social interactions and behaviours within collaborative learning environments. Observations provide rich and detailed real-time data on learners' behaviours, exchanges, and engagement. They offer an in-depth understanding of the collaborative learning process and can capture non-verbal cues and contextual information. Observational methods can be time-consuming and require trained observers. There may also be concerns about the observer effect, where learners may alter their behaviour when being observed. Furthermore, observational data may be limited to a specific time frame and not generalizable to all learning situations.

Social network analysis provides insights into the structure and dynamics of social interactions within collaborative learning environments. It helps identify influential individuals, information flow patterns, and subgroups within the network. It provides a quantitative perspective on collaboration and facilitates the identification of key players and knowledge brokers. Social network analysis relies on data that may only capture part of the complexity of social interactions. It may need to include informal interactions and contextual factors that influence collaboration. Data collection for social network analysis can be challenging and may require access to digital communication platforms or permission to collect data. Learning analytics platforms provide real-time data on learners' participation, performance, and progress within collaborative learning activities. They offer automated data collection and analysis, allowing educators to monitor and support learners' engagement and progress. Learning analytics platforms provide actionable insights for personalized feedback and interventions. Learning analytics platforms rely on the availability and accuracy of digital data within the learning environment. They may need to capture the full scope of social interactions or contextual factors that impact collaboration—analyzing online discussion forums or chat logs to collect data on learners' interactions, contributions, and engagement. It can involve tracking the frequency and quality of learners' posts, analyzing the content of their discussions, and identifying collaboration patterns.

They collect data through peer assessment and feedback processes where learners provide evaluations and feedback on their peers' work. This data can provide insights into learners' perceptions of their peers' contributions, collaboration skills, and the overall effectiveness of collaborative activities. This data can provide information on learners' participation, usage patterns, and progress in collaborative learning tasks and activities. They collect and analyze digital traces and artefacts generated during collaborative learning, such as shared documents, wikis, or cooperative project repositories. These traces can offer insights into the collaborative process, individual contributions, and the evolution of shared knowledge. Gathering data through peer ratings and evaluations, learners assess and rate their peers' performance, collaboration skills, or contributions to collaborative tasks. This data can provide insights into the quality of collaboration, peer influence, and the distribution of roles within cooperative groups.

They administer surveys and questionnaires to gather self-reported data on learners' perceptions, attitudes, and experiences in collaborative learning. Surveys can inquire about learners' satisfaction, perceived learning outcomes, collaboration effectiveness, and challenges. They conduct digital ethnographic studies that observe and analyze learners' online behaviours, interactions, and activities within collaborative learning platforms or virtual environments. This approach provides a deeper understanding of the social dynamics, norms, and cultural aspects of cooperative learning.

These data collection methods can provide valuable insights into learners' collaborative processes, interactions, engagement, and the effectiveness of collective learning experiences. Researchers and educators can comprehensively understand social learning dynamics and inform instructional design, interventions, and improvements in collaborative learning environments by combining multiple data sources and methods. Integrating virtual reality (VR), life skills, and the STEM approach into data collection methods for social learning analytics in collaborative learning can enhance the richness and depth of collected data. Using VR technology, data collection methods can capture learners' interactions, behaviours, and communication patterns within immersive and simulated collaborative environments. VR can provide a realistic and controlled setting for data collection, allowing researchers to observe and analyze learners' actions, decision-making processes, and problem-solving strategies. VR can also collect physiological data, such as heart rate or eye tracking, providing insights into learners' cognitive and affective states during collaborative activities.

Integrating life skills into data collection methods involves assessing and capturing learners' application of life skills during collaborative learning activities.

For example, observations or self-reporting methods can focus on how learners demonstrate effective communication, active listening, leadership, teamwork, and conflict-resolution skills during collaborative tasks. Develop data collection tools to gather information regarding learners' problem-solving methods, critical thinking capabilities, adaptability, and creativity. Enabling this integration provides a comprehensive understanding of the development and application of life skills within collaborative learning contexts. The integration of digital and non-digital learning media positively impacts the advancement of life skills among elementary education students after the COVID-19 pandemic, as demonstrated by Wardana et al. (2023). Customize data collection methods to capture learners' engagement with STEM concepts and practices during collaborative activities. For instance, observations or video recordings can focus on how learners utilize STEM knowledge, apply scientific inquiry, employ technology tools, and engage in engineering or mathematical problem-solving. Surveys or questionnaires can inquire about learners' perceptions of STEM integration, their confidence in STEM skills, and the relevance of STEM learning to their collaborative experiences. By aligning data collection methods with the STEM approach, researchers can assess the effectiveness of STEM collaboration, identify areas for improvement, and evaluate the impact of STEM integration on collaborative learning outcomes.

Researchers can capture a more comprehensive and holistic view of learners' experiences and behaviours within collaborative learning environments by integrating VR, life skills, and the STEM approach into data collection methods. This integration allows for the collection of data that reflects the immersive and realistic aspects of collaborative interactions in VR, the application and development of essential life skills, and engagement with STEM content and practices. The resulting data can provide deeper insights into the complex dynamics of collaborative learning and inform the design of interventions, instructional strategies, and personalized support for learners.

SOCIAL LEARNING ANALYTICS APPLICATIONS IN COLLABORATIVE LEARNING

Network analysis techniques examine the structure and dynamics of social networks within collaborative learning environments. Includes identifying key actors, analyzing communication patterns, and measuring centrality and influence. Network analysis provides insights into information flow, knowledge sharing, and social interactions among learners. Text mining and NLP techniques are employed to analyze textual data, such as online discussions or written reflections, to uncover patterns, themes, and sentiments. These techniques help identify key concepts, trends, and the quality of interactions within collaborative learning settings. Quantitative analysis involves statistical methods to analyze numerical data collected in social learning analytics. It can include descriptive statistics, correlation analysis, regression analysis, or multilevel modelling to examine relationships between variables, predict outcomes, or assess the impact of interventions on collaborative learning outcomes.

Researchers use content analysis techniques to analyze qualitative data, such as written responses or transcripts of collaborative discussions. They use coding and categorizing data to identify themes, patterns, and emerging concepts. The content analysis offers insights into the content and quality of cooperative interactions. LMS platforms often include built-in analytics tools that collect and analyze data on learners' interactions, engagement, and performance within collaborative learning activities. LMS analytics provide educators with dashboards, visualizations, and reports to monitor learners' progress and inform instructional decisions. Dedicated software tools for social network analysis facilitate the visualization and analysis of social networks within collaborative learning environments. These tools allow for identifying network structures, centrality measures, and the visualization of social interactions.

Text analysis tools and software leverage natural language processing algorithms to analyze textual data for collaborative learning. These tools can assist in sentiment analysis, topic modelling, and identifying key themes or concepts within written responses or online discussions. Data visualization tools help present social learning analytics data in visually appealing and meaningful ways. They enable educators and researchers to interpret and communicate complex data, patterns, and trends effectively. Visualization tools can include charts, graphs, and interactive visualizations. Social learning analytics can provide real-time feedback to learners and instructors, enabling timely interventions and personalized support. It allows educators to track learners' progress, identify areas for improvement, and provide targeted feedback on collaboration skills and knowledge acquisition.

Social learning analytics can assist in forming influential collaborative groups based on learners' profiles, skills, and compatibility. It can identify potential group dynamics issues, facilitate balanced participation, and support the forming diverse and productive teams. Social learning analytics can inform adaptive learning systems that dynamically adjust content, resources, and activities based on learners' collaborative interactions and individual needs. It enables personalized learning experiences that cater to learners' strengths, weaknesses, and preferences. Social learning analytics can support learners' metacognitive processes by providing visualizations and data on collaborative interactions. It encourages self-reflection and self-assessment and promotes metacognitive awareness of collaboration strategies, communication effectiveness, and group dynamics. Integrating virtual reality, life skills, and the STEM approach into social learning analytics applications in collaborative learning provides a more comprehensive understanding and supports learners' development. Virtual reality can collect data on learners' behaviours, decision-making processes, and problem-solving strategies within simulated collaborative environments. Social learning analytics techniques can analyze this data to gain insights into learners' collaboration patterns and inform instructional design.

Social learning analytics can include assessing life skills demonstrated during collaborative learning activities (Williams, 2017). Analyze data to evaluate learners' communication skills, teamwork, leadership abilities, and adaptability within a communal setting. Social learning analytics can examine integrating STEM concepts and practices within collaborative learning (Ouyang et al., 2022). It involves analyzing data to assess learners' application of STEM knowledge, problem-solving strategies, and collaboration in STEM-related projects. By integrating VR, life skills, and the STEM approach into social learning analytics applications, educators and researchers can better understand learners' collaborative processes, the development of essential skills, and the impact of STEM integration. This integration can inform instructional strategies, interventions, and personalized support to enhance collaborative learning outcomes and prepare learners for real-world challenges.

DESIGNING SOCIAL LEARNING ANALYTICS FOR COLLABORATIVE LEARNING

The design of social learning analytics should align with the specific learning objectives and goals of collaborative learning. Consider what insights and data are necessary to support those objectives and inform instructional decisions. Determine appropriate data collection methods that capture relevant aspects of cooperative learning, such as social interactions, communication patterns, knowledge sharing, and problem-solving processes. Consider the feasibility and ethical considerations of data collection. Select data analysis techniques that align with social learning analytics research questions and objectives. Choose methods that effectively analyze the collected data and provide meaningful insights into learners' collaborative experiences. Ensure that the design of social learning analytics respects learners' privacy and complies with ethical guidelines. Implement appropriate data anonymization, protection measures, and informed consent procedures, and ensure the ethical conduct of data collection and analysis processes.

Develop or utilize existing technologies to collect data on learners' collaborative interactions, communication, and engagement. It can include online platforms, learning management systems, virtual reality environments, or data collection apps. Create or utilize software tools to analyze social learning analytics data. It should support the application of relevant data analysis techniques and provide visualizations, dashboards, and reports to present the findings effectively. Create or utilize software tools to analyze social learning analytics data. These tools should support the application of relevant data analysis techniques and provide visualizations, dashboards, and reports to present the findings effectively. Incorporate visualization tools that enable the representation of social learning analytics data in a user-friendly and informative manner. Visualizations can help educators and researchers understand complex patterns, relationships, and trends within the collaborative learning context. Assess the validity and reliability of the social learning analytics methods and tools. Ensure that the data collected accurately reflects the intended constructs and that the analysis provides reliable and consistent results.

Evaluate the effects of social learning analytics on collaborative learning outcomes. Assess whether the insights gained from the analytics inform instructional decisions, enhance learners' engagement and performance, and contribute to achieving learning goals. Seek feedback from educators, learners, and other stakeholders regarding the usability, usefulness, and acceptance of the social learning analytics tools and findings. Incorporate user feedback to improve the design and effectiveness of the analytics tools. Incorporate virtual reality technology to collect data on learners' behaviours, interactions, and problem-solving strategies within simulated collaborative environments (Planey et al., 2023). This integration can provide a more immersive and realistic data collection and analysis context. Hsu and Liu's (2023) review study underscores that learner-centred pedagogies with personalized and contextual learning support, coupled with constructivist learning design and the promotion of collaborative learning and higher-order cognitive skills, yield positive effects on students' learning outcomes and interactions. The study presents a facilitation framework that combines situated learning, learning-by-doing, and social constructivist design to facilitate oral communication development through augmented reality. The study's findings provide practical guidance for educators and propose a theoretical framework aligned with research-proven theories to enhance student learning and engagement.

Develop social learning analytics for evaluating life skills exhibited during collaborative learning (Zheng et al., 2023). Analyze data to assess learners' communication, teamwork, and leadership skills, among others, to provide insights into their development and impact on collaboration. Integrate social learning analytics with the analysis of STEM integration within collaborative learning (Nungu et al., 2023). Examine data to assess learners' application of STEM knowledge, problem-solving approaches, and collaboration in STEM-related projects. The study by Sidekerskienė and Damaševičius (2023) explores digital escape rooms as a metaphor for breaking down barriers in STEM education. The study's core finding indicates that digital escape rooms positively impact student engagement, motivation, and learning outcomes in mathematics education. The results suggest that these immersive learning experiences enhance student learning by providing interactive and engaging activities. Through digital escape rooms, students develop critical thinking, problem-solving, and collaboration abilities.

Furthermore, the personalized nature of these rooms allows for tailored learning experiences that cater to individual student needs. The study emphasizes the versatility of digital escape rooms as a teaching tool applicable to various subjects. Suggestions for future work in this area include the development of more advanced and personalized puzzles, the implementation of rigorous assessment methods, the exploration of the potential of digital escape rooms for specific learning outcomes, and investigation in diverse educational settings and student populations. By integrating virtual reality, life skills, and the STEM approach into the design of social learning analytics, educators and researchers can better understand collaborative learning processes, the development of essential skills, and the impact of STEM integration. This integration can inform instructional strategies, interventions, and personalized support to enhance collaborative learning outcomes and prepare learners for real-world challenges.

FUTURE DIRECTIONS OF SOCIAL LEARNING ANALYTICS IN COLLABORATIVE LEARNING

Real-time analytics in social learning environments is an emerging trend. It involves collecting and analyzing real-time data to provide immediate feedback and interventions to learners, promoting active engagement and personalized support. Predictive analytics is gaining momentum in social learning analytics. By analyzing historical data and patterns, predictive models can forecast learners' performance, identify at-risk students, and recommend targeted interventions to improve collaborative learning outcomes. There is an increasing focus on integrating social-emotional learning analytics into collaborative learning environments. It involves analyzing data related to learners' social interactions, emotional states, and well-being to support the development of social and emotional skills. Future research should address ethical considerations in social learning analytics, such as privacy protection, data security, and informed consent. Establishing guidelines and frameworks to ensure the responsible and ethical use of learner data in collaborative learning contexts is essential.

Further research is needed to deepen our understanding of the learning processes that occur in collaborative environments. Includes investigating the impact of different types of social interactions, group dynamics, and individual contributions on learning outcomes. Longitudinal studies can provide valuable insights into the long-term effects of social learning analytics on collaborative learning outcomes. Examining the persistence and transferability of skills developed through collaborative learning can contribute to designing more effective interventions and instructional strategies. Social learning analytics can provide personalized learning experiences by tailoring interventions, resources, and feedback based on learners' collaborative interactions and individual needs. Prospects involve leveraging social learning analytics to create adaptive and customized learning environments. Dogan, Goru Dogan, and Bozkurt (2023) conducted a systematic review on using artificial intelligence (AI) in online learning and distance education processes. The study highlights the growing research interest and extensive application of AI technologies in this context. It identifies three main research themes: adaptive and personalized learning, exploration of ethics and human agency in algorithmic online educational spaces, and investigation of online learning through detection, identification, recognition, and prediction.

The study suggests that future research should consider the integration of pedagogy, curriculum, and instructional/learning design in AI applications for online distance education. It also emphasizes the need for regulations and ethical guidelines regarding the use of human-generated data in AI technologies. Developing policies and strategies to ensure a human-centred approach to online learning is crucial. The findings underscore the importance of technical and human-centred considerations in designing and implementing AI in online distance education. Social learning analytics can be essential in assessing and certifying collaborative skills and competencies. Prospects involve developing assessment frameworks and standards that recognize and validate learners' collective abilities within educational and professional contexts. Hsu, Chen, & Hwang (2023) studied the impacts of peer assessment and learning styles in vocational design certification courses. The core finding suggests peer assessment positively influences students' learning outcomes and motivation. Students who engaged in peer assessment activities showed better learning results and higher intrinsic motivation. Active learners benefited more from the peer assessment-based mobile learning approach. The study emphasizes the need for long-term planning to enhance learning retention in vocational education and the importance of integrating technology and pedagogical practices. However, the study acknowledges limitations in terms of the cognitive tests used. Future research should explore the effects of collaborative peer assessment in different vocational subjects. Technological advancements, including augmented and mixed reality, open up novel opportunities for enhanced collaboration. Possibilities encompass integrating these technologies with social learning analytics to craft immersive and interactive collaborative learning experiences. Virtual reality promises to improve data collection and analysis in social learning analytics. Prospects involve leveraging virtual reality to create more realistic and immersive collaborative learning environments, enabling the collection of rich data on learners' behaviours, interactions, and problem-solving processes. The integration of life skills assessment in social learning analytics has the potential to foster the development and evaluation of essential skills for collaboration. Prospects involve further refining the assessment methods and incorporating feedback mechanisms to support learners' life skill development.

Integrating STEM approaches in social learning analytics can support analyzing learners' application of STEM knowledge, problem-solving strategies, and collaboration in collaborative learning. Prospects involve exploring the integration of STEM-specific analytics to gain deeper insights into learners' STEM competencies and their impact on collective learning outcomes. The future of social learning analytics in collaborative learning holds great potential for personalized learning experiences, improved assessment and certification of collaborative skills, and the integration of emerging technologies and approaches such as virtual reality, life skills, and STEM. These advancements can enhance our understanding of collaborative learning processes and pave the way for more effective instructional strategies and interventions.

CONCLUSION

This chapter explored the design and application of social learning analytics in collaborative learning. It discussed the importance of social learning analytics in gaining insights into collaborative learning environments and enhancing learning outcomes. The presentation highlighted integrating virtual reality, life skills, and the STEM approach in social learning analytics, showcasing various theoretical perspectives. It discussed multiple data collection methods in social learning analytics, including their benefits and limitations. Data collection and analysis can provide insights into learners' collaborative interactions within collaborative learning. The chapter also probed into the applications of social learning analytics in collaborative learning, including data analysis techniques, tools, and technologies used. The exploration emphasized the potential of social learning analytics to inform instructional design and personalize learning experiences within pedagogical applications. Furthermore, it discussed the factors to consider in designing social learning analytics, including developing tools and assessing social learning analytics in collaborative learning.

Highlighting the integration of virtual reality, life skills, and the STEM approach in designing social learning analytics enhances the effectiveness and comprehensiveness of analytics. Finally, it examined the future directions and prospects of social learning analytics in collaborative learning, discussing emerging trends in real-time, predictive, and social-emotional learning analytics. We identified implications for future research, including ethical considerations and longitudinal studies. We explored the prospects of integrating social learning analytics into personalized learning, collaborative assessment and certification, and augmented collaboration, as well as the potential of incorporating virtual reality, life skills, and the STEM approach.

The chapter provides practical implications for educators and researchers in implementing social learning analytics. Consider incorporating social learning analytics to gain insights into learners' collaborative interactions and inform instructional decisions. Explore various data collection methods and tools that capture relevant aspects of cooperative learning while addressing privacy and ethical considerations. Use data analysis techniques and visualization tools to analyze and present data on social learning analytics effectively. Use social learning analytics to personalize learning experiences, assess collaborative skills, and support the development of life skills and STEM competencies.

Social learning analytics has the potential to revolutionize collaborative learning by providing actionable insights into learners' interactions and collaboration processes. Integrating virtual reality, life skills, and the STEM approach further enhances the capabilities of social learning analytics. As we progress, we must continue researching and refining the methodologies and technologies used in social learning analytics. Ethical considerations should always be at the forefront, ensuring learners' privacy and data protection. The thoughtful integration of social learning analytics enriches collaborative learning environments, promoting active engagement, personalized support, and the development of essential skills. By leveraging the power of social learning analytics and embracing emerging trends, educators and researchers can unlock the full potential of collaborative learning, leading to improved learning outcomes and preparing learners for future challenges.

This chapter has explored the importance of social learning analytics in collaborative learning and the integration of virtual reality, life skills, and STEM approaches in social learning analytics. The chapter has discussed different data collection methods, data analysis techniques, and pedagogical applications of social learning analytics in collaborative learning. Finally, the chapter has outlined the factors to consider in designing social learning analytics and the prospects for social learning analytics in collaborative learning.

REFERENCES

Dogan, M. E., Goru Dogan, T., & Bozkurt, A. (2023). The use of artificial intelligence (AI) in online learning and distance education processes: A systematic review of empirical studies. *Applied Sciences (Basel, Switzerland)*, *13*(5), 3056. doi:10.3390/app13053056

Hsu, K. C., & Liu, G. Z. (2023). Constructing a theory-based augmented reality-featured context-aware ubiquitous learning facilitation framework for oral communication development. *Journal of Computer Assisted Learning*, *39*(3), 883–898. Advance online publication. doi:10.1111/jcal.12792

Hsu, T. C., Chen, W. L., & Hwang, G. J. (2023). Impacts of interactions between peer assessment and learning styles on students' mobile learning achievements and motivations in vocational design certification courses. *Interactive Learning Environments*, *31*(3), 1351–1363. doi:10.1080/10494820.2020.1833351

Lee, W. W. S., & Yang, M. (2023). Effective collaborative learning from Chinese students' perspective: A qualitative study in a teacher-training course. *Teaching in Higher Education*, *28*(2), 221–237. doi:10.1080/13562517.2020.1790517

Nungu, L., Mukama, E., & Nsabayezu, E. (2023). Online collaborative learning and cognitive presence in mathematics and science education. Case study of the University of Rwanda, College of Education. *Education and Information Technologies*, 1–20. https://link.springer.com/article/10.1007/s10639-023-11607-w. doi:10.100710639-023-11607-w PMID:36779197

Ouyang, F., Dai, X., & Chen, S. (2022). Applying multimodal learning analytics to examine the immediate and delayed effects of instructor scaffoldings on small groups' collaborative programming. *International Journal of STEM Education*, *9*(1), 45. https://link.springer.com/article/10.1186/s40594-022-00361-z. doi:10.118640594-022-00361-z

Planey, J., Kim, T., Mercier, E., & Lindgren, R. (2023). Can you see Orion?: Knowledge construction and collaborative discourse while problem-solving with virtual reality. *Interactive Learning Environments*, •••, 1–14. doi:10.1080/10494820.2023.2239290

Sidekerskienė, T., & Damaševičius, R. (2023). Out-of-the-box learning: Digital escape rooms as a metaphor for breaking down barriers in STEM education. *Sustainability (Basel)*, *15*(9), 7393. doi:10.3390u15097393

Wardana, L. A., Rulyansah, A., Izzuddin, A., & Nuriyanti, R. (2023). Integration of digital and non-digital learning media to advance life skills of elementary education students post-pandemic COVID-19. *Pegem Journal of Education and Instruction*, 13(1), 211-222. https://www.pegegog.net/index.php/pegegog/article/view/1984

Williams, P. (2017). Assessing collaborative learning: Big data, analytics and university futures. *Assessment & Evaluation in Higher Education*, *42*(6), 978–989. doi:10.1080/02602938.2016.1216084

Zheng, L., Fan, Y., & Long, M. (2023). The impacts of the comprehensive learning analytics approach on learning performance in online collaborative learning. *Education and Information Technologies*, *28*(12), 1–24. https://link.springer.com/article/10.1007/s10639-023-11886-3. doi:10.100710639-023-11886-3 PMID:36688219

KEY TERMS AND DEFINITIONS

Collaborative Learning: Collaborative Learning is an instructional approach where students work in groups to achieve shared learning goals, fostering teamwork, communication, and critical thinking skills.

Emergent Practices: Emergent Practices in education refer to innovative, non-traditional approaches that evolve organically in response to the dynamic needs of learners and the changing educational landscape.

K-12 Classrooms: K-12 refers to primary and secondary education levels, typically encompassing kindergarten to 12th-grade students.

Learning Analytics: Learning Analytics involves the measurement, collection, analysis, and reporting of data about learners and their contexts to understand and optimize learning environments.

Life Skills: Life Skills encompass a range of abilities and competencies that enable individuals to navigate the challenges of everyday life effectively, including communication, critical thinking, and problem-solving.

Social Learning: Social Learning is a theory that suggests individuals learn through observing, imitating, and interacting with others, emphasizing the importance of social interactions in the learning process.

STEM Approach: STEM stands for Science, Technology, Engineering, and Mathematics. A STEM Approach in education emphasizes an interdisciplinary approach to teaching and learning, integrating these core subjects to promote problem-solving and innovation.

Virtual Reality: Virtual Reality (VR) involves using computer-generated simulations to create immersive, interactive environments, offering unique and often realistic experiences for educational purposes.

Chapter 8
Fostering K-12 Learners' Willingness to Communicate Through Technology-Enhanced Practices With a Perspective of Learner Analytics

Arzu Kanat-Mutluoglu
TED University, Turkey

Sibel Kahraman-Ozkurt:*Pamukkale University, Turkey*

ABSTRACT

As a result of the advancements in technology and the changes in the student profiles, which can be categorized as the digital natives, it is an indispensable practice for today's English as a Foreign Language (EFL) teachers to effectively apply digital tools to develop their students' language skills and increase their motivation and enthusiasm for communication in the target language. Based on this necessity, the current chapter of the book tries to give insights to EFL teachers to use digital tools for technology-enhanced practices with the aim of enhancing their students' willingness to communicate (WTC). It also suggests some ways for the teachers to collect data about their student's progress and the learning process, which is called learner analytics, while performing these technology-enhanced practices.

DOI: 10.4018/979-8-3693-0066-4.ch008

INTRODUCTION

Language learning as a life-long process is interwoven with intricate as well as diverse paths. These paths might include plenty of entrances and exits; however, each one of them commonly has one single direction, namely, being able to communicate. It is also interesting to reveal that communication is not only the goal of language learning, but it is also the tool of the process (Mystkowska-Wiertelak & Pietrzykowska, 2011). Learners of a language need to communicate in the target language both as a receiver and –better, as a producer of the language. This preferable outcome of language learning pursues communicative and interactive proficiency (Zarrinabadi et al., 2021), which could be shaped by actual practice.

In a setting where exposure to the target language is limited, foreign language (L2 hereafter) learning consists of deficiencies in access to the practice of communication. L2 learners are at a faulty position in utilizing the target language in communication as they are fenced by their first language (L1) (Baker & MacIntyre, 2000). In most cases, the L2 learning journey of these learners is only restricted to the classrooms, and they might fail to get opportunities to use the language daily (Chaisiri, 2023). Therefore, they are in essential need of emerging a stimulus for using the language in L2 communication.

In tandem with the search for stimulation in L2 communication, a series of proximal and distal influencing variables are shaped in L2 learners (MacIntyre et al., 2011). L2 learners might develop affective factors such as enjoyment, anxiety, or fear of communication, situational factors such as the effect of interlocutors or topics of communication, as well as individual factors such as their perceived proficiency level of L2. A full representation of the L2 communication process must conceptualize all these influences. Willingness to communicate (WTC) as a concept could unite these influencing variables and amend itself as a guide to real communication in L2 (Guo et al., 2023; Mystkowska-Wiertelak & Petrzykowska, 2011; Yashima et al., 2016). It is worth noting here that this real communication is a web of using all four language skills together. However, by following the tendency, communication or initiation to communication indicates speaking here and on in this chapter.

Originally shaped by the studies of Burgoon (1976) on the reticence, WTC is a multilayered concept that is intricately interwoven with individual, contextual, linguistic, and affective factors (Kanat-Mutluoğlu, 2020). The pioneering researcher of this concept, McCroskey, with an associate, described WTC in one of the earlier studies as the intention to communicate when free to do so (McCroskey & Baer, 1985). The emergence of and the emphasis on the intent in this description of WTC indicates the unnecessity of being in real communication. In a sense, WTC does not lead to a conclusion that an individual might turn this enthusiasm into an action of communication. Moreover, this identification refers to a stable tendency to be in communication, like a personality trait such as being emotional or talkative. However, when the concern is communication, the fluctuation of willingness is inevitable.

To identify WTC in an L2 context (L2 WTC hereafter), MacIntyre et al. (1998) also echoed the feature of intention, but they highlighted the fluctuation of WTC by its state and dynamic feature defining it as "readiness to enter into discourse at a specific time with a specific person or persons, using an L2 when free to do so" (ibid, 547). L2 WTC is further conceptualized as the final state predisposition before the explicit action of communication (MacIntyre et al., 2011; Peng et al., 2017). It is identified as the primary predictor for an individual to use the target language in communication (Bernales, 2016; MacIntyre & Legatto, 2011).

The conceptualization of L2 WTC as a readiness to communicate in certain settings with certain interlocutors in specific situations directs that it is not solely contingent upon possessing proficient language skills but also depends on a range of psychological, contextual, and individual variables (Mystkowska-Wiertelak, & Pawlak, 2016). The existing research on L2 WTC has identified these influential variables. Affective variables including anxiety (Hashimoto, 2002; Yu, 2011), self-confidence (Şener, 2014) and motivation (Yashima, 2002) as well as contextual variables such as the teachers (Cao, 2011; Khajavy et al., 2018), topics (Cao, 2011; Kang, 2005), tasks (Cao, 2011), and interlocutors (Cao & Philip, 2006), have been found to significantly impact an individual's L2 WTC. Additionally, individual variables such as perceived competence, personality (MacIntyre & Charos, 1996), and mood all play a significant effect in molding one's L2 WTC. These multilayers of the concept look for further attention while shaping, developing, and scaffolding it in the L2 learning process.

Paying this attention to the organization of L2 WTC, teachers all around the world who are teaching English as a foreign language (EFL) seek out ways to let learners communicate by using all dimensions of the target language effectively in L2 classrooms. Among the four essential skills for effective communication in English, namely, listening, reading, writing, and speaking, it is worth noting that speaking differs from the other three skills regarding the unique challenges learners encounter (Hsieh et al., 2023). As Chou (2018) indicates, speaking is a complex and compound skill enriched by different knowledge bases of English, including vocabulary, pronunciation, and listening all in all. As a result, the learners mostly have reluctance to talk in EFL classrooms, and for the teachers who aim to motivate the learners to talk in English, there are plenty of obstacles to overcome (Yashima et al., 2016).

The principal challenge might be related to the nature of EFL in L2 settings: the learners have very limited access to the language outside the classroom, and the learners might tend to reflect English as a subject rather than a language to use in communication (Rahimi & Fathi, 2022). This fact might lead to a decrease in the level of learners' L2 WTC along with their motivation to acquire the language (Aydın, 2014; Pawlak & Mystkowska-Wiertelak, 2015; Risatti, 2012). There exists a deficit regarding the necessity of employing various methodologies and techniques in the initial construction of L2 WTC and the subsequent enhancement of the one already shaped by the learners. In this vein, teachers are employing technology to establish a communicative atmosphere inside and outside the classroom. Digital learning tools are being utilized to facilitate English language learners in engaging in oral communication, so promoting and improving their second language (L2) speaking skills.

To gain a comprehensive understanding of the impact of this digital learning initially on L2 WTC and subsequently on L2 communication, the place of technology should be resolved. Then empirical studies on L2 WTC in digital contexts should be investigated. Lastly, to identify the impact of digital learning on L2 WTC, the successive effect of learning analytics, a base of the measurement, collection, analysis, and reporting of data about learners and their contexts should be addressed. All three of these proposed contents are respectively placed in this chapter. As a promising addition, this chapter also offers some practices by using three different technology-enhanced tools and certain ways to analyse the effect of this employment in the classroom via learning analytics.

MAIN FOCUS OF THE CHAPTER

Integrating Technology-Enhanced Practices Into EFL Classes

Technology is more commonplace today, influencing a wide range of social and educational factors, including our daily lives at home, work, and school as well as many of our leisure pursuits. As a direct result of these factors, the use of technology in schools for language teaching and learning purposes has gained great popularity and importance. It is widely contested by educational researchers (Archer et al., 2014; Chandra & Lloyd, 2008; Chauan, 2017; Polly et al., 2020; Scherer et al., 2020) and organizations such as TESOL Technology Standards Project Team and International Society for Technology in Education that student learning may be enhanced through effective administration of technological tools and practices. Although technology can raise student accomplishment in K-12 institutions (ages 5-18), concerns about teachers' readiness to successfully integrate technology into the classroom continue to emerge.

Technology integration in this chapter is addressed as "instances in which teachers and/or learners use technology as a tool to support the learning process" (Polly et al., 2020, p. 863). When technology is successfully integrated into education, it can help improving students' learning processes and creating a more effective, efficient, and appealing educational environment. Therefore, the role of the educator in this successful integration is crucial. Considering this sensitive and important role of the future teachers, many teacher education programs today offer introductory courses to develop basic technology skills of teachers. However, the problem here is that while teachers are equipped with technological skills such as word processing, preparing presentations or even developing simple software, they have little idea about implementing or integrating those skills into their teaching practices (Andersson, 2006; Farjon et al., 2019; Polly et al., 2020). Therefore, the current chapter of the book tries to give insights to language teachers on the integration of some digital tools into language teaching to analyse student development and achievement while accordingly raising the WTC levels of students.

Teachers' Technological Pedagogical and Content Knowledge (TPACK)

As discussed earlier, to equip EFL student teachers with the skills and qualifications needed for successful integration of technology, teacher education programs need to support these prospective teachers in developing not only technological skills but also pedagogical and methodological practices and content knowledge. They need to know what digital tools to use, how to utilize them correctly and how to make them pedagogically appropriate to the discipline (Kwangsawad, 2016). Based on this perspective, Mishra, and Koehler (2006), grounded in the work of Schulman (1987), developed Technological Pedagogical Content Knowledge (TPACK) as a theoretical framework for understanding the knowledge and skills teachers need for effective and efficient integration of technology. TPACK framework includes seven domains as illustrated in Figure 1: Technology Knowledge (TK), Pedagogy Knowledge (PK), Content Knowledge (CK), Technological Content Knowledge (TCK), Technological Pedagogical Knowledge (TPK), Pedagogical Content Knowledge (PCK), and Technological Pedagogical Content Knowledge (TPACK).

The framework in Figure 1 has three main components that relate and align with one another: content (subject matter), pedagogy (teaching methodology) and technology. A successful practitioner teacher is required to understand and interpret the relations and interplay among these three components (Koehler & Mishra, 2009). Technology knowledge (TK) means that teachers must have a thorough understanding of information technology to effectively implement it in their classrooms. They must also know how to modify the goals of technologies to make better use of them. Teachers' knowledge of the procedures and methods used in teaching and learning is known as pedagogy knowledge (PK). It offers information on instructional methodologies, learner characteristics, and methods for assessing students' comprehension (Harris et al., 2009). Content knowledge (CK) is teachers' knowledge about the subject matter they teach including concepts, theories, or conceptual frameworks.

Although there are some studies indicating a problematic distinction among the components of the framework (Graham, 2011; Niess, 2011; Voogt et al., 2013), TPACK is regarded as a useful framework for describing the information that pre-service teachers must acquire to properly integrate technology into their teaching, regardless of the subject matter (Baran et al., 2011). A teacher internalizing TPACK framework can understand the technological concepts and pedagogical methods that effectively teach curriculum by using technology.

Figure 1. TPACK framework
(Retrieved from www.tpack.org)

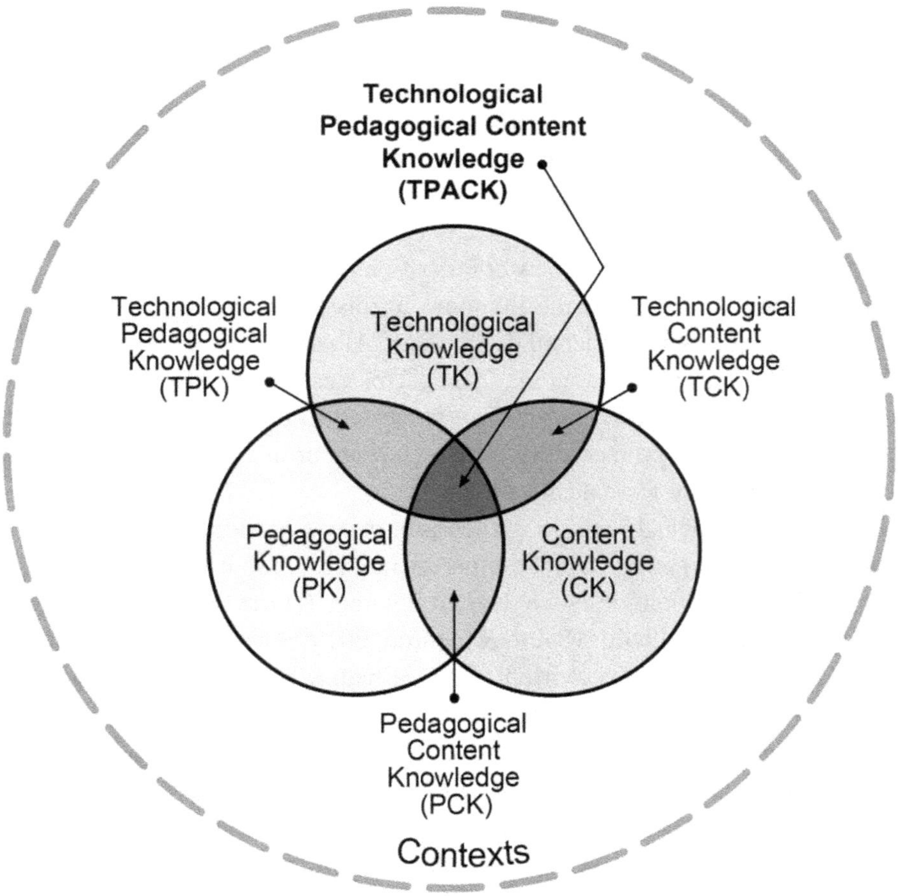

L2 WTC in Digital Contexts

Empirically supported, the role of technology is overarching in L2 classrooms. L2 WTC also gets its share of this increased attention to digital technology use, and recently, a growing number of studies have been conducted to explore the nature of L2 WTC in digital contexts in which the use of technology-enhanced tools or practices is habitually exemplified (e.g., Alqarni, 2021; Ebadi & Ebadijalal, 2022; Lee, 2019; Zarrinabadi et al., 2021). Contemporary research in the field of L2 WTC tends to conceptualize L2 WTC both in classroom contexts and extracurricular or extramural contexts (Soyoof, 2022). The division of extracurricular and extramural contexts is bounded by the idea of autonomous learning and teacher interference. In the previous one, the learners are included in a setting of digital learning where teachers are evaluating the process and guiding the students by assigning digitally-enhanced activities to learners inside or outside the classroom, whereas the latter one is totally attached to the learners that they are intentionally initiating the use of digital tools or platforms to communicate in L2. In a sense, while extracurricular digital learning is based on formal education and the teacher's initiation, extramural digital learning is free from these prerequisites and germane to the learner's autonomy (Lee, 2019; Soyoof, 2022; Sylvén & Sundqvist, 2017).

With the primary aim of offering some activities for teachers to use in EFL classrooms while enhancing learners' L2 WTC and evaluating this enhancement, this chapter might be regarded as a new contribution to the L2 WTC in extracurricular digital learning. A review of the literature in this field reveals that most studies have utilized a quasi-experimental design (e.g., Alqarni, 2021; Ebadi & Ebadijalal, 2022; Lee, 2019; Zarrinabadi et al., 2021). This design involves the allocation of two distinct groups of learners who are subjected to different language teaching practices, either within the confines of a classroom or in an external setting, as an integral component of formal education.

In different ecological conditions, such as in-class or outside the class, the learners are having some interventions in the experimental groups that are engaged in a wide range of digital technologies such as digital games (Horowitz, 2019; Reinders & Wattana, 2015), digital wilds (Sauro & Zourou, 2019; Soyoof et al., 2023), Google Assistant (Tai & Chen, 2023), virtual reality (Ebadi & Ebadijalal, 2022), and social media (Chotipaktanasook & Reinders, 2016). The impacts of these interventions via technology-enhanced practices on L2 WTC are explored by comparing the L2 WTC levels of learners both in the experiment and control groups. Employing such a design, Chaisiri (2023) recently examined the influence of technology-mediated oral tasks on Thai EFL learners' WTC. The participants of the study were taking synchronous EFL classes virtually. However, the ones in the experiment groups were offered some oral tasks through the asynchronously mediated self-taken videos by using the digital application Flip (formerly known as Flipgrid). The results suggested that the learners performing the tasks promoted by Flip increased their L2 WTC more and they suggested that they had a less-anxiety provoked atmosphere there so that they felt more willing and ready to communicate in English. As an echo of Chaisiri (2023) in methodological and implication manners, Cherrez (2023) also explored the influence of technology-mediated tasks on the Spanish L2 learners' L2 WTC by using the same application, Flip. The study quantitatively suggested that the group of learners who had access to the digital tasks by using Flip enhanced their L2 WTC and communicative performance in Spanish. It further elaborated that the learners felt more confident and willing without the fear of making mistakes and being evaluated while doing the tasks in Flip, and in conclusion, it indicated that technology-mediated tasks could be identified as possible ways of promoting L2 use with a potential of empowering autonomy in learners by creating awareness of aims of learning an L2 and taking the responsibility of the process.

With a different group of Thai EFL learners, Chhum and Champakaew (2019) explored the role of an online application, namely, Hello English, in the enhancement of L2 WTC by having a similar research design. They found that after the intervention to the experiment group by using Hello English as an extra online tool outside the classroom, the students in both groups increased their level of WTC. However, the ones in the experimental group increased their level of WTC more than the other group.

Focusing on providing a stress-free environment to enhance L2 WTC, some studies suggested using virtual reality (VR) tools (e.g., Ebadi & Ebadijalal, 2022; Wu & Hung, 2022). VR could be defined as "an immersive computer-enabled technology that replicates an environment and allows a simulation of the user to be present and interact in that environment" (Lloyd et al., 2017, p. 222). By using specifically designed applications, the learners in L2 classrooms could be equipped with the opportunity to use the target language in real-life-like situations. For instance, in their mixed-method study, Ebadi & Ebadijalal (2022) let the experiment group learners become museum guides or visitors for twenty minutes through ten weeks by using Google Expeditions while they are all using the VR tools in the whole process. In these ten weeks, the ones in the control group were also provided the same activity requesting role-plays; however, they did not have the VR tools. In the end, it was found that the learners with the VR tool outperformed the ones without the VR tool in terms of developing their oral skills and L2 WTC. In contrast to Ebadi & Ebadijalal (2022), Wu & Hung (2022) failed to support the positive influence of VR tools on the Taiwanese EFL learners' level of L2 WTC. The VR software was Cospaces this time and a total of 56 learners were divided into experiment and control groups. Before the actual visit to a museum, the learners in both groups were provided with the necessary vocabulary, grammar, and dialogue logs. The ones in the experiment group had access to the Cospaces through VR headsets during the instruction, while the ones in the control group received the instructions with the use of traditional teaching materials such as use of pictures, PowerPoint presentations, and flashcards. They found that this VR tool engagement in the L2 learning process had no impact on the learners' L2 WTC, learning autonomy, pronunciation, and fluency, but it influenced grammar and vocabulary knowledge. In this vein, the differences in the applications and the demographic background of the learners, such as age, might have a mediating effect on VR tools and software use to enhance L2 WTC.

These studies examining the effect of VR tools on L2 WTC emerged with the objective of creating authentic communication environments inside a virtual context. The primary goal is to alleviate the anxiety associated with interpersonal communication, particularly verbal interaction with others. In the same vein, thanks to the accelerated innovation in technology, a more stress-free environment for learners might be built around the idea of facilitating human-to-non-human interaction, which creates novel opportunities for communication without the fear of judgment by others (Ayedoun et al., 2019; Hsieh et al., 2023; Tai & Chen, 2023). With a relatively young group of Taiwanese learners aged 10-11, Hsieh et al. (2023) conducted research to comprehend the impact of human-to-robot interaction on the learners' L2 WTC and pronunciation knowledge. By letting the learners interact with a robot while using some extra materials such as a tablet, a cell phone, and a set of tangible objects, the L2 WTC was hypothesized to be augmented. Consequently, they found that the human-to-robot interaction influenced the learners' L2 WTC and pronunciation positively, and they reported active engagement of interaction with several tries based on video-recorded observations. We could deduce that robots possess qualities such as patience and non-judgment, which might enable them to provide learners with a feeling of psychological security and mitigate the stress of social assessment that learners may experience when engaging with human individuals.

With the same concerns, Tai and Chen (2023) created a learning atmosphere where an intelligent personal assistant (IPA) application, namely, Google Assistant, is used for communication in precisely designed tasks in the flow of the English classes for two weeks. The findings of the study indicated that the utilization of Google Assistant had a substantial impact on the improvement of the learners' L2 WTC, bolstered their confidence in communication abilities, and mitigated their levels of anxiety when speaking. The qualitative data indicated that individuals derived enjoyment from engaging in gaming activities with Google Assistant and conversing with chatbots. These interactions served to alleviate anxiety and fostered a sense of motivation to utilize the English language for authentic and purposeful communication. In a sense, the results of the study revealed that the use of IPA-based interaction created a more conducive and less intimidating atmosphere for learners. Thus, learners might have demonstrated increased levels of engagement, motivation, confidence, and, subsequently, their willingness to communicate in the target language. Dizon (2020) echoed the results of Tai and Chen (ibid) and found an IPA advanced the L2 WTC and took a role in the process of outperforming the linguistic knowledge in an experimental study in which Alexa developed by Amazon appeared to be the IPA that the undergraduate Japanese learners interacted with.

In addition to this contemporary research on the enhancement of L2 WTC and, consequently, L2 communication as well as their methods of studying these concepts, the highlight of flipped learning is noticeable in the literature. Rather than having all the features of a real flipped education approach in which the learners had opportunities to use digital learning sources before and after the face-to-face classes for preparation, practices, or continuum, the studies were mostly conducted to reveal the differences of L2 WTC levels inside, outside, and digital classroom settings. Without having the mixture of inside the classroom and virtual classroom in the process of English instruction, Alqarni (2021) questioned the differences of the tertiary level Arabic learners' L2 WTC in face-to-face classes and online classes based on the learners' previous and current experiences. They found that their L2 WTC level is higher in online settings, which could promote the experience of flipped learning for EFL instruction. Zarrinabadi et al. (2021) also tested the effect of flipped learning approach on enhancing L2 WTC. They worked with two groups of learners in two EFL classes and one group received EFL education through flipped learning, while the other had conventional English teaching. In the end, they found that the flipped learning approach remained ahead of the L2 WTC enhancement due to its influences on increasing the joy of learning and motivation, as well as decreasing the anxiety of learning. In the tandem use of offline (in-class and out-of-class) and digital settings as a way of flipped learning, the influencing effect of digital setting on shaping the learners' L2 WTC was also indicated by Lee and Hsieh (2019). The Taiwanese EFL learners in this study had higher level of L2 WTC when they felt confident and persistent to initiate communication in English in both offline and digital settings. However, receiving digital learning while learning English had more influences on the increase of L2 WTC with the reasons of being less anxious and more confident in this setting.

The current attempts are gathered mostly around the use of social media when the concern is blending the digital and offline teaching and investigating its effect on the development of L2 WTC. By assigning some before or after in-class tasks through use of Telegram (Jafarigohar et al., 2019; Mohammadi et al., 2019; Zarrinabadi et al., 2021), Facebook (Kasuma, 2021; Nugroho & Atmojo, 2020), YouTube (Lee & Lu, 2021), and a combination of applicable applications, it was revealed that the enhancement of L2 WTC and speaking skills is possible. The reasons for this enhancement are bound to the nature of social media, where the users had a more stress-free environment and felt less anxious about communication in an L2 (Sharma,

2019; Su & Fatmawati, 2019) and more motivated to learn new things (Dirjal et al., 2020) when it is mostly and specifically used in extracurricular settings.

Indicated deeply, a consensus has been reached about the influencing effect of digital settings on L2 WTC in the process of foreign language learning. The fact that various learners are hesitant to speak in the target language for fear of making mistakes in front of others, getting negative feedback from their peers and teachers, and being a mockery of others makes the enhancement of L2 WTC a big challenge for language teachers in the formal language teaching (Peng, 2019; Tai & Chen, 2023). This challenge is growing when the limited chances of oral communication are presented to the learners in L2 settings outside the classroom (Cherrez, 2023; MacIntyre et al., 1998). The rapid advancements in digital environments have presented significant prospects for augmenting these chances of communication and raising the possibility of initiation of communication (Hsieh et al., 2023). Learners in digital contexts are indicated to feel more confident and more engaged in communicating in L2 orally without the effect of communication anxiety (Chaisiri, 2023; Ebadi & Ebadijalal, 2022; Fan, 2022; Hsieh et al., 2023; Lee & Hsieh, 2019). Moreover, they are given an extra setting to practice oral communication being free from the limits of the classroom. This significantly suggested fact, however, fails to provide alternatives to language teachers when they consider how they could incorporate digital contexts in their teaching setting and how they could evaluate the effect of such incorporation. The objective of this chapter is to advocate for the implementation of three technology-enhanced tools in second language (L2) classrooms. The aim is to enhance L2 learners' willingness to communicate (WTC) by outlining the objectives and procedures of these tools. Additionally, the chapter explores the applicability of these tools across different levels of K-12 education, specifically primary, secondary, and high schools. Additionally, this chapter also aims to present the potential use of research methods to the language teachers to detect the effect of these practices in K-12 classrooms because teachers could be the perfect researchers by being in the action actively. These suggestions of research are discussed with the concepts of learning analytics, which will be argued in the following.

The Place of Learning Analytics for L2 WTC in Digital Contexts

A very few years ago, with an immediate and unexpected need, teachers found themselves as subjects of virtual teaching journeys as a side effect of Covid 19 outbreak. Most of them sought out ways to adopt effective ways of teaching in this novel setting. For EFL teachers, it could be identified as being a bit more challenging because they should have detected techniques and tools open to interaction, particularly oral interaction. At the end of the process that took more than a year, almost all EFL teachers in the classrooms happened to use digital management platforms and/or digital tools to engage learners in oral interaction.

This fictional reality that the whole world experienced made the digital learning context an actual case to be implemented as part of formal language education. Some applications were regarded as useful in developing learners' initiation to use English in communication, in other words, their L2 WTC given in detail in the previous section. Under these circumstances, the use of digital applications in EFL classrooms becomes inevitable. However, still, teachers might still need some answers to the questions whether the students get the benefits of digital tools and whether the tools are in good fit for the students. The digital learning systems are providing a good source of data for the answers to these questions and more (Gafandzhieva et al., 2020). The concern is to decide how to analyse these data in the process of assisting teaching and learning practices in the schools (Jivet et al., 2018).

This potential analysis concern might be sorted out with the emergence of learning analytics (LA hereafter). LA deals with the collection, analysis, and description of data about learners and contexts where learning takes place (Siemens & Gasevic, 2012). This perspective of LA about investigating learning and teaching, chasing student progress, studying school or university data, and looking for evidence to improve teaching and learning is not a novel issue. LA is formed on these ambitions; however, it aims to activate opportunities after the emergence of digital data in learning contexts and use computational analysis methods from data science (SoLAR, 2023). It includes "...an educational application of web analytics aimed at learner profiling, a process of gathering and analysing details of individual student interactions in online learning activities" (NMC Horizon Project, 2016). In this sense, for the concerns about the effect of any digital learning tool, LA is a good choice with its defined aims in NMC Horizon Project (2016) as "to build better pedagogies, empower active learning, target at-risk student populations, and assess factors affecting completion and student success" and with its features described by Reinders (2018) as "more available, easier, and quicker than ever before".

As inferred from its definition, there is no restriction to use LA in almost all fields of education. In language learning, it could be applied to understand the indicators of L2 learning over time by using the already gathered data and evaluating the metrics of the learners. Then it could also be manipulated to diagnose why some language parts are achieved while others failed and to prescribe effective ways of learning an L2 based on the data (Reinders, 2018; SoLAR, 2023).

All these methods of LA seek data mining and analysis, and the higher education institutions appear to have an advantage in that point, especially when it is considered their mature level of using and accessing data collection tools (Leitner et al., 2017; Sousa et al., 2021). With some fair worries about educational and institutional politics, language teachers in K-12 schools tend to be sceptical of utilizing LA tools

(Brown, 2020), or they simply resist applying LA tools because they do not know how to utilize them (Reinders, 2018). With support provided to the language teachers in K -12 schools, it could be stressed that the emerged data could be analysed only through spreadsheets and basic statistical packages that many teachers are already equipped with (Sousa et al., 2021) because LA could supply solutions to many of the practical problems of language teachers meet daily Reinders, 2018.

In a classroom where a language teacher uses a digitally enhanced tool to improve the learners' oral interaction or L2 WTC, it is possible to suspect its influence. LA might take the stage here to analyse how the adopted tools take roles in improving these concepts. Such tools present data for student engagement in interaction by not only providing actual interaction but also delivering the tries. The number of tries, along with the percentage of interaction, could work as indicators of influence on the learners' L2 WTC.

With the aim of guiding language teachers in the process of enhancing L2 WTC, this chapter will offer three digitally enhanced practices to be applied in three different K-12 schools. Then to serve the aim of letting the teachers to become researchers of their own practices, this chapter will extend some suggestions for using LA to analyse the influence of these potentially effective practices. This section will encompass the design of presenting the procedure, including the stated objectives, the intended group of learners, and the integration of a digital tool within an L2 classroom at a K-12 educational institution to foster L2 interaction and L2 WTC. Additionally, it will explore potential approaches for implementing learning analytics (LA) methods to assess the impact of this intervention.

Technology-Enhanced Practices With Digital Tools

In this part of the chapter, the audience of the book is presented with information about some Web 2.0 tools and how to utilize them for language learning purposes with the aim of developing learners' WTC and analysing learners' progress and achievement. Three different digital tools are introduced, and sample activity plans are shared for language teachers to give insights and inspiration for their current and future classroom practices. To have better insights of the influences of these tools on the learners' L2 WTC, teachers are encouraged to become researchers and apply learning analytics (LA) as a method of research. This encouragement is supported by providing some applicable suggestions for each digital tool while exploring its effect on L2 WTC. Through the activity plans suggested for language teachers, they can find their way in using the digital tools both for teaching purposes and applying LA to enhance their students' WTC.

1. Voki

Voki, as an educational digital tool, allows teachers and language learners to create their own speaking animated characters. Learners can give voice to their animated characters by recording their voices or using text-to-speech. They can choose among the characters and make them talk freely with Basic Voki. Teachers can also use Voki to create animated presentations for their classrooms and assign tasks, homework or projects to their students through Voki Classroom.

Voki does not require downloading any software or application, but it simply works through the Web browser. Today's language learners, called as digital natives, can easily understand the principles and design of the tool, and associate it with other digital tools they have already used. As Voki is accessible for most language teachers and learners at home and in the classroom, it makes learners feel motivated and encouraged to use Voki for language learning purposes, increases student autonomy and responsibility for learning, and creates a distancing effect that appeals to hesitant and reluctant students (Aikina & Zubkova, 2015; Ramdani, 2018; Yeşilbağ & Korkmaz, 2021).

To use Voki for educational purposes as a teacher or learner, there are some steps to follow. First, one needs to sign up for Voki at www.voki.com and create an account according to the role (as a teacher, student, administrator, or parent). By using the create button, students can design their own avatars using various options for customizing their Voki animations. To add voice to their avatars, they can text for speech, record synchronously by their microphones, or upload a pre-recorded audio file. Then, they can publish and send it to their classmates or teachers.

An Activity Plan to Apply Voki for Language Teaching

Prior to the activity: The function and useful language addressed by the teacher and the syllabus focus on greeting and meeting people, expressing likes and dislikes, and making simple inquiries. Prior to the class, the teacher creates 3 different characters using Voki and makes them talk about themselves. By doing so, s/he also introduces the students to the Voki as a digital tool.

Students' Proficiency Level: A1
Students' Age: 9

Aims of the Activity:

- Students will be able to introduce themselves.
- Students will be able to meet new people.
- Students will be able to exchange simple personal information.

Procedure: The teacher comes to the class and greets the students. Then, s/he tells the students they are going to watch 3 different people talking about themselves. S/he says one of these characters is the teacher and asks the students to guess which video includes information about the teacher. S/he plays the videos and asks for students' opinions. When they give their answers, s/he asks the reasons for this. Following the discussion, s/he asks for their opinions about these 3 videos and whether they like creating such videos. Then, s/he asks the students to go to their homes and record themselves by choosing and designing a character in Voki to introduce themselves. S/he elaborates on the assignment by giving some details such as using at least one greeting expression, talking about favorite classes, telling the school's name etc. S/he also tells the students they can use teacher's videos as samples to prepare their own recordings through Voki. S/he says s/he has already created a Voki classroom and added the students in that classroom. At that point, s/he shows the interface of Voki, how to sign up for it and a few buttons that can be useful for students when creating their own avatars. Students are given 3 days to complete that assignment and send it to the teacher. S/he says they will play a game in the class by watching these recordings in the next class. S/he also tells the students to contact with him/her whenever they seek for help for creating their avatars through Voki.

In the given time duration, the students create their own avatars, make them speak about themselves, record the audio, and send it to the teacher. In the class time, the teacher tells the students s/he has already watched their recordings, and thanks them for their efforts and work. S/he says they will play a 'Guess Who?' game right now. S/he says she is going to show some recordings prepared by the students in their class, and they are going to guess who this is. S/he tells the class they will find the opportunity to get to know their classmates in a better way. S/he also asks for comments on the recordings to get peer feedback.

Applying LA for Voki practices to investigate its influence on L2 WTC: Voki, as a digital tool designed for synchronous or asynchronous purposes, enables users to have an avatar. When we consider the age of the target group as young learners at a secondary school, the fear of making mistakes in front of others might increase their reluctance to communicate by using English. However, the use of avatars rather than the actual identity would work to decrease the level of this fear (Kruk, 2016; Wehner, 2014) because they could think that the mistakes did not belong to them but to the avatars, which might lead to the enhancement of L2 WTC.

In order to test this assumption, the teachers could conduct such a piece of research that does not bring much burden to them. Before using the Voki as a tool in the class, teachers had better observe the learners and seek to develop an understanding of learners. S/he could identify the learners who had anxiety sourced from the fear of making mistakes. Rather than this observation, it is also possible to adopt a communication anxiety (CA) scale and measure the level of learners' anxiety. After acquiring information about the anxiety level, teachers might conduct semi-structured interviews with the more anxious learners and less anxious learners. During this interview, s/he could direct questions about having Voki with a feature of using an avatar while speaking in English and its effect on CA. Then indirectly, she could question the effect of Voki on learners L2 WTC as mentioned, the anxiety level is one of the strongest indicators of L2 WTC.

While analysing the collected data, it is not vital that teachers have access to well-developed analysis packages or an acquired knowledge of analysis methods. It is possible to use spreadsheet programs to report the learners' answers gathered in the interviews to the questions about the influence of Voki on CA and L2 WTC. Then by reading these answers thoroughly and recurrently, s/he could comprehend the effect of Voki based on a novel research study and develop some key terms germane to the reasons for the influence of the current digital tool.

2. Flip

Flip (formerly known as Flipgrid) is an online video discussion platform. It enables the teachers to create their own online classes to let their students share their opinions and ideas asynchronously in short videos or audio messages. Teachers create a classroom group and send an invite link or join code for the students. Students can also be invited by adding their emails. This makes access to the tool easier for the students as they do not have to create an account or sign up for it. In that online group, the teacher or the students post a topic to spark a discussion, and the responses to that discussion can be given through short videos. The teacher can give prompts or guidelines for the students on topics so that they can follow them to create their video thread responses. Time duration (min 30 seconds and max 2 minutes) for video responses can also be specified by the teacher.

As one of the contemporary video response technologies, Flip can be used as a video-based learning tool for discussion, reflections, or presentations (Keiper et al., 2021). Students find the opportunity to video and edit themselves by using different strategies without the pressure related to others watching (Taylor & Hinchman, 2020). When it is addressed in terms of L2 WTC, Flip has the potential to enhance student confidence, collaboration and cooperation, participation in discussion and speaking time (Delmas & Moore, 2019; Gurjar, 2020; Saçak & Kavun, 2020). It offers students the chance to connect with their teachers and classmates whenever they want and in their comfort zone. Thus, this may increase their WTC and give a more proactive role to the students.

To register for free to Flip, one needs to go to the website www.flip.com. Then, teachers can create their own safe and private classroom groups by adding their students to the groups they create and start the online video discussions under various topics they determine.

An Activity Plan to Apply Flip for Language Teaching

Prior to the Activity: The teacher finds out that some of the students in his/her class avoid risk-taking in the class and hence refrain from speaking L2. Also, s/he thinks limited time is advocated for speaking activities, and not all the students find the opportunity to speak L2 because of limited weekly class hours. S/he decides to apply Flip as an out-of-class activity to engage his/her students with various speaking tasks. Considering the number of students in class, s/he creates three different groups with 10 students in each group to make the administration of the groups easier and to give more chances for speaking to the students.

Students' Proficiency Level: B1
Students' Age: 15

Aims of the Activity:

- Students will be able to practice their speaking skills.
- Students will be able practice their pronunciation skills.
- Students will be able to discuss contemporary topics.

Procedure: The teacher comes to the class and greets the students. Then, s/he tells the students they are going to start a new project to develop their speaking and pronunciation skills by posting in an online group. S/he says they will use Flip as a Web 2.0 tool during one semester, shows the web site, and introduces its interface. They also watch a video on the uses of Flip, and s/he aims at making the students familiar with the website. S/he tells the students she has already divided them into 3 groups, and the groups will be rearranged every month so that they can find the opportunity to interact with all their classmates on that online platform. S/he shares the names in Group 1, Group 2 and Group 3 and asks the groups to find a name for their group. The students in each group come together, find a name for their group, and the teacher renames the groups. S/he also gives the invitation links to the students so that they can be a member of these groups. S/he says they will start a discussion on a topic each week in class, and the discussion will go on in Flip. They will have a one-week duration to post their video discussions in their groups. They will take turns to post video responses to the themes, with discussion emerging via replies to that initial response and each other's replies. They will have at least 20 seconds and a maximum of 2 minutes for their video recordings. S/he says that they will get feedback about the clarity, coherence, and cohesion of the content of their videos and their pronunciation skills via the inbuilt feedback mechanism Flip offers. S/he says she has already chosen the topics for the first discussion in the groups but asks for their ideas on themes that can be discussed in the coming weeks. The first discussion topic is what three adjectives their family would use to describe their personality. They need to elaborate on it in their video response.

Applying LA for Flip practices to investigate its influence on L2 WTC: The current group using Flip that provides asynchronous video recording is a group of teenagers. For this age group, the opinions of their peers have a role in their further moves. The teacher in the provided practice is asking the students in three different groups to provide feedback on each other's posts with this knowledge in mind. Here, for this teacher, two points to explore have arisen: (1) s/he could explore the effect of using an asynchronous digital tool for enabling learners to talk, and (2) s/he might investigate the influence of peer feedback that the learners gathered from their groupmates in three different cycles.

For the first research aim, s/he should ask the students to report the time of recording the videos and uploading them to Flip and the number of trials until reaching the finalized recorded video. By using the log of the tool, s/he should also check whether the students reupload their videos or not. These records might give the teacher some numerical data that would become meaningful with a triangulation of qualitative data collected through interviews. For these interviews, the teacher could invite the students who log in to Flip and upload their videos at different times of the day and who have more than one trial. The opinions of the students could be gathered in the interview by asking about the influence of these features of Flip on their initiation to communicate and eagerness to participate in the task. These overall data would provide empirical findings about the effect of using such features of an asynchronous technology-enhanced tool because the students encompass the chance to record the video when they are ready, willing, and motivated at most. Additionally, the assumption about watching their own videos could be tested when it is asked how many times they upload the video and how it takes a role in shaping WTC. The students are able to watch themselves in Flip and correct their mistakes if they find any.

In Flip, the students could watch not only their own videos but also their peer's videos. The tool also enables peer feedback that each student acquires from the watchers. In the given practice sample, the teacher asks the students to provide feedback to their friends. In a sense, a student in a group is going to watch nine videos apart from his or her own one. Then they are required to provide feedback to each other. For teenagers, receiving peer feedback would have an impact on their L2 WTC. This requirement of getting feedback might enhance their L2 WTC if they receive positive feedback. However, the influence of negative feedback might endure the enhancement. One fact is clear: all these individual-specific and situational assumptions should be tested. The teacher could collect the data by asking the students to keep a journal in which they mention their overall reactions to the Flip task, their perceived level of L2 WTC, and how the delivery of peer feedback influences this willingness. To elaborate on the input in the journal, the teacher might invite three students to interviews. The overall data could be analysed though coding and reaching key factors about the impact of peer feedback on L2 WTC so that the teacher could consider applying peer feedback as a learning and teaching technique with the same group of students and similar students.

3. ELSA Speak

ELSA, English Language Speech Assistant, is a speech recognition application that was created specifically to assist language learners in polishing their English pronunciation. The users of ELSA app have an artificial intelligence (AI) coach giving 95% immediate feedback and study tips to the students. The AI coach or tutor of the app pays attention to all the steps learners take forward and prompts them when they veer off course. The AI used by ELSA was created from voice recordings of English speakers with varying accents. Therefore, voice recognition algorithm of ELSA enables it to recognize the speech patterns of non-native speakers.

To grasp the rationale of the application, it would be sensible to look at the story of the app. The co-founder of the app, Vu Van, wanted to pursue a master's degree at Stanford University. However, she had problems about her Vietnamese accent as her professors and classmates had some difficulty in understanding her speech. She found out that she was not the only one experiencing this difficulty. All her international friends had the same problem especially in their earlier years of study and this decreased their WTC levels. To give more confidence and encouragement to these non-native speakers of English, they developed the app together with a speech technologist, Dr. Xavier Anguera.

To get full access to the whole application and its exercises, users need to subscribe to the application. Yet, it has free materials for educators. Teachers can create personalized learning paths for their classes to develop all important speaking skills: pronunciation, fluency, intonation, word stress, listening, and contextual vocabulary. The app also gives real-time learners analytics to the teachers by measuring students' study time and progress according to their classes and departments. With all these benefits and advantages offered to the students through the app, they can enhance their English pronunciation with a variety and up-to-date resources (Anggraini, 2022; Kholis, 2021; Samad & Ismail, 2020).

An Activity Plan to Apply ELSA for Language Teaching

Prior to the Activity: The teacher detects problems about his/her students' English pronunciation skills and decides to engage them with pronunciation improving activities out of school in addition to classroom practices. S/he asks them to download ELSA speak app to their mobile phones and start using it. She says ELSA will give them a percentage about their levels of sounding like a native speaker first. The app also asks the practice goal of the learners to keep them on track to reach their goals. The teacher wants the students to choose 'serious practice', which is 20 minutes for each day. They will create their accounts by adding their names and e-mails to the app.

Students' Proficiency Level: B1
Students' Age: 18

Aims of the Activity:

- Students will be able to practice their pronunciation skills.
- Students will be able to detect the problems in their pronunciation.

Procedure: The teacher comes to the class and greets the students. S/he then starts talking about his/her concerns about the students' pronunciation skills and tells them s/he would like to introduce an application to the students. S/he shows the interface of ELSA Speak and explains the basic rationale of the app. S/he then asks all the students to download the app and give a few minutes to the students to get their accounts by signing up. S/he also wants them to surf the application so that they can self-discover some of the properties. S/he tells the students that they are going to start studying by topic. S/he asks them to go to the 'study by topic' part, click on it and then choose English Basic. There are 50 easy lessons under this topic. S/he tells the students that they are going to learn to distinguish sounds between similar words. They are going to choose the right answers to complete the lesson. S/he says they will get some scores at the end of the lessons and get a rank on the leader board. S/he also tells them they are able to share these results and scores with him/her so that s/he can follow their progress in the application. S/he informs the students that they will use the application during the term and complete all the topics.

Applying LA for ELSA practices to investigate its influence on L2 WTC: The teacher of the current class can also choose a control group to see the effects of using ELSA on the pronunciation skills of the students and their WTC, specifically in terms of pronunciation. That is, in another class consisting of the students with the same education level or age as in the intervention class, s/he can just apply conventional methods of teaching pronunciation such as 'repeat after me' sessions in the class or working and practicing on the phonetic alphabet. Prior to the both classes, the teacher can do small interviews or focus-group meetings with the students in both classes to see their WTC levels especially in terms of pronunciation. S/he can ask questions such as 'Do you like practicing English pronunciation?', 'What is difficult/easy for you in English pronunciation?', 'Do you feel motivated to speak in the class?', 'How do you feel about sounding non-native like in class?'. Based on the analysis (that does not have to be an academic data analysis, instead, the teacher can check students' answers to get a general stance about their WTC and willingness to develop their pronunciation) of the questions, the teacher can develop a perspective on their WTC prior to the classes. While the teacher applies traditional pronunciation practice activities in the control group (such as drills as in Audio Lingual Method or working on the International Phonetic Alphabet), the experimental group is responsible for the activities and lessons in ELSA speak. S/he receives learner analytics each week from ELSA about the students' progress, study time and their ranks on the leader board. For the control group, s/he traditional assessment methods such as using rubrics for evaluation to check student progress. Completing the practices in both the control group and the experimental group, the teacher can have semi-structured interviews with the students in both groups to collect information of the effectiveness of the ELSA and conventional methods. S/he can also ask questions about their levels of motivation or willingness for speaking and pronunciation. S/he can especially try to detect whether the students in the experimental group enjoyed using ELSA during the term and it enhanced their enthusiasm for speaking and pronunciation.

CONCLUSION

Many language teachers today need to deal with the issue of encouraging learners to produce the target language, to feel relaxed, and not to worry about making mistakes when producing the language. When the students are doing this, their level of WTC is believed to influence the frequency and amount of target language communication and hence successful language acquisition. Therefore, language teachers exert a lot of effort to come up with a wide range of methods and activities to foster their students' WTC. At that point, using some contemporary technological tools can be the simplest, or the most complicated for some language teachers, solution for overcoming the barriers of anxiety and inhibition.

Language learners of this age needs to effectively use and critically evaluate technology-based tools as aids in the development of their language learning competence as part of formal instruction (Healey et al., 2008). They should be able to use technology-based productivity tools collaboratively and individually in order to enhance their language learning competence. Therefore, their teachers need to demonstrate an understanding of a wide range of technology supports for language learning and options for using them in a given setting. The use of such tools many increase their levels of WTC as their inhibition and anxiety levels will lower at the same time. They can take a different identity or role through these contemporary technological tools. Even though it depends on the students' readiness and motivation, digital tools can be a catalyst as well as the tool for speaking. Considering the concerns and barriers of the language learners in communication and the use of technology for overcoming these barriers, the current chapter of the book has tried to give some insights to language teachers to design and create some language activities to foster their learners' speaking skills by using some digital tools. The chapter has also attempted to shed light on the issue of learner analytics by giving ideas to EFL teachers while integrating the digital tools into the learning process for the enhancement of their students' WTC. In conclusion, the present chapter is believed to provoke EFL teachers to gain new perspectives on collecting data about the learning process and the technology integration for their students' WTC by using many other digital tools in their current and future practices.

REFERENCES

Aikina, T., & Zubkova, O. (2015). Integrating online services into English language teaching and learning: The case of Voki. *International Journal of Emerging Technologies in Learning*, *10*(3), 66–68. doi:10.3991/ijet.v10i3.4546

Al-AmraniS. N. (2021, March). Omani learners' willingness to communicate in English: Can university learning management system help? doi:10.2139/ssrn.3777023

Alqarni, N. (2021). Language learners' willingness to communicate and speaking anxiety in online versus face-to-face learning contexts. *International Journal of Learning. Teaching and Educational Research*, *20*(11), 57–77.

Andersson, S. (2006). Newly qualified teachers' learning related to their use of information and communication technology: A Swedish perspective. *British Journal of Educational Technology*, *37*(5), 665–682. doi:10.1111/j.1467-8535.2006.00563.x

Anggraini, A. (2022). Improving students' pronunciation skill using ELSA speak application. *Journal of English Language and Pedagogy*, *5*(1), 135–141. doi:10.33503/journey.v5i1.1840

Archer, K., Savage, R., Sanghera-Sidhu, S., Wood, E., Gottardo, A., & Chen, V. (2014). Examining the effectiveness of technology use in classrooms: A tertiary meta-analysis. *Computers & Education*, *78*, 140–149. doi:10.1016/j.compedu.2014.06.001

Aydin, S. (2014). Foreign language learners' interactions with their teachers on Facebook. *System*, *42*, 155–163. doi:10.1016/j.system.2013.12.001

Ayedoun, E., Hayashi, Y., & Seta, K. (2019). Adding communicative and affective strategies to an embodied conversational agent to enhance second language learners' willingness to communicate. *International Journal of Artificial Intelligence in Education*, *29*(1), 29–57. doi:10.100740593-018-0171-6

Baker, S. C., & MacIntyre, P. D. (2000). The role of gender and immersion in communication and second language orientations. *Language Learning*, *50*(2), 311–341. doi:10.1111/0023-8333.00119

Baran, E., Chuang, H., & Thompson, A. (2011). TPACK: An emerging research and development tool for teacher educators. *The Turkish Online Journal of Educational Technology*, *10*(4), 370–377.

Bernales, C. (2016). Towards a comprehensive concept of willingness to communicate: Learners' predicted and self-reported participation in the foreign language classroom. *System*, *56*, 1–12. doi:10.1016/j.system.2015.11.002

Brown, M. (2020). Seeing students at scale: How faculty in large lecture courses act upon learning analytics dashboard data. *Teaching in Higher Education*, *25*(4), 384–400. doi:10.1080/13562517.2019.1698540

Burgoon, J. K. (1976). The unwillingness-to-communicate scale: Development and validation. *Communication Monographs*, *43*(1), 60–69. doi:10.1080/03637757609375916

Cao, Y. (2011). Investigating situational willingness to communicate within second language classrooms from an ecological perspective. *System*, *39*(4), 468–479. doi:10.1016/j.system.2011.10.016

Cao, Y., & Philp, J. (2006). Interactional context and willingness to communicate: A comparison of behavior in whole class, group and dyadic interaction. *System*, *34*(4), 480–493. doi:10.1016/j.system.2006.05.002

Chaisiri, P. (2023). Promoting Thai EFL learners' willingness to communicate in the virtual classroom through technology-mediated oral tasks. *LEARN Journal: Language Education and Acquisition Research Network*, *16*(1), 97–120.

Chandra, V., & Lloyd, M. (2008). The methodological nettle: ICT and student achievement. *British Journal of Educational Technology*, *39*(6), 1087–1098. doi:10.1111/j.1467-8535.2007.00790.x

Chauhan, S. (2017). A meta-analysis of the impact of technology on learning effectiveness of elementary students. *Computers & Education*, *105*, 14–30. doi:10.1016/j.compedu.2016.11.005

Chhum, C., & Champakaew, W. (2019). Effects of mobile assisted language learning on learners' willingness to communicate in English. *Proceeding of National and International Conference, 1*(10), 40-54.

Chotipaktanasook, N., & Reinders, H. (2016). Willingness to communicate in social media: An investigation of the long-term effects. *Asian EFL Journal*, *18*(4), 6–25.

Chou, M.-H. (2018). Speaking anxiety and strategy use for learning English as a foreign language in full and partial English-medium instruction contexts. *TESOL Quarterly*, *52*(3), 611–633. doi:10.1002/tesq.455

Delmas, P. M., & Moore, P. R. (2019). Student perceptions of video-based discussions in online and blended learning. *Proceedings of the E-Learn 2019 Annual Conference* (pp. 1280–1286). Association for the Advancement of Computing in Education.

Dirjal, A. H., Ghapanchi, Z., & Ghonsooly, B. (2020). Role of social media application in promoting motivation and listening skill of Iraqi EFL learners: A Skype-Based study. *Asian Social Science*, *16*(8), 20–32. doi:10.5539/ass.v16n8p20

Dizon, G. (2020). Evaluating intelligent personal assistants for L2 listening and speaking development. *Language Learning & Technology*, *24*(1), 16–26.

Ebadi, S., & Ebadijalal, M. (2022). The effect of Google Expeditions virtual reality on EFL learners' willingness to communicate and oral proficiency. *Computer Assisted Language Learning*, *35*(8), 1975–2000. doi:10.1080/09588221.2020.1854311

Fan, X. (2022). The development of EFL learners' willingness to communicate and self-efficacy: The role of flipped learning approach with the use of social media. *Frontiers in Psychology*, *13*, 1–12. doi:10.3389/fpsyg.2022.1001283 PMID:36389595

Farjon, D., Smits, A., & Voogt, J. (2019). Technology integration of pre-service teachers explained by attitudes and beliefs, competency, access and experience. *Computers & Education*, *130*, 81–93. doi:10.1016/j.compedu.2018.11.010

Gaftandzhieva, S., Docheva, M., & Doneva, R. (2020). A Comprehensive approach to learning analytics in Bulgarian school education. *Education and Information Technologies*, *26*(1), 145–163. doi:10.100710639-020-10261-w

Graham, C. R. (2011). Theoretical considerations for understanding technological pedagogical content knowledge (TPACK). *Computers & Education*, *57*(3), 1953–1960. doi:10.1016/j.compedu.2011.04.010

Guo, Y., Wang, Y., & Ortega-Martin, J. L. (2023). The impact of blended learning-based scaffolding techniques on learners' self-efficacy and willingness to communicate. *Porta Linguarum An International Journal of Foreign Language Teaching and Learning*, *40*(40), 253–273. doi:10.30827/portalin.vi40.27061

Gurjar, N. (2020). Reducing transactional distance with synchronous and asynchronous video-based discussions in distance learning. *Proceedings of the SITE 2020: Society for Information Technology & Teacher Education International Conference* (pp. 268–272). Association for the Advancement of Computing in Education.

Harris, J., Mishra, P., & Koehler, M. (2009). Teachers' technological pedagogical content knowledge and learning activity types. *Journal of Research on Technology in Education*, *41*(4), 393–416. doi:10.1080/15391523.2009.10782536

Hashimoto, Y. (2002). Motivation and willingness to communicate as predictors of reported L2 use: The Japanese ESL context. *Second Language Studies*, *20*(2), 29–70. 10125/40649

Healey, D., Hegelheimer, V., Hubbard, P., Ioannou-Georgiou, S., Kessler, G., & Ware, P. (2008). *TESOL technology standards framework*. TESOL. https://www.tesol.org

Horowitz, K. S. (2019). Video games and English as a second language: The effect of massive multiplayer online video games on the willingness to communicate and communicative anxiety of college students in Puerto Rico. *American Journal of Play*, *11*(3), 379–410.

Hsieh, W., Yeh, H., & Chen, N. (2023). Impact of a robot and tangible object (R&T) integrated learning system on elementary EFL learners' English pronunciation and willingness to communicate. *Computer Assisted Language Learning*, 1–26. doi:10.1080/09588221.2023.2228357

Jafarigohar, M., Khoshsima, H., Haghighi, H., & Vahdany, F. (2019). Incorporation of flipped learning into EFL classrooms: Performance and perception. *Iranian Journal of English Academy Purposes*, *8*, 1–14.

Jivet, I., Scheffel, M., Specht, M., & Drachsler, H. (2018). License to evaluate: Preparing learning analytics dashboards for educational practice. The *Proceedings of the 8th International Conference on Learning Analytics and Knowledge* (pp. 31–40). ACM. 10.1145/3170358.3170421

Kanat-Mutluoğlu, A. (2020). *A multiphase study on willingness to communicate in English as a foreign learning context* [Unpublished doctoral dissertation, Hacettepe University, Ankara].

Kang, S. J. (2005). Dynamic emergence of situational willingness to communicate in a second language. *System, 33*(2), 277–292. doi:10.1016/j.system.2004.10.004

Kasuma, S. A. A. (2021). ESL Learning via Facebook among science and non-science university students. *International Journal of Virtual and Personal Learning Environments, 11*(2), 1–17. doi:10.4018/IJVPLE.2021070101

Keiper, M. C., White, A., Carlson, C. D., & Lupinek, J. M. (2021). Student perceptions on the benefits of Flipgrid in a HyFlex learning environment. *Journal of Education for Business, 96*(6), 343–351. doi:10.1080/08832323.2020.1832431

Khajavy, G. H., MacIntyre, P. D., & Barabadi, E. (2018). Role of the emotions and classroom environment in willingness to communicate: Applying doubly latent multilevel analysis in second language acquisition research. *Studies in Second Language Acquisition, 40*(3), 605–624. doi:10.1017/S0272263117000304

Kholis, A. (2021). Elsa speak app: Automatic speech recognition (ASR) for supplementing English pronunciation skills. Pedagogy. *Journal of English Language Teaching, 9*(1), 1–14. doi:10.32332/joelt.v9i1.2723

Koehler, M., & Mishra, P. (2009). What is technological pedagogical content knowledge (TPACK)? *Contemporary Issues in Technology & Teacher Education, 9*(1), 60–70.

Kruk, M. (2016). Variations in motivation, anxiety and boredom in learning English in Second Life. *The EuroCALL Review, 24*(1), 25–39. doi:10.4995/eurocall.2016.5693

Kwangsawad, T. (2016). Examining EFL pre-service teachers' TPACK trough self-report, lesson plans and actual practice. *Journal of Education and Learning, 10*(2), 103–108.

Lee, J. S. (2019). EFL students' views of willingness to communicate in the extramural digital context. *Computer Assisted Language Learning, 32*(7), 692–712. doi:10.1080/09588221.2018.1535509

Lee, J. S., & Hsieh, J. C. (2019). Affective variables and willingness to communicate of EFL learners in in-class, out-of-class, and digital contexts. *System, 82*, 63–73. doi:10.1016/j.system.2019.03.002

Lee, J. S., & Lu, Y. (2021). L2 motivational self-system and willingness to communicate in the classroom and extramural digital contexts. *Computer Assisted Language Learning, 2*, 1–23.

Leitner, P., Khalil, M., & Ebner, M. (2017). Learning analytics in higher education: A literature review. *Learning Analytics: Fundaments, Applications, and Trends,* 1–23.

Lloyd, A., Rogerson, S., & Stead, G. (2017). Imagining the potential for using virtual reality technologies in language learning. In M. Carrier, R. M. Damerow, & K. M. Bailey (Eds.), *Digital language learning and teaching: Research, theory, and practice* (pp. 222–234). Routledge. doi:10.4324/9781315523293-19

MacIntyre, P. D., Burns, C., & Jessome, A. (2011). Ambivalence about communicating in a second language: A qualitative study of French immersion students' willingness to communicate. *Modern Language Journal, 95*(1), 81–96. doi:10.1111/j.1540-4781.2010.01141.x

MacIntyre, P. D., & Charos, C. (1996). Personality, attitudes, and affect as predictors of second language communication. *Journal of Language and Social Psychology, 15*(1), 3–26. doi:10.1177/0261927X960151001

MacIntyre, P. D., Clément, R., Dörnyei, Z., & Noels, K. A. (1998). Conceptualizing willingness to communicate in a L2: A situational model of L2 confidence and affiliation. *Modern Language Journal, 82*(4), 545–562. doi:10.1111/j.1540-4781.1998.tb05543.x

MacIntyre, P. D., & Legatto, J. J. (2011). A dynamic system approach to willingness to communicate: Developing an idiodynamic method to capture rapidly changing affect. *Applied Linguistics, 32*(2), 149–171. doi:10.1093/applin/amq037

McCroskey, J. C., & Baer, J. E. (1985, November 7–10). *Willingness to communicate: The construct and its measurement* [Paper presentation]. Annual Meeting of the Speech Communication Association, Denver, Colorado, United States.

Mishra, P., & Koehler, M. J. (2006). Technological pedagogical content knowledge: A new framework for teacher knowledge. *Teachers College Record, 108*(6), 1017–1054. doi:10.1111/j.1467-9620.2006.00684.x

Mohammadi, J., Barati, H., & Youhanaee, M. (2019). The effectiveness of using flipped classroom model on Iranian EFL learners' English achievements and their willingness to communicate. *English Language Teaching, 12*(5), 101–115. doi:10.5539/elt.v12n5p101

Mystkowska-Wiertelak, A., & Pawlak, M. (2016). Designing a tool for measuring the interrelationships between L2 WTC, confidence, beliefs, motivation, and context. In M. Pawlak (Ed.), *Classroom-oriented research* (pp. 19–37). Springer. doi:10.1007/978-3-319-30373-4_2

Mystkowska-Wiertelak, A., & Pietrzykowska, A. (2011). L2 willingness to communicate (WTC) and international posture in the Polish educational context. *Studies in Second Language Learning and Teaching, 1*(1), 119–134. doi:10.14746sllt.2011.1.1.7

Niess, M. L. (2005). Preparing teachers to teach science and mathematics with technology: Developing a technology pedagogical content knowledge. *Teaching and Teacher Education, 21*(5), 509–523. doi:10.1016/j.tate.2005.03.006

NMC Horizon Project. (2016). *Higher education edition wiki on learning analytics*. NMC. http://horizon.wiki.nmc.org/Learning+Analytics

Nugroho, A. (2021). Learners Willingness to Communicate in a Foreign Language: The Role of Informal Digital Learning of English. *ELE Reviews: English Language Education Reviews, 1*(2), 125–133. doi:10.22515/ele-reviews.v1i2.4396

Nugroho, A., & Atmojo, A. E. P. (2020). Digital Learning of English Beyond Classroom: EFL Learners' Perception and Teaching Activities. [Journal of English Education and Linguistics Studies]. *JEELS, 7*(2), 219–243. doi:10.30762/jeels.v7i2.1993

Pawlak, M., & Mystkowska-Wiertelak, A. (2015). Investigating the dynamic nature of willingness to communicate. *System, 50*, 1–9. doi:10.1016/j.system.2015.02.001

Peng, J. E. (2019). The roles of multimodal pedagogic effects and classroom environment in willingness to communicate in English. *System, 82*, 161–173. doi:10.1016/j.system.2019.04.006

Peng, J. E., Zhang, L., & Chen, Y. (2017). The mediation of multimodal affordances on willingness to communicate in the English as a foreign language classroom. *TESOL Quarterly, 51*(2), 302–331. doi:10.1002/tesq.298

Polly, D., Mims, C., Shepherd, C. E., & Inan, F. (2010). Evidence of impact: Transforming teacher education with preparing tomorrow's teachers to teach with technology (PT3) grants. *Teaching and Teacher Education, 26*(4), 863–870. doi:10.1016/j.tate.2009.10.024

Rahimi, M., & Fathi, J. (2022). Employing e-tandem language learning method to enhance speaking skills and willingness to communicate: The case of EFL learners. *Computer Assisted Language Learning*, 1–37. doi:10.1080/09588221.2022.2064512

Ramdani, A. S. (2018). The use of Voki as a media to support the enhancement of first grade students speaking skills at SMPN 4 Tambun Selatan. *Jurnal Inovasi Pendidikan MH Thamrin, 2*(1), 12–25. doi:10.37012/jipmht.v2i1.32

Reinders, H. (2018). Learning analytics for language learning and teaching. *The JALT CALL Journal, 14*(1), 77–86. doi:10.29140/jaltcall.v14n1.225

Reinders, H., & Wattana, S. (2015). Affect and willingness to communicate in digital game-based learning. *ReCALL, 27*(1), 38–57. doi:10.1017/S0958344014000226

Riasati, M. J. (2012). EFL learners' perception of factors influencing willingness to speak English in language classrooms: A qualitative study. *World Applied Sciences Journal, 17*(10), 1287–1297.

Saçak, B., & Kavun, N. (2020). Rethinking Flipgrid and VoiceThread in the context of online collaborative learning theory. In E. Alqurashi (Ed.), *Handbook of research on fostering student engagement with instructional technology in higher education* (pp. 211–228). IGI Global. doi:10.4018/978-1-7998-0119-1.ch012

Samad, I., & Ismail, I. (2020). ELSA speak application as a supporting media in enhancing students' pronunciation skill. *MAJESTY JOURNAL, 2*(2), 1–7. doi:10.33487/majesty.v2i2.510

Sauro, S., & Zourou, K. (2019). What are the digital wilds? *Language Learning & Technology, 23*(1), 1–7. 10125/44666

Scherer, R., Siddiq, F., & Tondeur, J. (2020). All the same or different? Revisiting measures of teachers' technology acceptance. *Computers & Education, 143*, 1–17. doi:10.1016/j.compedu.2019.103656

Schulman, L. S. (1987). Knowledge and teaching: Foundations of the new form. *Harvard Educational Review, 57*(1), 1–23. doi:10.17763/haer.57.1.j463w79r56455411

Şener, S. (2014). Turkish ELT students' willingness to communicate in English. *ELT Research Journal, 3*(2), 91–109.

Sharma, V. (2019). Saudi students' perspective on social media usage to promote EFL learning. *International Journal of Linguistics. Literature and Translation, 2*(1), 129–139.

Siemens, G., & Gasevic, D. (2012). Guest editorial-learning and knowledge analytics. *Journal of Education and Technology, 15*(3), 1–2.

Society for Learning Analytics Research. (2023). *What is learning analytics?* Solar Research. https://www.solaresearch.org/about/what-is-learning-analytics/

Sousa, E. B. G., Alexandre, B., Ferreira Mello, R., Pontual Falcão, T., Vesin, B., & Gašević, D. (2021). Applications of learning analytics in high schools: A systematic literature review. *Frontiers in Artificial Intelligence*, *4*, 1–14. doi:10.3389/frai.2021.737891 PMID:34647016

Soyoof, A. (2022). Iranian EFL students' perception of willingness to communicate in an extramural digital context. *Interactive Learning Environments*.

Soyoof, A., Reynolds, B. L., Vazquez-Calvo, B., & McLay, K. (2023). Informal digital learning of English (IDLE): A scoping review of what has been done and a look towards what is to come. *Computer Assisted Language Learning*, *36*(4), 608–640. doi:10.1080/09588221.2021.1936562

Su, Y. R., & Fatmawati, F. (2019). Fostering students' self-Esteem in speaking by extending speaking activities in social media. *Pedagogy Journal of English Language Teaching*, *7*(1), 65–74. doi:10.32332/pedagogy.v7i1.1544

Sylvén, L. K., & Sundqvist, P. (2017). Computer-assisted language learning (CALL) in extracurricular/extramural contexts. *CALICO Journal*, *34*(1), i–iv. doi:10.1558/cj.31822

Tai, T.-Y., & Chen, H. H.-J. (2023). The impact of Google Assistant on adolescent EFL learners' willingness to communicate. *Interactive Learning Environments*, *31*(3), 1485–1520. doi:10.1080/10494820.2020.1841801

Taylor, C., & Hinchman, T. (2020). Strategies for using Flipgrid in the education. *US-China Education Review B*, *10*(1), 26–31.

Üstünbaş, Z. (2021). *The effects of flipped instruction through authentic videos on Turkish EFL learners' use of speech acts and willingness to communicate* [Unpublished MA thesis, Bursa Uludağ University, Bursa].

Voogt, J., Fisser, P., Pareja Roblin, N., Tondeur, J., & Van Braak, J. (2013). Technological Pedagogical Content Knowledge (TPACK) - a review of the literature. *Journal of Computer Assisted Learning*, *29*(2), 109–121. doi:10.1111/j.1365-2729.2012.00487.x

Wehner, A. K. (2014). *Exploring the relationship of motivation, anxiety, and virtual worlds in the experiences of two Spanish language learners: a case study.* [Unpublished doctoral dissertation, University of South Florida].

Wu, Y.-H., & Hung, S.-T. (2022). The effects of virtual reality infused instruction on elementary school students' English-speaking performance, willingness to communicate, and learning autonomy. *Journal of Educational Computing Research*, *60*(6), 1558–1587. doi:10.1177/07356331211068207

Yashima, T. (2002). Willingness to communicate in a second language: The Japanese EFL context. *Modern Language Journal*, *86*(1), 54–66. doi:10.1111/1540-4781.00136

Yashima, T., MacIntyre, P. D., & Ikeda, M. (2016). Situated willingness to communicate in an L2: Interplay of individual characteristics and context. *Language Teaching Research*, *22*(1), 115–137. doi:10.1177/1362168816657851

Yeşilbağ, S., & Korkmaz, Ö. (2021). The effect of Voki application on students' academic achievements and attitudes towards English course. *Education and Information Technologies*, *26*(1), 465–487. doi:10.100710639-020-10264-7 PMID:32837235

Yu, M. (2011). Effect of communication variables, affective variables, and teacher immediacy on willingness to communicate of foreign language learners. *Chinese Journal of Communication*, *4*(02), 218–236. doi:10.1080/17544750.2011.565678

Zarrinabadi, N., Khodarahmi, E., & Shahbazi, H. (2021). On the effect of using a flipped classroom methodology on Iranian EFL learners' willingness to communicate. In N. Zarrinabadi & M. Pawlak (Eds.), *New Perspectives on Willingness to Communicate in a Second Language* (pp. 155–167). Springer. doi:10.1007/978-3-030-67634-6_8

ADDITIONAL READING

Dooly, M., & Sadler, R. (2020). "If you don't improve, what's the point?": Investigating the impact of a "flipped" online exchange in teacher education. *ReCALL*, *32*(1), 4–24. doi:10.1017/S0958344019000107

Elias, T. (2011). *Learning analytics: Definitions, processes, and potential*. Springer.

Hubbard, L., & Levy, M. (Eds.). (2006). *Teacher education in CALL*. John Benjamins. doi:10.1075/lllt.14

Knoke, D., & Yang, S. (2019). *Social network analysis*. Sage Publications.

Long, P., & Siemens, G. (2011). Penetrating the fog: Analytics in learning and education. *EDUCAUSE Review*, *46*(5), 31–40.

McCroskey, J. C. (1992). Reliability and validity of the willingness to communicate scale. *Communication Quarterly*, *40*(1), 16–25. doi:10.1080/01463379209369817

Mystkowska-Wiertelak, A., & Pawlak, M. (2017). *Willingness to communicate in instructed second language acquisition: Combining a macro and micro perspective*. Multilingual Matters. doi:10.21832/9781783097173

Nami, F., Marandi, S. S., & Sotoudehnama, E. (2016). CALL teacher professional growth through lesson study practice: An investigation into EFL teachers' perceptions. *Computer Assisted Language Learning*, *29*(4), 658–682. doi:10.1080/09588221.2015.1016439

KEY TERMS AND DEFINITIONS

Learning Analytics: It is the collection, analysis, and description of data about learners and contexts where learning takes place.

Technological Pedagogical Content Knowledge (TPACK): It is a theoretical framework for understanding the knowledge and skills teachers need for effective and efficient integration of technology.

Technology Integration: It is referred to technology integration when teachers and/or students use technology as a tool to support the learning process.

Technology-Enhanced Practices: These are the practices carried out using digital tools by integrating them into learning process.

Willingness to Communicate: It is identified as an intention to communicate orally in the target language. It mainly focuses on the willingness in spoken interaction and neglects the eagerness of communication in other skills.

Chapter 9
Rethinking Learning Engagement Through Emotional Learning Analytics in K-12 Classrooms Through Social-Emotional Learning and Mindfulness

Nurdan Kavaklı Ulutaş
https://orcid.org/0000-0001-9572-9491
Izmir Demokrasi University, Turkey

ABSTRACT

Since human beings are not only physical entities, albeit constituted by complex social and emotional features, their well-being also depends on learning how to communicate their needs to the others in an effective way, and to manage their emotions in a healthy way. From the learning perspective, emotional health also contributes to enhanced academic success, leading to improvement in learning. It is, thus, of critical importance to develop an understanding for learning engagement through the utilization of a novel concept of emotional learning analytics (ELA) to transform education systems with the purpose of molding a future that strengthens improved academic success as well as nestling peace and well-being. Accordingly, this review aims to provide a double dividend to the learners in K-12 classrooms to embrace the significance of social-emotional learning (SEL) and mindfulness to rethink learning engagement by synthesizing the findings, challenges, and recommendations from latest research through ELA to nurture emphatic learners for a sustainable society across the world.

DOI: 10.4018/979-8-3693-0066-4.ch009

INTRODUCTION

In the continuous flow of life, individuals complete their day without realizing what they do, see, and hear during the day. However, even with a short but effective breathing exercise, the awareness of the mind can be increased. Mindfulness, which includes many more of such exercises and practices, has been mentioned in many religions, cultures, and wisdom traditions from the past to the present. In recent times, mindfulness practices have taken a significant place in therapeutic, educational, and government settings, with an increasing number of studies supporting their individual and societal benefits (Mischenko, 2021). To provide a brief definition, mindfulness is the process of participating openly with awareness of one's current experiences (Creswell, 2017). Furthermore, the importance of mindfulness practices in education has increased with the success in applications related to various psychological development goals, including learning (Zeilhofer, 2020).

In the field of education, mindfulness has been unified to an increasing extent with Social Emotional Learning (SEL), which is related to the improvement of self-awareness, self- management, social-awareness, and relationship skills (Mischenko, 2021). In other words, SEL is about the objectives that are surely fundamental for learners such as managing emotions, building healthy relationships with people, and problem-solving skills (Zins & Elias, 2006). According to an article from National University (2022), SEL encompasses social and emotional skills that people of all ages can learn and practice. Moreover, SEL can be encountered frequently in many educational plans today, notably since its acquisition from a young age will positively affect one's future success. As a result, learners could be more likely to engage and could be less prone to mentally drift off during their classes when teachers personalize and relate educational subjects to them. In that, SEL can have a beneficial lifetime effect by encouraging self-awareness, empathy, and emotions of safety and inclusivity in language classrooms (National University, 2022).

To give a synopsis, mindfulness cultivates the disposition of sympathy and ethical ways of living, while SEL offers how to make that happen (Lantieri & Zakrzewski, 2015). Taking all these factors into account, mindfulness and SEL, when combined, have a chance to impact learners as a catalyst for improving learners' performance as rooted in learning analytics (LA), and more specifically emotional learning analytics (ELA). Thus, in this review chapter, previous research studies around mindfulness and SEL together with their application in language classrooms are scrutinized. Subsequently, some pedagogical implications and suggestions are listed for practitioners in the field of language education.

BACKGROUND

Mindful learning is based on the learners' ability to be aware of what they are doing in the present moment. Thus, it is thought that it is an intrinsic process that requires focus and discipline. Therefore, the main goals of the research and the programs applied have revealed that the main cores that SEL and mindfulness can add up to the learners' performance can be listed as self-awareness, self-management, self-regulation, social awareness, relationship skills, and responsible decision- making. With the help of these five main components, English as a foreign language (EFL) teachers aim to enhance students' awareness of learning and boost their concentration. That is why all the components have a crucial importance in language classrooms.

Firstly, self-awareness involves understanding one's values, and personal goals, and increasing emotional regulation. Secondly, self-management and/or self-regulation concentrates on thoughts, behaviors, and emotions. It also requires attitudes and skills to regulate emotions and behaviors. When learners are faced with a stressful situation, it concerns them about what they do and how they react. Together with these, inhibitory control is captured, as well. Inhibitory control is defined as the ability to stop oneself from making an inappropriate response (Lyons & DeLange, 2016). In school settings, this means when learners are dealing with a task, they prevent themselves from chatting with their friends by obeying the classroom rules, and by providing positive relationships. Although inhibitory control is not one of the main goals of the training, it arises indirectly. Namely, self-regulation and/or self-management has a great effect on the learning process.

In terms of social awareness, as the name suggests, it includes empathizing and being kind towards people who are from different backgrounds or cultures. Social awareness also supports the feeling of respect and acceptance toward diverse perceptions. This situation is also associated with emotional well-being. That is, everyone starts to accept everyone as they are, thus the psychological pressure from differences disappears, and self-esteem level starts to rise. Relationship skills and social awareness are interrelated. Relationship skills competency is associated with communicating clearly, listening actively, and negotiating with problems. It means the ability to keep healthy relationships with everybody regardless of their background. Lastly, responsible decision-making competency requires making the right choices based on personal behavior and social interactions. Therefore, if a person considers ethical and safety issues and takes a realistic view of the possible consequences, s/he is assumed to be competent in responsible decision-making.

Additionally, there are several attitudes presented with mindfulness, the first one is acceptance. It is defined as accepting all feelings regardless of good or bad. With the application of it, individuals begin to accept that everyone's life is unique. Consequently, they learn not to judge and label people. They also start to trust themselves, which means that they take their own responsibilities patiently. For a lifetime, patience has an undeniable significance because everything takes time such as language learning. Without a doubt, individuals can also learn to appreciate themselves even for the smallest thing in their lives. They should have the courage to take the necessary steps to achieve their goals and be aware that nothing is permanent. With this mindset, it will be easier for them to cope with the difficulties they face with the help of a letting go attitude of mindfulness.

To generalize, if students receive mindfulness training for a certain period, they may greatly improve themselves in above mentioned competencies. In such a manner, they start to feel more comfortable, their life becomes stress-free, and their self-esteem levels get higher and higher. As a trade-off, a better life and success are inevitable since it feeds noticing together with acceptance by avoiding negative thoughts and feelings (Caballero et al., 2019) as well as having a transformational effect on the learners' choices and reactions in teaching and learning environments which has a direct effect on learning. In this context, learning analytics (LA) come to the forefront to collect and analyze learner data through a deeper analysis. To note more, emotional learning analytics (ELA) adopts a data-driven approach to analyze the impact of emotions on learners' performance and engagement since if learners can overcome negative thoughts and emotions, they can get positive learning gains; otherwise, their learning may be impeded (Atapattu et al., 2019).

Recently, it is clearly seen that mindfulness and SEL have been the core of many studies (Zeilhofer & Sasao, 2022) since mostly over the last ten years, there has been a growing curiosity about the effects of mindfulness training on both children and adults. It is proven that even short-term mindfulness training may lead to a development in brain functioning. For example, mindfulness training has been found to improve the brain's ability to selectively focus attention (Jha et al., 2007; Napoli et al., 2005, as cited in Lyons & DeLange, 2016). Because, during the training, learners learn how they be aware of the moment. They question what is happening right now, and they can better focus on what they are doing. It can be an exam or an activity, it does not matter, because they ignore distractors and just do their work.

In terms of adolescents, there is preliminary evidence to suggest that mindfulness training administered in a clinical setting reduces parent-reported attention problems among early adolescents (e.g., Semple et al., 2010, as cited in Lyons & DeLange, 2016). As attention problems decrease, it is seen that working memory improves. To give a brief definition, working memory is the ability to keep in mind and manipulate information (Baddeley, 1992, as cited in Lyons & DeLange, 2016). Thus, it is a fact that there is a direct proportion between attention development and working memory. Hence, it can be said that it brings academic success when it is thought working memory is used to solve problems in the academy.

Beyond question, SEL can be defined as the cognitive and behavioral mechanisms by which individuals, including children and adults, develop proficiency in recognizing, regulating, and expressing emotions, establish and pursue constructive objectives, exhibit empathic concern towards others, cultivate and sustain healthy interpersonal connections, and exercise informed judgment in decision-making (CASEL, 2023). Research, herein, suggests that SEL can be used for every stage of learning starting from preschool to adulthood (Pentón Herrera, 2020). The recent surge in attention towards SEL could be attributed to empirical investigations and scholarly literature that have highlighted the advantageous outcomes of SEL in terms of promoting individuals' self-development, academic achievement, and behavioral enhancement (Allbright & Hough, 2020; Jones & Khan, 2017; Rogers, 2019). The Collaborative for Academic, Social, and Emotional Learning (CASEL) has proposed a widely recognized framework for SEL, comprising five distinct competencies: self- awareness, self-management, social-awareness, relationships skills and responsible decision making. These competencies underscore the significance of equipping children with social, behavioral, and emotional skills that are critical for their academic and social achievements as well as for their overall success in life (CASEL, 2023).

SEL encompasses the various steps individuals go through to gain and utilize the essential knowledge, attitudes, and abilities needed to comprehend and handle emotions, demonstrate empathy, set and accomplish positive objectives, cultivate and sustain healthy relationships, and exercise sound judgment. (Weissberg et al., 2015). Moreover, numerous interventions focused on SEL, primarily conducted with children in the United States, have been extensively analyzed and evaluated in various reviews and meta-analytic studies. These investigations have yielded robust and consistent evidence indicating that SEL programs of excellent implementation and quality produce immediate and enduring favorable effects on children's and youth's social, emotional, behavioral, and academic outcomes. (Durlak et al., 2011; Sklad et al., 2012; Weare & Nind, 2011).

To exemplify, a study conducted in Uganda was to assess whether a mindfulness-based school program called MindUp, focused on SEL, could be implemented successfully, and yield positive results for children residing in post-conflict (Matsuba et al., 2021). The program, MindUp, consists of 45 minutes of a lesson which was taught periodically every week practicing SEL and mindfulness. The instructional session combined mindfulness techniques with engaging activities to facilitate learning about the brain, comprehending the influence of thoughts and emotions on behavior, and acquiring strategies to cultivate empathy and compassion (Matsuba et al., 2021). In addition, children gained an understanding of how cultivating focused awareness through training could impact their brain and nervous system, providing them with a self-regulation technique to manage overwhelming emotions and attain a state of calmness. 5th and 6th graders contributed to this program during two years of implementation. At the same time, they had been compared to other 5th and 6th graders from a different school but without the implementation of the program.

As a result, the group which took the program for two years, teachers observed a noticeable enhancement in children's behavior, resulting in reduced disciplinary concerns. Additionally, teachers reported that the program contributed to their professional growth, expanding their teaching knowledge and skills, while fostering improved relationships with their students. The program also aided teachers in effectively managing their own stress. These perceived advantages served as significant motivators for teachers, increasing the likelihood of their continued implementation of the program. For the second group, teachers noted that children who participated in the MindUp program exhibited higher levels of positive emotions and displayed more empathic behavior when compared to children who did not have exposure to the program. An important finding was worthy of highlighting which purported that children who participated in the MindUp program demonstrated superior academic performance compared to children who did not have exposure to the program. This finding aligned with previous research that indicated an improvement in Math grades among children (Schonert-Reichl et al., 2015). Additionally, previous studies have revealed that children's social competencies have played a crucial role in predicting their academic success (Oberle et al., 2014), suggesting that programs like MindUp may have a significant indirect impact on academic achievement by enhancing social skills.

PEDAGOGICAL IMPLICATIONS TO CONCEPTUALIZE MINDFULNESS BASED SEL IN LANGUAGE CLASSROOMS

In the current era, educational institutions have become a great part of the daily lives of the learners. They have a variety of course subjects and a lot to cover in each of them. However, most of the learners cannot help themselves to feel lost at schools. One of the moments in which students feel alienated at school is English language courses. When a student is not interested in language learning and has some prejudice towards foreign languages, overcoming these barriers becomes so tough for EFL teachers. In this point, mindfulness based SEL practices take the stage and offer a wide range of activities with the aim of promoting well-being, emotional regulation, and self-awareness, and reducing anxiety, depression, and stress of the learners (Maloney et al., 2016).

To implement mindfulness based SEL in language classrooms, Cowan (2010) suggests some steps to follow. As a starter point, EFL teachers should practice mindfulness in their own lives to increase the effectiveness of future practices in their classrooms. In terms of the classroom application, they should allocate specific times for these practices, and let the students know about the specialness of those moments. Then, as in any other school subject, they should choose exercises that are suitable for their learners' cognitive abilities. They also need to create a mindful environment by clearing benches or moving furniture while doing these exercises. Most important after all is learner engagement and involvement, so teachers, with the help of their guidance, should make sure that their learners are trying to be in the moment. Moreover, there should also be a wisdom sharing part in which both the teacher and learners share their experiences with the whole class to establish interpersonal relationships and not to be disturbed by their feelings. Finally, EFL teachers should cultivate mindfulness based SEL activities in their classrooms every day, since the more they integrate it, the easier it is to engage their learners. Below, a detailed review of mindfulness based SEL activities for language classrooms is listed for young, adolescent, and adult learners.

Young Learners

When considering young learners (YL), there are several factors to consider for an EFL teacher. These factors are the age, proficiency level, and cognitive capacity of the students, as well as the engagement and authenticity of the materials. First and foremost, breathing exercise is the one that is suitable for all the stated factors for YL classes. Kuru Gönen (2022) suggests various types of breathing exercises for YL, named as "Rainbow Breathing", and "Worm Breathing". These breathing exercises are very appealing for YLs with their colorful illustrations. There are even instructions on the website of Mindfulness-Enhanced Language Teaching (MELT) with suggested audio to be played while applying these exercises in the classroom. After the application, there seems to be a big difference in the classroom environment in a good way as the YLs are invited to relax and overcome their problems by realizing the sound of their breath, which is like an ocean.

Besides, YLs are mostly known for their love of stories, one of the most beneficial materials to teach various types of topics, including value education, and mindfulness. In addition to integrating the stories into an EFL classroom in which mindfulness based SEL is applied, there are hundreds of stories for teachers to choose from based on their learners' needs. For instance, a wonderful story source for YLs is the book series called "Shapes' Adventures" (Islah, 2022) which consists of six books that include cute illustrations of shapes by focusing on different values. Moreover, read aloud story videos are another option when considering the YLs who are not literate yet. The suggestions of read aloud stories consisted of videos named "I'm Calm" (Reading to Flourish London, 2020), "The Lemonade Hurricane" (Northern Bright Bookshelf, 2020), and "Bee Calm" (KidLit TV, 2019). Thanks to the stories,

YLs may have a chance to improve their reading and listening skills in the target language while increasing their well-being implicitly.

Finally, it is important to carry mindfulness based SEL activities outside of the school to relate them to the daily life of the learners. To do this, EFL teachers may give some handouts as homework or summer/semester break assignments. In the process of practicing at home, parents may also play a role by accompanying their children. As an example, a poster named “I can Pause and” aims to make students realize that life is all about choices. Hence, this activity may help them to change their point of view and focus on the good by doing the given actions on the poster like hugging someone. Additionally, creating daily routines may provide a mindful environment in the students’ homes. For instance, “Morning Routine” and “Evening Routine” posters are effective ways to implement mindfulness at home. After being inspired by these posters, YLs may add or remove some parts in their own routines with the help of their parents. Overall, the “Morning Mindfulness Routine” is to activate the sleepy minds of YLs, and enable them to start the day energetically, while the “Evening Mindfulness Routine” is to relax the body and prepare sleep. Following these routines for a period may improve the life quality of YLs.

Adolescent Learners

Regarding adolescent learners, there are numerous ways to conduct mindfulness based SEL in EFL classes. As a warm-up activity, teachers may determine the “question of the day” in their classes such as controversial conversation starter questions so that they can give each learner the opportunity to express their feelings or thoughts, as well as create a space for speaking practice. Apart from that, meditation is another common way to practice mindfulness, just like breathing exercises. There are various types, such as mindfulness meditation in which one pays attention to one’s own thoughts by focusing on the present moment without judgment. Considering meditation, learners can become aware of their thoughts and feelings, including an increase in their self-confidence and motivation.

Furthermore, mobile apps are excellent sources to bring technology both inside and outside of mindful classes. Because they give learners the freedom of choosing mindfulness activities in line with their needs and interests, and they can help learners to build mindful habits in their lives. “Calm” (Tew & Smith, 2012), “Headspace” (Puddicombe, 2010), and “Smiling Mind” (Martino & Tutton, 2010) are among the most popular applications in recent times. They may help learners to establish healthy sleeping routines, relax through guided mediations, and provide a quick break from the complexity of life.

Adult Learners

As for adult learners, individual activities are the ones that are most common when compared to group or pair ones. Therefore, literature is a great way to practice mindfulness on their own. EFL teachers should encourage their learners to read books that will contribute to their well-being. Some books that have been suggested within mindfulness encompass "Growing Up Mindful" by Willard (2016), "Wherever You Go, There You Are" by Kabat-Zinn (2005), "Mindsight" by Siegel (2010), and "Emotional Intelligence" by Goleman (2012). With the help of these and such books, learners may also improve their English reading skills.

Additionally, podcasts are among the efficient materials for mindfulness based SEL practices for adult learners. They offer listening practice while relaxing and overwhelming brains by touching upon topics like yoga meditation, and rituals. There are numerous podcasts on these topics, some of the most popular ones are "The JOY Factor" (Hanson, 2019-present), "The Anxiety Coaches" (Ryan, 2015-present), "The Overwhelmed Brain" (Colaianni, 2013-present), and "Wake Me Up" (Brown, 2019-present). Finally, community services are a way to practice mindfulness experientially by contributing to students' moral identity and collaboration skills (Lawlor, 2016). As a result of these types of activities, learners have a chance to reflect on their experiences by either writing or speaking in the target language. Besides, they may foster SEL competencies such as self-awareness.

An increasing amount of research proves the vital role of mindfulness techniques and demonstrates their enormous influence on a variety of areas of an individual's life (Williams et al., 2015). Mindful actions support individuals' career activities, relationships with others, and overall happiness together with helping them succeed academically. People who practice mindfulness can improve their mental capacities, concentrate more effectively, efficiently handle stress, and increase their level of productivity, all of which will ultimately result in higher accomplishments in education and other areas of life.

According to relevant literature (Jha et al., 2007; Napoli et al., 2005, as cited in Lyons & DeLange, 2016), even simple mindfulness training can significantly alter how the brain functions, such as increasing the brain's capacity for selective attention. Learners who practice mindfulness gain the ability to reflect on and observe their current circumstances, which helps them focus more successfully on what they are doing. As a result, EFL teachers can start each lesson with a short mindfulness exercise to get learners engaged and receptive. This might include body scans, short meditations, or guided breathing exercises. Thus, a short but effective result may be obtained. As another finding of the research conducted, it is stated that competency in relationship skills is correlated with effective communication, active listening, and problem-solving. It refers to the capacity to maintain positive relationships with everyone, regardless of their background. Consequently, activities that encourage active listening can be combined by the teacher since EFL teachers may encourage learners to fully participate in conversations with each other by listening intently and responding with interest and empathy.

Moreover, the MindUp program, a mindfulness-based educational initiative with SEL focus for children who have experienced conflict, was examined for effectiveness in a study carried out in Uganda (Matsuba, et al., 2021). The results imply that the MindUp program had a positive effect on the learners' emotional and social health, giving them useful abilities to control their feelings and enhance their behavior while lowering disciplinary issues in comparison to a control group. Furthermore, teachers stated that the training program helped their professional development by broadening their expertise and abilities in teaching while establishing stronger connections with their learners. The training also helped teachers manage their stress to a greater extent; thus, it could be said that mindfulness based SEL practices in education programs not only improved students but also contributed to teachers. By being a great example for their learners to practice mindful communication, EFL teachers can show mindfulness in their language and actions by expressing valid attention and compassion while communicating with them.

In addition, as stated in another study (Pentón Herrera, 2020), SEL has had a wide range of usability which means it can be used from young learners to adult learners. SEL also can promote individuals' self-development and behavioral enhancement without considering their age range. Also, SEL enables individuals to participate actively in social activities, and promotes their mental and physical well-being. Furthermore, the academic success of adult students can be supported by SEL. Individual activities are counted as more appropriate for adult learners, consequently reading activities related to SEL can be an accurate choice for them.

Accordingly, it can be stipulated that mindfulness based SEL practices can promote positive emotional learning analytics with the advantages and positive aspects they offer. Because it is a well-designed system for both educators and students, myriad of studies have shown that SEL has a lot of benefits not only for learners of all ages but also for teachers themselves as well as improving their mental capacity, concentration, creativity, and productivity.

CONCLUSION

All things considered, mindfulness and SEL, which are regarded as beneficial tools for EFL classrooms, are common techniques that prioritize the well-being of the students. While the main aim of SEL is to develop the social and emotional skills of the individuals, such as responsible decision making, the main aim of mindfulness is to cultivate awareness of the present moment with an attitude of acceptance. Studies and discussions on mindfulness and SEL frequently point to the significant impact that they can both have on the psychological wellbeing, academic achievement, and potential future success of the students.

When implementing mindfulness based SEL in language classrooms, EFL teachers should put an emphasis on the needs of their students. Accordingly, they should choose suitable materials with the aim of both practicing mindfulness based SEL and the target language in the classroom. In the light of these, it can be stated that mindfulness based SEL facilitates learning especially for YLs who become more willing to speak up, take risks, and engage in their own learning process. There are numerous ways to conduct activities on this topic, for instance, breathing exercises and storytelling are among the most popular ways to do it in YL classrooms. However, apps and meditation are more accurate choices for adolescent learners, while literature and podcast are the ones that are mostly chosen for adult learners. Thus, EFL teachers should be the ones who make the right choices among many activities for their own learners.

In conclusion, mindfulness based SEL helps to create a mindful atmosphere, that results in mutual respect among the members of the classroom. As a result of this atmosphere various mindful attitudes such as acceptance, gratitude, non-judging, and patience are promoted in the classrooms. Learners realize that sometimes feeling blue is also normal, and it is part of life that they should not escape. That's why, in the personal growth journey of the learners, their EFL teachers should try to play a positive role, instead of classifying them according to their achievement scores or any other external rewards. Because the world is desperately in need of more peaceful, creative, emotional, and at the same time assertive minds that can be revealed with the help of mindfulness-based SEL.

REFERENCES

Allbright, T., & Hough, H. (2020). Measures of SEL and school climate in California. *The State Education Standard, 20*(2), 28–50.

Atapattu, T., Thilakaratne, M., Vivian, R., & Falkner, K. (2019). Detecting cognitive engagement using word embeddings within an online teacher professional development community. *Computers & Education, 140*, 103594. doi:10.1016/j.compedu.2019.05.020

Brown, T. (Host). (2019-present). *Wake Me Up: Morning meditation and motivation*. Wake Me Up. https://www.wakemeuppodcast.com

Caballero, C., Scherer, E., West, M. R., Mrazek, M. D., Gabrieli, C. F., & Gabrieli, J. D. (2019). Greater mindfulness is associated with better academic achievement in middle school. *Mind, Brain and Education : the Official Journal of the International Mind, Brain, and Education Society*, *13*(3), 157–166. doi:10.1111/mbe.12200

Colaianni, P. (2013-present). *The Overwhelmed Brain*. The Overwhelmed Brain. https://theoverwhelmedbrain.com/podcasts/

Collaborative for Academic, Social, and Emotional Learning (CASEL). (2023). *Fundamentals of SEL*. CASEL. https://casel.org/what-is-sel/

Cowan, M. (2010). *Tips for teaching mindfulness to dids*. Greater Good. https://greatergood.berkeley.edu/article/item/tips_for_teaching_mindfulness_to_kids

Creswell, J. D. (2017). Mindfulness Interventions. *Annual Review of Psychology*, *68*(1), 491–516. doi:10.1146/annurev-psych-042716-051139 PMID:27687118

Durlak, J. A., Weissberg, R. P., Dymnicki, A. B., Taylor, R. D., & Schellinger, K. B. (2011). The impact of enhancing students' social and emotional learning: A meta-analysis of schoolbased universal interventions. *Child Development*, *82*(1), 405–432. doi:10.1111/j.1467-8624.2010.01564.x PMID:21291449

Goleman, D. (2012). *Emotional Intelligence: Why It Can Matter More Than IQ*. Bantam.

Hanson, J. (Host). (2019-present). *The JOY Factor: Mindfulness, Compassion, Positive Psychology, Healing, Yoga*. Apple. https://podcasts.apple.com/tr/podcast/the-joy-factor- mindfulness-compassion-positive/id1108263766

Islah, Y. (2022). *Shapes' Adventures Book Series*. Universal ELT. https://universalelt.com/?s=Shapes+Adventures

Kabat-Zinn, J. (2005). *Wherever you go, there you are: Mindfulness meditation in everyday life*. Hyperion.

KidLit TV. (2019, June 18). *Read Out Loud BEE CALM: THE BUZZ ON YOGA* [Video]. YouTube. https://www.youtube.com/watch?v=oOYA8Sg4JBk

Kuru Gönen, S. İpek. (2022). Mindfulness-based practices for EFL teachers: sample tasks and insights to cultivate mindfulness. *Focus on ELT Journal, 4*(3), 78–93. doi:10.14744/felt.2022.4.3.6

Lantieri, L., & Zakrzewski, V. (2015). *How SEL and mindfulness can work together*. Greater Good. https://greatergood.berkeley.edu/article/item/how_social_emotional_learning_and_ mindfulness_can_work_together

Lawlor, M. S. (2016). Mindfulness and Social Emotional Learning (SEL): A conceptual framework. In K. A. Schonert-Reichl & R. W. Roeser (Eds.), *Handbook of mindfulness in education: Integrating theory and research into practice* (pp. 65–80). Springer. doi:10.1007/978-1-4939-3506-2_5

Lyons, K. E., & DeLange, J. (2016). Mindfulness matters in the classroom: The effects of mindfulness training on brain development and behavior in children and adolescents. In K. A. Schonert-Reichl & R. W. Roeser (Eds.), *Handbook of mindfulness in education: Integrating theory and research into practice* (pp. 271–283). Springer. doi:10.1007/978-1-4939-3506-2_17

Maloney, J. E., Lawlor, M. S., Schonert-Reichl, K. A., & Whitehead, J. (2016). A Mindfulness- based social and emotional learning curriculum for school-aged children: The MindUP program. In K. A. Schonert-Reichl & R. W. Roeser (Eds.), *Handbook of mindfulness in education: Integrating theory and research into practice* (pp. 313–334). doi:10.1007/978-1-4939-3506-2_20

Martino, J., & Tutton, J. (Founders). (2012). *Smiling Mind* [Mobile app]. https://www.smilingmind.com.au

Matsuba, M. K., Schonert-Reichl, K. A., McElroy, T., & Katahoire, A. (2021). Effectiveness of a SEL/mindfulness program on Northern Ugandan children. *International Journal of School & Educational Psychology*, *9*(1), 113–131. doi:10.1080/21683603.2020.1760977

Mischenko, P. P. (2021). *Mindfulness-based Social Emotional Learning in a Hybrid Education Environment* (Programme Document IBE/2021/WP/CD/48). https://unesdoc.unesco.org/ark:/48223/pf0000379403

National University. (2022). *What is social emotional Learning (SEL): Why it matters*. NU. https://www.nu.edu/blog/social-emotional-learning-sel-why-it-matters-for- educators/#how-educators-approach-sel

Northern Bright Bookshelf. (2020, April 13). *The Lemonade Hurricane: a story of mindfulness and meditation - a read out loud story book* [Video]. YouTube. https://www.youtube.com/watch?v=Olqt-Ghi-zo

Oberle, E., Schonert-Reichl, K. A., Hertzman, C., & Zumbo, B. D. (2014). Social–emotional competencies make the grade: Predicting academic success in early adolescence. *Journal of Applied Developmental Psychology*, *35*(3), 138–147. doi:10.1016/j.appdev.2014.02.004

Pentón Herrera, L. J. (2020). Social-emotional learning in TESOL: What, why, and how. *Journal of English Learner Education*, *10*(1), 1.

Puddicombe, A. (Founder). (2010). *Headspace* [Mobile app]. https://www.headspace.com

Ryan, G. (Host). (2015-present). *The Anxiety Coaches Podcast*. The Anxiety Coaches Podcast. https://www.theanxietycoachespodcast.com

Schonert-Reichl, K. A., Oberle, E., Lawlor, M. S., Abbott, D., Thomson, K., Oberlander, T. F., & Diamond, A. (2015). Enhancing cognitive and social-emotional development through a simple-to-administer school program. *Developmental Psychology*, *51*(1), 52–66. doi:10.1037/a0038454 PMID:25546595

Siegel, D. J. (2010). *Mindsight: The new science of personal transformation*. Bantam.

Tew, A., & Smith, M. A. (Founders). (2012). *Calm* [Mobile app]. https://www.calm.com

Weissberg, R. P., Durlak, J. A., Domitrovich, C. E., & Gullotta, T. P. (2015). Social and emotional learning: Past, present, and future. In J. A. Durlak, C. E. Domitrovich, R. P. Weissberg, & T. P. Gullotta (Eds.), *Handbook for social and emotional learning* (pp. 3–19). Guilford.

Willard, C. (2016). *Growing Up mindful: Essential practices to help children, teens, and families find balance, calm, and resilience*. Sounds True.

Williams, M., Teasdale, J., Segal, Z., & J. Kabat-Zinn, J. (2015). *İyi hissetme sanatı, kronik mutsuzlukla baş etme rehberi*. (Z. H. Haktanır, Çev.). Diyojen Yayıncılık.

Zeilhofer, L. (2020). Mindfulness in the foreign language classroom: Influence on academic achievement and awareness. *Language Teaching Research*, *27*(1), 96–114. doi:10.1177/1362168820934624

Zeilhofer, L., & Sasao, Y. (2022). Mindful language learning: The effects of college students' mindfulness on short-term vocabulary retention. *System*, *110*(6), 102909. doi:10.1016/j.system.2022.102909

Zins, J. E., & Elias, M. (2006). Social and emotional learning. *Children's Needs III: Development, Prevention, and Intervention*, 1–13.

ADDITIONAL READING

Abuşka, A., & Kavaklı Ulutaş. (forthcoming). An inquiry on the psychological well-being of the university students during emergency remote teaching: Application of the EMPATHICS Model. *Smart Learning Environments*.

Kabat-Zinn, J. (2013). *Full catastrophe living: Using the wisdom of your body and mind to face stress, pain, and illness*. Bantham Books.

Meiklejohn, J., Phillips, C., Freedman, M. L., Griffin, M. L., Biegel, G., Roach, A., & Saltzman, A. (2012). Integrating mindfulness training into K-12 education: Fostering the resilience of teachers and students. *Mindfulness*, *3*(4), 291–307. doi:10.100712671-012-0094-5

Pekrun, R., Vogl, E., Muis, K. R., & Sinatra, G. M. (2017). Measuring emotions during epistemic activities: The epistemically related emotion scales. *Cognition and Emotion*, *31*(6), 1268–1276. doi:10.1080/02699931.2016.1204989 PMID:27448030

Schmidt, R. (1990). The role of consciousness in second language learning. *Applied Linguistics*, *11*(2), 129–158. doi:10.1093/applin/11.2.129

Vogl, E., Pekrun, R., Murayama, K., & Loderer, K. (2020). Surprised–curious–confused: Epistemic emotions and knowledge exploration. *Emotion (Washington, D.C.)*, *20*(4), 625–641. doi:10.1037/emo0000578 PMID:30883147

Zeilhofer, L. (2020). Mindfulness in the foreign language classroom: Influence on academic achievement and awareness. *Language Teaching Research*, *13*, 1–19. doi:10.1177/1362168820934624

KEY TERMS AND DEFINITIONS

Emotional Learning Analytics (ELA): It is a kind of analysis of learning, processing emotionally driven data to improve students' learning using computational methods and techniques.

K-12 Education: It is the 12 years of compulsory education from kindergarten to Grade 12.

Learner Engagement: It reflects both quality and quantity of a student's participation into an educational program through efficiency echoed by interaction and cooperation with other students and teachers in the learning environment.

Learning Analytics (LA): It is a kind of an analysis of learning, processing data to improve students' learning using computational methods and techniques.

Mindfulness: It is the mental state of being aware of something on the present moment, acknowledging one's feelings and thoughts, accepting bodily sensations by means of a therapeutic technique.

Social-Emotional Learning (SEL): It is the process through which students learn how to apply social and emotional sets of knowledge, skills, and values to manage success at school.

Chapter 10
The Value of Learning Analytics in Educational Settings and Future Directions

Devrim Höl
https://orcid.org/0000-0001-5151-2581
Pamukkale University, Turkey

Nurdan Kavaklı Ulutaş
https://orcid.org/0000-0001-9572-9491
Izmir Demokrasi University, Turkey

ABSTRACT

This chapter highlights the significance of learning analytics (LA) in educational settings. A growing number of studies have been conducted in lieu of LA. LA is a notion that has emerged as a technique of exploiting the massive amount of learner data created by electronic system operations for educational purposes. As a recent learner-cantered method that strives to understand and optimize learning and learning environments, LA holds some pivotal benefits to enhance the teaching-learning process and makes a significant contribution to the field of educational design by analysing, storing, and processing the relevant data and provides an evidence-based decision-making process for all stakeholders ranging from institutions to researchers. The chapter then moves toward the theoretical framework on LA by exploring and understanding of the nature of learning and improve educational environments. In the final part, the significance of LA in educational settings and higher institutions is presented.

DOI: 10.4018/979-8-3693-0066-4.ch010

INTRODUCTION

Learning analytics (LA) is a new learner-centred approach which aims to understand and optimize learning and learning environment (Khuzairi et al., 2020). It employs a variety of analytical methods that effectively collect and identify significant information from large amounts of data, such as identifying patterns and adapting them to the educational process (Ruipérez-Valiente et al., 2017). According to Virgili (2019), LA is a collection of approaches and strategies which consists of gathering, processing, and analysing data that are stored on relevant software. The goal of this collection and analysis is to enhance educational procedures and draw conclusions about student performance levels.

LA offers several benefits. First, LA can be used to enhance the teaching-learning process by analysing data to make better decisions and benefit all parties involved. For instance, teachers can utilize LA as a foundation for enhancing their teaching methods in the learning environment as well as monitoring, examining, estimating, and making inferences about student performance throughout their teaching process (Oliva-Córdova et al., 2021). Second, according to Šereš et al. (2020), LA can provide opportunities to expedite enhancement of student achievement inside educational institutions via examining learning experiences and organizational practices of students. Third, relevant stakeholders could obtain insights about the behaviours of learners to enhance their learning circumstances (Calvo-Morata et al., 2018). Finally, LA can provide valuable information about individual differences between learners, which adaptive learning systems can be employed to tailor the changing needs of individual learners (Sense et al., 2021). Although LA has made a significant contribution to the field of educational design, most of its innovations have been centred on finding solutions for developed countries. This suggests that there is a need for future investigation in underdeveloped countries (Mahmoud et al., 2022). Also, LA could create a new space for students' motivational dispositions and expectations of educational support (Schumacher, 2018).

In a nutshell, LA seems to hold the potential to improve educational processes with different options. These options range from evidence-based decision-making to personalized learning techniques. Thus, it can be claimed that LA can revolutionize educational settings, improve teaching techniques, and ultimately improve student learning results.

THE SIGNIFICANCE OF LEARNING ANALYTICS IN EDUCATIONAL SETTINGS

An approach to decision-making and understanding student learning that is informed by data has evolved as an effective instrument in educational settings (Banihashem et al., 2018). In this vein, LA has emerged as a valuable tool in educational settings and has been used by educational institutions more and more to detect and support students who may suffer from low performance or disorder (Oliva-Córdova, 2021). According to Banihashem et al. (2018), the capacity to comprehend how students learn is one of the potential benefits of LA. Another potential benefit is the move from speculative decision-making toward practices that are based on evidence. This can be actualized by the substantial use of digital resources for self-directed learning, which is within the scope of LA based-on data from student questionnaires (Scott et al., 2017). Thus, LA has the potential to yield significant advantages in education, including enhanced service quality, enhanced student engagement, enhanced learning outcomes, accessibility to immediate feedback, and personalization of learning experiences (Mian et al., 2022). In addition, LA is dependent on a tailored approach for both teachers and students, which highlights its ability to cater to the specific learning requirements of individuals (Maseleno et al., 2018).

Based on the study of Wilkinson et al. (2019), LA is currently being implemented in tertiary education with the purpose of enhancing learning and teaching processes and improving the overall educational experiences. In this context, higher education institutions have been increasingly gathering data by utilizing various types of Learning Management Systems (LMS), Content Management Systems (CMS), tutoring systems, and educational platforms, which incorporate both traditional and blended learning methods (Klašnja-Milićević & Ivanović, 2018). However, to employ and implement data governance for learning analytics in higher education, it is necessary to have a common understanding of the objectives and aims of LA (Elouazizi, 2014).

Higher education institutions have been utilizing LA to enhance the facilities offered to students as well as the other stakeholders in education. The aim is to improve the visible and quantifiable results of learning such as grades, achievement rates, rewards, challenges, and barriers (Cooper, 2013). According to the findings of a scoping assessment (Quadri & Shukor, 2021), LA offers several advantages to stakeholders in higher education, including students, teaching staff, and administrative staff in educational institutions. In addition, the incorporation of research that pertains to both learning design and LA provides educators and researchers with the evidence that they need to enhance both teaching and learning practices (Macfadyen et al., 2020). According to Sagarika et al. (2021), assessment and LA have limited impact on education transformation. However, the potential effect of LA on transformative learning emerges when these two elements are combined. The synergy between assessment and LA creates a powerful inquiry into the factors that support authentic, deep, and transformative learning experiences for students. In this study, to facilitate an efficient educational experience, LA was utilized to analyse formative assessments, which can then be used to inform changes in teaching techniques and ultimately aid in the improvement of the overall educational arena. In this line of thinking, data science methodologies can be implemented to offer actionable educational insights and benefits for learning practices via LA (Ochoa & Wise, 2020). These benefits include enhancement of teaching quality, management of educational institutions, detection of students who are at risk (Mian et al., 2022), and continuous improvement initiatives in higher education institutions (Alfy et al., 2019). However, there could be some challenges regarding ethical and privacy concerns, data collection and analysis, and evaluation process (Mian et al., 2022).

FUTURE DIRECTIONS OF LA

In recent years, there have been an increasing number of research studies on the field of learning analytics. The concept of learning analytics has surfaced as a means of utilizing the vast quantity of learner data generated by electronic system operations for instructional purposes (Greller et al., 2014). Learning analytics is the process of measuring, collecting, analyzing, and reporting data about learners and the educational contexts (Clow, 2013). The goal of this process is to gain an understanding of the nature of learning and improve educational environments accordingly. When we look at the historical background of learning analytics, it is traced back to the early 2010s when several authors attempted to establish a theoretical foundation for learning analytics (Clow, 2013). In 2011, the Society for Learning Analytics Research (SOLAR) introduced the most widely accepted explanation for Learning Analytics (LA) at the First Learning Analytics and Knowledge Conference. According to this definition, LA involves the systematic process of measuring, collecting, analysing, and reporting data about learners and their contexts (Ferguson, 2017; Siemens & Long, 2011). Since then, LA has attracted the attention of scholars in different contexts with an aim to investigate its possibilities and current and future directions for educational purposes.

The impact of LA on the design of learning and the improvement of learning outcomes is one of its most important components. By providing a comprehensive background of the current landscape of learning and educational contexts, LA attracts the attention to the significance of making decisions about the ongoing design patterns and learning phenomena to improve learning (Mangaroska & Giannakos, 2017). In this sense, the future of LA is intricately connected to the concept of individualized learning. To illustrate, in their study, Maseleno et al. (2018) highlighted the importance of LA as a foundation for enhancing personalized learning. The authors also reported the potential for individualized and adaptive learning experiences, which implies that the future of LA may involve a shift toward personalized and adaptive learning environments through utilizing data to cater to the specific requirements and preferences of individual learners. Also, Gašević et al. (2017) have stressed the consolidation of LA as a discipline of study and practice on multiple occasions. To specify, the authors indicated the significance of multi-perspective approaches to LA, which include ensuring a healthy development of the field, a sustainable impact on research, and practice. The amalgamation of these approaches implies that educational domains are laying the groundwork of LA for future developments. Additionally, the incorporation of LA into learning design has been a primary focus of attention for scholars. To exemplify the potential of informed LA development with learning design, Nguyen et al. (2020) aimed to close the loop between LA and learning design, which demonstrates the possibility of LA to be integrated with learning design. In this way, as a future direction, LA will play a vital role in defining and informing the design of educational interventions and learning experiences.

The development and deployment of technologies could be specifically suited for the future of LA. In this sense, Srinivasa and Kurni (2021) examined the significance of tools of LA, pointing out that there is an increasing emphasis on the creation of specialized tools that can facilitate the gathering, analysis, and interpretation of learning data. Thus, it can be claimed that LA technologies will grow more advanced and play a vital role in educational practices and decision-making procedures. In a similar vein, Giannakos et al. (2016) underlined the potential of intelligent LA in that LA may include intelligent technologies and algorithms to enhance learning experiences and outcomes, which creates a need for further research in smart LA.

Considering the increasing number of research in recent years together with the recommendations of the studies, it appears that LA is an exceptionally promising area of research. Therefore, it is expected that the future of LA will involve judgments that are based on evidence to improve learning, including improvement of learning experiences, integration of learning design, creation of specialized tools, and the possibility of utilizing smart learning technologies.

REFERENCES

Alfy, S., Gómez, J., & Dani, A. (2019). Exploring the benefits and challenges of learning analytics in higher education institutions: A systematic literature review. *Information Discovery and Delivery*, *47*(1), 25–34. doi:10.1108/IDD-06-2018-0018

Banihashem, S., Aliabadi, K., Ardakani, S., Delaver, A., & Ahmadabadi, M. (2018). Learning analytics: A systematic literature review. *Interdisciplinary Journal of Virtual Learning in Medical Sciences, 9*(2). doi:10.5812/ijvlms.63024

Calvo-Morata, A., Alonso-Fernández, C., Martínez-Ortiz, I., & Fernández-Manjón, B. (2018). Making understandable game learning analytics for teachers., 112-121. doi:10.1007/978-3-319-96565-9_11

Clow, D. (2013). An overview of learning analytics. *Teaching in Higher Education, 18*(6), 683–695. doi:10.1080/13562517.2013.827653

Elouazizi, N. (2014). Critical factors in data governance for learning analytics. *Journal of Learning Analytics, 1*(3), 211–222. doi:10.18608/jla.2014.13.25

Ferguson, R. (2012). Learning analytics: Drivers, developments, and challenges. *International Journal of Technology Enhanced Learning, 4*(5-6), 304–317. doi:10.1504/IJTEL.2012.051816

Gašević, D., Kovanović, V., & Joksimovíc, S. (2017). Piecing the learning analytics puzzle: A consolidated model of a field of research and practice. *Learning Research and Practice, 3*(1), 63–78. doi:10.1080/23735082.2017.1286142

Giannakos, M., Sampson, D., & Kidziński, Ł. (2016). Introduction to smart learning analytics: Foundations and developments in video-based learning. *Smart Learning Environments, 3*(1), 12. Advance online publication. doi:10.118640561-016-0034-2

Khuzairi, N., Sidhu, M., & Cob, Z. (2020). Learning analytics and teaching analytics: The similarities and differences. *International Journal of Humanities Management and Social Science, 3*(2), 52–58. doi:10.36079/lamintang.ij-humass-0302.135

Klašnja-Milićević, A., & Ivanović, M. (2018). Learning analytics: New flavor and benefits for educational environments. *Informatics Educ., 17*(2), 285–300. doi:10.15388/infedu.2018.15

Macfadyen, L., Lockyer, L., & Rienties, B. (2020). Learning design and learning analytics: Snapshot 2020. *Journal of Learning Analytics, 7*(3), 6–12. doi:10.18608/jla.2020.73.2

Mahmoud, M., Dafoulas, G., ElAziz, R., & Saleeb, N. (2022). Factors affecting the deployment of learning analytics in developing countries: Case of Egypt. *International Journal of Emerging Technologies in Learning, 17*(03), 279–298. doi:10.3991/ijet.v17i03.24405

Mangaroska, K., & Giannakos, M. (2017). *Learning analytics for learning design: Towards evidence-driven decisions to enhance learning,* 428-433. doi:10.1007/978-3-319-66610-5_38

Maseleno, A., Sabani, N., Huda, M., Ahmad, R., Jasmi, K., & Basiron, B. (2018). Demystifying learning analytics in personalised learning. *IACSIT International Journal of Engineering and Technology*, *7*(3), 1124. doi:10.14419/ijet.v7i3.9789

Mian, Y., Khalid, F., Qun, A., & Ismail, S. (2022). Learning analytics in education, advantages, and issues: A systematic literature review. *Creative Education*, *13*(09), 2913–2920. doi:10.4236/ce.2022.139183

Nguyen, A., Gardner, L., & Sheridan, D. (2020). *A design methodology for learning analytics information systems: Informing learning analytics development with learning design.* Scholar Space. doi:10.24251/HICSS.2020.014

Ochoa, X., & Wise, A. (2020). Supporting the shift to digital with student-centered learning analytics. *Educational Technology Research and Development*, *69*(1), 357–361. doi:10.100711423-020-09882-2 PMID:33250614

Oliva-Córdova, L. M., Garcia-Cabot, A., & Amado-Salvatierra, H. R. (2021). Learning analytics to support teaching skills: A systematic literature review. *IEEE Access : Practical Innovations, Open Solutions*, *9*, 58351–58363. doi:10.1109/ACCESS.2021.3070294

Quadri, A., & Shukor, N. (2021). The benefits of learning analytics to higher education institutions: A scoping review. *International Journal of Emerging Technologies in Learning*, *16*(23), 4–15. doi:10.3991/ijet.v16i23.27471

Ruipérez-Valiente, J. A., Muñoz-Merino, P. J., Pijeira Díaz, H. J., Santofimia Ruiz, J., & Delgado Kloos, C. (2017). Evaluation of a learning analytics application for open EdX platform. *Computer Science and Information Systems*, *14*(1), 51–73. doi:10.2298/CSIS160331043R

Sagarika, R., Kandakatla, R., & Gulhane, A. (2021). Role of learning analytics to evaluate formative assessments: Using a data driven approach to inform changes in teaching practices. *Journal of Engineering Education Transformations*, *34*(0), 550–556. doi:10.16920/jeet/2021/v34i0/157212

Schumacher, C., & Ifenthaler, D. (2018). The importance of students' motivational dispositions for designing learning analytics. *Journal of Computing in Higher Education*, *30*(3), 599–619. doi:10.100712528-018-9188-y

Scott, K., Morris, A., & Marais, B. (2017). Medical student use of digital learning resources. *The Clinical Teacher*, *15*(1), 29–33. doi:10.1111/tct.12630 PMID:28300343

Sense, F., Velde, M., & Rijn, H. (2021). Predicting university students' exam performance using a model-based adaptive fact-learning system. *Journal of Learning Analytics*, *8*(3), 155–169. doi:10.18608/jla.2021.6590

Šereš, L., Pavlicevic, V., & Petrović, G. (2020). *Learning analytics: An updated view*. UNS. doi:10.46541/978-86-7233-386-2_38

Siemens, G., & Long, P. (2011). Penetrating the fog: Analytics in learning and education. *EDUCAUSE Review*, *46*(5), 30.

Srinivasa, K., & Kurni, M. (2021). Tools for learning analytics. In S. K. G., & M. Kurni (Eds.), A Beginner's Guide to Learning Analytics (pp. 121-159). Springer. doi:10.1007/978-3-030-70258-8_5

Virgili, E. (2019). Learning analytics: Online higher education in management. *Sociology and Anthropology (Alhambra, Calif.)*, *7*(2), 66–75. doi:10.13189a.2019.070202

Wilkinson, K., McNamara, I., Wilson, D., & Riggs, K. (2019). Using learning analytics to evaluate course design and student behavior in an online wine business course. *International Journal of Innovation in Science and Mathematics Education*, *27*(4). doi:10.30722/IJISME.27.04.008

ADDITIONAL READING

Baker, R. S., & Koedinger, K. R. (2018). Towards demonstrating the value of learning analytics for K-12 education. *Learning Analytics in Education*, 49-62.

Fischer, C., Pardos, Z. A., Baker, R. S., Williams, J. J., Yu, P., Sm, R., Slater, S., & Baker, S. (2020). Mining big data in education: Affordances and challenges. *Review of Research in Education*, *44*(1), 130–160. doi:10.3102/0091732X20903304

Herodotou, C., Rienties, B., Boroowa, A., Zdrahal, Z., & Hlosta, M. (2019). A large-scale implementation of predictive learning analytics in higher education: The teachers' role and perspective. *Educational Technology Research and Development*, *67*(5), 1273–1306. doi:10.100711423-019-09685-0

Ifenthaler, D., & Yau, J. Y. K. (2020). Utilising learning analytics to support study success in higher education: A systematic review. *Educational Technology Research and Development*, *68*(4), 1961–1990. doi:10.100711423-020-09788-z

Jones, K. M. (2019). Learning analytics and higher education: A proposed model for establishing informed consent mechanisms to promote student privacy and autonomy. *International Journal of Educational Technology in Higher Education*, *16*(1), 1–22. doi:10.118641239-019-0155-0

Leitner, P., Khalil, M., & Ebner, M. (2017). Learning analytics in higher education—a literature review. *Learning analytics: Fundaments, applications, and trends: A view of the current state of the art to enhance. E-learning*, 1–23.

Monroy, C., Rangel, V. S., & Whitaker, R. (2014). A strategy for incorporating learning analytics into the design and evaluation of a K-12 science curriculum. *Journal of Learning Analytics*, *1*(2), 94–125. doi:10.18608/jla.2014.12.6

KEY TERMS AND DEFINITIONS

Content Management System (CMS): It serves as an application to help users create, edit, publish, and store digital content through a software system.

Learning Analytics (LA): It is the process of measuring, collecting, analyzing, and reporting data about learners and educational contexts.

Learning Management System (LMS): It provide virtual classroom environments that support the learning process.

Compilation of References

Aaron, P. G. (1994). *Dyslexia and hyperlexia: Diagnosis and management of developmental reading disabilities*. Springer Dordrecht., doi:10.1007/978-94-009-1065-2

Aguerrebere, C., He, H., Kwet, M., Laakso, M. J., Lang, C., Price-Dennis, C. M. D., & Zhang, H. (2022). Global perspectives on learning analytics in K12 education. In C. Lang, A. F. Wise, A. Merceron, D. Gašević, & G. Siemens (Eds.), *The handbook of learning analytics* (pp. 223–231). SOLAR. doi:10.18608/hla22.022

Aikina, T., & Zubkova, O. (2015). Integrating online services into English language teaching and learning: The case of Voki. *International Journal of Emerging Technologies in Learning*, *10*(3), 66–68. doi:10.3991/ijet.v10i3.4546

Akhtar, S. (2009). *The nature of developmental dyslexia.* [Unpublished MA thesis, Long Island University, Brooklyn].

Alam, A. (2021, December). Should robots replace teachers? Mobilisation of AI and learning analytics in education. *The Proceedings of the International Conference on Advances in Computing, Communication, and Control* (ICAC3) (pp. 1-12). ACM.

Al-AmraniS. N. (2021, March). Omani learners' willingness to communicate in English: Can university learning management system help? doi:10.2139/ssrn.3777023

Alfy, S., Gómez, J., & Dani, A. (2019). Exploring the benefits and challenges of learning analytics in higher education institutions: A systematic literature review. *Information Discovery and Delivery*, *47*(1), 25–34. doi:10.1108/IDD-06-2018-0018

Alhudithi, E. (2017). *A corpus-based analysis of English vocabulary input provided in K-12 textbooks used in Saudi Arabia* [Unpublished Doctoral dissertation, Colorado State University]. ProQuest Dissertations and Theses Global.

Allbright, T., & Hough, H. (2020). Measures of SEL and school climate in California. *The State Education Standard*, *20*(2), 28–50.

Allen, L. K., Perret, C., Likens, A., & McNamara, D. S. (2017). What'd you say again? *The Proceedings of the Seventh International Learning Analytics & Knowledge Conference.* Association for Computing Machinery. 10.1145/3027385.3027445

Almalki, S. (2016). Integrating quantitative and qualitative data in mixed methods research--challenges and benefits. *Journal of education and learning, 5*(3), 288-296.

Alqarni, N. (2021). Language learners' willingness to communicate and speaking anxiety in online versus face-to-face learning contexts. *International Journal of Learning. Teaching and Educational Research, 20*(11), 57–77.

Anderson, J. R., Boyle, C. F., & Reiser, B. J. (1985). Intelligent tutoring systems. *Science, 228*(4698), 456–462. doi:10.1126cience.228.4698.456 PMID:17746875

Andersson, S. (2006). Newly qualified teachers' learning related to their use of information and communication technology: A Swedish perspective. *British Journal of Educational Technology, 37*(5), 665–682. doi:10.1111/j.1467-8535.2006.00563.x

Anggraini, A. (2022). Improving students' pronunciation skill using ELSA speak application. *Journal of English Language and Pedagogy, 5*(1), 135–141. doi:10.33503/journey.v5i1.1840

Apolinar-Gotardo, M. (2019). Using decision tree algorithm to predict student performance. *Indian Journal of Science and Technology, 12*, 5.

Apriani, E., & Supardan, D. (2018). Language learning disabilities: How can I help my students with dyslexia. *English Franca, 2*(2), 187–200. doi:10.29240/ef.v2i2.598

Archer, K., Savage, R., Sanghera-Sidhu, S., Wood, E., Gottardo, A., & Chen, V. (2014). Examining the effectiveness of technology use in classrooms: A tertiary meta-analysis. *Computers & Education, 78*, 140–149. doi:10.1016/j.compedu.2014.06.001

Atapattu, T., Thilakaratne, M., Vivian, R., & Falkner, K. (2019). Detecting cognitive engagement using word embeddings within an online teacher professional development community. *Computers & Education, 140*, 103594. doi:10.1016/j.compedu.2019.05.020

Avella, J. T., Kebritchi, M., Nunn, S. G., & Kanai, T. (2016). Learning analytics methods, benefits, and challenges in higher education: A systematic literature review. *Online Learning : the Official Journal of the Online Learning Consortium, 20*(2), 13–29.

Aydin, S. (2014). Foreign language learners' interactions with their teachers on Facebook. *System, 42*, 155–163. doi:10.1016/j.system.2013.12.001

Ayedoun, E., Hayashi, Y., & Seta, K. (2019). Adding communicative and affective strategies to an embodied conversational agent to enhance second language learners' willingness to communicate. *International Journal of Artificial Intelligence in Education, 29*(1), 29–57. doi:10.100740593-018-0171-6

Ayşenur, A. V., & Höl, D. (2023). DigiFlyers:a digital storytelling program to improve the listening performance of young learners. *Mehmet Akif Ersoy Üniversitesi Eğitim Fakültesi Dergisi*, (66), 446–474.

Azevedo, R., Bouchet, F., Duffy, M., Harley, J., Taub, M., Trevors, G., Cloude, E., Dever, D., Wiedbusch, M., Wortha, F., & Cerezo, R. (2022). Lessons learned and future directions of MetaTutor: Leveraging multichannel data to scaffold self-regulated learning with an intelligent tutoring system. *Frontiers in Psychology, 13*, 813632. doi:10.3389/fpsyg.2022.813632 PMID:35774935

Badal, Y. T., & Sungkur, R. K. (2023). Predictive modelling and analytics of students' grades using machine learning algorithms. *Education and Information Technologies, 28*(3), 3027–3057. doi:10.100710639-022-11299-8 PMID:36097545

Bailie, J. L. (2020). Online learner analytics of asynchronous discussions as a predictor of final grades. *Journal of Instructional Pedagogies, 24.*

Baker, R. S. (2016). Stupid tutoring systems, intelligent humans. *International Journal of Artificial Intelligence in Education, 26*(2), 600–614. doi:10.100740593-016-0105-0

Baker, R. S., & Koedinger, K. R. (2018). Towards demonstrating the value of learning analytics for K-12 education. In *Learning analytics in education* (pp. 49–62). Information Age Publishing.

Baker, S. C., & MacIntyre, P. D. (2000). The role of gender and immersion in communication and second language orientations. *Language Learning, 50*(2), 311–341. doi:10.1111/0023-8333.00119

Baneres, D., Rodríguez-Gonzalez, M. E., & Serra, M. (2019). An early feedback prediction system for learners at-risk within a first-year higher education course. *IEEE Transactions on Learning Technologies, 12*(2), 249–263. doi:10.1109/TLT.2019.2912167

Banihashem, S., Aliabadi, K., Ardakani, S., Delaver, A., & Ahmadabadi, M. (2018). Learning analytics: A systematic literature review. *Interdisciplinary Journal of Virtual Learning in Medical Sciences, 9*(2). doi:10.5812/ijvlms.63024

Baran, E., Chuang, H., & Thompson, A. (2011). TPACK: An emerging research and development tool for teacher educators. *The Turkish Online Journal of Educational Technology, 10*(4), 370–377.

Barmaki, R., & Hughes, C. E. (2015). Providing real-time feedback for student teachers in a virtual rehearsal environment. *The Proceedings of the 2015 ACM on International Conference on Multimodal Interaction* (pp. 531–537). ACM.

Bayyurt, Y. (2012). Proposing a model for English language education in the Turkish sociocultural context. In Y. Bayyurt & Y. Bektaş-Çetinkaya (Eds.), *Research perspectives on teaching and learning English in Turkey: Policies and practices* (pp. 301–312). Peter Lang.

Bernales, C. (2016). Towards a comprehensive concept of willingness to communicate: Learners' predicted and self-reported participation in the foreign language classroom. *System, 56*, 1–12. doi:10.1016/j.system.2015.11.002

Bernardini, S. (2001). Spoilt for choice: A learner explores general language corpora. In G. Aston (Ed.), *Learning with corpora* (pp. 220–249). Athelstan.

Bharadiya, J. P. (2023). A comparative study of business intelligence and artificial intelligence with big data analytics. *American Journal of Artificial Intelligence, 7*(1), 24.

Biber, D., Conrad, S., & Reppen, R. (1998). *Corpus linguistics: Investigating language structure and use*. Cambridge University Press. doi:10.1017/CBO9780511804489

Bienkowski, M., Feng, M., & Means, B. (2012). *Enhancing Teaching and Learning through Educational Data Mining and Learning Analytics: An Issue Brief.* Office of Educational Technology, US Department of Education. https://files.eric.ed.gov/fulltext/ED611199.pdf

Blumenstein, M. (2020). Synergies of learning analytics and learning design: A systematic review of student outcomes. *Journal of Learning Analytics*, *7*(3), 13–32. doi:10.18608/jla.2020.73.3

Bond, M., Viberg, O., & Bergdahl, N. (2023, March). The current state of using learning analytics to measure and support K-12 student engagement: A scoping review. *13th International Learning Analytics and Knowledge (LAK) Conference* (pp. 240-249). Arlington: ACM.

Bozkurt, A. (2016). Öğrenme analitiği: E-öğrenme, büyük veri ve bireyselleştirilmiş öğrenme. *Açıköğretim Uygulamaları ve Araştırmaları Dergisi*, *2*(4), 55–81.

Bradley, L., & Bryant, P. E. (1983). Categorizing sounds and learning to read: A casual connection. *Nature*, *301*(3), 419–421. doi:10.1038/301419a0

Brady, S. (1986). Short-term memory, phonological processing, and reading ability. *Annals of Dyslexia*, *36*(1), 138–153. doi:10.1007/BF02648026 PMID:24243456

British Dyslexia Association. (2007). *What is Dyslexia?* BDA. https://www.bdadyslexia.org.uk/dyslexia/about-dyslexia/what-is-dyslexia

British Psychological Society. (1999). *Dyslexia, literacy, and psychological assessment*. British Psychological Society.

Brookhart, S. M. (2017). *How to give effective feedback to your students*. ASCD.

Brooks, C., Thompson, C., & Teasley, S. (2015, March). A time series interaction analysis method for building predictive models of learners using log data. *The Proceedings of the fifth international conference on learning analytics and knowledge* (pp. 126-135).

Brousseau, R. G. (2006). *An Investigation into the progression of early acquired dyslexia* [Unpublished Doctoral dissertation, University of Windsor]. https://scholar.uwindsor.ca/cgi/viewcontent.cgi?article=8216&context=etd

Brown, T. (Host). (2019-present). *Wake Me Up: Morning meditation and motivation*. Wake Me Up. https://www.wakemeuppodcast.com

Brown, M. (2012). Learning analytics: Moving from concept to practice. *EDUCAUSE Learning Initiative*, *7*, 1–5.

Brown, M. (2020). Seeing students at scale: How faculty in large lecture courses act upon learning analytics dashboard data. *Teaching in Higher Education*, *25*(4), 384–400. doi:10.1080/13562517.2019.1698540

Bryant, P., & Bradley, L. (1985). *Children's reading problems*. Blackwell.

Bulut, O., Gorgun, G., Yildirim-Erbasli, S. N., Wongvorachan, T., Daniels, L. M., Gao, Y., Lai, K. W., & Shin, J. (2022). Standing on the shoulders of giants: Online formative assessments as the foundation for predictive learning analytics models. *British Journal of Educational Technology*, *54*(1), 19–39. doi:10.1111/bjet.13276

Burgoon, J. K. (1976). The unwillingness-to-communicate scale: Development and validation. *Communication Monographs*, *43*(1), 60–69. doi:10.1080/03637757609375916

Buxbaum-Conradi, S., Redlich, T., & Branding, J. H. (2016, January). Conceptualizing hybrid human-machine systems and interaction. *The 49th Hawaii International Conference on System Sciences (HICSS)* (pp. 551-559). IEEE. 10.1109/HICSS.2016.75

Caballero, C., Scherer, E., West, M. R., Mrazek, M. D., Gabrieli, C. F., & Gabrieli, J. D. (2019). Greater mindfulness is associated with better academic achievement in middle school. *Mind, Brain and Education : the Official Journal of the International Mind, Brain, and Education Society*, *13*(3), 157–166. doi:10.1111/mbe.12200

Calvo-Morata, A., Alonso-Fernández, C., Martínez-Ortiz, I., & Fernández-Manjón, B. (2018). Making understandable game learning analytics for teachers., 112-121. doi:10.1007/978-3-319-96565-9_11

Campbell, J. P., DeBlois, P. B., & Oblinger, D. G. (2007). Academic analytics: A new tool for a new era. *EDUCAUSE Review*, *42*(4), 40.

Cantiani, C., Lorusso, M. L., Perego, P., Molteni, M., & Guasti, M. T. (2015). Developmental dyslexia with and without language impairment: ERPs reveal qualitative differences in morphosyntactic processing. *Developmental Neuropsychology*, *40*(5), 291–312. doi:10.1080/87565641.2015.1072536 PMID:26285096

Cao, Y. (2011). Investigating situational willingness to communicate within second language classrooms from an ecological perspective. *System*, *39*(4), 468–479. doi:10.1016/j.system.2011.10.016

Cao, Y., & Philp, J. (2006). Interactional context and willingness to communicate: A comparison of behavior in whole class, group and dyadic interaction. *System*, *34*(4), 480–493. doi:10.1016/j.system.2006.05.002

Carroll, J. B. (1993). *Human cognitive abilities: A survey of factor-analytic studies*. Cambridge University Press. doi:10.1017/CBO9780511571312

Castles, A., Bates, T. C., & Coltheart, M. (2006). John Marshall and the developmental dyslexia. *Aphasiology*, *20*(9-11), 871–892. doi:10.1080/02687030600738952

Chaisiri, P. (2023). Promoting Thai EFL learners' willingness to communicate in the virtual classroom through technology-mediated oral tasks. *LEARN Journal: Language Education and Acquisition Research Network*, *16*(1), 97–120.

Chandra, V., & Lloyd, M. (2008). The methodological nettle: ICT and student achievement. *British Journal of Educational Technology*, *39*(6), 1087–1098. doi:10.1111/j.1467-8535.2007.00790.x

Chatti, M. A., Dyckhoff, A. L., Schroeder, U., & Thüs, H. (2012). A reference model for learning analytics. *International Journal of Technology Enhanced Learning*, *4*(5/6), 318–331. doi:10.1504/IJTEL.2012.051815

Chauhan, S. (2017). A meta-analysis of the impact of technology on learning effectiveness of elementary students. *Computers & Education*, *105*, 14–30. doi:10.1016/j.compedu.2016.11.005

Chen, L., Lu, M., Goda, Y., & Yamada, M. (2019, November). Design of learning analytics dashboard supporting metacognition. *The Proceedings of the 16th International Conference on Cognition and Exploratory Learning in the Digital Age (CELDA)* (pp. 175-182). IADIS. 10.33965/celda2019_201911L022

Chen, F., & Cui, Y. (2020). Utilizing student time series behavior in learning management systems for early prediction of course performance. *Journal of Learning Analytics*, *7*(2), 1–17. doi:10.18608/jla.2020.72.1

Chen, L., Chen, P., & Lin, Z. (2020). Artificial intelligence in education: A review. *IEEE Access : Practical Innovations, Open Solutions*, *8*, 75264–75278. doi:10.1109/ACCESS.2020.2988510

Chhum, C., & Champakaew, W. (2019). Effects of mobile assisted language learning on learners' willingness to communicate in English. *Proceeding of National and International Conference*, *1*(10), 40-54.

Chotipaktanasook, N., & Reinders, H. (2016). Willingness to communicate in social media: An investigation of the long-term effects. *Asian EFL Journal*, *18*(4), 6–25.

Chou, C. C., Block, L., & Jesness, R. (2012). A case study of mobile learning pilot project in K-12 schools. [JETDE]. *Journal of Educational Technology Development and Exchange*, *5*(2), 11–26. doi:10.18785/jetde.0502.02

Chou, C. Y., Tseng, S. F., Chen, Z. H., Chao, P. Y., Peng, K. C., & Lin, Y. L. (2015). *Learning analytics of core competencies: A comparative study of students, academics, and industries. 23rd International Conference on Computers in Education (ICCE)*. Asia-Pacific Society for Computers in Education. https://scholar.lib.ntnu.edu.tw/en/publications/learning-analytics-of-core-competencies-a-comparative-study-of-st-2

Chou, C. Y., Tseng, S. F., Chih, W. C., Chen, Z. H., Chao, P. Y., Lai, K. R., Chan, C.-L., Yu, L.-C., & Lin, Y. L. (2015). Open student models of core competencies at the curriculum level: Using learning analytics for student reflection. *IEEE Transactions on Emerging Topics in Computing*, *5*(1), 32–44. https://ieeexplore.ieee.org/document/7335629. doi:10.1109/TETC.2015.2501805

Chou, C. Y., Tseng, S. F., Wang, C. J., Chao, P. Y., Chen, Z. H., Lai, K. R., Chan, C.-L., & Yu, L. C. (2018). Learning analytics on graduates' academic records to reflect on a competency-based curriculum. *Computer Applications in Engineering Education*, *26*(6), 2168–2182. doi:10.1002/cae.22019

Chou, M.-H. (2018). Speaking anxiety and strategy use for learning English as a foreign language in full and partial English-medium instruction contexts. *TESOL Quarterly*, *52*(3), 611–633. doi:10.1002/tesq.455

Chung, K. K. H., & Ho, C. S. (2010). Second language learning difficulties in Chinese children with dyslexia: What are the reading-related cognitive skills that contribute to English and Chinese word reading? *Journal of Learning Disabilities*, *43*(3), 195–211. doi:10.1177/0022219409345018 PMID:19897734

Ciolacu, M., Tehrani, A. F., Beer, R., & Popp, H. (2017, October). Education 4.0—Fostering student's performance with machine learning methods. *IEEE 23rd International Symposium for Design and Technology in Electronic Packaging (SIITME)* (pp. 438-443). IEEE. https://doi.org/10.1109/SIITME.2017.8259941

Ciolacu, M., Tehrani, A. F., Binder, L., & Svasta, P. M. (2018, October). Education 4.0-Artificial Intelligence assisted higher education: Early recognition system with machine learning to support students' success. *IEEE 24th International Symposium for Design and Technology in Electronic Packaging (SIITME)* (pp. 23-30). IEEE. 10.1109/SIITME.2018.8599203

Clow, D. (2012). The learning analytics cycle: Closing the loop effectively. *The Proceedings of the 2nd International Conference on Learning Analytics and Knowledge* (LAK12), (pp. 134-138). IEEE.

Clow, D. (2013). An overview of learning analytics. *Teaching in Higher Education*, *18*(6), 683–695. doi:10.1080/13562517.2013.827653

Colaianni, P. (2013-present). *The Overwhelmed Brain.* The Overwhelmed Brain. https://theoverwhelmedbrain.com/podcasts/

Collaborative for Academic, Social, and Emotional Learning (CASEL). (2023). *Fundamentals of SEL.* CASEL. https://casel.org/what-is-sel/

Cook, D. J., Augusto, J. C., & Jakkula, V. R. (2009). Ambient intelligence: Technologies, applications, and opportunities. *Pervasive and Mobile Computing*, *5*(4), 277–298. doi:10.1016/j.pmcj.2009.04.001

Corrin, L., Kennedy, G., French, S., Buckingham Shum, S., Kitto, K., Pardo, A., West, D., Mirriahi, N., & Colvin, C. (2019). *The ethics of learning analytics in Australian higher education: A discussion paper.*

Coskun, N., & Mitrani, C. (2020). An instructional design for vocabulary acquisition with a hidden disability of dyslexia. *New Trends and Issues Proceedings on Humanities and Social Sciences*, *7*(1), 220–241. doi:10.18844/prosoc.v7i1.4901

Cowan, M. (2010). *Tips for teaching mindfulness to dids.* Greater Good. https://greatergood.berkeley.edu/article/item/tips_for_teaching_mindfulness_to_kids

Creswell, J. D. (2017). Mindfulness Interventions. *Annual Review of Psychology*, *68*(1), 491–516. doi:10.1146/annurev-psych-042716-051139 PMID:27687118

Cui, Y., Chen, F., & Shiri, A. (2020). Scale up predictive models for early detection of at-risk students: A feasibility study. *Information and Learning Science*, *121*(3/4), 97–116. doi:10.1108/ILS-05-2019-0041

Currier, C. (2021). Unresolved privacy and ethics issues related to learning analytics in higher education and academic librarianship. *Emerging Library & Information Perspectives*, *4*(1), 117–142. doi:10.5206/elip.v4i1.13463

Da Fontoura, H. A., & Siegel, L. S. (1995). Reading, syntactic, and working memory skills of bilingual Portuguese-English Canadian children. *Reading and Writing*, *7*(1), 139–153. doi:10.1007/BF01026951

Darvishi, A., Khosravi, H., Sadiq, S., & Gašević, D. (2022). Incorporating AI and learning analytics to build trustworthy peer assessment systems. *British Journal of Educational Technology*, *53*(4), 844–875. doi:10.1111/bjet.13233

Davenport, T. H., Harris, J. G., & Morison, R. (2010). *Analytics at work: Smarter decisions, better results*. Harvard Business Press.

Davis, R. D., & Braun, E. M. (1997). *The gist of dyslexia*. Perigee Books.

Dazo, S. L., Stepanek, N. R., Chauhan, A., & Dorn, B. (2017). Examining instructor use of learning analytics. *Paper presented at the Proceedings of the 2017 CHI Conference Extended Abstracts on Human Factors in Computing Systems*. ACM. 10.1145/3027063.3053256

Del Blanco, Á., Serrano, Á., Freire, M., Martínez-Ortiz, I., & Fernández-Manjón, B. (2013, March). E-Learning standards and learning analytics. Can data collection be improved by using standard data models? *Global Engineering Education Conference (EDUCON)* (pp. 1255-1261). IEEE. 10.1109/EduCon.2013.6530268

Delgardo, M., Higgins, D., McCormick, K. L., Reid, P., Canoll, P., & McCormick, P. C. (2022). Clinical characteristics, outcomes, and pathology analysis in patients with dorsal arachnoid web. *Neurosurgery*, *90*(5), 581–587. doi:10.1227/neu.0000000000001884 PMID:35290255

Delmas, P. M., & Moore, P. R. (2019). Student perceptions of video-based discussions in online and blended learning. *Proceedings of the E-Learn 2019 Annual Conferenc*e (pp. 1280–1286). Association for the Advancement of Computing in Education.

Demirpolat, B. C. (2015). *Türkiye'nin yabancı dil öğretimiyle imtihanı: Sorunlar ve çözüm önerileri*. SETA. http://file.setav.org/Files/Pdf/20150707131308_131_yabancidil_web.pdf

Department for Education and Skills. (2004). *A framework for understanding Dyslexia*. https://www.achieveability.org.uk/files/1270740075/dfes-framework-for-understanding-dyslexia.pdf

Dewey, J. (1938). *Experience and education*. Macmillan.

Dhamija, A., & Dhamija, D. (2020). Impact of innovative and interactive instructional strategies on student classroom participation. In M. Montebello (Ed.), Handbook of Research on Digital Learning (pp. 20-37). IGI Global. doi:10.4018/978-1-5225-9304-1.ch002

DiCerbo, K., Shute, V., & Kim, Y. J. (2017). The future of assessment in technology rich environments: Psychometric considerations. In *Learning, design, and technology: An international compendium of theory, research, practice, and policy* (pp. 1–21). Springer. doi:10.1007/978-3-319-17727-4_66-1

Dietz-Uhler, B., & Hurn, J. E. (2013). Using learning analytics to predict (and improve) student success: A faculty perspective. *Journal of Interactive Online Learning*, *12*(1), 17–26.

Dietz-Uhler, B., & Hurn, J. E. (2015). Strategies for engagement in online courses: Engaging with the content, instructor, and other students. In *Quick Hits for Adjunct Faculty and Lecturers* (pp. 41–44). Indiana University Press.

Dignum, V., Penagos, M., Pigmans, K., & Vosloo, S. (2020). *Policy guidance on AI for children.* UNICEF Office of Global Insight and Policy.

Dimililer, C., & Istek, E. (2018). Experiences of a dyslexic child in an English as a foreign language class. *Springer Science+Business Media B.V., part of Springer Nature, 20*(52), 1391-1398.

Dirjal, A. H., Ghapanchi, Z., & Ghonsooly, B. (2020). Role of social media application in promoting motivation and listening skill of Iraqi EFL learners: A Skype-Based study. *Asian Social Science*, *16*(8), 20–32. doi:10.5539/ass.v16n8p20

Dizon, G. (2020). Evaluating intelligent personal assistants for L2 listening and speaking development. *Language Learning & Technology*, *24*(1), 16–26.

Dogan, M. E., Goru Dogan, T., & Bozkurt, A. (2023). The use of artificial intelligence (AI) in online learning and distance education processes: A systematic review of empirical studies. *Applied Sciences (Basel, Switzerland)*, *13*(5), 3056. doi:10.3390/app13053056

Dringus, L. P. (2012). Learning analytics considered harmful. *Journal of Asynchronous Learning Networks*, *16*(3), 87–100.

Durlak, J. A., Weissberg, R. P., Dymnicki, A. B., Taylor, R. D., & Schellinger, K. B. (2011). The impact of enhancing students' social and emotional learning: A meta-analysis of schoolbased universal interventions. *Child Development*, *82*(1), 405–432. doi:10.1111/j.1467-8624.2010.01564.x PMID:21291449

Du, X., Yang, J., Shelton, B. E., Hung, J. L., & Zhang, M. (2021). A systematic meta-review and analysis of learning analytics research. *Behaviour & Information Technology*, *40*(1), 49–62. doi:10.1080/0144929X.2019.1669712

Ebadi, S., & Ebadijalal, M. (2022). The effect of Google Expeditions virtual reality on EFL learners' willingness to communicate and oral proficiency. *Computer Assisted Language Learning*, *35*(8), 1975–2000. doi:10.1080/09588221.2020.1854311

Ehsanzadehsorati, S. (2018). *A corpus-driven approach toward teaching vocabulary and reading to English language learners in US-based K-12 context through a mobile app.* [*Dissertation, FIU*]. https://digitalcommons.fiu.edu/etd/3860

Elias, T. (2011). *Learning analytics: The definitions, the processes, and the potential.* Learning Analytics. http://learninganalytics.net/LearningAnalyticsDefinitionsProcesses Potential.pdf

Elouazizi, N. (2014). Critical factors in data governance for learning analytics. *Journal of Learning Analytics, 1*(3), 211–222. doi:10.18608/jla.2014.13.25

Everatt, J., Steffert, B., & Smythe, I. (1999). An eye for the unusual: Creative thinking in dyslexics. *Dyslexia (Chichester, England), 5*(1), 28–46. doi:10.1002/(SICI)1099-0909(199903)5:1<28::AID-DYS126>3.0.CO;2-K

Fabriz, S., Mendzheritskaya, J., & Stehle, S. (2021). Impact of synchronous and asynchronous settings of online teaching and learning in higher education on students' learning experience during COVID-19. *Frontiers in Psychology, 12*, 4544. doi:10.3389/fpsyg.2021.733554 PMID:34707542

Fan, X. (2022). The development of EFL learners' willingness to communicate and self-efficacy: The role of flipped learning approach with the use of social media. *Frontiers in Psychology, 13*, 1–12. doi:10.3389/fpsyg.2022.1001283 PMID:36389595

Farjon, D., Smits, A., & Voogt, J. (2019). Technology integration of pre-service teachers explained by attitudes and beliefs, competency, access and experience. *Computers & Education, 130*, 81–93. doi:10.1016/j.compedu.2018.11.010

Ferguson, R., & Clow, D. (2017). Learning analytics: avoiding failure. *Educause Review Online, 31*. https://oro.open.ac.uk/50385/

Ferguson, R. (2012). Learning analytics: Drivers, developments, and challenges. *International Journal of Technology Enhanced Learning, 4*(5-6), 304–317. doi:10.1504/IJTEL.2012.051816

Ferguson, R., Clow, D., Griffiths, D., & Brasher, A. (2019). Moving forward with learning analytics: Expert views. *Journal of Learning Analytics, 6*(3), 43–59. doi:10.18608/jla.2019.63.8

Fernandez, C. J., Ramesh, R., & Manivannan, A. S. R. (2022). Synchronous learning and asynchronous learning during COVID-19 pandemic: A case study in India. *Asian Association of Open Universities Journal, 17*(1), 1–14. doi:10.1108/AAOUJ-02-2021-0027

Fernsel, L., & Simbeck, K. (2022). Data synthesis for fairness audits of learning analytics algorithms. Monographien (AKWI-Tagungsband zur 35), 316-320. https://doi.org/ doi:10.30844/AKWI_2022_21

Ferraro, M. P., & Doyle, B. A. (1981, April 12-17). *Syntactic and reading abilities in normal and learning disabled high school students.* [Paper Presentation]. Annual International Convention of the Council for Exceptional Children 59th Council for Exceptional Children, New York. https://journals.sagepub.com/doi/abs/10.1177/001440298104700514

Fisher, M., & Schneider, Z. (2016). Analysing data in quantitative research. In Z. Schneider, D. Whitehead, G. Lo-Biondo-Wood, & J. Haber (Eds.), *Nursing and midwifery research methods and appraisal for evidence-based practice* (pp. 213–235). Elsevier.

Frith, U. (1981). Experimental approaches to developmental dyslexia: An introduction. *Psychological Research*, *43*(2), 97–109. doi:10.1007/BF00309824 PMID:7302094

Full Fabric. (n.d.). How predictive analytics can boost student success rates. *Full Fabric*. https://www.fullfabric.com/

Gabrielatos, C. (2005). Corpora and language teaching: Just a fling or wedding bells? *Tesl-Ej*, *8*(4), 1–35.

Gabriel, F., Cloude, E. B., & Azevedo, R. (2022). Using learning analytics to measure motivational and affective processes during self-regulated learning with advanced learning technologies. In *Social and Emotional Learning and Complex Skills Assessment: An Inclusive Learning Analytics Perspective* (pp. 93–108). Springer. doi:10.1007/978-3-031-06333-6_6

Gaftandzhieva, S., Docheva, M., & Doneva, R. (2020). A Comprehensive approach to learning analytics in Bulgarian school education. *Education and Information Technologies*, *26*(1), 145–163. doi:10.100710639-020-10261-w

Gandhi, Y. (2022). *What is learning analytics? Challenges and types*. Analytics Steps – A leading source of Technical & Financial content. https://www.analyticssteps.com/blogs/what-learning-analytics-challenges-and-types

Gandomi, A., & Haider, M. (2015). Beyond the hype: Big data concepts, methods, and analytics. *International Journal of Information Management*, *35*(2), 137–144. doi:10.1016/j.ijinfomgt.2014.10.007

Gašević, D., Dawson, S., & Siemens, G. (2015). Let's not forget: Learning analytics are about learning. *TechTrends*, *59*(1), 64–71. doi:10.100711528-014-0822-x

Gašević, D., Kovanović, V., & Joksimovíc, S. (2017). Piecing the learning analytics puzzle: A consolidated model of a field of research and practice. *Learning Research and Practice*, *3*(1), 63–78. doi:10.1080/23735082.2017.1286142

Gašević, D., Kovanović, V., & Joksimović, S. (2017). Piecing the learning analytics puzzle: A consolidated model of a field of research and practice. *Learning: Research and Practice*, *3*(1), 63–78.

Ghilay, Y. (2022). Quantitative courses in higher education: A comparison between asynchronous and synchronous distance learning. *Journal of Education and Learning*, *11*(5), 93. doi:10.5539/jel.v11n5p93

Ghotit Dyslexia Writing and Reading Assistant. (n.d.). *Grammar corrections* [Data set]. https://www.ghotit.com/dyslexia-grammar-corrections

Giannakos, M., Sampson, D., & Kidziński, Ł. (2016). Introduction to smart learning analytics: Foundations and developments in video-based learning. *Smart Learning Environments*, *3*(1), 12. Advance online publication. doi:10.118640561-016-0034-2

Glaser, B. G. (1965). The constant comparative method of qualitative analysis. *Social Problems*, *12*(4), 436–445. doi:10.2307/798843

Glaser, B., & Strauss, A. (1967). *The discovery of grounded theory*. Aldine Publishing Company.

Goggins, S. P., Galyen, K., Petakovic, E., & Laffey, J. M. (2016). Connecting performance to social structure and pedagogy as a pathway to scaling learning analytics in MOOCs: An exploratory study. *Journal of Computer Assisted Learning*, *32*(3), 244–266. doi:10.1111/jcal.12129

Goleman, D. (2012). *Emotional Intelligence: Why It Can Matter More Than IQ*. Bantam.

Goosen, L. (2018). Sustainable and inclusive quality education through research informed practice on information and communication technologies in education. In L. Webb (Ed.), *Proceedings of the 26th Conference of the Southern African Association for Research in Mathematics, Science and Technology Education (SAARMSTE)* (pp. 215-228). Gabarone: University of Botswana.

Goosen, L., & Van Heerden, D. (2017). Beyond the horizon of learning programming with educational technologies. In U. I. Ogbonnaya, & S. Simelane-Mnisi (Ed.), *Proceedings of the South Africa International Conference on Educational Technologies* (pp. 78 - 90). Pretoria: African Academic Research Forum.

Gorgun, G., Yildirim-Erbasli, S. N., & Demmans Epp, C. (2022). Predicting cognitive engagement in online course discussion forums. In A. Mitrovic, & N. Bosch (Eds.), *Proceedings of the 15th International Conference on Educational Data Mining*, (pp. 276-289). Durham, UK: International Educational Data Mining Society. 10.5281/zenodo.6853149

Graham, C. R. (2011). Theoretical considerations for understanding technological pedagogical content knowledge (TPACK). *Computers & Education*, *57*(3), 1953–1960. doi:10.1016/j.compedu.2011.04.010

Gray, E. S. (2008). Understanding dyslexia and its instructional implications: A case to support intense intervention. *Literacy Research and Instruction*, *47*(2), 116–123. doi:10.1080/19388070701878790

Griffiths, D. (2020). The ethical issues of learning analytics in their historical context. In *Radical solutions and open science: An open approach to boost higher education* (pp. 39–55). Springer. doi:10.1007/978-981-15-4276-3_3

Grimm, A., Steegh, A., Kubsch, M., & Neumann, K. (2023). Learning analytics in physics education. *Journal of Learning Analytics*, *10*(1), 71–84. doi:10.18608/jla.2023.7793

Guba, E. G. (1981). Criteria for assessing the trustworthiness of naturalistic inquiries. *Educational Communication and Technology*, *29*(2), 75–91. doi:10.1007/BF02766777

Guo, L. (2022). Using metacognitive prompts to enhance self-regulated learning and learning outcomes: A meta-analysis of experimental studies in computer-based learning environments. *Journal of Computer Assisted Learning*, *38*(3), 811–832. doi:10.1111/jcal.12650

Guo, Y., Wang, Y., & Ortega-Martin, J. L. (2023). The impact of blended learning-based scaffolding techniques on learners' self-efficacy and willingness to communicate. *Porta Linguarum An International Journal of Foreign Language Teaching and Learning*, *40*(40), 253–273. doi:10.30827/portalin.vi40.27061

Gurjar, N. (2020). Reducing transactional distance with synchronous and asynchronous video-based discussions in distance learning. *Proceedings of the SITE 2020: Society for Information Technology & Teacher Education International Conference* (pp. 268–272). Association for the Advancement of Computing in Education.

Haiyang, L., Wang, Z., Benachour, P., & Tubman, P. (2018, July). A time series classification method for behavior-based dropout prediction. *IEEE 18th international conference on advanced learning technologies (ICALT)* (pp. 191-195). IEEE.

Hancı-Azizoglu, E. B., & Kavaklı Ulutaş, N. (2021). Creative digital writing: A multilingual perspective. In *Digital pedagogies and the transformation of language education* (pp. 250–266). IGI Global. doi:10.4018/978-1-7998-6745-6.ch013

Hanson, J. (Host). (2019-present). *The JOY Factor: Mindfulness, Compassion, Positive Psychology, Healing, Yoga*. Apple. https://podcasts.apple.com/tr/podcast/the-joy-factor- mindfulness-compassion-positive/id1108263766

Harris, J., Mishra, P., & Koehler, M. (2009). Teachers' technological pedagogical content knowledge and learning activity types. *Journal of Research on Technology in Education*, *41*(4), 393–416. doi:10.1080/15391523.2009.10782536

Hashimoto, Y. (2002). Motivation and willingness to communicate as predictors of reported L2 use: The Japanese ESL context. *Second Language Studies*, *20*(2), 29–70. 10125/40649

Haznedar, B. (2003). *Neden erken yaşta yabancı dil eğitimi. İ. Erdoğan (Haz.), Türk eğitim sisteminde yabancı dil eğitimi ve kalite arayışları*. Özel Okullar Derneği Yayınları.

Healey, D., Hegelheimer, V., Hubbard, P., Ioannou-Georgiou, S., Kessler, G., & Ware, P. (2008). *TESOL technology standards framework*. TESOL. https://www.tesol.org

Heigham, J., & Croker, R. A. (2009). *Qualitative research in applied linguistics: A practical introduction*. Palgrave Macmillan. doi:10.1057/9780230239517

Heiser, R., Stritto, M., Brown, A., & Croft, B. (2023). Amplifying student and administrator perspectives on equity and bias in learning analytics. *Journal of Learning Analytics*, *10*(1), 8–23. doi:10.18608/jla.2023.7775

Helland, T., & Kaasa, R. (2005). Dyslexia in English as a second language. *Dyslexia (Chichester, England)*, *11*(1), 41–60. doi:10.1002/dys.286 PMID:15747806

Herodotou, C., Hlosta, M., Boroowa, A., Rienties, B., Zdrahal, Z., & Mangafa, C. (2019). Empowering online teachers through predictive learning analytics. *British Journal of Educational Technology*, *50*(6), 3064–3079. doi:10.1111/bjet.12853

Herodotou, C., Maguire, C., McDowell, N., Hlosta, M., & Boroowa, A. (2021). The engagement of university teachers with predictive learning analytics. *Computers & Education*, *173*, 104285. doi:10.1016/j.compedu.2021.104285

Herodotou, C., Naydenova, G., Boroowa, A., Gilmour, A., & Rienties, B. (2020). How can predictive learning analytics and motivational interventions increase student retention and enhance administrative support in distance education? *Journal of Learning Analytics*, *7*(2), 72–83. doi:10.18608/jla.2020.72.4

Herodotou, C., Rienties, B., Boroowa, A., Zdrahal, Z., & Hlosta, M. (2019). A large-scale implementation of predictive learning analytics in higher education: The teachers' role and perspective. *Educational Technology Research and Development*, *67*(5), 1273–1306. doi:10.100711423-019-09685-0

Herodotou, C., Rienties, B., Hlosta, M., Boroowa, A., Mangafa, C., & Zdrahal, Z. (2020). The scalable implementation of predictive learning analytics at a distance learning university: Insights from a longitudinal case study. *The Internet and Higher Education*, *45*, 100725. doi:10.1016/j.iheduc.2020.100725

Hirsto, L., Saqr, M., López-Pernas, S., & Valtonen, T. (2022). A systematic narrative review of learning analytics research in K-12 and schools. *Proceedings of the Finnish Learning Analytics and Artificial Intelligence in Education Conference (FLAIEC)*. Joensuu, Finland. https://ceur-ws.org/Vol-3383/FLAIEC22_paper_9536.pdf

Hoel, T., & Chen, W. (2018). Privacy and data protection in learning analytics should be motivated by an educational maxim—Towards a proposal. *Research and Practice in Technology Enhanced Learning*, *13*(1), 1–14. doi:10.118641039-018-0086-8 PMID:30595748

Höl, D. (2022). A bibliometric analysis of twenty-eight years on 'assessing pronunciation in English as a second/foreign language classes' (1993-2021). *International Online Journal of Education & Teaching*, *9*(4), 2057–2075.

Höl, D. (2023). Standardized testing in Turkey: EFL teachers' perceptions and experiences on Cambridge YLE exams. *International Journal of Curriculum and Instruction*, *15*(2), 984–1007.

Höl, D., & Akman, E. (2023). A bibliometric analysis on "e-assessment in teaching English as a foreign language" publications in web of science (WoS). In D. Köksal, N. Kavaklı Ulutaş, & S. Arslan (Eds.), *Handbook of Research on Perspectives in Foreign Language Assessment* (pp. 329–355). IGI Global. doi:10.4018/978-1-6684-5660-6.ch016

Höl, D., & Kasımi, Y. (2022). A growing dilemma: English speaking anxiety-in-EFL classrooms: A review of research. *RumeliDE Dil ve Edebiyat Araştırmaları Dergisi*, (28), 421–438. doi:10.29000/rumelide.1132581

Höl, D., & Küçük, O. (2023). Pre-service teacher and student shyness: English language teaching context. *Van Yüzüncü Yıl Üniversitesi Eğitim Fakültesi Dergisi*, *20*(1), 228–253. doi:10.33711/yyuefd.1118901

Holstein, K., & Doroudi, S. (2019, March). Fairness and equity in learning analytics systems (FairLAK). *The Proceedings of the 9th International Conference on Learning Analytics & Knowledge* (LAK 2019) (pp. 1-2).

Hooper, S. R., & Hynd, G. W. (1985). Differential diagnosis of subtypes of developmental dyslexia with the Kaufman Assessment Battery for children (K- ABC). *Journal of Clinical Child Psychology*, *14*(2), 145–152. doi:10.120715374424jccp1402_8

Horowitz, K. S. (2019). Video games and English as a second language: The effect of massive multiplayer online video games on the willingness to communicate and communicative anxiety of college students in Puerto Rico. *American Journal of Play*, *11*(3), 379–410.

Hsieh, W., Yeh, H., & Chen, N. (2023). Impact of a robot and tangible object (R&T) integrated learning system on elementary EFL learners' English pronunciation and willingness to communicate. *Computer Assisted Language Learning*, 1–26. doi:10.1080/09588221.2023.2228357

Hsu, K. C., & Liu, G. Z. (2023). Constructing a theory-based augmented reality-featured context-aware ubiquitous learning facilitation framework for oral communication development. *Journal of Computer Assisted Learning*, *39*(3), 883–898. Advance online publication. doi:10.1111/jcal.12792

Hsu, T. C., Chen, W. L., & Hwang, G. J. (2023). Impacts of interactions between peer assessment and learning styles on students' mobile learning achievements and motivations in vocational design certification courses. *Interactive Learning Environments*, *31*(3), 1351–1363. doi:10.1080/10494820.2020.1833351

Hudson, R. F., High, L., & Otaiba, S. A. (2007). Dyslexia and the brain: What does current research tell us? *The Reading Teacher*, *60*(6), 506–515. doi:10.1598/RT.60.6.1

Hunston, S. (2022). *Corpora in applied linguistics* (2nd ed.). Cambridge University Press. doi:10.1017/9781108616218

Hwang, G. J., Chu, H. C., & Yin, C. (2017). Objectives, methodologies, and research issues of learning analytics. *Interactive Learning Environments*, *25*(2), 143–146. doi:10.1080/10494820.2017.1287338

Ifenthaler, D., Gibson, D., & Dobozy, E. (2018). Informing learning design through analytics: Applying network graph analysis. *Australasian Journal of Educational Technology*, *34*(2), 117–132. doi:10.14742/ajet.3767

Ifenthaler, D., & Schumacher, C. (2019). Releasing Personal Information Within Learning Analytics Systems. In D. Sampson, J. M. Spector, D. Ifenthaler, P. Isaías, & S. Sergis (Eds.), *Learning Technologies for Transforming Large-Scale Teaching, Learning, and Assessment* (pp. 3–18). Springer. doi:10.1007/978-3-030-15130-0_1

Ifenthaler, D., Schumacher, C., & Kuzilek, J. (2023). Investigating students' use of self-assessments in higher education using learning analytics. *Journal of Computer Assisted Learning*, *39*(1), 255–268. doi:10.1111/jcal.12744

Ifenthaler, D., & Tracey, M. W. (2016). Exploring the relationship of ethics and privacy in learning analytics and design: Implications for the field of educational technology. *Educational Technology Research and Development*, *64*(5), 877–880. doi:10.100711423-016-9480-3

Islah, Y. (2022). *Shapes' Adventures Book Series*. Universal ELT. https://universalelt.com/?s=Shapes+Adventures

Jafarigohar, M., Khoshsima, H., Haghighi, H., & Vahdany, F. (2019). Incorporation of flipped learning into EFL classrooms: Performance and perception. *Iranian Journal of English Academy Purposes*, *8*, 1–14.

Järvelä, S., Malmberg, J., Haataja, E., Sobocinski, M., & Kirschner, P. A. (2021). What multimodal data can tell us about the students' regulation of their learning process? *Learning and Instruction*, *72*, 101203. doi:10.1016/j.learninstruc.2019.04.004

Jivet, I., Scheffel, M., Specht, M., & Drachsler, H. (2018, March). License to evaluate: Preparing learning analytics dashboards for educational practice. *Proceedings of the 8th international conference on learning analytics and knowledge* (pp. 31-40). Sydney, NSW, Australia: ACM. 10.1145/3170358.3170421

Johns, T. (1991). Should you be persuaded - Two examples of data-driven learning materials. In T. Johns & P. King (Eds.), *Classroom concordancing: English language research journal* (pp. 1–16). Birmingham University.

Joksimović, S., Kovanović, V., & Dawson, S. (2019). The journey of learning analytics. *HERDSA Review of Higher Education*, *6*, 27–63.

Jones, H. (2019, January). Barriers, enablers, and motivations for staff adoption of learning analytics: Insights for professional learning opportunities from an Australian university. *Proceedings of the 36th International Conference on Innovation, Practice and Research in the Use of Educational Technologies in Tertiary Education (ASCILITE)* (pp. 149-158). Singapore: University of Social Sciences.

Jones, K. M., Briney, K. A., Goben, A., Salo, D., Asher, A., & Perry, M. R. (2020). A comprehensive primer to library learning analytics practices, initiatives, and privacy issues. *College & Research Libraries*, *81*(3), 570–591. doi:10.5860/crl.81.3.570

Jones, K. M., & Hinchliffe, L. J. (2023). Ethical issues and learning analytics: Are academic library practitioners prepared? *Journal of Academic Librarianship*, *49*(1), 102621. doi:10.1016/j.acalib.2022.102621

Jordan, R., & Bake, R. (2022). Implementing flipped classroom that used an intelligent tutoring system into learning process: Formative assessment in the design of instructional systems. *AI and Ethics*, 1–10. doi10.1002374543681-022-0001274-z

Joseph, R. C., & Johnson, N. A. (2013). Big data and transformational government. *IT Professional*, *15*(6), 43–48. doi:10.1109/MITP.2013.61

Judge, L. (n.d.). *Predictive analytics in education: An introduction.* Tribal Group. https://www.tribalgroup.com/blog/predictive-analytics-in-education-an-introduction

K, S. (2022, October 18). *Role of predictive analytics in transforming education.* Bold BI. https://www.boldbi.com/blog/role-of-predictive-analytics-in-transforming-education

Kabat-Zinn, J. (2005). *Wherever you go, there you are: Mindfulness meditation in everyday life.* Hyperion.

Kabudi, T., Pappas, I., & Olsen, D. H. (2021). AI-enabled adaptive learning systems: A systematic mapping of the literature. *Computers and Education: Artificial Intelligence, 2*, 100017. doi:10.1016/j.caeai.2021.100017

Kanat-Mutluoğlu, A. (2020). *A multiphase study on willingness to communicate in English as a foreign learning context* [Unpublished doctoral dissertation, Hacettepe University, Ankara].

Kang, S. J. (2005). Dynamic emergence of situational willingness to communicate in a second language. *System, 33*(2), 277–292. doi:10.1016/j.system.2004.10.004

Kara, S. (2020). *EFL teachers' views and corpus analysis of English coursebooks used in Turkish state schools in terms of authentic grammatical and lexical contents with a specific focus to the use of "must".* [Unpublished MA thesis, Karadeniz Technical University, Trabzon].

Karkhanis, S. P., & Dumbre, S. S. (2015). A study of application of data mining and analytics in education domain. *International Journal of Computer Applications, 120*(22). doi:10.5120/21393-4436

Kasimi, Y., & Höl, D. (2023). A qualitative study on listening skills in Turkish EFL classes. [Research on Youth and Language]. *Novitas-ROYAL, 17*(1), 91–107.

Kasuma, S. A. A. (2021). ESL Learning via Facebook among science and non-science university students. *International Journal of Virtual and Personal Learning Environments, 11*(2), 1–17. doi:10.4018/IJVPLE.2021070101

Kavaklı Ulutaş, N., & Abuşka, A. (2023). Language teachers' investment in digital multimodal composing (DMC) as a manifold application of computer-mediated communication. In Multidisciplinary Applications of Computer-Mediated Communication (pp. 17-30). IGI Global.

Kavaklı Ulutaş, N. (2023). Revisiting the past to shape the future: Assessment of foreign language abilities. In D. Köksal, N. Kavaklı Ulutaş, & S. Arslan (Eds.), *Handbook of Research on Perspectives in Foreign Language Assessment* (pp. 1–10). IGI Global. doi:10.4018/978-1-6684-5660-6.ch001

Keiper, M. C., White, A., Carlson, C. D., & Lupinek, J. M. (2021). Student perceptions on the benefits of Flipgrid in a HyFlex learning environment. *Journal of Education for Business, 96*(6), 343–351. doi:10.1080/08832323.2020.1832431

Khajavy, G. H., MacIntyre, P. D., & Barabadi, E. (2018). Role of the emotions and classroom environment in willingness to communicate: Applying doubly latent multilevel analysis in second language acquisition research. *Studies in Second Language Acquisition*, *40*(3), 605–624. doi:10.1017/S0272263117000304

Kholis, A. (2021). Elsa speak app: Automatic speech recognition (ASR) for supplementing English pronunciation skills. Pedagogy. *Journal of English Language Teaching*, *9*(1), 1–14. doi:10.32332/joelt.v9i1.2723

Khuzairi, N., Sidhu, M., & Cob, Z. (2020). Learning analytics and teaching analytics: The similarities and differences. *International Journal of Humanities Management and Social Science*, *3*(2), 52–58. doi:10.36079/lamintang.ij-humass-0302.135

Kidecha, S. (2022, June 4). *Extensive guide on the role of predictive analytics in education*. Kody Technolab. https://kodytechnolab.com/blog/predictive-analytics-in-education/

KidLit TV. (2019, June 18). *Read Out Loud BEE CALM: THE BUZZ ON YOGA* [Video]. YouTube. https://www.youtube.com/watch?v=oOYA8Sg4JBk

Kilgarriff, A., Pavel, R., Pavel, S., & David, T. (2008). The sketch engine. In T. Fontenelle (Ed.), *Practical lexicography: A reader* (pp. 297–306). Oxford University Press. doi:10.1093/oso/9780199292332.003.0020

Kılıçkaya, F. (2022). Teaching vocabulary online using internet resources: A language teacher's experience. In E. Duruk (Ed.), *The New Normal of Online Language Education* (pp. 109–124).

Kim, K., & Moon, N. (2019). Activity index model for self-regulated learning with learning analysis in a TEL environment. *The Journal of Supercomputing*, *75*(4), 1971–1989. doi:10.100711227-018-2446-y

Kirkgöz, Y. (2007). Language planning and implementation in Turkish primary schools. *Current Issues in Language Planning*, *8*(2), 174–191. doi:10.2167/cilp114.0

Kitto, K., Lupton, M., Bruza, P., Mallett, D., Banks, J., Dawson, S., & Siemens, G. (2020). *Learning analytics beyond the LMS: Enabling connected learning via open source analytics in "the wild"*. Australian Government Department of Education, Skills and Employmen. https://opus.lib.uts.edu.au/bitstream/10453/152210/2/ID14-3821_Kitto_Report_2020.pdf

Kizilcec, R. F., & Davis, D. (2023). Learning analytics education: A case study, review of current programs, and recommendations for instructors. In O. Viberg & A. Grönlund (Eds.), *Practicable Learning Analytics* (pp. 133–176). Springer. doi:10.1007/978-3-031-27646-0_8

Klašnja-Milićević, A., & Ivanović, M. (2018). Learning analytics: New flavor and benefits for educational environments. *Informatics Educ.*, *17*(2), 285–300. doi:10.15388/infedu.2018.15

Klein, C., Lester, J., Rangwala, H., & Johri, A. (2019). Technological barriers and incentives to learning analytics adoption in higher education: Insights from users. *Journal of Computing in Higher Education*, *31*(3), 604–625. doi:10.100712528-019-09210-5

Knudsen, I. (2012). *Dyslexia and foreign language learning*. [Unpublished MA thesis, Malmö University, Malmö]. https://www.diva-portal.org/smash/get/diva2:1498521/FULLTEXT01.pdf

Koehler, M., & Mishra, P. (2009). What is technological pedagogical content knowledge (TPACK)? *Contemporary Issues in Technology & Teacher Education*, *9*(1), 60–70.

Kostagiolas, P., Lavranos, C., & Korfiatis, N. (2019). Learning analytics: Survey data for measuring the impact of study satisfaction on students' academic self-efficacy and performance. *Data in Brief*, *25*, 104051. doi:10.1016/j.dib.2019.104051 PMID:31211203

Krasowicz-Kupis, G. (1999). *Rozwój metajęzykowy a osiągnięcia w czytaniu u dzieci 6-9 letnich*. Wydawnictwo UMCS.

Krikun, I. (2017, November). Applying learning analytics methods to enhance learning quality and effectiveness in virtual learning environments. *5th IEEE workshop on Advances in Information, Electronic and Electrical Engineering (AIEEE)* (pp. 1-6). IEEE. https://doi.org/10.1109/AIEEE.2017.8270532

Kruk, M. (2016). Variations in motivation, anxiety and boredom in learning English in Second Life. *The EuroCALL Review*, *24*(1), 25–39. doi:10.4995/eurocall.2016.5693

Kuru Gönen, S. İpek. (2022). Mindfulness-based practices for EFL teachers: sample tasks and insights to cultivate mindfulness. *Focus on ELT Journal*, *4*(3), 78–93. doi:10.14744/felt.2022.4.3.6

Kwangsawad, T. (2016). Examining EFL pre-service teachers' TPACK trough self-report, lesson plans and actual practice. *Journal of Education and Learning*, *10*(2), 103–108.

Lantieri, L., & Zakrzewski, V. (2015). *How SEL and mindfulness can work together*. Greater Good. https://greatergood.berkeley.edu/article/item/how_social_emotional_learning_and_mindfulness_can_work_together

Lawlor, M. S. (2016). Mindfulness and Social Emotional Learning (SEL): A conceptual framework. In K. A. Schonert-Reichl & R. W. Roeser (Eds.), *Handbook of mindfulness in education: Integrating theory and research into practice* (pp. 65–80). Springer. doi:10.1007/978-1-4939-3506-2_5

Law, N., & Liang, L. (2020). A multilevel framework and method for learning analytics integrated learning design. *Journal of Learning Analytics*, *7*(3), 98–117. doi:10.18608/jla.2020.73.8

Lawson, C., Beer, C., Rossi, D., Moore, T., & Fleming, J. (2016). Identification of 'at risk' students using learning analytics: The ethical dilemmas of intervention strategies in a higher education institution. *Educational Technology Research and Development*, *64*(5), 957–968. doi:10.100711423-016-9459-0

Lee, H. S., Pallant, A., Pryputniewicz, S., Lord, T., Mulholland, M., & Liu, O. L. (2019). Automated text scoring and real-time adjustable feedback: Supporting revision of scientific arguments involving uncertainty. *Science Education*, *103*(3), 590–622. doi:10.1002ce.21504

Lee, J. S. (2019). EFL students' views of willingness to communicate in the extramural digital context. *Computer Assisted Language Learning, 32*(7), 692–712. doi:10.1080/09588221.2018.1535509

Lee, J. S., & Hsieh, J. C. (2019). Affective variables and willingness to communicate of EFL learners in in-class, out-of-class, and digital contexts. *System, 82*, 63–73. doi:10.1016/j.system.2019.03.002

Lee, J. S., & Lu, Y. (2021). L2 motivational self-system and willingness to communicate in the classroom and extramural digital contexts. *Computer Assisted Language Learning, 2*, 1–23.

Lee, W. W. S., & Yang, M. (2023). Effective collaborative learning from Chinese students' perspective: A qualitative study in a teacher-training course. *Teaching in Higher Education, 28*(2), 221–237. doi:10.1080/13562517.2020.1790517

Leitner, P., Khalil, M., & Ebner, M. (2017). Learning analytics in higher education: A literature review. *Learning Analytics: Fundaments, Applications, and Trends,* 1–23.

Li, M., & Wong, K. K. (2019). Pedagogical shifts: Learning analytics of mobile learning using rain classroom in theater arts classes. *International Conference on Applied Education, Technology and Innovation.* https://repository.vtc.edu.hk/thei-aeti-2019/Day3-Session13/Session13/1/

Lim, L., Bannert, M., van der Graaf, J., Singh, S., Fan, Y., Surendrannair, S., Rakovic, M., Molenaar, I., Moore, J., & Gašević, D. (2023). Effects of real-time analytics-based personalized scaffolds on students' self-regulated learning. *Computers in Human Behavior, 139*, 107547. doi:10.1016/j.chb.2022.107547

Lim, L., Dawson, S., Joksimovic, S., & Gašević, D. (2019, March). Exploring students' sensemaking of learning analytics dashboards: Does frame of reference make a difference? *Proceedings of the 9th international conference on learning analytics & knowledge* (pp. 250-259). ACM. 10.1145/3303772.3303804

Liontou, T. (2019). The effect of data-driven learning activities on young EFL learners' processing of English idioms. In P. Crosthwaite (Ed.), *Data-driven learning for the next generation: Corpora and DDL for pre-tertiary learners* (pp. 208–227). Routledge., doi:10.4324/9780429425899-12

Liu, D. Y. T., Bartimote-Aufflick, K., Pardo, A., & Bridgeman, A. J. (2017). Data-driven personalization of student learning support in higher education. In A. Peña-Ayala (Ed.), *Learning analytics: Fundaments, applications, and trends: A view of the current state of the art to enhance e-learning* (pp. 143–169). Springer., doi:10.1007/978-3-319-52977-6_5

Liu, R. (2022). Data analysis of educational evaluation using K-means clustering method. *Computational Intelligence and Neuroscience, 31*, 3762431. doi:10.1155/2022/3762431 PMID:35958764

Liu, Y., Ng, J., Hu, X., Ma, Z., & Lai, X. (2023). Adopt or abandon: Facilitators and barriers of in-service teachers' integration of game learning analytics in K–12 classrooms? *Computers & Education.* doi:10.1016/j.compedu.2023.104951

Lloyd, A., Rogerson, S., & Stead, G. (2017). Imagining the potential for using virtual reality technologies in language learning. In M. Carrier, R. M. Damerow, & K. M. Bailey (Eds.), *Digital language learning and teaching: Research, theory, and practice* (pp. 222–234). Routledge. doi:10.4324/9781315523293-19

Łockiewicz, M., & Jaskulska, M. (2015). Mental lexicon, working memory and L2 (English) vocabulary in Polish students with and without dyslexia. *Center for Educational Policy Studies Journal*, *5*(1), 71–89. doi:10.26529/cepsj.155

Lyell, D., & Coiera, E. (2017). Automation bias and verification complexity: A systematic review. *Journal of the American Medical Informatics Association : JAMIA*, *24*(2), 423–431. doi:10.1093/jamia/ocw105 PMID:27516495

Lyon, G. R., Shaywitz, S. E., & Shaywitz, B. A. (2003). A definition of dyslexia. *Annals of Dyslexia*, *53*(1), 1–14. doi:10.100711881-003-0001-9 PMID:24234186

Lyons, K. E., & DeLange, J. (2016). Mindfulness matters in the classroom: The effects of mindfulness training on brain development and behavior in children and adolescents. In K. A. Schonert-Reichl & R. W. Roeser (Eds.), *Handbook of mindfulness in education: Integrating theory and research into practice* (pp. 271–283). Springer. doi:10.1007/978-1-4939-3506-2_17

Macarini, L. A., Lemos dos Santos, H., Cechinel, C., Ochoa, X., Rodés, V., Pérez Casas, A., Lucas, P. P., Maya, R., Alonso, G. E., & Díaz, P. (2020). Towards the implementation of a countrywide K-12 learning analytics initiative in Uruguay. *Interactive Learning Environments*, *28*(2), 166–190. doi:10.1080/10494820.2019.1636082

Macfadyen, L., Lockyer, L., & Rienties, B. (2020). Learning design and learning analytics: Snapshot 2020. *Journal of Learning Analytics*, *7*(3), 6–12. doi:10.18608/jla.2020.73.2

MacIntyre, P. D., Burns, C., & Jessome, A. (2011). Ambivalence about communicating in a second language: A qualitative study of French immersion students' willingness to communicate. *Modern Language Journal*, *95*(1), 81–96. doi:10.1111/j.1540-4781.2010.01141.x

MacIntyre, P. D., & Charos, C. (1996). Personality, attitudes, and affect as predictors of second language communication. *Journal of Language and Social Psychology*, *15*(1), 3–26. doi:10.1177/0261927X960151001

MacIntyre, P. D., Clément, R., Dörnyei, Z., & Noels, K. A. (1998). Conceptualizing willingness to communicate in a L2: A situational model of L2 confidence and affiliation. *Modern Language Journal*, *82*(4), 545–562. doi:10.1111/j.1540-4781.1998.tb05543.x

MacIntyre, P. D., & Legatto, J. J. (2011). A dynamic system approach to willingness to communicate: Developing an idiodynamic method to capture rapidly changing affect. *Applied Linguistics*, *32*(2), 149–171. doi:10.1093/applin/amq037

Mahmoud, M., Dafoulas, G., ElAziz, R., & Saleeb, N. (2022). Factors affecting the deployment of learning analytics in developing countries: Case of Egypt. *International Journal of Emerging Technologies in Learning*, *17*(03), 279–298. doi:10.3991/ijet.v17i03.24405

Mair, C. (2002). Empowering non-native speakers: The hidden surplus value of corpora in continental English departments. In B. Kettemann & G. Marko (Eds.), *Teaching and learning by doing corpus analysis* (pp. 119–130). Rodopi. doi:10.1163/9789004334236_011

Maloney, J. E., Lawlor, M. S., Schonert-Reichl, K. A., & Whitehead, J. (2016). A Mindfulness-based social and emotional learning curriculum for school-aged children: The MindUP program. In K. A. Schonert-Reichl & R. W. Roeser (Eds.), *Handbook of mindfulness in education: Integrating theory and research into practice* (pp. 313–334). doi:10.1007/978-1-4939-3506-2_20

Mangaroska, K., & Giannakos, M. (2017). *Learning analytics for learning design: Towards evidence-driven decisions to enhance learning,* 428-433. doi:10.1007/978-3-319-66610-5_38

Mangaroska, K., & Giannakos, M. (2018). Learning analytics for learning design: A systematic literature review of analytics-driven design to enhance learning. *IEEE Transactions on Learning Technologies*, *12*(4), 516–534. doi:10.1109/TLT.2018.2868673

Mangaroska, K., Sharma, K., Gašević, D., & Giannakos, M. (2022). Exploring students' cognitive and affective states during problem solving through multimodal data: Lessons learned from a programming activity. *Journal of Computer Assisted Learning*, *38*(1), 40–59. doi:10.1111/jcal.12590

Marlowe, B. A., & Page, M. L. (2005). *Creating and sustaining the constructivist classroom* (2nd ed.). Corwin Press.

Marmo, R. (2023). Artificial intelligence in e-learning systems. In *Encyclopedia of Data Science and Machine Learning* (pp. 1531–1545). IGI Global. https://www.igi-global.com/chapter/artificial-intelligence-in-e-learning-systems/317567

Martinez-Maldonado, R., Pardo, A., Mirriahi, N., Yacef, K., Kay, J., & Clayphan, A. (2015). LATUX: An iterative workflow for designing, validating, and deploying learning analytics visualizations. *Journal of Learning Analytics*, *2*(3), 9–39. doi:10.18608/jla.2015.23.3

Martino, J., & Tutton, J. (Founders). (2012). *Smiling Mind* [Mobile app]. https://www.smilingmind.com.au

Martin, T., & Sherin, B. (2013). Learning analytics and computational techniques for detecting and evaluating patterns in learning: An introduction to the special issue. *Journal of the Learning Sciences*, *22*(4), 511–520. doi:10.1080/10508406.2013.840466

Maseleno, A., Sabani, N., Huda, M., Ahmad, R., Jasmi, K., & Basiron, B. (2018). Demystifying learning analytics in personalised learning. *IACSIT International Journal of Engineering and Technology*, *7*(3), 1124. doi:10.14419/ijet.v7i3.9789

Masutto, C., Bravar, L., & Fabbro, F. (1994). Neurolinguistic differentiation of children with subtypes of dyslexia. *Journal of Learning Disabilities*, *27*(8), 520–526. doi:10.1177/002221949402700807 PMID:7989856

Matcha, W., Gasevic, D., Uzir, N. A. A., Jovanovic, J., Pardo, A., Lim, L., & Tsai, Y. S. (2020). Analytics of learning strategies: Role of course design and delivery modality. *Journal of Learning Analytics*, *7*(2), 45–71. doi:10.18608/jla.2020.72.3

Mather, N., & Wendling, B. J. (2012). *Essentials of dyslexia assessment and intervention*. John Wiley & Sons, Inc.

Matsuba, M. K., Schonert-Reichl, K. A., McElroy, T., & Katahoire, A. (2021). Effectiveness of a SEL/mindfulness program on Northern Ugandan children. *International Journal of School & Educational Psychology*, *9*(1), 113–131. doi:10.1080/21683603.2020.1760977

McCroskey, J. C., & Baer, J. E. (1985, November 7–10). *Willingness to communicate: The construct and its measurement* [Paper presentation]. Annual Meeting of the Speech Communication Association, Denver, Colorado, United States.

McGavisk, T. (2023, May 2). *Using predictive analytics to improve student education*. Time and Data security. https://www.timedatasecurity.com/blogs/using-predictive-analytics-to-improve-student-education

McKenney, S., & Mor, Y. (2015). Supporting teachers in data-informed educational design. *British Journal of Educational Technology*, *46*(2), 265–279. doi:10.1111/bjet.12262

McLoughlin, C. E. (2013, June). The pedagogy of personalised learning: exemplars, MOOCS and related learning theories. *EdMedia+ Innovate Learning* (pp. 266-270). Association for the Advancement of Computing in Education (AACE).

Merceron, A., Blikstein, P., & Siemens, G. (2015). Learning analytics: From big data to meaningful data. *Journal of Learning Analytics*, *2*(3), 4–8. doi:10.18608/jla.2015.23.2

Merriam, S. B. (1998). *Qualitative research and case study applications in education*. Jossey-Bass Publishers.

Mian, Y. S., Khalid, F., Qun, A. W., & Ismail, S. S. (2022). Learning analytics in Education, advantages and issues: A systematic literature review. *Creative Education*, *13*(9), 2913–2920. doi:10.4236/ce.2022.139183

Minasi, R. (2023). Industry revolution 4.0 and its impact on education. In J. Wang (Ed.), *Encyclopedia of Data Science and Machine Learning* (pp. 2211–2222). IGI Global. https://www.igi-global.com/chapter/industry-revolution-40-and-its-impact-on-education/317617

Mischenko, P. P. (2021). *Mindfulness-based Social Emotional Learning in a Hybrid Education Environment* (Programme Document IBE/2021/WP/CD/48). https://unesdoc.unesco.org/ark:/48223/pf0000379403

Mishra, P., & Koehler, M. J. (2006). Technological pedagogical content knowledge: A new framework for teacher knowledge. *Teachers College Record*, *108*(6), 1017–1054. doi:10.1111/j.1467-9620.2006.00684.x

Mohammadi, J., Barati, H., & Youhanaee, M. (2019). The effectiveness of using flipped classroom model on Iranian EFL learners' English achievements and their willingness to communicate. *English Language Teaching, 12*(5), 101–115. doi:10.5539/elt.v12n5p101

Molenaar, I. (2022). The concept of hybrid human-AI regulation: Exemplifying how to support young learners' self-regulated learning. *Computers and Education: Artificial Intelligence, 3*, 100070. doi:10.1016/j.caeai.2022.100070

Molenaar, I., de Mooij, S., Azevedo, R., Bannertd, M., Järveläe, S., & Gaševićf, D. (2023). Measuring self-regulated learning and the role of AI: Five years of research using multimodal multichannel data. *Computers in Human Behavior, 107540*, 107540. doi:10.1016/j.chb.2022.107540

Molenaar, I., Horvers, A., & Dijkstra, R. (2019). Young learners' regulation of practice behavior in adaptive learning technologies. *Frontiers in Psychology, 10*, 2792. doi:10.3389/fpsyg.2019.02792 PMID:31920837

Monroy, C., Rangel, V. S., & Whitaker, R. (2014). A strategy for incorporating learning analytics into the design and evaluation of a K-12 science curriculum. *Journal of Learning Analytics, 1*(2), 94–125. doi:10.18608/jla.2014.12.6

Moorhouse, B. L., & Wong, K. M. (2022). Blending asynchronous and synchronous digital technologies and instructional approaches to facilitate remote learning. *Journal of Computers in Education, 9*(1), 51–70. doi:10.100740692-021-00195-8

Morente, B. Y. (2020). *Learning an L2 with dyslexia: Phonological working memory effects, accuracy, and lexical richness.* [Unpublished MA thesis, University of Wyoming, Laremie].

Munshi, A., Biswas, G., Baker, R., Ocumpaugh, J., Hutt, S., & Paquette, L. (2023). Analysing adaptive scaffolds that help students develop self-regulated learning behaviours. *Journal of Computer Assisted Learning, 39*(2), 351–368. doi:10.1111/jcal.12761

Murphy, R. F. (2019). Artificial intelligence applications to support K-12 teachers and teaching. Rand Corporation, 10.

Muter, V. (2003). *Early reading development and dyslexia.* Whurr Publishers.

Mystkowska-Wiertelak, A., & Pawlak, M. (2016). Designing a tool for measuring the interrelationships between L2 WTC, confidence, beliefs, motivation, and context. In M. Pawlak (Ed.), *Classroom-oriented research* (pp. 19–37). Springer. doi:10.1007/978-3-319-30373-4_2

Mystkowska-Wiertelak, A., & Pietrzykowska, A. (2011). L2 willingness to communicate (WTC) and international posture in the Polish educational context. *Studies in Second Language Learning and Teaching, 1*(1), 119–134. doi:10.14746sllt.2011.1.1.7

National University. (2022). *What is social emotional Learning (SEL): Why it matters.* NU. https://www.nu.edu/blog/social-emotional-learning-sel-why-it-matters-for- educators/#how-educators-approach-sel

Ndukwe, I. G., & Daniel, B. K. (2020). Teaching analytics, value, and tools for teacher data literacy: A systematic and tripartite approach. *International Journal of Educational Technology in Higher Education*, *17*(1), 1–31. doi:10.118641239-020-00201-6

Neuropedia Children's Neuroscience Center. (2021). 7 common myths about dyslexia. *Neuropedia. ae*. https://neuropedia.ae/Blog/7-common-myths-about-dyslexia

New Media Consortium (NMC). (2015). *NMC Horizon Report*. British Columbia Teachers' Federation.

Nguyen, A., Gardner, L., & Sheridan, D. (2020). *A design methodology for learning analytics information systems: Informing learning analytics development with learning design*. Scholar Space. doi:10.24251/HICSS.2020.014

Niemi, D., Pea, R. D., Saxberg, B., & Clark, R. E. (Eds.). (2018). *Learning analytics in education*. Information Age Publishing, Inc.

Niess, M. L. (2005). Preparing teachers to teach science and mathematics with technology: Developing a technology pedagogical content knowledge. *Teaching and Teacher Education*, *21*(5), 509–523. doi:10.1016/j.tate.2005.03.006

NMC Horizon Project. (2016). *Higher education edition wiki on learning analytics*. NMC. http://horizon.wiki.nmc.org/Learning+Analytics

Northern Bright Bookshelf. (2020, April 13). *The Lemonade Hurricane: a story of mindfulness and meditation - a read out loud story book* [Video]. YouTube. https://www.youtube.com/watch?v=Olqt-Ghi-zo

Nugroho, A. (2021). Learners Willingness to Communicate in a Foreign Language: The Role of Informal Digital Learning of English. *ELE Reviews: English Language Education Reviews*, *1*(2), 125–133. doi:10.22515/ele-reviews.v1i2.4396

Nugroho, A., & Atmojo, A. E. P. (2020). Digital Learning of English Beyond Classroom: EFL Learners' Perception and Teaching Activities. [Journal of English Education and Linguistics Studies]. *JEELS*, *7*(2), 219–243. doi:10.30762/jeels.v7i2.1993

Nungu, L., Mukama, E., & Nsabayezu, E. (2023). Online collaborative learning and cognitive presence in mathematics and science education. Case study of the University of Rwanda, College of Education. *Education and Information Technologies*, •••, 1–20. https://link.springer.com/article/10.1007/s10639-023-11607-w. doi:10.100710639-023-11607-w PMID:36779197

O'Sullivan, Í. (2007). Enhancing a process-oriented approach to literacy and language learning: The role of corpus consultation literacy. *ReCALL*, *19*(3), 269–286. doi:10.1017/S095834400700033X

Oberle, E., Schonert-Reichl, K. A., Hertzman, C., & Zumbo, B. D. (2014). Social–emotional competencies make the grade: Predicting academic success in early adolescence. *Journal of Applied Developmental Psychology*, *35*(3), 138–147. doi:10.1016/j.appdev.2014.02.004

Ochoa, X., & Wise, A. (2020). Supporting the shift to digital with student-centered learning analytics. *Educational Technology Research and Development*, *69*(1), 357–361. doi:10.100711423-020-09882-2 PMID:33250614

Oliva-Córdova, L. M., Garcia-Cabot, A., & Amado-Salvatierra, H. R. (2021). Learning analytics to support teaching skills: A systematic literature review. *IEEE Access : Practical Innovations, Open Solutions*, *9*, 58351–58363. doi:10.1109/ACCESS.2021.3070294

Ölmez, R., & Kavaklı Ulutaş, N. (2023). A diachronic view into an understanding of technology acceptance: Where to go through TAM for teacher education from global to local? [IJELTAL]. *Indonesian Journal of English Language Teaching and Applied Linguistics*, *7*(2), 359–377.

Ott, P. (1997). *How to detect and manage dyslexia – A reference and resource manual*. Heinemann Educational Books.

Ouellette, G. P. (2006). What's meaning got to do with it: The role of vocabulary in word reading and reading comprehension. *Journal of Educational Psychology*, *98*(3), 554–566. doi:10.1037/0022-0663.98.3.554

Ouyang, F., Dai, X., & Chen, S. (2022). Applying multimodal learning analytics to examine the immediate and delayed effects of instructor scaffoldings on small groups' collaborative programming. *International Journal of STEM Education*, *9*(1), 45. https://link.springer.com/article/10.1186/s40594-022-00361-z. doi:10.118640594-022-00361-z

Ouyang, F., Wu, M., Zheng, L., Zhang, L., & Jiao, P. (2023). Integration of artificial intelligence performance prediction and learning analytics to improve student learning in online engineering course. *International Journal of Educational Technology in Higher Education*, *20*(1), 1–23. doi:10.118641239-022-00372-4 PMID:36683653

Özbay, A. Ş. (2015). *Corpus analysis of the support verb construction development and use by EFL learners*. [Unpublished Doctoral dissertation, Karadeniz Technical University, Trabzon].

Pallathadka, H., Wenda, A., Ramirez-Asís, E., Asís-López, M., Flores-Albornoz, J., & Phasinam, K. (2023). Classification and prediction of student performance data using various machine learning algorithms. *Materials Today: Proceedings*, *80*, 3782–3785. doi:10.1016/j.matpr.2021.07.382

Panadero, E., & Alonso-Tapia, J. (2014). How do students self-regulate? Review of Zimmerman's cyclical model of self-regulated learning. *Anales de Psicología*, *30*(2), 450–462. doi:10.6018/analesps.30.2.167221

Papamitsiou, Z., & Economides, A. A. (2014). Learning analytics and educational data mining in practice: A systematic literature review of empirical evidence. *Journal of Educational Technology & Society*, *17*(4), 49–64.

Pardo, A., Dawson, S., Gaševic, D., & Siemens, G. (2019). *Supporting feedback processes at scale with ontask a hands-on tutorial*. International Learning Analytics & Knowledge Conference.

Pardo, A., & Siemens, G. (2014). Ethical and privacy principles for learning analytics. *British Journal of Educational Technology*, *45*(3), 438–450. doi:10.1111/bjet.12152

Park, Y., & Jo, I. H. (2015). Development of the learning analytics dashboard to support students' learning performance. *Journal of Universal Computer Science*, *21*(1), 110.

Patel, H. H., & Prajapati, P. (2018). Study and analysis of decision tree-based classification algorithms. *International Journal on Computer Science and Engineering*, *6*(10).

Pavlidou, E. V., & Williams, J. M. (2010). Developmental dyslexia and implicit learning: Evidence from an AGL transfer study. *Procedia: Social and Behavioral Sciences*, *2*(2), 3289–3296. doi:10.1016/j.sbspro.2010.03.503

Pawlak, M., & Mystkowska-Wiertelak, A. (2015). Investigating the dynamic nature of willingness to communicate. *System*, *50*, 1–9. doi:10.1016/j.system.2015.02.001

Peng, J. E. (2019). The roles of multimodal pedagogic effects and classroom environment in willingness to communicate in English. *System*, *82*, 161–173. doi:10.1016/j.system.2019.04.006

Peng, J. E., Zhang, L., & Chen, Y. (2017). The mediation of multimodal affordances on willingness to communicate in the English as a foreign language classroom. *TESOL Quarterly*, *51*(2), 302–331. doi:10.1002/tesq.298

Pentón Herrera, L. J. (2020). Social-emotional learning in TESOL: What, why, and how. *Journal of English Learner Education*, *10*(1), 1.

Piaget, J. (1983). Piaget's Theory. In Handbook of Child Psychology. New York: Wiley.

Planey, J., Kim, T., Mercier, E., & Lindgren, R. (2023). Can you see Orion?: Knowledge construction and collaborative discourse while problem-solving with virtual reality. *Interactive Learning Environments*, •••, 1–14. doi:10.1080/10494820.2023.2239290

Polly, D., Mims, C., Shepherd, C. E., & Inan, F. (2010). Evidence of impact: Transforming teacher education with preparing tomorrow's teachers to teach with technology (PT3) grants. *Teaching and Teacher Education*, *26*(4), 863–870. doi:10.1016/j.tate.2009.10.024

Prieto, L. P., Sharma, K., Dillenbourg, P., & Jesús, M. (2016). Teaching analytics: towards automatic extraction of orchestration graphs using wearable sensors. *The Proceedings of the Sixth International Conference on Learning Analytics & Knowledge* (pp. 148–157). ACM.

Prieto, L. P., Sharma, K., Kidzinski, Ł., Rodríguez-Triana, M. J., & Dillenbourg, P. (2018). Multimodal teaching analytics: Automated extraction of orchestration graphs from wearable sensor data. *Journal of Computer Assisted Learning*, *34*(2), 193–203. doi:10.1111/jcal.12232 PMID:29686446

Puddicombe, A. (Founder). (2010). *Headspace* [Mobile app]. https://www.headspace.com

Quadri, A., & Shukor, N. (2021). The benefits of learning analytics to higher education institutions: A scoping review. *International Journal of Emerging Technologies in Learning*, *16*(23), 4–15. doi:10.3991/ijet.v16i23.27471

Rahimi, M., & Fathi, J. (2022). Employing e-tandem language learning method to enhance speaking skills and willingness to communicate: The case of EFL learners. *Computer Assisted Language Learning*, 1–37. doi:10.1080/09588221.2022.2064512

Rahman, A. M., Al Mamun, A., & Islam, A. (2017, December). Programming challenges of chatbot: Current and future prospective. *IEEE Region 10 Humanitarian Technology Conference (R10-HTC)* (pp. 75-78). IEEE.

Ramdani, A. S. (2018). The use of Voki as a media to support the enhancement of first grade students speaking skills at SMPN 4 Tambun Selatan. *Jurnal Inovasi Pendidikan MH Thamrin*, *2*(1), 12–25. doi:10.37012/jipmht.v2i1.32

Ramírez-Mera, U., & Tur, G. (2023). Metacognitive skills and emotions in the construction of Personal Learning Environments. [RED]. *Revista de Educación a Distancia*, *23*(71). Advance online publication. doi:10.6018/red.526831

Ranney, S. (2012). Defining and teaching academic language: Developments in K-12 ESL. *Language and Linguistics Compass*, *6*(9), 560–574. doi:10.1002/lnc3.354

Raut, A. B., & Nichat, M. A. A. (2017). Students performance prediction using decision tree. *International Journal of Computational Intelligence Research*, *13*(7), 1735–1741.

Regehr, S. M. (1987). The genetic aspects of developmental dyslexia. *Canadian Journal of Behavioral Science/Revue Canadienne. Science et Comportement*, *19*(3), 239–253.

Reid, G., Fawcett, A., Manis, F., & Siegel, L. (2008). *Handbook of dyslexia*. SAGE Publications. doi:10.4135/9780857020987

Reinders, H. (2018). Learning analytics for language learning and teaching. *The JALT CALL Journal*, *14*(1), 77–86. doi:10.29140/jaltcall.v14n1.225

Reinders, H., & Wattana, S. (2015). Affect and willingness to communicate in digital game-based learning. *ReCALL*, *27*(1), 38–57. doi:10.1017/S0958344014000226

Rets, I., Herodotou, C., & Gillespie, A. (2023). Six practical recommendations enabling ethical use of predictive learning analytics in distance education. *Journal of Learning Analytics*.

Rets, I., Herodotou, C., Bayer, V., Hlosta, M., & Rienties, B. (2021). Exploring critical factors of the perceived usefulness of a learning analytics dashboard for distance university students. *International Journal of Educational Technology in Higher Education*, *18*(1), 1–23. doi:10.118641239-021-00284-9 PMID:34778534

Rhalmi, M. (2021, February 25). Discovery learning: Guiding language discovery. *My English Pages*. https://www.myenglishpages.com/blog/discovery-learning-guiding-languagediscovery/

Riasati, M. J. (2012). EFL learners' perception of factors influencing willingness to speak English in language classrooms: A qualitative study. *World Applied Sciences Journal*, *17*(10), 1287–1297.

Roberts, L., Howell, J., Seaman, K., & Gibson, D. (2016). Student attitudes toward learning analytics in higher education: "The Fitbit version of the learning world". *Frontiers in Psychology*, *7*. doi:10.3389/fpsyg.2016.01959 PMID:28066285

Roblyer, M. D., & Doering, A. H. (2013). *Integrating educational technology into teaching* (6th ed.). Pearson.

Roll, I., Russell, D. M., & Gašević, D. (2018). Learning at scale. *International Journal of Artificial Intelligence in Education*, *28*(4), 471–477. doi:10.100740593-018-0170-7

Roos, S. (2018). *Chatbots in education: A passing trend or a valuable pedagogical tool?* Diva Portal. https://www.diva-portal.org/smash/get/diva2:1223692/FULLTEXT01.pdf

Ruipérez-Valiente, J. A., & Kim, Y. J. (2020). Effects of solo vs. collaborative play in a digital learning game on geometry: Results from a K12 experiment. *Computers & Education*, *159*, 104008. doi:10.1016/j.compedu.2020.104008

Ruipérez-Valiente, J. A., Muñoz-Merino, P. J., Pijeira Díaz, H. J., Santofimia Ruiz, J., & Delgado Kloos, C. (2017). Evaluation of a learning analytics application for open EdX platform. *Computer Science and Information Systems*, *14*(1), 51–73. doi:10.2298/CSIS160331043R

Ryan, G. (Host). (2015-present). *The Anxiety Coaches Podcast*. The Anxiety Coaches Podcast. https://www.theanxietycoachespodcast.com

Saadati, Z., Zeki, C. P., & Vatankhah Barenji, R. (2021). On the development of blockchain-based learning management system as a metacognitive tool to support self-regulation learning in online higher education. *Interactive Learning Environments*, *31*(5), 1–24. doi:10.1080/10494820.2021.1920429

Sabourin, J. L., Shores, L. R., Mott, B. W., & Lester, J. C. (2013). Understanding and predicting student self-regulated learning strategies in game-based learning environments. *International Journal of Artificial Intelligence in Education*, *23*(1-4), 94–114. doi:10.100740593-013-0004-6

Saçak, B., & Kavun, N. (2020). Rethinking Flipgrid and VoiceThread in the context of online collaborative learning theory. In E. Alqurashi (Ed.), *Handbook of research on fostering student engagement with instructional technology in higher education* (pp. 211–228). IGI Global. doi:10.4018/978-1-7998-0119-1.ch012

Sagarika, R., Kandakatla, R., & Gulhane, A. (2021). Role of learning analytics to evaluate formative assessments: Using a data driven approach to inform changes in teaching practices. *Journal of Engineering Education Transformations*, *34*(0), 550–556. doi:10.16920/jeet/2021/v34i0/157212

Saint, J., Whitelock-Wainwright, A., Gašević, D., & Pardo, A. (2020). Trace-SRL: A framework for analysis of microlevel processes of self-regulated learning from trace data. *IEEE Transactions on Learning Technologies*, *13*(4), 861–877. doi:10.1109/TLT.2020.3027496

Salas-Pilco, S. Z., Xiao, K., & Hu, X. (2022). Artificial intelligence and learning analytics in teacher education: A systematic review. *Education Sciences*, *12*(8), 569. doi:10.3390/educsci12080569

Salend, S. J. (1998). *Effective mainstreaming creating inclusive classrooms*. Prentice Hall.

Samad, I., & Ismail, I. (2020). ELSA speak application as a supporting media in enhancing students' pronunciation skill. *MAJESTY JOURNAL*, *2*(2), 1–7. doi:10.33487/majesty.v2i2.510

Sarker, I. H., Kayes, A. S. M., & Watters, P. (2019). Effectiveness analysis of machine learning classification models for predicting personalized context-aware smartphone usage. *Journal of Big Data*, *6*(1), 1–28. doi:10.118640537-019-0219-y

Sauro, S., & Zourou, K. (2019). What are the digital wilds? *Language Learning & Technology*, *23*(1), 1–7. 10125/44666

Scherer, R., Siddiq, F., & Tondeur, J. (2020). All the same or different? Revisiting measures of teachers' technology acceptance. *Computers & Education*, *143*, 1–17. doi:10.1016/j.compedu.2019.103656

Schneider, B., Reilly, J., & Radu, I. (2020). Lowering barriers for accessing sensor data in education: Lessons learned from teaching multimodal learning analytics to educators. *Journal for STEM Education Research*, *3*(1), 91–124. doi:10.100741979-020-00027-x

Schonert-Reichl, K. A., Oberle, E., Lawlor, M. S., Abbott, D., Thomson, K., Oberlander, T. F., & Diamond, A. (2015). Enhancing cognitive and social-emotional development through a simple-to-administer school program. *Developmental Psychology*, *51*(1), 52–66. doi:10.1037/a0038454 PMID:25546595

Schulman, L. S. (1987). Knowledge and teaching: Foundations of the new form. *Harvard Educational Review*, *57*(1), 1–23. doi:10.17763/haer.57.1.j463w79r56455411

Schumacher, C., & Ifenthaler, D. (2018). The importance of students' motivational dispositions for designing learning analytics. *Journal of Computing in Higher Education*, *30*(3), 599–619. doi:10.100712528-018-9188-y

Sclater, N. (2016). Developing a code of practice for learning analytics. *Journal of Learning Analytics*, *3*(1), 16–42. doi:10.18608/jla.2016.31.3

Scott, K., Morris, A., & Marais, B. (2017). Medical student use of digital learning resources. *The Clinical Teacher*, *15*(1), 29–33. doi:10.1111/tct.12630 PMID:28300343

Selwyn, N. (2019). What's the problem with learning analytics? *Journal of Learning Analytics*, *6*(3), 11–19. doi:10.18608/jla.2019.63.3

Şener, S. (2014). Turkish ELT students' willingness to communicate in English. *ELT Research Journal*, *3*(2), 91–109.

Sense, F., Velde, M., & Rijn, H. (2021). Predicting university students' exam performance using a model-based adaptive fact-learning system. *Journal of Learning Analytics*, *8*(3), 155–169. doi:10.18608/jla.2021.6590

Seo, K., Fels, S., Yoon, D., Roll, I., Dodson, S., & Fong, M. (2020b). Artificial intelligence for video-based learning at scale. *The Proceedings of the Seventh ACM Conference on Learning@ Scale* (pp. 215–217). ACM.

Šereš, L., Pavlicevic, V., & Petrović, G. (2020). *Learning analytics: An updated view*. UNS. doi:10.46541/978-86-7233-386-2_38

Sghir, N., Adadi, A., & Lahmer, M. (2022). Recent advances in predictive learning analytics: A decade systematic review (2012–2022). *Education and Information Technologies*, 1–35. PMID:36571084

Sharma, V. (2019). Saudi students' perspective on social media usage to promote EFL learning. *International Journal of Linguistics. Literature and Translation*, *2*(1), 129–139.

Shaywitz, S. E. (1998). Current Concepts: Dyslexia. *The New England Journal of Medicine*, *338*(5), 307–312. doi:10.1056/NEJM199801293380507 PMID:9445412

Shaywitz, S. E. (2003). *Overcoming dyslexia*. Alfred A. Knopf.

Shen, H., Liang, L., Law, N., Hemberg, E., & O'Reilly, U. M. (2020, August). Understanding learner behavior through learning design informed learning analytics. *Proceedings of the Seventh Conference on Learning@Scale* (pp. 135-145). ACM. 10.1145/3386527.3405919

Shenton, A. K. (2004). Strategies for ensuring trustworthiness in qualitative research projects. *Education for Information*, *22*(2), 63–75. doi:10.3233/EFI-2004-22201

Sidekerskienė, T., & Damaševičius, R. (2023). Out-of-the-box learning: Digital escape rooms as a metaphor for breaking down barriers in STEM education. *Sustainability (Basel)*, *15*(9), 7393. doi:10.3390u15097393

Siegel, D. J. (2010). *Mindsight: The new science of personal transformation*. Bantam.

Siemens, G. (2012, April). Learning analytics: Envisioning a research discipline and a domain of practice. *The Proceedings of the 2nd International Conference on Learning Analytics and Knowledge* (pp. 4-8).

Siemens, G., Dawson, S., & Lynch, G. (2013, December). *Improving the quality and productivity of the higher education sector. Policy and Strategy for Systems-Level Deployment of Learning Analytics*. Canberra: Society for Learning Analytics Research for the Australian Office for Learning and Teaching. https://ltr.edu.au/resources/SoLAR_Report_2014.pdf

Siemens, G. (2013). Learning analytics: The emergence of a discipline. *The American Behavioral Scientist*, *57*(10), 1380–1400. doi:10.1177/0002764213498851

Siemens, G., & Gasevic, D. (2012). Guest editorial-learning and knowledge analytics. *Journal of Education and Technology*, *15*(3), 1–2.

Siemens, G., & Gašević, D. (2012). Special issue on learning and knowledge analytics. *Journal of Educational Technology & Society*, *15*(3), 1–163.

Siemens, G., & Long, P. (2011). Penetrating the fog: Analytics in learning and education. *EDUCAUSE Review*, *46*(5), 30.

Sinclair, J. (1991). *Corpus, concordance, collocation*. Oxford University Press.

Skinner, B. F. (1974). *About behaviorism*. Knopf.

Šlibar, B., Zlatić, L., &Ređep, N. B. (2021). *Ethical and privacy issues of learning analytics in higher education. 14th annual International Conference of Education, Research and Innovation (ICERI) Proceedings*. IATED. https://library.iated.org/view/SLIBAR2021ETH

Smith, C., Butler, N. L., Griffith, K. G., & Allan, W. (2007). The role of communication context, corpus-based grammar, and scaffolded interaction in ESL/EFL instruction. *Online Submission, 4*.

Snowling, M. J. (2006). *Dyslexia speech and language: The practitioner's handbook*. Wiley.

Snowling, M. J. (2013). Early identification and interventions for dyslexia: A contemporary view. *Journal of Research in Special Educational Needs*, *13*(1), 7–14. doi:10.1111/j.1471-3802.2012.01262.x PMID:26290655

Snowling, M., & Hulme, C. (1989). A longitudinal case study of developmental phonological dyslexia. *Cognitive Neuropsychology*, *6*(4), 379–401. doi:10.1080/02643298908253289

Society for Learning Analytics Research. (2023). *What is learning analytics?* Solar Research. https://www.solaresearch.org/about/what-is-learning-analytics/

Sousa, E. B. G., Alexandre, B., Ferreira Mello, R., Pontual Falcão, T., Vesin, B., & Gašević, D. (2021). Applications of learning analytics in high schools: A systematic literature review. *Frontiers in Artificial Intelligence*, *4*, 1–14. doi:10.3389/frai.2021.737891 PMID:34647016

Soyoof, A. (2022). Iranian EFL students' perception of willingness to communicate in an extramural digital context. *Interactive Learning Environments*.

Soyoof, A., Reynolds, B. L., Vazquez-Calvo, B., & McLay, K. (2023). Informal digital learning of English (IDLE): A scoping review of what has been done and a look towards what is to come. *Computer Assisted Language Learning*, *36*(4), 608–640. doi:10.1080/09588221.2021.1936562

Srinivasa, K., & Kurni, M. (2021). Tools for learning analytics. In S. K. G., & M. Kurni (Eds.), A Beginner's Guide to Learning Analytics (pp. 121-159). Springer. doi:10.1007/978-3-030-70258-8_5

Stark, S. (2015, February 19-21). *The dyslexia debate* [Conference session]. International Association for Cognitive Education, Southern Africa. http://www.iacesa.co.za/wp-content/uploads/2015/07/Stark-Sandra.-The-ReadingBrain1.pdf

Stefanakos, M., & Stefanakos, M. (2023). Predictive Analytics in Education: How can it help | AnalyticVue. https://analyticvue.com/predictive-analytics-in-education/

Stewart, C. (2017). Learning Analytics: Shifting from theory to practice. *Journal on Empowering Teaching Excellence*, *1*(1), 95–105.

Suehiro, D., Taniguchi, Y., Shimada, A., & Ogata, H. (2017). Face-to-face teaching analytics: Extracting teaching activities from e-book logs via time-series analysis. *IEEE 17th International Conference On Advanced Learning Technologies (ICALT)*, 2017 (pp. 267–268). IEEE.

Sungkur, R. K., & Maharaj, M. (2022). A review of intelligent techniques for implementing SMART learning environments. In B. Sikdar, S. Prasad Maity, J. Samanta, & A. Roy (Eds.), *Proceedings of the 3rd International Conference on Communication, Devices and Computing: Lecture Notes in Electrical Engineering (*Vol. 851*)*. Springer. 10.1007/978-981-16-9154-6_69

Su, Y. R., & Fatmawati, F. (2019). Fostering students' self-Esteem in speaking by extending speaking activities in social media. *Pedagogy Journal of English Language Teaching*, *7*(1), 65–74. doi:10.32332/pedagogy.v7i1.1544

Sykes, J. (2008). *Dyslexia, design and reading: Making print work for college students with dyslexia a qualitative interaction design study*. [Unpublished Doctoral dissertation, Carnegie Merlon University, Pennsylvania].

Sylvén, L. K., & Sundqvist, P. (2017). Computer-assisted language learning (CALL) in extracurricular/extramural contexts. *CALICO Journal*, *34*(1), i–iv. doi:10.1558/cj.31822

Tai, T.-Y., & Chen, H. H.-J. (2023). The impact of Google Assistant on adolescent EFL learners' willingness to communicate. *Interactive Learning Environments*, *31*(3), 1485–1520. doi:10.1080/10494820.2020.1841801

Tan, J. P. L., Koh, E., Jonathan, C., & Yang, S. (2017). Learner dashboards a double-edged sword? Students' sense-making of a collaborative critical reading and learning analytics environment for fostering 21st-century literacies. *Journal of Learning Analytics*, *4*(1), 117–140. doi:10.18608/jla.2017.41.7

Taylor, C., & Hinchman, T. (2020). Strategies for using Flipgrid in the education. *US-China Education Review B*, *10*(1), 26–31.

Team, P. (2022, August 9). *Asynchronous learning explained: Examples, benefits, and more*. Panopto Video Platform. https://www.panopto.com/blog/asynchronous-learning-explained-examples-benefits-and-more/

Tew, A., & Smith, M. A. (Founders). (2012). *Calm* [Mobile app]. https://www.calm.com

Thomas, H. (2020). Critical literature review on chatbots in education. *IJTSRD*, *4*(6), 786–788.

Thorwarth, C. (2014). Debunking the myths of dyslexia. *Leadership and Research in Education*, *1*, 51–66.

Tlili, A., Essalmi, F., Jemni, M., Kinshuk, P., & Chen, N. S. (2019). A complete validated learning analytics framework: Designing issues from data use perspective. [IJICTE]. *International Journal of Information and Communication Technology Education*, *15*(3), 42–59. doi:10.4018/IJICTE.2019070104

Toetenel, L., & Rienties, B. (2016). Analysing 157 learning designs using learning analytic approaches as a means to evaluate the impact of pedagogical decision making. *British Journal of Educational Technology*, *47*(5), 981–992. doi:10.1111/bjet.12423

Tsai, Y. S., Rates, D., Moreno-Marcos, P. M., Muñoz-Merino, P. J., Jivet, I., Scheffel, M., Drachsler, H., Delgado Kloos, C., & Gašević, D. (2020). Learning analytics in European higher education—Trends and barriers. *Computers & Education*, *155*, 103933. doi:10.1016/j.compedu.2020.103933

Tutsun, E. (2020). Öğrenme analitikleri ve yükseköğretimdeki uygulama alanları. *Bilişim Teknolojileri Dergisi*, *13*(3), 243–254. doi:10.17671/gazibtd.688052

Tzimas, D., & Demetriadis, S. (2021). Ethical issues in learning analytics: A review of the field. *Educational Technology Research and Development*, *69*(2), 1101–1133. doi:10.100711423-021-09977-4

Üstünbaş, Z. (2021). *The effects of flipped instruction through authentic videos on Turkish EFL learners' use of speech acts and willingness to communicate* [Unpublished MA thesis, Bursa Uludağ University, Bursa].

Uunona, G. N., & Goosen, L. (2023). Leveraging ethical standards in artificial intelligence technologies: A guideline for responsible teaching and learning applications. In M. Garcia, M. Lopez Cabrera, & R. de Almeida (Eds.), *Handbook of Research on Instructional Technologies in Health Education and Allied Disciplines* (pp. 310–330). IGI Global., doi:10.4018/978-1-6684-7164-7.ch014

van Leeuwen, A., Janssen, J., Erkens, G., & Brekelmans, M. (2014). Supporting teachers in guiding collaborating students: Effects of learning analytics in CSCL. *Computers & Education*, *79*, 28–39. doi:10.1016/j.compedu.2014.07.007

van Leeuwen, A., Janssen, J., Erkens, G., & Brekelmans, M. (2015). Teacher regulation of cognitive activities during student collaboration: Effects of learning analytics. *Computers & Education*, *90*, 80–94. doi:10.1016/j.compedu.2015.09.006

van Leeuwen, A., Knoop-van Campen, C. A., Molenaar, I., & Rummel, N. (2021). How teacher characteristics relate to how teachers use dashboards: Results from two case studies in K-12. *Journal of Learning Analytics*, *8*(2), 6–21. doi:10.18608/jla.2021.7325

VanLehn, K. (2011). The relative effectiveness of human tutoring, intelligent tutoring systems, and other tutoring systems. *Educational Psychologist*, *46*(4), 197–221. doi:10.1080/00461520.2011.611369

Varkey, T. C., Varkey, J. A., Ding, J. B., Varkey, P. K., Zeitler, C., Nguyen, A. M., Merhavy, Z. I., & Thomas, C. R. (2022). Asynchronous learning: A general review of best practices for the 21st century. *Journal of Research in Innovative Teaching & Learning*, *16*(1), 4–16. doi:10.1108/JRIT-06-2022-0036

Veena, A., & Gowrishankar, S. (2021). *Healthcare Analytics: Overcoming the barriers to health information using machine learning algorithms. Image Processing and Capsule Networks (ICIPCN 2020)*. Springer.

Veluri, R. K., Patra, I., Naved, M., Prasad, V. V., Arcinas, M. M., Beram, S. M., & Raghuvanshi, A. (2022). Learning analytics using deep learning techniques for efficiently managing educational institutes. *Materials Today: Proceedings*, *51*, 2317–2320. doi:10.1016/j.matpr.2021.11.416

Verbert, K., Duval, E., Klerkx, J., Govaerts, S., & Santos, J. L. (2013). Learning analytics dashboard applications. *The American Behavioral Scientist*, *57*(10), 1500–1509. doi:10.1177/0002764213479363

Villegas-Ch, W., & Luján-Mora, S. (2017, March). Analysis of data mining techniques applied to LMS for personalized education. *IEEE 2017 World Engineering Education Conference (EDUNINE)* (pp. 85-89). IEEE.

Villegas-Ch, W., Luján-Mora, S., & Buenaño-Fernandez, D. (2017, December). Data mining toolkit for extraction of knowledge from LMS. *The Proceedings of the 9th International Conference on Education Technology and Computers* (pp. 31-35). ACM.

Villegas-Ch, W., Palacios-Pacheco, X., Ortiz-Garcés, I., & Luján-Mora, S. (2019). *Management of educative data in university students with the use of big data techniques*. Página personal - Sergio Luján Mora. https://sergiolujanmora.es/management-educative-data-university-students-use-big-data-techniques

Villegas-Ch, W., Román-Cañizares, M., & Palacios-Pacheco, X. (2020). Improvement of an online education model with the integration of machine learning and data analysis in an LMS. [MDPI AG.]. *Applied Sciences (Basel, Switzerland)*, *10*(15), 5371. doi:10.3390/app10155371

Virgili, E. (2019). Learning analytics: Online higher education in management. *Sociology and Anthropology (Alhambra, Calif.)*, *7*(2), 66–75. doi:10.13189a.2019.070202

Voogt, J., Fisser, P., Pareja Roblin, N., Tondeur, J., & Van Braak, J. (2013). Technological Pedagogical Content Knowledge (TPACK) - a review of the literature. *Journal of Computer Assisted Learning*, *29*(2), 109–121. doi:10.1111/j.1365-2729.2012.00487.x

Vygotsky, L. (1994). Academic concepts in school aged children. In R. van der Veer, & J. Valsiner (Eds.), The Vygotsky reader (Original work published 1934 ed., pp. 111–126). Oxford: Blackwell.

Waller, M. A., & Fawcett, S. E. (2013). Data science, predictive analytics, and big data: A revolution that will transform supply chain design and management. *Journal of Business Logistics*, *34*(2), 77–84. doi:10.1111/jbl.12010

Wandera, H., Marivate, V., & Sengeh, M. D. (2019). Predicting national school performance for policy making in South Africa. *6th International Conference on Soft Computing Machine Intelligence (ISCMI)* (pp. 23–28). Springer. 10.1109/ISCMI47871.2019.9004323

Wardana, L. A., Rulyansah, A., Izzuddin, A., & Nuriyanti, R. (2023). Integration of digital and non-digital learning media to advance life skills of elementary education students post-pandemic COVID-19. *Pegem Journal of Education and Instruction*, 13(1), 211-222. https://www.pegegog.net/index.php/pegegog/article/view/1984

Wehner, A. K. (2014). *Exploring the relationship of motivation, anxiety, and virtual worlds in the experiences of two Spanish language learners: a case study.* [Unpublished doctoral dissertation, University of South Florida].

Weissberg, R. P., Durlak, J. A., Domitrovich, C. E., & Gullotta, T. P. (2015). Social and emotional learning: Past, present, and future. In J. A. Durlak, C. E. Domitrovich, R. P. Weissberg, & T. P. Gullotta (Eds.), *Handbook for social and emotional learning* (pp. 3–19). Guilford.

Westbrook, L. (1994). Qualitative research methods: A review of major stages, data analysis techniques, and quality controls. *Library & Information Science Research, 16*(3), 241–254. doi:10.1016/0740-8188(94)90026-4

Whitelock-Wainwright, A., Gašević, D., Tejeiro, R., Tsai, Y. S., & Bennett, K. (2019). The student expectations of learning analytics questionnaire. *Journal of Computer Assisted Learning, 35*(5), 633–666. doi:10.1111/jcal.12366

Wilkinson, K., McNamara, I., Wilson, D., & Riggs, K. (2019). Using learning analytics to evaluate course design and student behavior in an online wine business course. *International Journal of Innovation in Science and Mathematics Education, 27*(4). doi:10.30722/IJISME.27.04.008

Willard, C. (2016). *Growing Up mindful: Essential practices to help children, teens, and families find balance, calm, and resilience*. Sounds True.

Williams, M., Teasdale, J., Segal, Z., & J. Kabat-Zinn, J. (2015). *İyi hissetme sanatı, kronik mutsuzlukla baş etme rehberi.* (Z. H. Haktanır, Çev.). Diyojen Yayıncılık.

Williams, P. (2017). Assessing collaborative learning: Big data, analytics and university futures. *Assessment & Evaluation in Higher Education, 42*(6), 978–989. doi:10.1080/02602938.2016.1216084

Wolff, A., Zdrahal, Z., Herrmannova, D., Kuzilek, J., & Hlosta, M. (2014). Developing predictive models for early detection of at-risk students on distance learning modules. *Machine Learning and Learning Analytics Workshop at The 4th International Conference on Learning Analytics and Knowledge (LAK14)*, Indianapolis, Indiana, USA.

Wolpers, M., Najjar, J., Verbert, K., & Duval, E. (2007). Tracking actual usage: The attention metadata approach. *Journal of Educational Technology & Society, 10*(3), 106–121.

Wong, B. T. M. (2017). Learning analytics in higher education: An analysis of case studies. *Asian Association of Open Universities Journal, 12*(1), 21–40. doi:10.1108/AAOUJ-01-2017-0009

Wu, Y.-H., & Hung, S.-T. (2022). The effects of virtual reality infused instruction on elementary school students' English-speaking performance, willingness to communicate, and learning autonomy. *Journal of Educational Computing Research*, *60*(6), 1558–1587. doi:10.1177/07356331211068207

Xia, Q., Chiu, T. K., & Chai, C. S. (2022). The moderating effects of gender and need satisfaction on self-regulated learning through Artificial Intelligence (AI). *Education and Information Technologies*, *28*(7), 8691–8713. doi:10.100710639-022-11547-x

Xing, W., & Du, D. (2019). Dropout prediction in MOOCs: Using deep learning for personalized intervention. *Journal of Educational Computing Research*, *57*(3), 547–570. doi:10.1177/0735633118757015

Yadav, S. K., & Pal, S. (2012). Data mining: A prediction for performance improvement of engineering students using classification. *arXiv preprint arXiv:1203.3832.*

Yang, T. C., Chen, M. C., & Chen, S. Y. (2018). The influences of self-regulated learning support and prior knowledge on improving learning performance. *Computers & Education, 126*, 37-52. https://doi.org/. compedu.2018.06.025 doi:10.1016/j

Yashima, T. (2002). Willingness to communicate in a second language: The Japanese EFL context. *Modern Language Journal*, *86*(1), 54–66. doi:10.1111/1540-4781.00136

Yashima, T., MacIntyre, P. D., & Ikeda, M. (2016). Situated willingness to communicate in an L2: Interplay of individual characteristics and context. *Language Teaching Research*, *22*(1), 115–137. doi:10.1177/1362168816657851

Yaylali, A., Banat, H., & Novikov, A. (2021). Use of corpus-based materials in K-12 language classrooms. *TESOL SLWIS Newsletter*. http://newsmanager.commpartners.com/tesolslwis/issues/2021-02-26/3.html

Yazıcıoğlu, T. (2018). Kaynaştırma uygulamalarının tarihsel süreci ve Türkiye'de uygulanan kaynaştırma modelleri. *Nevşehir Hacı Bektaş Veli Üniversitesi SBE Dergisi*, *8*(1), 92–110. doi:10.30783/nevsosbilen.420028

Yeşilbağ, S., & Korkmaz, Ö. (2021). The effect of Voki application on students' academic achievements and attitudes towards English course. *Education and Information Technologies*, *26*(1), 465–487. doi:10.100710639-020-10264-7 PMID:32837235

Yu, X. (2020). *Examining and comparing English textbooks and high-stakes exams in Turkey: A Corpus-based study*. Corpora and Discourse International Conference, Brighton, England. https://hdl.handle.net/11511/92609

Yu, M. (2011). Effect of communication variables, affective variables, and teacher immediacy on willingness to communicate of foreign language learners. *Chinese Journal of Communication*, *4*(02), 218–236. doi:10.1080/17544750.2011.565678

Zabell, C. (2003). *Individual differences in dyslexia.* [Unpublished Doctoral dissertation, University of Surrey, Guildford]. https://openresearch.surrey.ac.uk/esploro/outputs/doctoral/Individual-Differences-in-Dyslexia/99516562702346#file-0

Zarrinabadi, N., Khodarahmi, E., & Shahbazi, H. (2021). On the effect of using a flipped classroom methodology on Iranian EFL learners' willingness to communicate. In N. Zarrinabadi & M. Pawlak (Eds.), *New Perspectives on Willingness to Communicate in a Second Language* (pp. 155–167). Springer. doi:10.1007/978-3-030-67634-6_8

Zeilhofer, L. (2020). Mindfulness in the foreign language classroom: Influence on academic achievement and awareness. *Language Teaching Research, 27*(1), 96–114. doi:10.1177/1362168820934624

Zeilhofer, L., & Sasao, Y. (2022). Mindful language learning: The effects of college students' mindfulness on short-term vocabulary retention. *System, 110*(6), 102909. doi:10.1016/j.system.2022.102909

Zheng, L., Fan, Y., & Long, M. (2023). The impacts of the comprehensive learning analytics approach on learning performance in online collaborative learning. *Education and Information Technologies, 28*(12), 1–24. https://link.springer.com/article/10.1007/s10639-023-11886-3. doi:10.100710639-023-11886-3 PMID:36688219

Zhu, M., Sari, A. R., & Lee, M. M. (2022). Trends and issues in MOOC learning analytics empirical research: A systematic literature review (2011–2021). *Education and Information Technologies, 27*(7), 10135–10160. doi:10.100710639-022-11031-6

Zimmerman, B. J. (1990). Self-regulated learning and academic achievement: An overview. *Educational Psychologist, 25*(1), 3–17. doi:10.120715326985ep2501_2

Zimmerman, B. J. (2000). Attaining self-regulation: A social cognitive perspective. In M. Boekaerts, P. R. Pintrich, & M. Zeidner (Eds.), *Handbook of self-regulation* (pp. 13–39). Academic Press. doi:10.1016/B978-012109890-2/50031-7

Zins, J. E., & Elias, M. (2006). Social and emotional learning. *Children's Needs III: Development, Prevention, and Intervention*, 1–13.

About the Contributors

Nurdan Kavaklı Ulutaş received her PhD degree in English Language Teaching at Hacettepe University. During her PhD years, she was awarded by the graduate scholarship program of the Scientific and Technological Research Council of Turkey. She is currently a full-time academic at the department of English Language Teaching at Izmir Demokrasi University. She divides her loyalties between teaching undergraduate and graduate classes, and academic research. She has book chapters, and articles published in national and international academic journals. She has coordinated or participated in the steering committees of several national and international education projects. She is the editor-in-chief of a fledgling international academic journal, Futuristic Implementations of Research in Higher Education (FIRE). Her research interests include language teacher education, language testing and assessment, second language writing, and language attrition.

Devrim Höl earned his PhD in English Language Teaching from Çanakkale Onsekiz Mart University, Turkey. He is currently working as Assistant Professor at Pamukkale University, Faculty of Education English Language Teaching Department, Denizli, Turkey. His main research interests are Testing, Evaluation and Assessment and teacher education in foreign language teaching.

***

Ömer Akpınar is a teacher at the Ministry of National Education. His main interests are professional development, inclusive education, and language teaching methods.

Okan Bulut is an Associate Professor of psychometrics and data science at the University of Alberta. His areas of expertise include instrument development (e.g., digital assessments, tests, surveys, and scales), statistical modeling and visualization of big data, educational data mining, and learning analytics.

Tuğba Çıtlak is a PhD candidate at Hacettepe University, who is working as an instructor at the University of Turkish Aeronautical Association. Her research interests include English for specific purposes, corpus linguistics, data-driven learning approach, learner corpora, and academic writing. She has presented papers on English for specific purposes, corpus linguistics, and academic writing.

Feryal Çubukçu has been teaching at Dokuz Eylul University as a professor. Her main interests are applied linguistics, psycholinguistics, sociolinguistics, and literary theories.

Ankit Dhamija is an Associate Professor at Amity Business School, Amity University, Gwalior. He received his PhD degree from Amity School of Engineering & Technology, Amity University Haryana in 2021 and his master's degree from Kurukshetra University Kurukshetra in 2008. He has published research papers in international peer reviewed journals, conferences, and published book chapters with international publishers. His research interests include software maintenance, cyber-security, database efficiency and innovative instructional strategy.

Deepika Dhamija is an academician having more that 14 years of experience as Assistant Professor (Information Technology). She is comfortable with blended-teaching learning. She has published more than 20 research papers and book chapters in reputed journal and presented papers in national/International Conferences. She also has Scopus indexed book chapters with leading publishers and published an e-book. She has also attended various FDP's, workshops and seminars with highly reputed organizations and Researchers. She has won Best paper award, Young Scientist Award, Woman Researcher Award in different conferences and seminars. She is also skilled in teaching the Undergraduate and Postgraduate students.

G. Sabeena is a PhD Research Scholar at the School of Law, Christ University, Bengaluru, India.

Leila Goosen is a full professor in the Department of Science and Technology Education of the University of South Africa. Prof. Goosen was an Associate Professor in the School of Computing, and the module leader and head designer of the fully online signature module for the College for Science, Engineering and Technology, rolled out to over 92,000 registered students since the first semester of 2013. She also supervises ten Masters and Doctoral students, and has successfully completed supervision of 43 students at postgraduate level. Previously, she was a

Deputy Director at the South African national Department of Education. In this capacity, she was required to develop ICT strategies for implementation. She also promoted, coordinated, managed, monitored and evaluated ICT policies and strategies, and drove the research agenda in this area. Before that, she had been a lecturer of Information Technology (IT) in the Department for Science, Mathematics and Technology Education in the Faculty of Education of the University of Pretoria. Her research interests have included cooperative work in IT, effective teaching and learning of programming and teacher professional development.

Guher Gorgun is a PhD candidate in the Measurement, Evaluation, and Data Science program at the University of Alberta. Her research interests include student modeling, educational data mining, automated item quality evaluation, and human-centered AI applications in education.

Alphonsa Diana Haokip is a PhD Research Scholar at Rajiv Gandhi University, Rono-Hills, Doimukh, Arunachal Pradesh, India.

Arzu Kanat-Mutluoglu holds a PhD degree in the field of English Language Teaching (ELT), and she is currently working as a lecturer in the Department of Foreign Language Teaching at TED University in Ankara, Türkiye. Her main research interests focus on willingness to communicate of foreign language learners, psychology of language learning and teaching, and language teacher education. She currently offers the classes of Instructional Design in ELT, Teaching Practice, and Teaching Speaking Skill.

Ronelle Klinck-Van der Merwe's career in the Education and specifically Technology in Education spans over 25 years. Starting out as an IT educator in High School and then supporting educators as an EdTech coach with integrating technology into the teaching and learning environment. A few highlights in her career include managing a Teacher Development centre i.e. Thandulwazi, interviews on SABC on Game Based Learning and promoting the Microsoft Innovator Educator Experts programme and achieving the EduTech Leadership Award at the 6th edition World Education Congress in Mumbai, India. Her focus and passion projects includes a Masters in ICT - Augmented Reality in the classroom and more recently pursuing her Doctorate in Technology Education.

Melita Stephen Natal is an Assistant Professor at Amity Business School, Amity University, Greater Noida, UP, India.

Ali Şükrü Özbay holds his PhD from the English Language and Literature department of KTU. His main areas of interest include corpus linguistics and learner corpora, pragmatics, sociolinguistics, translation studies, academic writing and error analysis and phraseology. He has published research articles and book chapters on corpus linguistics, phraseology, data driven learning, meta-discourse, semantic prosody, and lexical priming. Assoc. Prof. Dr. Özbay is currently the departmental coordinator of Erasmus Exchange Programs and a faculty member at Karadeniz Technical University, Türkiye.

Sibel Kahraman-Ozkurt holding a PhD works as a research assistant at the Foreign Languages Education Department of Pamukkale University. Her research interests include second language acquisition, teacher autonomy, use of technology in language education, and continuing professional development. She is currently giving lectures on language acquisition, computer-assisted language learning (CALL) and language skills.

Ranjit Singha is a Doctorate Research Fellow at Christ (Deemed to be University) and a distinguished American Psychological Association (APA) member. His expertise lies in research and development across various domains, including Mindfulness, Addiction Psychology, Women Empowerment, UN Sustainable Development Goals, and Data Science. He has earned certifications from renowned institutions, including IBM and The University of Oxford Mindfulness Centre, UK, in Mindfulness. Additionally, he holds certifications as a Microsoft Innovative Educator, Licensed Yoga Professional, Certified Mindfulness Teacher, and CBCT Teachers Training from Emory University, USA. His educational qualifications include PGDBA (GM), MBA (IB), MSc. in Counseling Psychology, and completion of a Senior Diploma in Tabla (Musical Instrumentation). His dedication to continuous learning is evident through his involvement in the SEE Learning® (Social, Emotional, and Ethical) Learning program. As a committed researcher and educator, He focuses on mindfulness and compassion-based interventions. He has an impressive publication record, having authored twenty-three research papers, ten chapters, four books, and five edited books. His research interests encompass various aspects of mindfulness, such as assessment, benefits of mindfulness-based programs, change mechanisms, professional training, mindfulness ethics, cognitive and neuropsychology, and studies related to high-risk behaviors. Apart from his research endeavors, he has extensive teaching experience, instructing courses in diverse subjects like Forensic Psychology, Positive Psychology, Organizational Planning, Strategic Management, Psycho

Metric Tests, Counseling Skills, Disaster Management, Basic Computer Science, Business Planning, Business Law, and Auditing. He has mentored numerous Post-graduate and undergraduate research projects, demonstrating his commitment to nurturing young minds in psychology. Furthermore, he actively provides personal counseling services, showcasing his genuine concern for his students' well-being and academic success. His unwavering dedication to research and education has solidified his position as a valuable contributor to psychology.

Surjit Singha is a dedicated researcher actively involved in Research & Development (R&D) and publishing on a wide range of topics, including UN Sustainable Development Goals, Organizational Climate, Workforce Diversity, Organizational Culture, HRM, Marketing, Finance, IB, Global Business, Business, AI, Women Studies, Cultural Studies, and Data Science. Currently serving as a faculty member in the Department of Commerce at Kristu Jayanti College (Autonomous), Dr. Surjit holds the position of Editor, reviewer, and author for various esteemed Global Publications and Journals. With over 13 years of experience in Administration, Teaching, and Research in both Industry and Higher Education Institutions (HEIs), Dr. Surjit is committed to imparting knowledge and guiding students in their research pursuits. As a research mentor for students, Dr. Surjit plays a vital role in nurturing young minds and fostering their academic growth. Additionally, Dr. Surjit heads the website management, promotion, and social media publicity, leading a team of approximately 35 faculty members. Dr. Surjit's dedication to continuous learning is evident through certifications as a Life Skill Trainer by RGNYID (An Institution of National Importance introduced by the Act of Parliament), a Microsoft Innovative Educator by Microsoft, and a Yoga Volunteer certified by The Yoga Certification Board, Ministry of AYUSH, Gov. of India, and evaluated by Morarji Desai National Institute of Yoga. As a dedicated leader in academia, Dr. Surjit has guided and mentored 21 student projects in the academic year 2022-23, resulting in all 21 students publishing papers under Dr. Surjit's astute guidance. As NSS Faculty Mentor, Dr. Surjit has successfully mentored 65 students in the academic year 2022-23, ensuring all students achieve credits and qualifications. Dr. Surjit has an impressive track record with over 65 publications in SCOPUS-indexed articles, including chapters in books, edited books, and various textbooks. Granted 2 US Copyright and received two fully funded minor research projects (Completed and Published) from Kristu Jayanti College (Autonomous). With an unwavering commitment to excellence in education and research, Dr. Surjit Singha continues to impact various domains profoundly, elevating the institution's status and fostering an environment of knowledge dissemination and growth.

Jishamol Thomas is a PhD Research Scholar at Department of Social Work, Christ University, Bengaluru.

Seyma N. Yildirim-Erbasli is an Assistant Professor in the Department of Psychology at the Concordia University of Edmonton. She is interested in investigating, developing, and applying state-of-the-art techniques to advance the assessment experiences of diverse populations. Driven by an interdisciplinary approach, her research spans the realms of data science, artificial intelligence, and digital assessments within the fields of education and psychology.

Index

I

K

L

M

N

O

P

Q

R

S

T

U

V

W

www.ingramcontent.com/pod-product-compliance
Lightning Source LLC
LaVergne TN
LVHW080647011026
849160LV00014B/1345